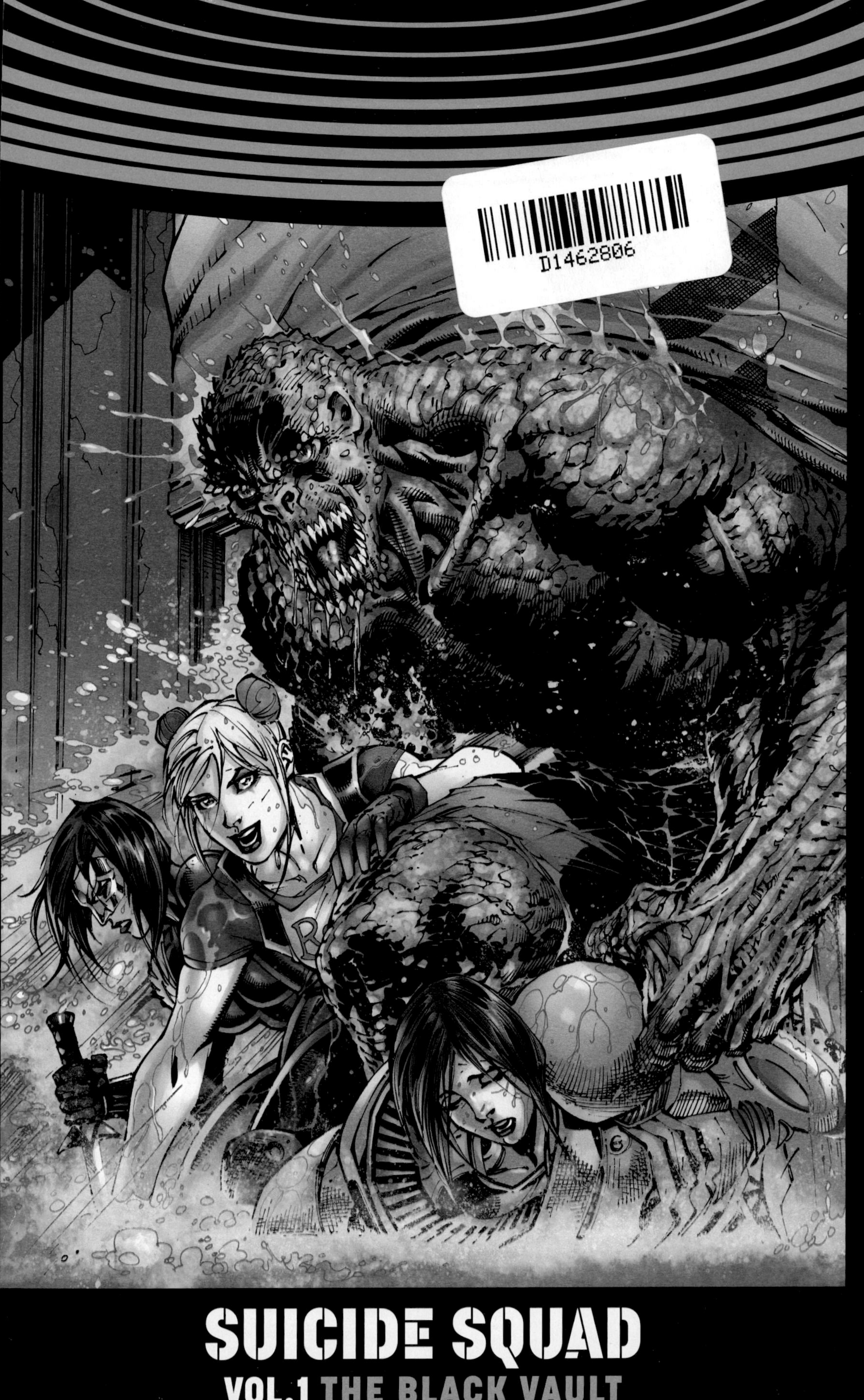

SUICIDE SQUAD
VOL.1 THE BLACK VAULT

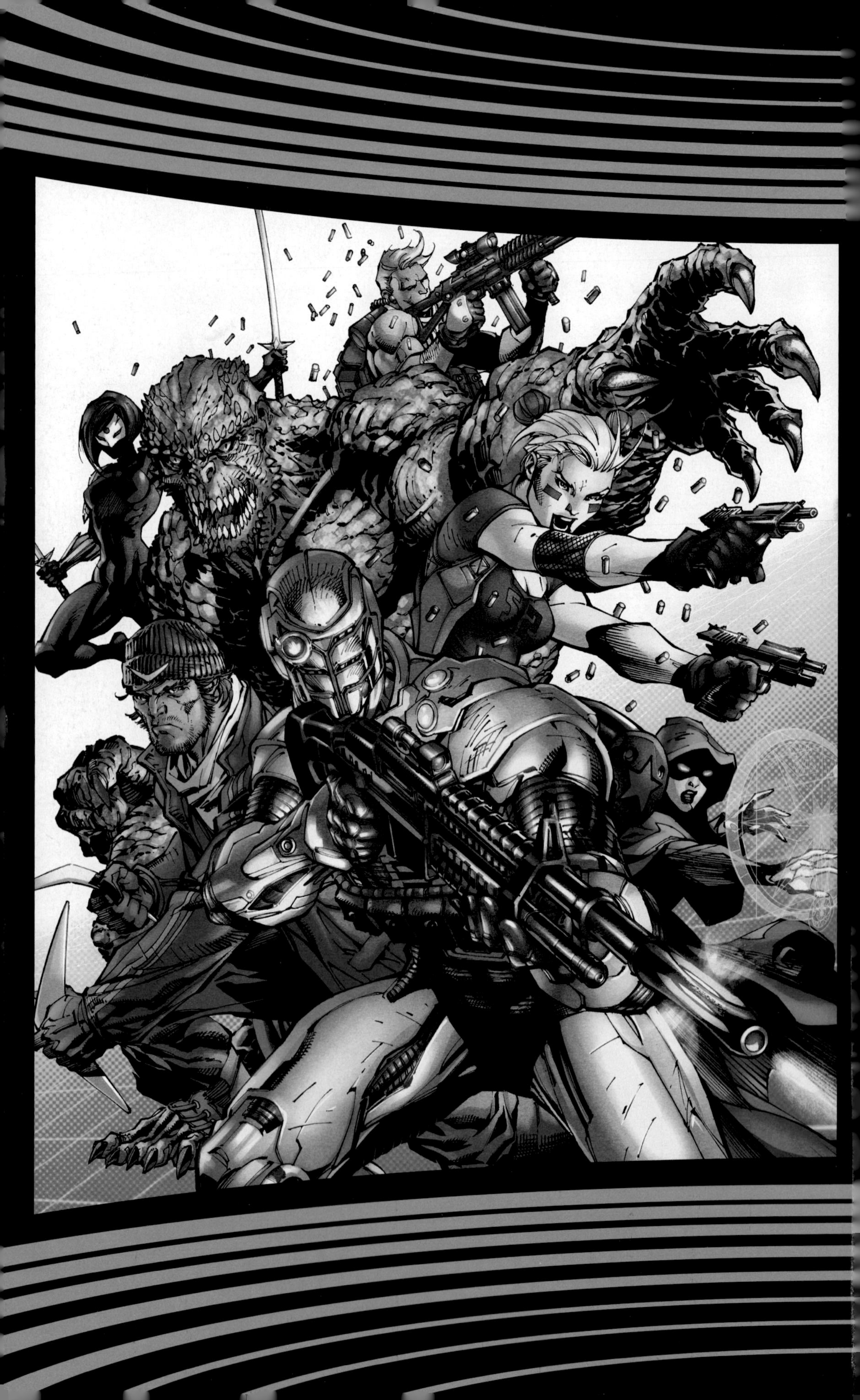

SUICIDE SQUAD
VOL.1 THE BLACK VAULT

ROB WILLIAMS
writer

**JIM LEE * PHILIP TAN * JASON FABOK
IVAN REIS * GARY FRANK * SCOTT WILLIAMS
JONATHAN GLAPION * SCOTT HANNA * SANDU FLOREA
OCLAIR ALBERT * SANDRA HOPE * TREVOR SCOTT**
artists

**ALEX SINCLAIR * BRAD ANDERSON
MARCELO MAIOLO * ELMER SANTOS * HI-FI**
colorists

**NATE PIEKOS OF BLAMBOT®
TRAVIS LANHAM
ROB LEIGH**
letterers

JIM LEE, SCOTT WILLIAMS & ALEX SINCLAIR
collection cover art

**JIM LEE, SCOTT WILLIAMS & ALEX SINCLAIR
PHILIP TAN, JONATHAN GLAPION & ALEX SINCLAIR**
original series covers

BRIAN CUNNINGHAM ANDY KHOURI Editors - Original Series * **HARVEY RICHARDS** Associate Editor - Original Series
DIEGO LOPEZ Assistant Editor - Original Series * **JEB WOODARD** Group Editor - Collected Editions
SCOTT NYBAKKEN Editor - Collected Edition * **STEVE COOK** Design Director - Books * **MONIQUE GRUSPE** Publication Design

BOB HARRAS Senior VP - Editor-in-Chief, DC Comics

DIANE NELSON President * **DAN DiDIO** Publisher * **JIM LEE** Publisher * **GEOFF JOHNS** President & Chief Creative Officer
AMIT DESAI Executive VP - Business & Marketing Strategy, Direct to Consumer & Global Franchise Management
SAM ADES Senior VP - Direct to Consumer * **BOBBIE CHASE** VP - Talent Development
MARK CHIARELLO Senior VP - Art, Design & Collected Editions * **JOHN CUNNINGHAM** Senior VP - Sales & Trade Marketing
ANNE DePIES Senior VP - Business Strategy, Finance & Administration * **DON FALLETTI** VP - Manufacturing Operations
LAWRENCE GANEM VP - Editorial Administration & Talent Relations * **ALISON GILL** Senior VP - Manufacturing & Operations
HANK KANALZ Senior VP - Editorial Strategy & Administration * **JAY KOGAN** VP - Legal Affairs
THOMAS LOFTUS VP - Business Affairs * **JACK MAHAN** VP - Business Affairs
NICK J. NAPOLITANO VP - Manufacturing Administration * **EDDIE SCANNELL** VP - Consumer Marketing
COURTNEY SIMMONS Senior VP - Publicity & Communications
JIM (SKI) SOKOLOWSKI VP - Comic Book Specialty Sales & Trade Marketing
NANCY SPEARS VP - Mass, Book, Digital Sales & Trade Marketing

SUICIDE SQUAD VOL. 1: THE BLACK VAULT

DC Comics, 2900 West Alameda Ave., Burbank, CA 91505
Printed by LSC Communications, Salem, VA, USA. 1/27/17. First Printing.
ISBN: 978-1-4012-6981-4

Library of Congress Cataloging-in-Publication Data is available.

PEFC Certified
Printed on paper from sustainably managed forests, controlled sources
PEFC/29-31-337
www.pefc.org

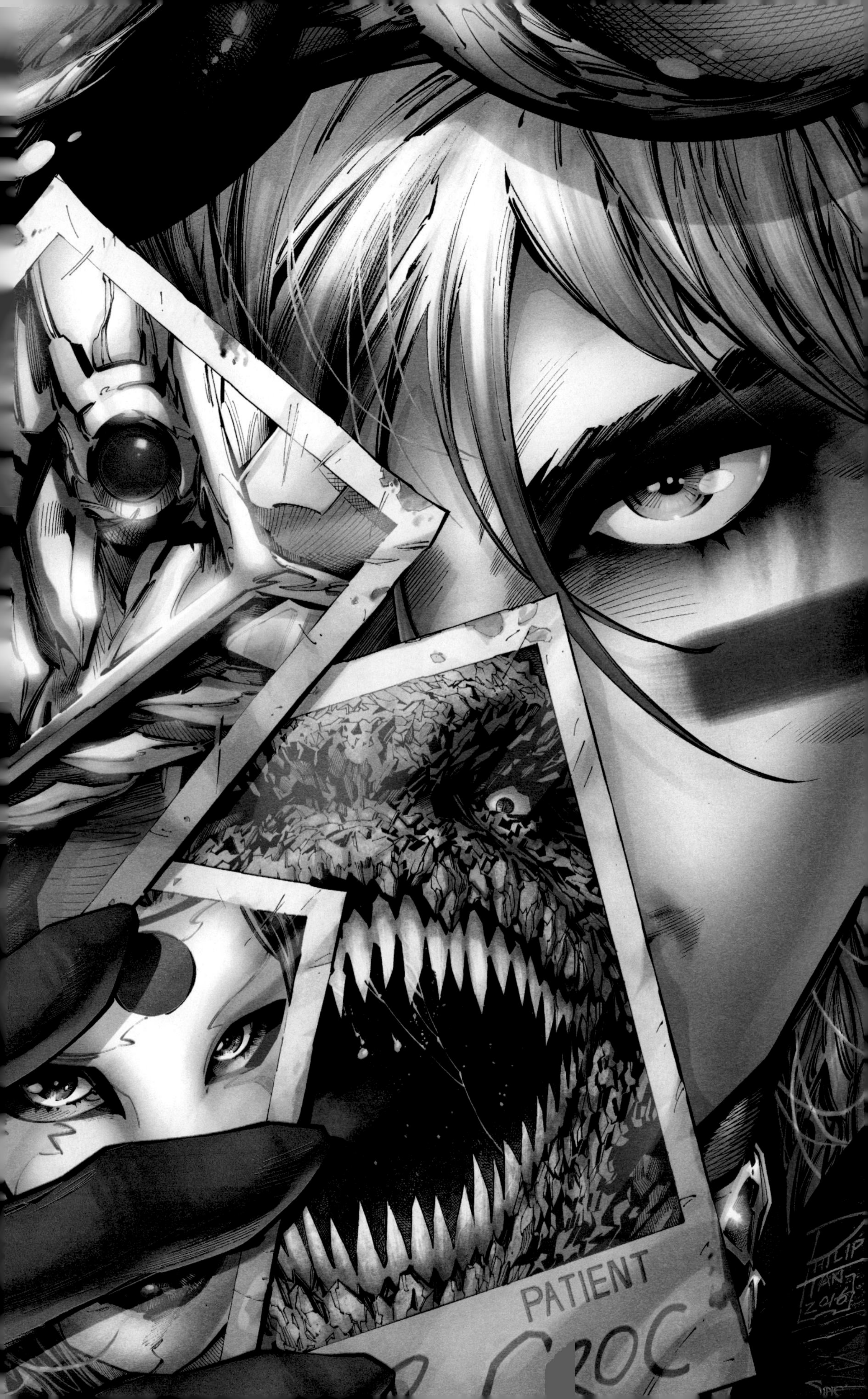
PATIENT
CROC

REBIRTH

ROB WILLIAMS writer * PHILIP TAN penciller
JONATHAN GLAPION SCOTT HANNA SANDU FLOREA inkers * ALEX SINCLAIR colorist * TRAVIS LANHAM letterer
Cover by PHILIP TAN, JONATHAN GLAPION and ALEX SINCLAIR

HARVEY RICHARDS associate editor * BRIAN CUNNINGHAM ANDY KHOURI editors

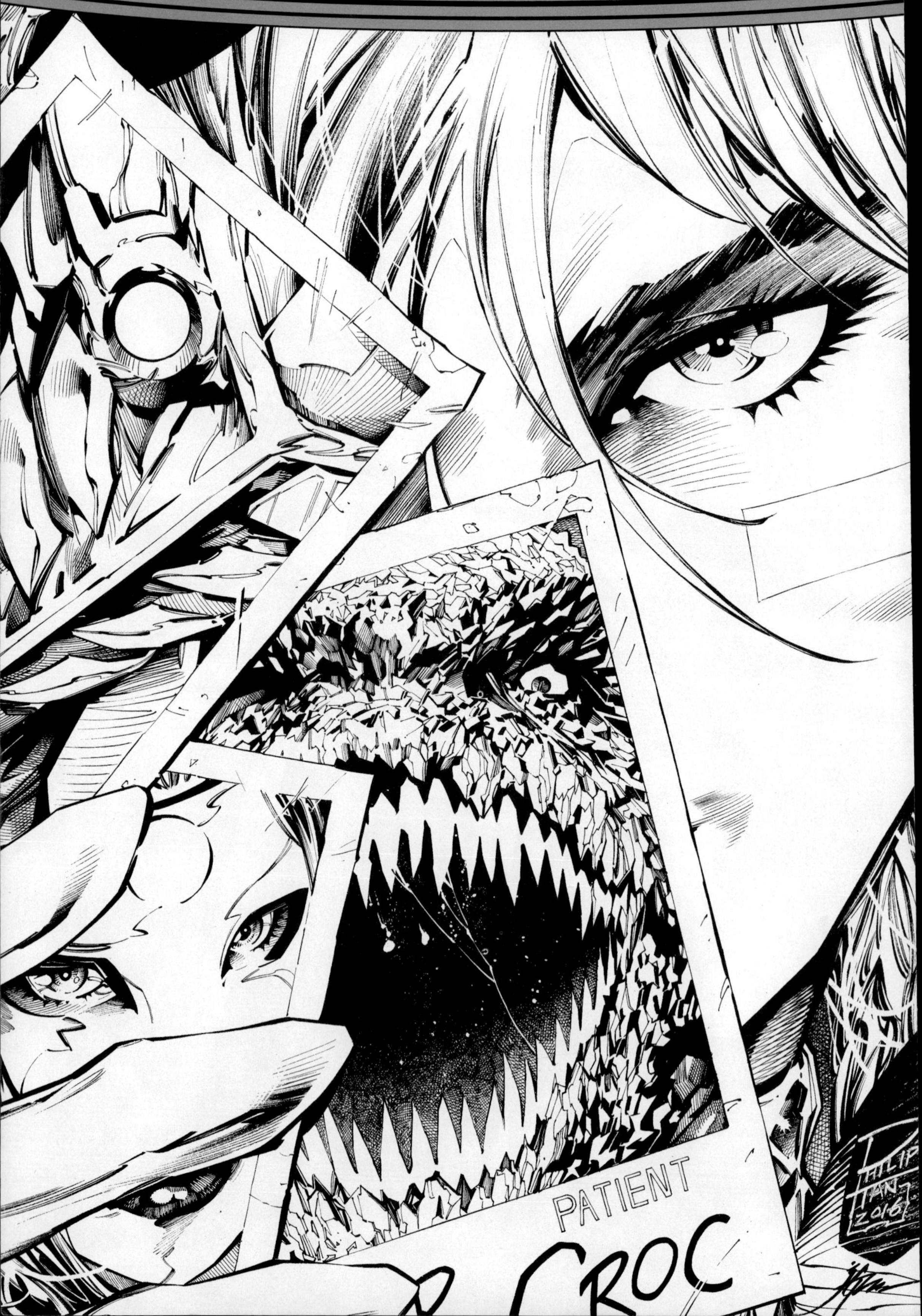

PATIENT
CROC
PHILIP TAN 2016

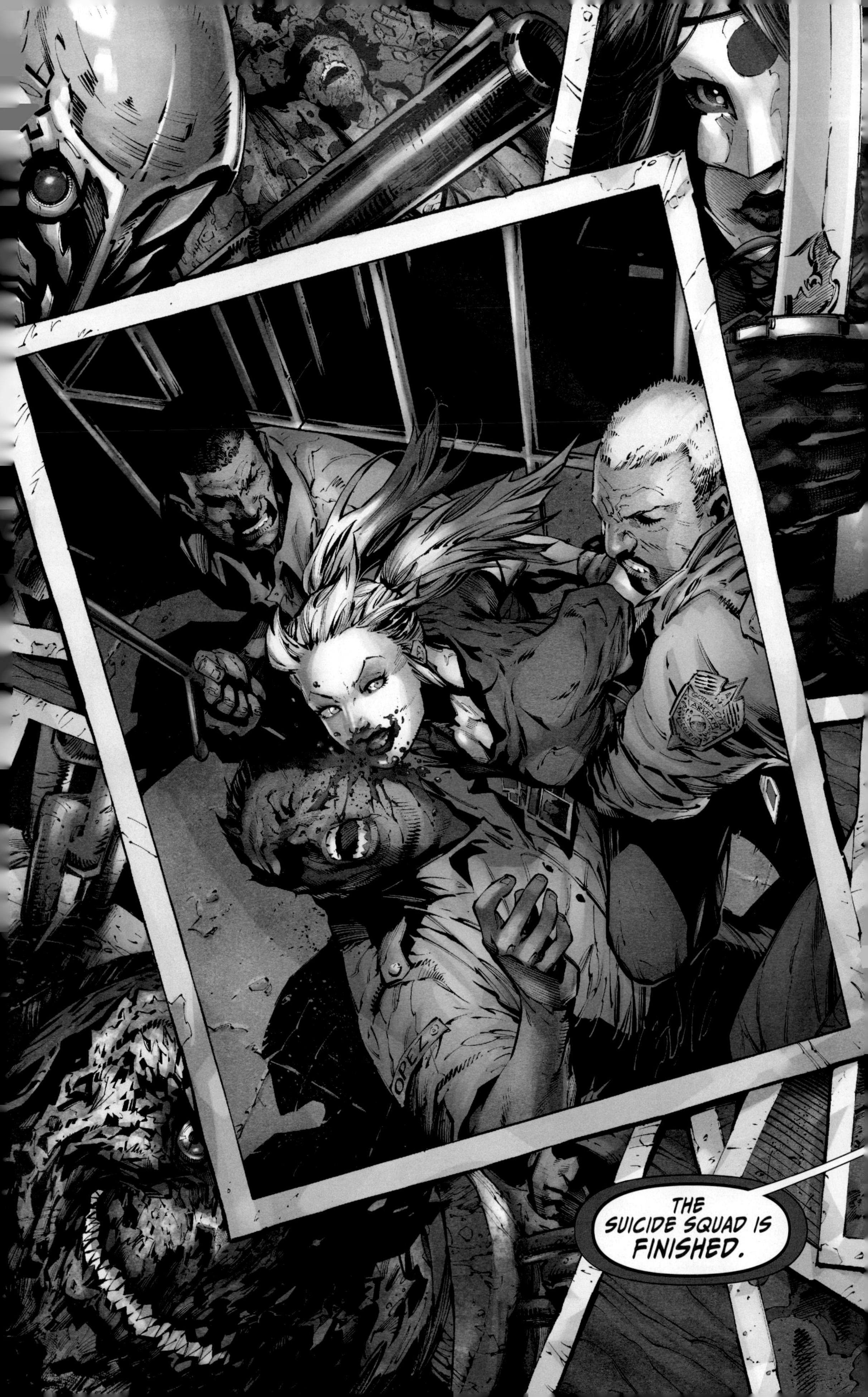
THE SUICIDE SQUAD IS FINISHED.

FINISHED, *DIRECTOR WALLER.* PERIOD.

FRANKLY, I WOULD HAVE MADE THIS DECISION A LOT SOONER, BUT IT WASN'T UNTIL I WAS ALREADY IN MY SECOND TERM THAT I WAS EVEN MADE AWARE OF YOUR... PROGRAM.

WHICH IS EXACTLY THE WAY YOU *LIKED* IT, I'M SURE.

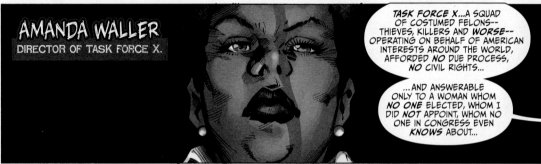

AMANDA WALLER
DIRECTOR OF TASK FORCE X.

TASK FORCE X...A SQUAD OF COSTUMED FELONS-- THIEVES, KILLERS AND *WORSE*-- OPERATING ON BEHALF OF AMERICAN INTERESTS AROUND THE WORLD, AFFORDED *NO DUE PROCESS,* *NO* CIVIL RIGHTS...

...AND ANSWERABLE ONLY TO A WOMAN WHOM *NO ONE* ELECTED, WHOM I DID *NOT* APPOINT, WHOM NO ONE IN CONGRESS EVEN *KNOWS* ABOUT...

...I DON'T KNOW HOW THIS WHOLE THING GOT STARTED, DIRECTOR WALLER, BUT THE SUICIDE SQUAD IS NOT ONLY A *BETRAYAL* OF OUR IDEALS...IT'S MANIFESTLY A *BOMB* WAITING TO BLOW UP IN OUR *FACES.*

I SWORE AN OATH TO DEFEND THIS *COUNTRY.* WE DO *NOT* DO THIS.

NOT *HERE.*

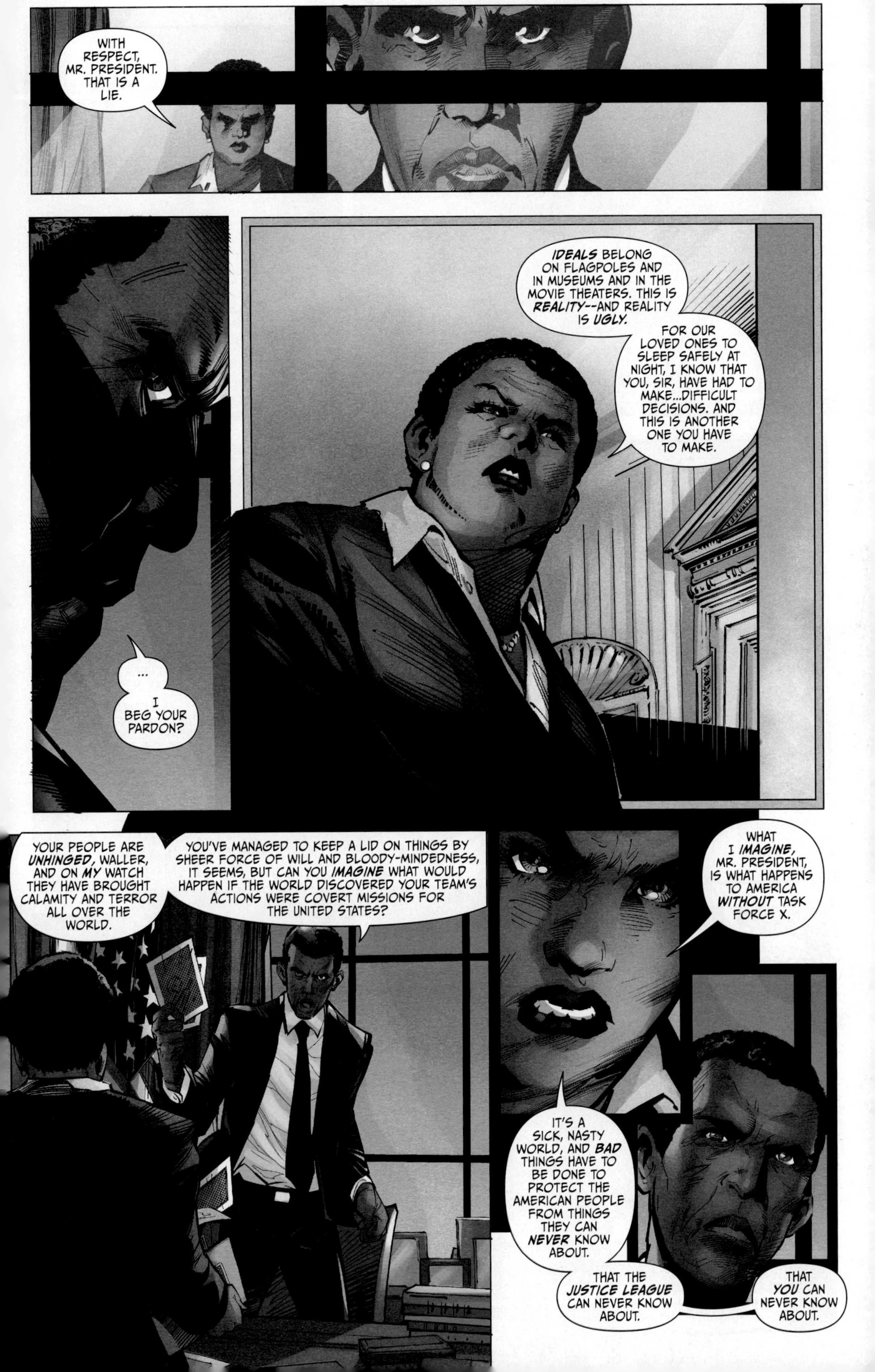
WITH RESPECT, MR. PRESIDENT. THAT IS A LIE.
IDEALS BELONG ON FLAGPOLES AND IN MUSEUMS AND IN THE MOVIE THEATERS. THIS IS REALITY--AND REALITY IS UGLY.
FOR OUR LOVED ONES TO SLEEP SAFELY AT NIGHT, I KNOW THAT YOU, SIR, HAVE HAD TO MAKE...DIFFICULT DECISIONS. AND THIS IS ANOTHER ONE YOU HAVE TO MAKE.
...
I BEG YOUR PARDON?
YOUR PEOPLE ARE UNHINGED, WALLER, AND ON MY WATCH THEY HAVE BROUGHT CALAMITY AND TERROR ALL OVER THE WORLD.
YOU'VE MANAGED TO KEEP A LID ON THINGS BY SHEER FORCE OF WILL AND BLOODY-MINDEDNESS, IT SEEMS, BUT CAN YOU IMAGINE WHAT WOULD HAPPEN IF THE WORLD DISCOVERED YOUR TEAM'S ACTIONS WERE COVERT MISSIONS FOR THE UNITED STATES?
WHAT I IMAGINE, MR. PRESIDENT, IS WHAT HAPPENS TO AMERICA WITHOUT TASK FORCE X.
IT'S A SICK, NASTY WORLD, AND BAD THINGS HAVE TO BE DONE TO PROTECT THE AMERICAN PEOPLE FROM THINGS THEY CAN NEVER KNOW ABOUT.
THAT THE JUSTICE LEAGUE CAN NEVER KNOW ABOUT.
THAT YOU CAN NEVER KNOW ABOUT.

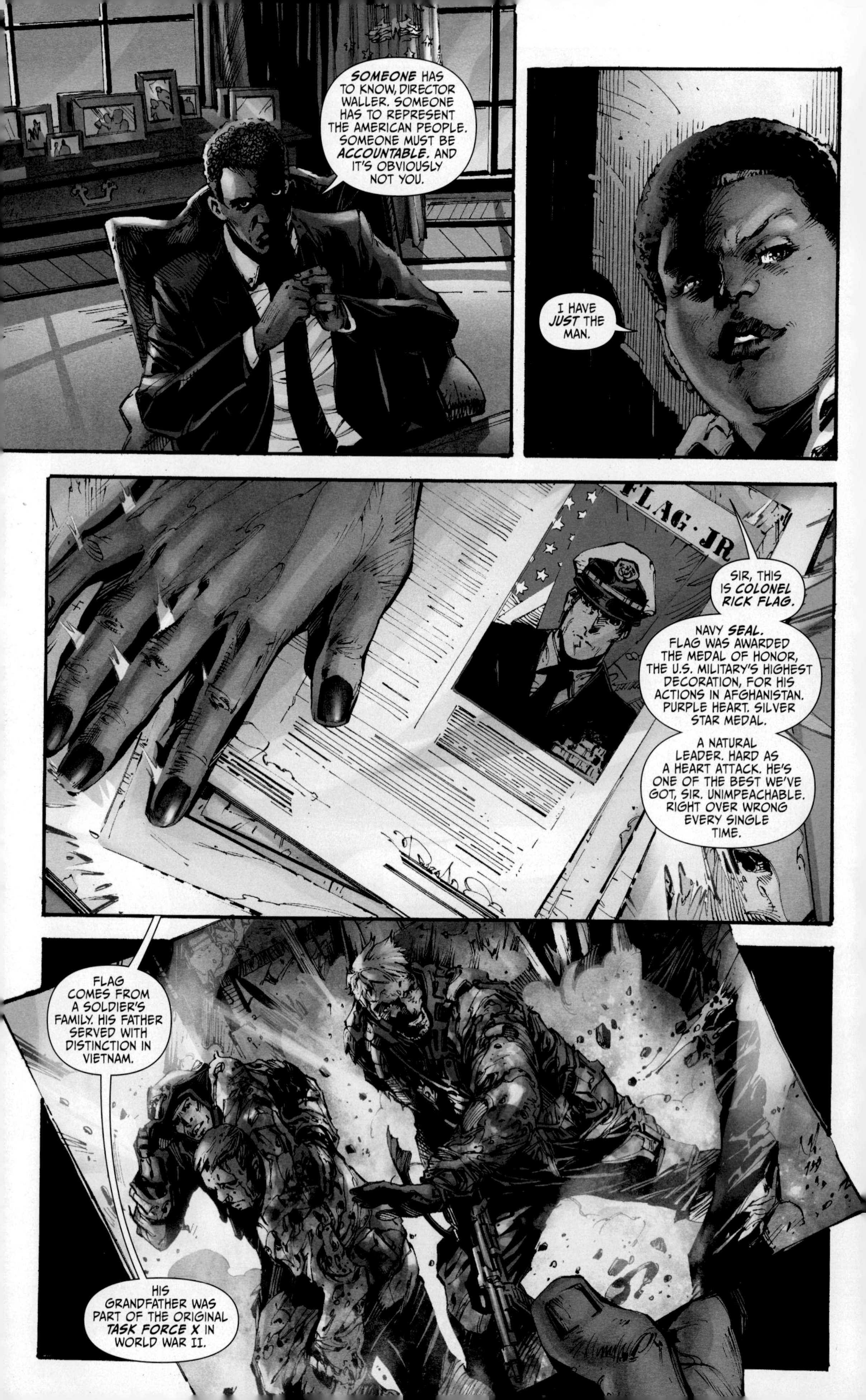
SOMEONE HAS TO KNOW, DIRECTOR WALLER. SOMEONE HAS TO REPRESENT THE AMERICAN PEOPLE. SOMEONE MUST BE ACCOUNTABLE. AND IT'S OBVIOUSLY NOT YOU.
I HAVE JUST THE MAN.
FLAG · JR
SIR, THIS IS COLONEL RICK FLAG.
NAVY SEAL. FLAG WAS AWARDED THE MEDAL OF HONOR, THE U.S. MILITARY'S HIGHEST DECORATION, FOR HIS ACTIONS IN AFGHANISTAN. PURPLE HEART. SILVER STAR MEDAL.
A NATURAL LEADER. HARD AS A HEART ATTACK. HE'S ONE OF THE BEST WE'VE GOT, SIR. UNIMPEACHABLE. RIGHT OVER WRONG EVERY SINGLE TIME.
FLAG COMES FROM A SOLDIER'S FAMILY. HIS FATHER SERVED WITH DISTINCTION IN VIETNAM.
HIS GRANDFATHER WAS PART OF THE ORIGINAL TASK FORCE X IN WORLD WAR II.

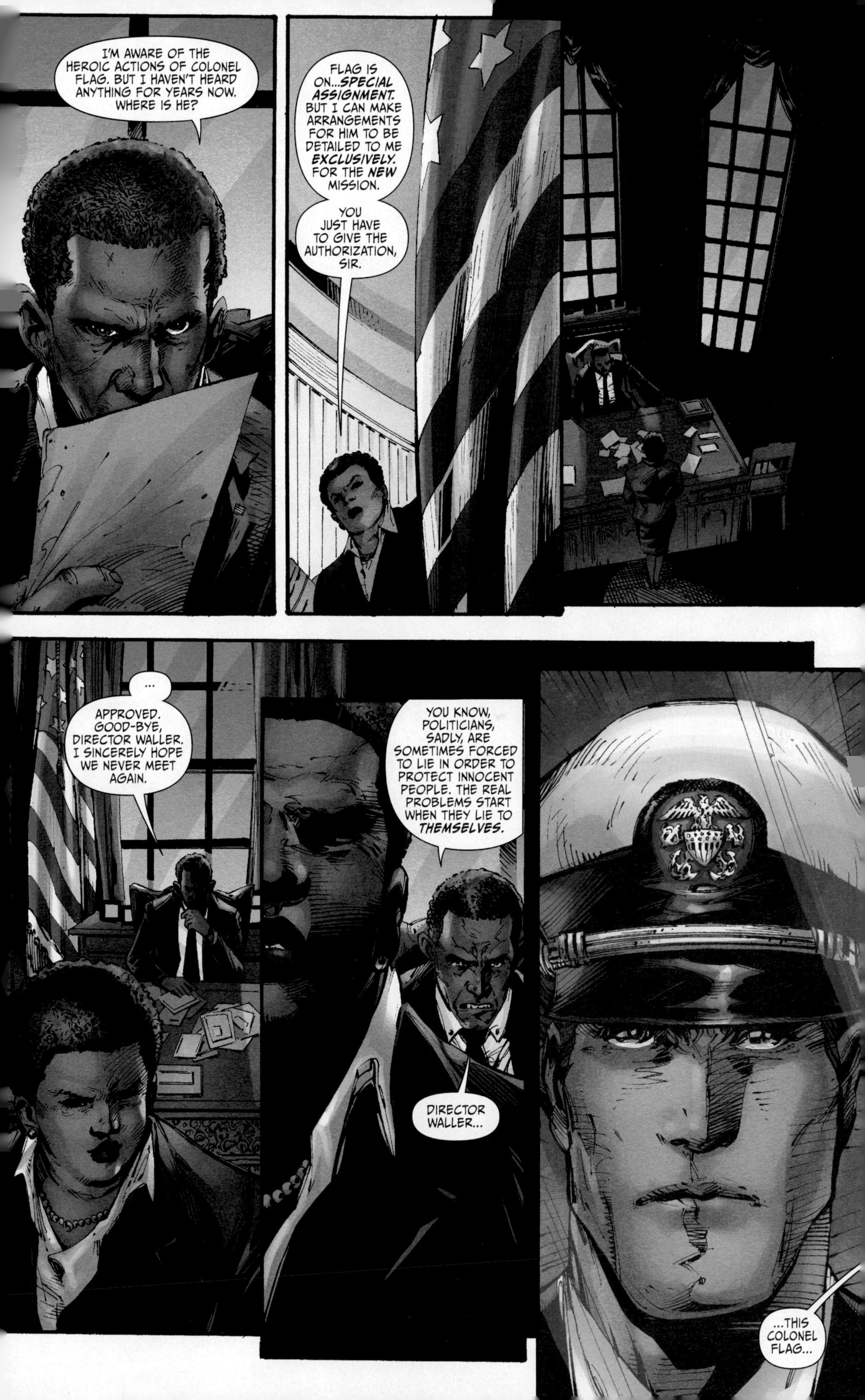
I'M AWARE OF THE HEROIC ACTIONS OF COLONEL FLAG. BUT I HAVEN'T HEARD ANYTHING FOR YEARS NOW. WHERE IS HE?
FLAG IS ON...SPECIAL ASSIGNMENT. BUT I CAN MAKE ARRANGEMENTS FOR HIM TO BE DETAILED TO ME EXCLUSIVELY. FOR THE NEW MISSION.
YOU JUST HAVE TO GIVE THE AUTHORIZATION, SIR.
...
APPROVED. GOOD-BYE, DIRECTOR WALLER. I SINCERELY HOPE WE NEVER MEET AGAIN.
YOU KNOW, POLITICIANS, SADLY, ARE SOMETIMES FORCED TO LIE IN ORDER TO PROTECT INNOCENT PEOPLE. THE REAL PROBLEMS START WHEN THEY LIE TO THEMSELVES.
DIRECTOR WALLER...
...THIS COLONEL FLAG...

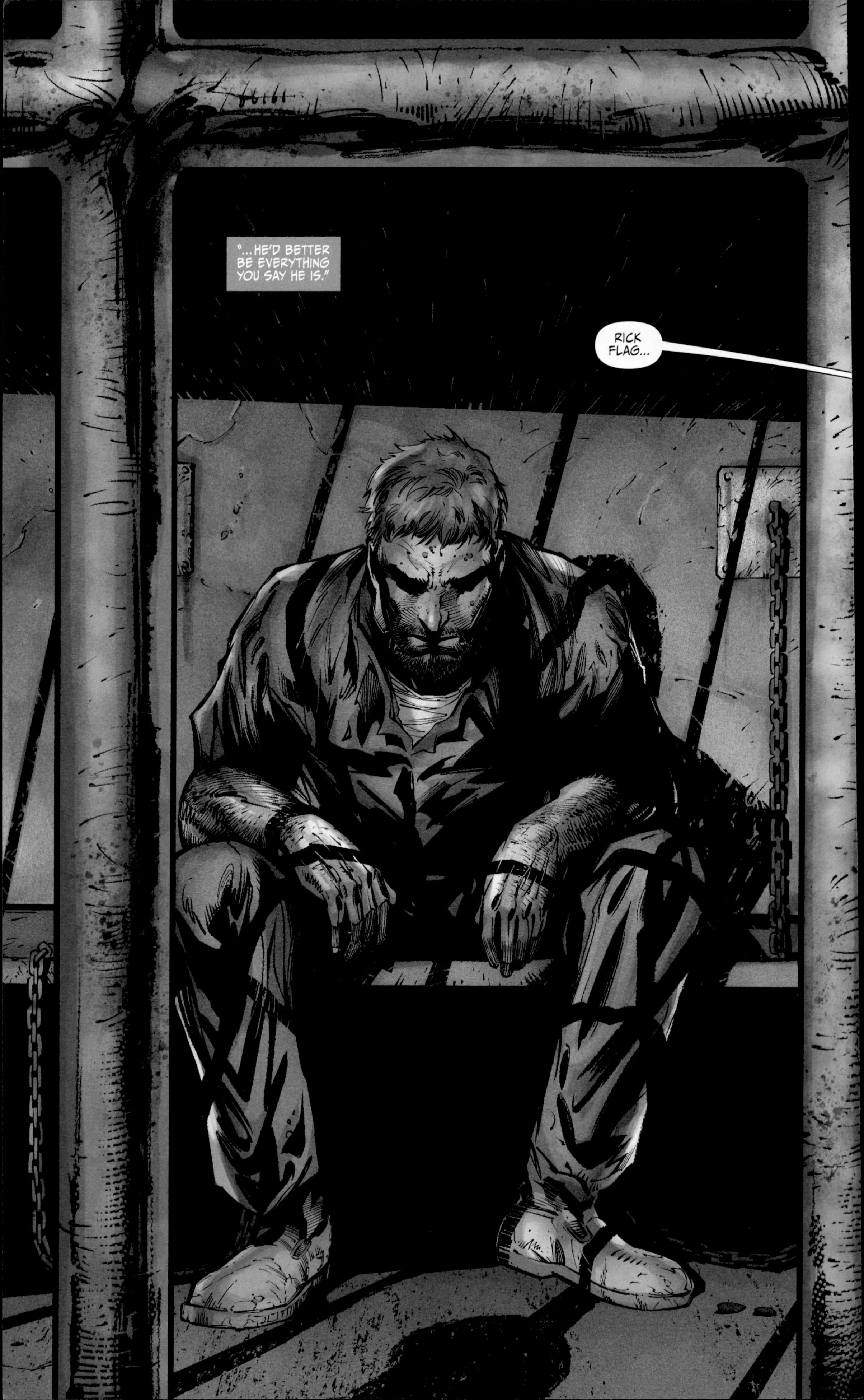
"...HE'D BETTER BE EVERYTHING YOU SAY HE IS."
RICK FLAG...

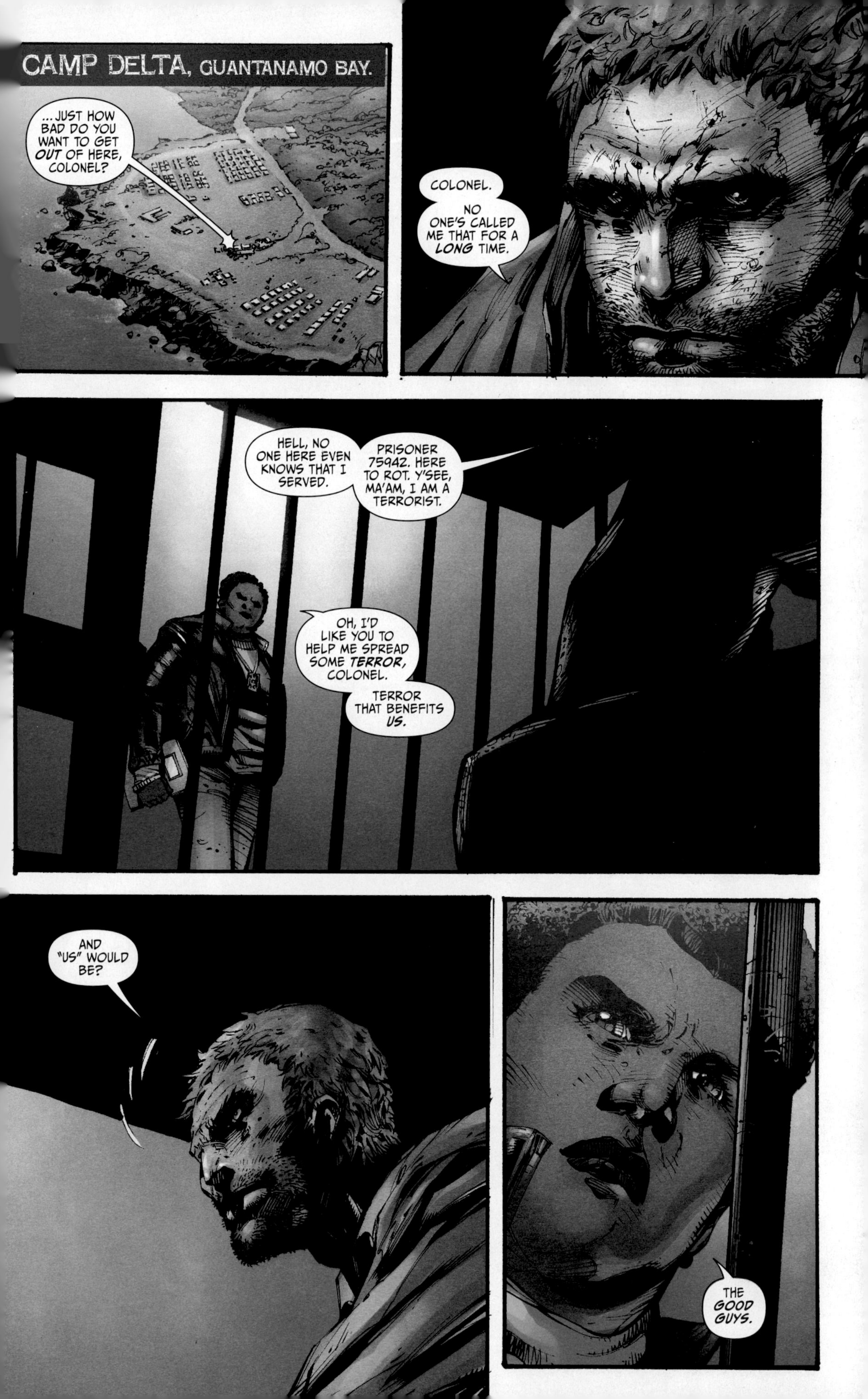
CAMP DELTA, GUANTANAMO BAY.
...JUST HOW BAD DO YOU WANT TO GET *OUT* OF HERE, COLONEL?
COLONEL.
NO ONE'S CALLED ME THAT FOR A *LONG* TIME.
HELL, NO ONE HERE EVEN KNOWS THAT I SERVED.
PRISONER 75942. HERE TO ROT. Y'SEE, MA'AM, I AM A TERRORIST.
OH, I'D LIKE YOU TO HELP ME SPREAD SOME *TERROR,* COLONEL.
TERROR THAT BENEFITS *US.*
AND "US" WOULD BE?
THE *GOOD GUYS.*

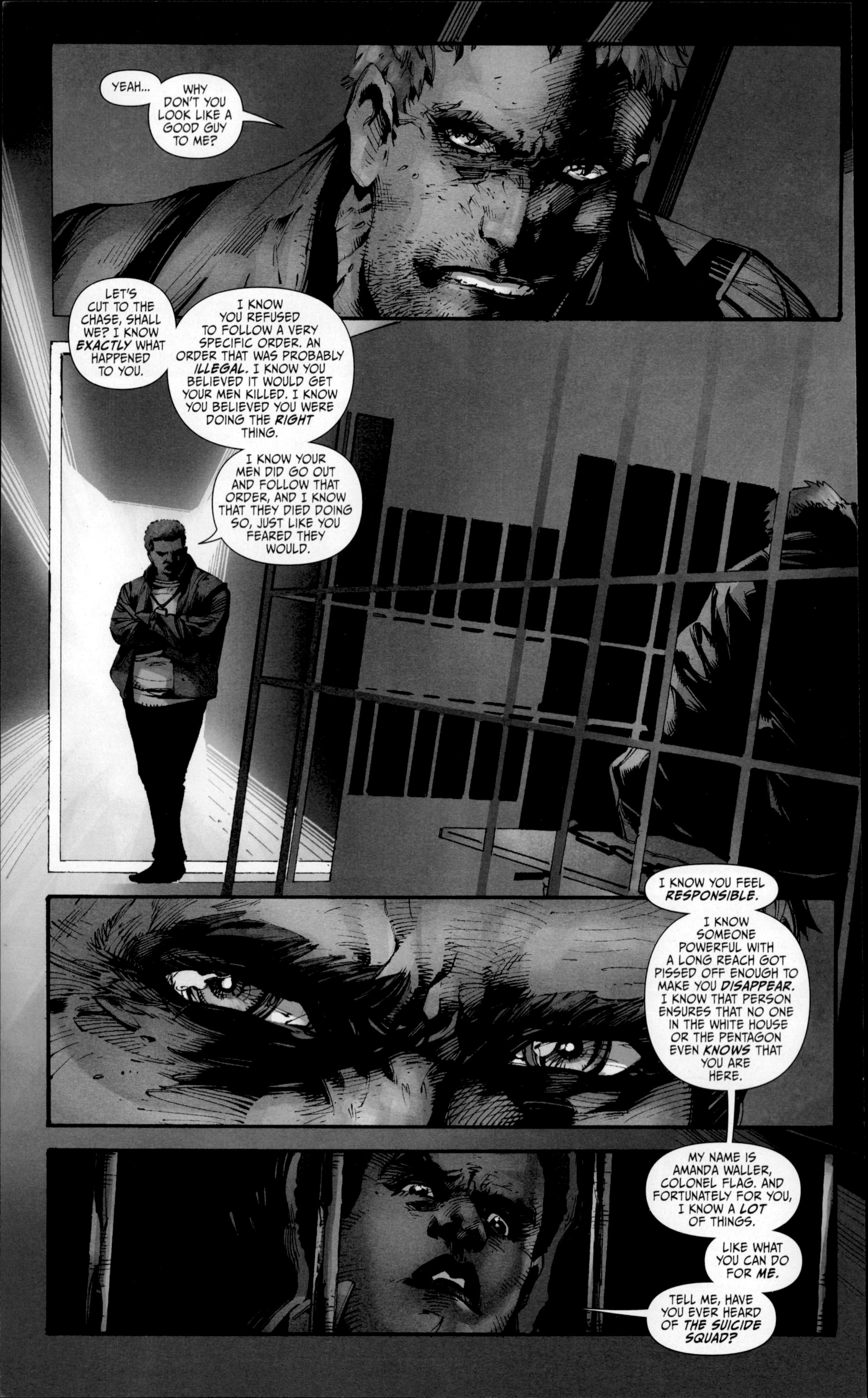
YEAH...
WHY DON'T YOU LOOK LIKE A GOOD GUY TO ME?
LET'S CUT TO THE CHASE, SHALL WE? I KNOW EXACTLY WHAT HAPPENED TO YOU.
I KNOW YOU REFUSED TO FOLLOW A VERY SPECIFIC ORDER. AN ORDER THAT WAS PROBABLY ILLEGAL. I KNOW YOU BELIEVED IT WOULD GET YOUR MEN KILLED. I KNOW YOU BELIEVED YOU WERE DOING THE RIGHT THING.
I KNOW YOUR MEN DID GO OUT AND FOLLOW THAT ORDER, AND I KNOW THAT THEY DIED DOING SO, JUST LIKE YOU FEARED THEY WOULD.
I KNOW YOU FEEL RESPONSIBLE.
I KNOW SOMEONE POWERFUL WITH A LONG REACH GOT PISSED OFF ENOUGH TO MAKE YOU DISAPPEAR. I KNOW THAT PERSON ENSURES THAT NO ONE IN THE WHITE HOUSE OR THE PENTAGON EVEN KNOWS THAT YOU ARE HERE.
MY NAME IS AMANDA WALLER, COLONEL FLAG. AND FORTUNATELY FOR YOU, I KNOW A LOT OF THINGS.
LIKE WHAT YOU CAN DO FOR ME.
TELL ME, HAVE YOU EVER HEARD OF THE SUICIDE SQUAD?

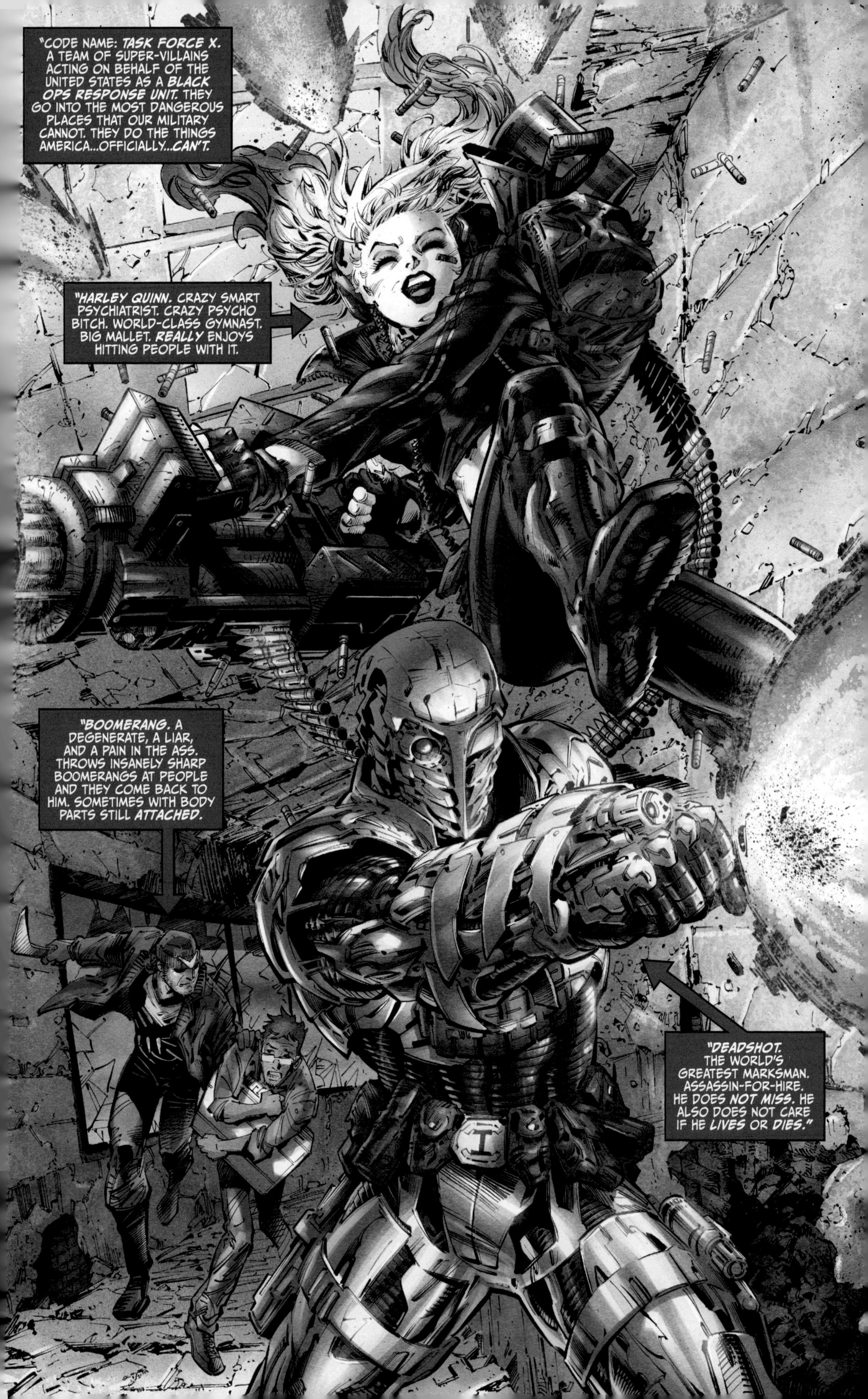
"CODE NAME: TASK FORCE X. A TEAM OF SUPER-VILLAINS ACTING ON BEHALF OF THE UNITED STATES AS A BLACK OPS RESPONSE UNIT. THEY GO INTO THE MOST DANGEROUS PLACES THAT OUR MILITARY CANNOT. THEY DO THE THINGS AMERICA...OFFICIALLY...CAN'T.
"HARLEY QUINN. CRAZY SMART PSYCHIATRIST. CRAZY PSYCHO BITCH. WORLD-CLASS GYMNAST. BIG MALLET. REALLY ENJOYS HITTING PEOPLE WITH IT.
"BOOMERANG. A DEGENERATE, A LIAR, AND A PAIN IN THE ASS. THROWS INSANELY SHARP BOOMERANGS AT PEOPLE AND THEY COME BACK TO HIM. SOMETIMES WITH BODY PARTS STILL ATTACHED.
"DEADSHOT. THE WORLD'S GREATEST MARKSMAN. ASSASSIN-FOR-HIRE. HE DOES NOT MISS. HE ALSO DOES NOT CARE IF HE LIVES OR DIES."

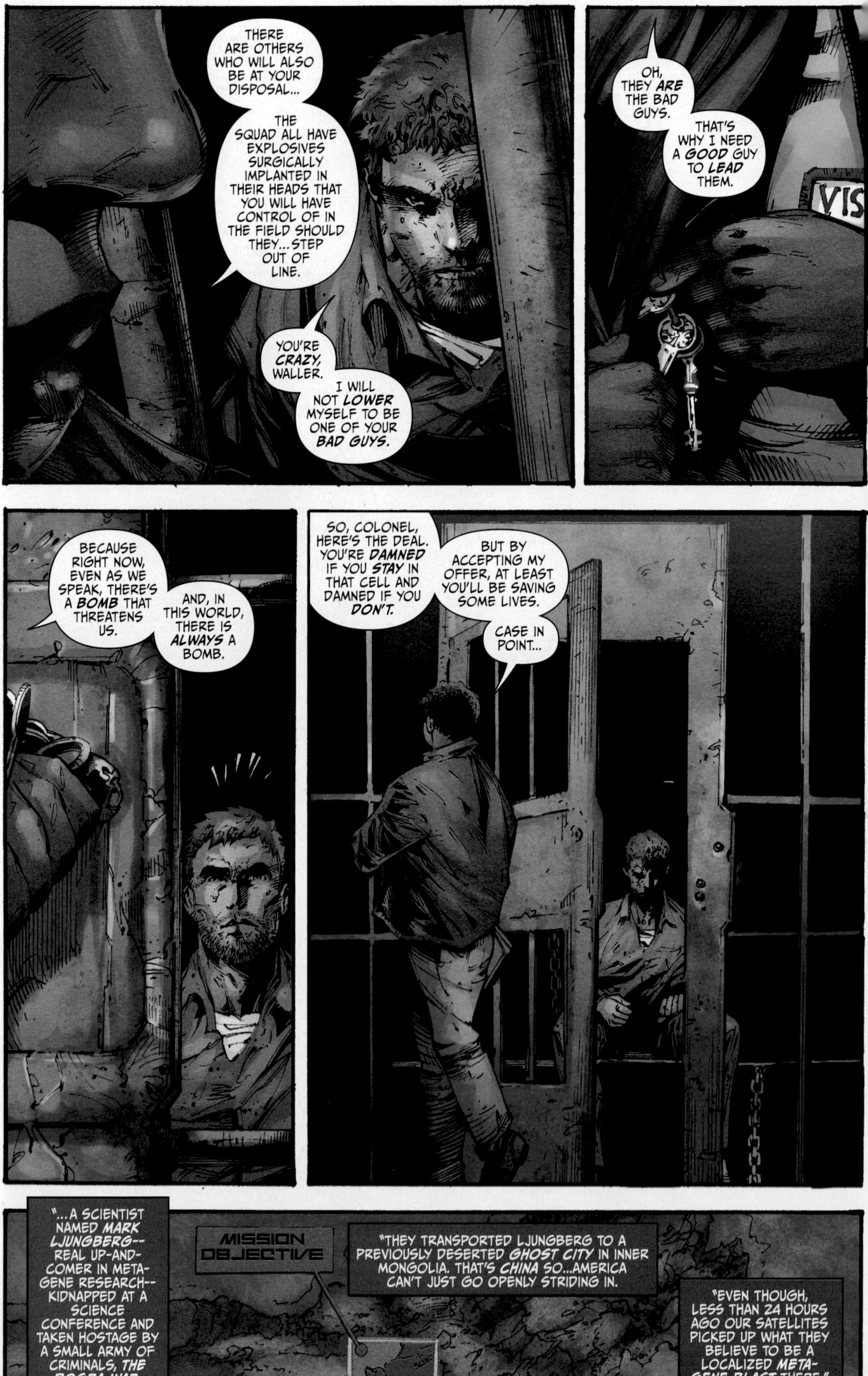
THERE ARE OTHERS WHO WILL ALSO BE AT YOUR DISPOSAL...
THE SQUAD ALL HAVE EXPLOSIVES SURGICALLY IMPLANTED IN THEIR HEADS THAT YOU WILL HAVE CONTROL OF IN THE FIELD SHOULD THEY... STEP OUT OF LINE.
YOU'RE CRAZY, WALLER.
I WILL NOT LOWER MYSELF TO BE ONE OF YOUR BAD GUYS.
OH, THEY ARE THE BAD GUYS.
THAT'S WHY I NEED A GOOD GUY TO LEAD THEM.
VIS
BECAUSE RIGHT NOW, EVEN AS WE SPEAK, THERE'S A BOMB THAT THREATENS US.
AND, IN THIS WORLD, THERE IS ALWAYS A BOMB.
SO, COLONEL, HERE'S THE DEAL. YOU'RE DAMNED IF YOU STAY IN THAT CELL AND DAMNED IF YOU DON'T.
BUT BY ACCEPTING MY OFFER, AT LEAST YOU'LL BE SAVING SOME LIVES.
CASE IN POINT...
"...A SCIENTIST NAMED MARK LJUNGBERG-- REAL UP-AND-COMER IN META-GENE RESEARCH-- KIDNAPPED AT A SCIENCE CONFERENCE AND TAKEN HOSTAGE BY A SMALL ARMY OF CRIMINALS, THE DOGRA WAR.
MISSION OBJECTIVE
"THEY TRANSPORTED LJUNGBERG TO A PREVIOUSLY DESERTED GHOST CITY IN INNER MONGOLIA. THAT'S CHINA SO...AMERICA CAN'T JUST GO OPENLY STRIDING IN.
"EVEN THOUGH, LESS THAN 24 HOURS AGO OUR SATELLITES PICKED UP WHAT THEY BELIEVE TO BE A LOCALIZED META-GENE BLAST THERE."

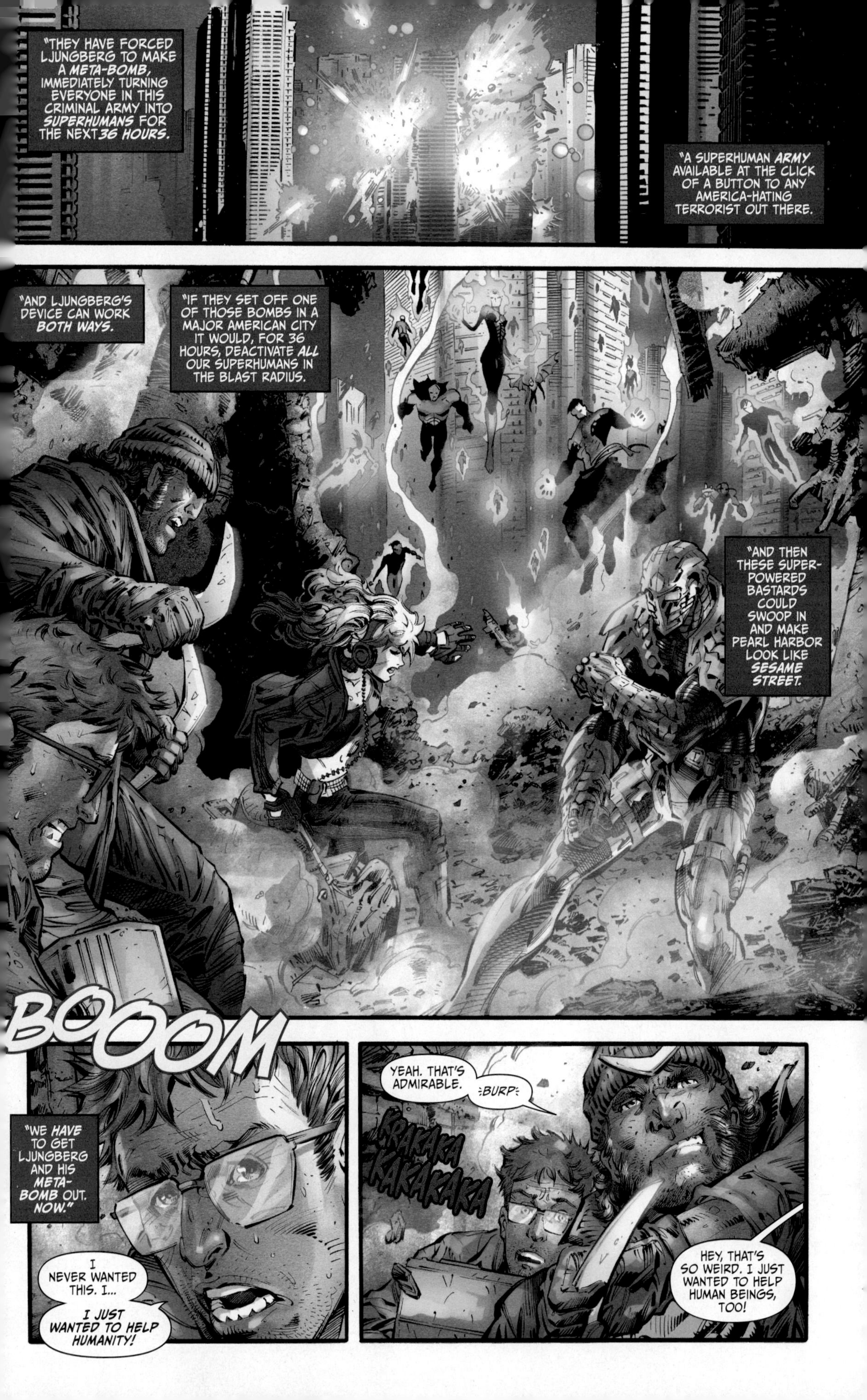
"THEY HAVE FORCED LJUNGBERG TO MAKE A META-BOMB, IMMEDIATELY TURNING EVERYONE IN THIS CRIMINAL ARMY INTO SUPERHUMANS FOR THE NEXT 36 HOURS.
"A SUPERHUMAN ARMY AVAILABLE AT THE CLICK OF A BUTTON TO ANY AMERICA-HATING TERRORIST OUT THERE.
"AND LJUNGBERG'S DEVICE CAN WORK BOTH WAYS.
"IF THEY SET OFF ONE OF THOSE BOMBS IN A MAJOR AMERICAN CITY IT WOULD, FOR 36 HOURS, DEACTIVATE ALL OUR SUPERHUMANS IN THE BLAST RADIUS.
"AND THEN THESE SUPER-POWERED BASTARDS COULD SWOOP IN AND MAKE PEARL HARBOR LOOK LIKE SESAME STREET.
BOOOOM
"WE HAVE TO GET LJUNGBERG AND HIS META-BOMB OUT. NOW."
I NEVER WANTED THIS. I...
I JUST WANTED TO HELP HUMANITY!
YEAH. THAT'S ADMIRABLE.
BURP
KRAKAKA KAKAKAKA
HEY, THAT'S SO WEIRD. I JUST WANTED TO HELP HUMAN BEINGS, TOO!

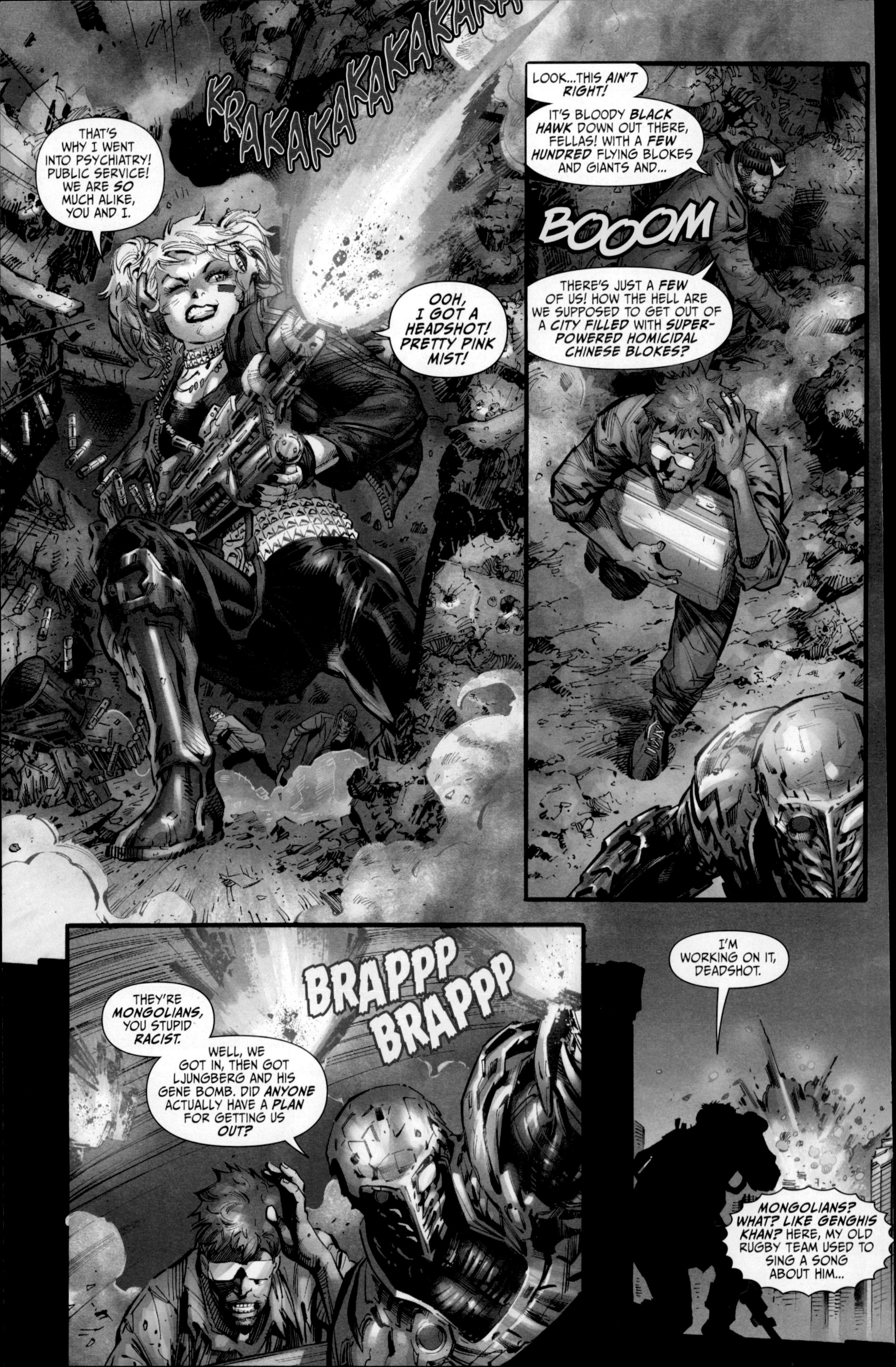
KRAKAKAKAKAKAKAKA
THAT'S WHY I WENT INTO PSYCHIATRY! PUBLIC SERVICE! WE ARE SO MUCH ALIKE, YOU AND I.
OOH, I GOT A HEADSHOT! PRETTY PINK MIST!
LOOK...THIS AIN'T RIGHT!
IT'S BLOODY BLACK HAWK DOWN OUT THERE, FELLAS! WITH A FEW HUNDRED FLYING BLOKES AND GIANTS AND...
BOOOM
THERE'S JUST A FEW OF US! HOW THE HELL ARE WE SUPPOSED TO GET OUT OF A CITY FILLED WITH SUPER-POWERED HOMICIDAL CHINESE BLOKES?
BRAPPP BRAPPP
THEY'RE MONGOLIANS, YOU STUPID RACIST.
WELL, WE GOT IN, THEN GOT LJUNGBERG AND HIS GENE BOMB. DID ANYONE ACTUALLY HAVE A PLAN FOR GETTING US OUT?
I'M WORKING ON IT, DEADSHOT.
MONGOLIANS? WHAT? LIKE GENGHIS KHAN? HERE, MY OLD RUGBY TEAM USED TO SING A SONG ABOUT HIM...

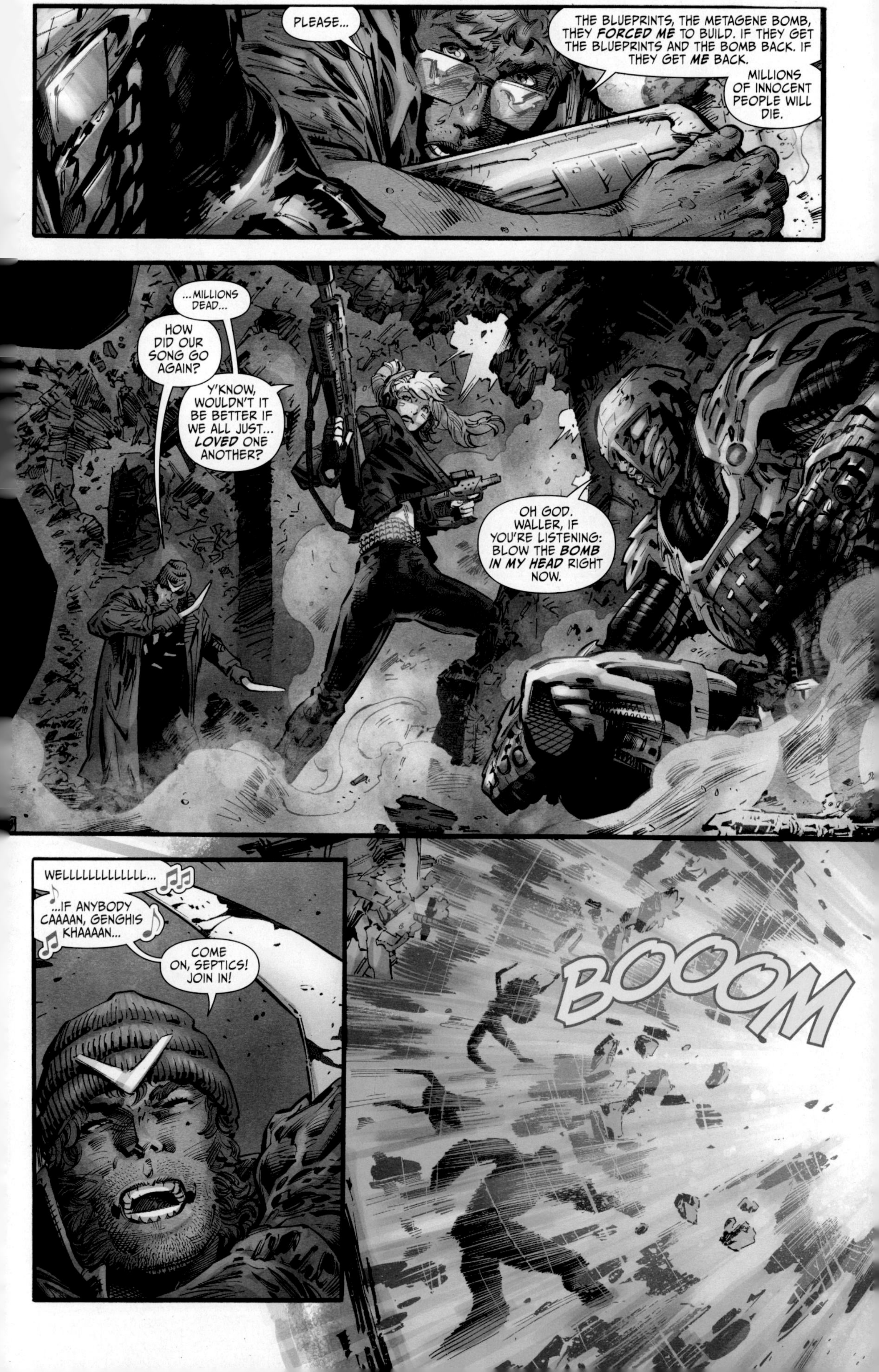
PLEASE...
THE BLUEPRINTS, THE METAGENE BOMB, THEY FORCED ME TO BUILD. IF THEY GET THE BLUEPRINTS AND THE BOMB BACK. IF THEY GET ME BACK.
MILLIONS OF INNOCENT PEOPLE WILL DIE.
...MILLIONS DEAD...
HOW DID OUR SONG GO AGAIN?
Y'KNOW, WOULDN'T IT BE BETTER IF WE ALL JUST... LOVED ONE ANOTHER?
OH GOD. WALLER, IF YOU'RE LISTENING: BLOW THE BOMB IN MY HEAD RIGHT NOW.
WELLLLLLLLLLLLLL...
...IF ANYBODY CAAAAN, GENGHIS KHAAAAN...
COME ON, SEPTICS! JOIN IN!
BOOOM

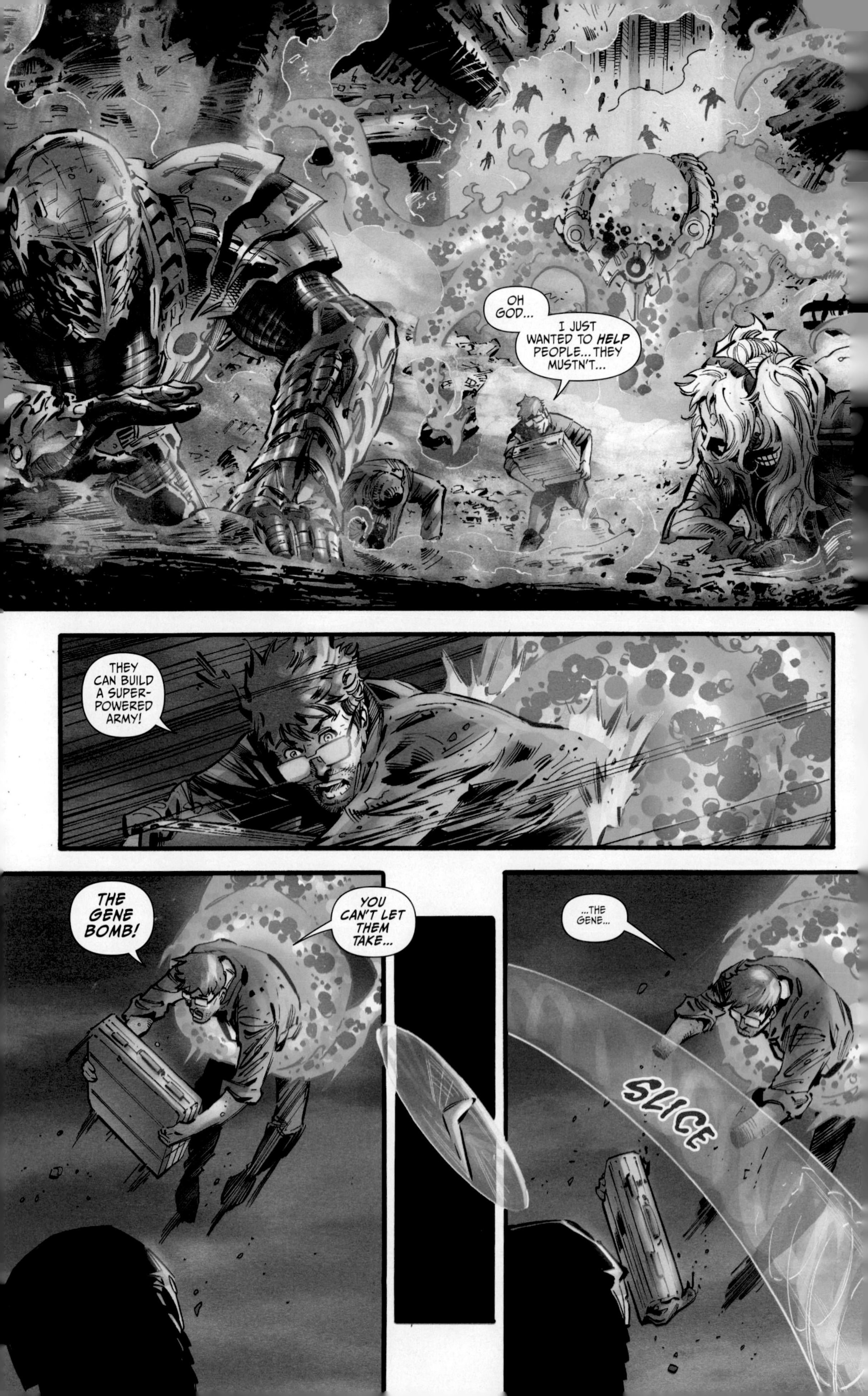
OH GOD...
I JUST WANTED TO HELP PEOPLE... THEY MUSTN'T...
THEY CAN BUILD A SUPER-POWERED ARMY!
THE GENE BOMB!
YOU CAN'T LET THEM TAKE...
...THE GENE...
SLICE

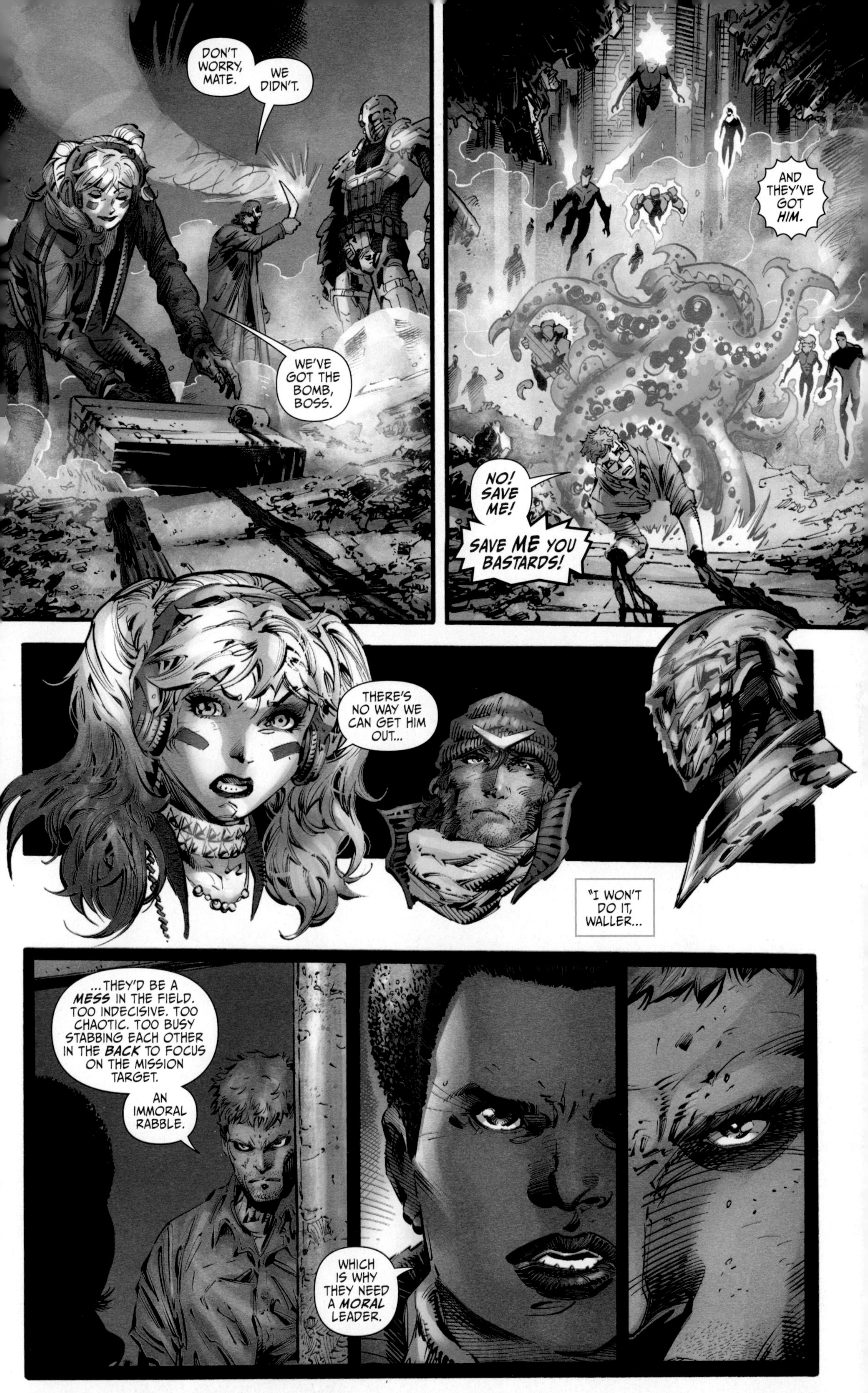
DON'T WORRY, MATE.
WE DIDN'T.
WE'VE GOT THE BOMB, BOSS.
AND THEY'VE GOT HIM.
NO! SAVE ME!
SAVE ME YOU BASTARDS!
THERE'S NO WAY WE CAN GET HIM OUT...
"I WON'T DO IT, WALLER...
...THEY'D BE A MESS IN THE FIELD. TOO INDECISIVE. TOO CHAOTIC. TOO BUSY STABBING EACH OTHER IN THE BACK TO FOCUS ON THE MISSION TARGET.
AN IMMORAL RABBLE.
WHICH IS WHY THEY NEED A MORAL LEADER.

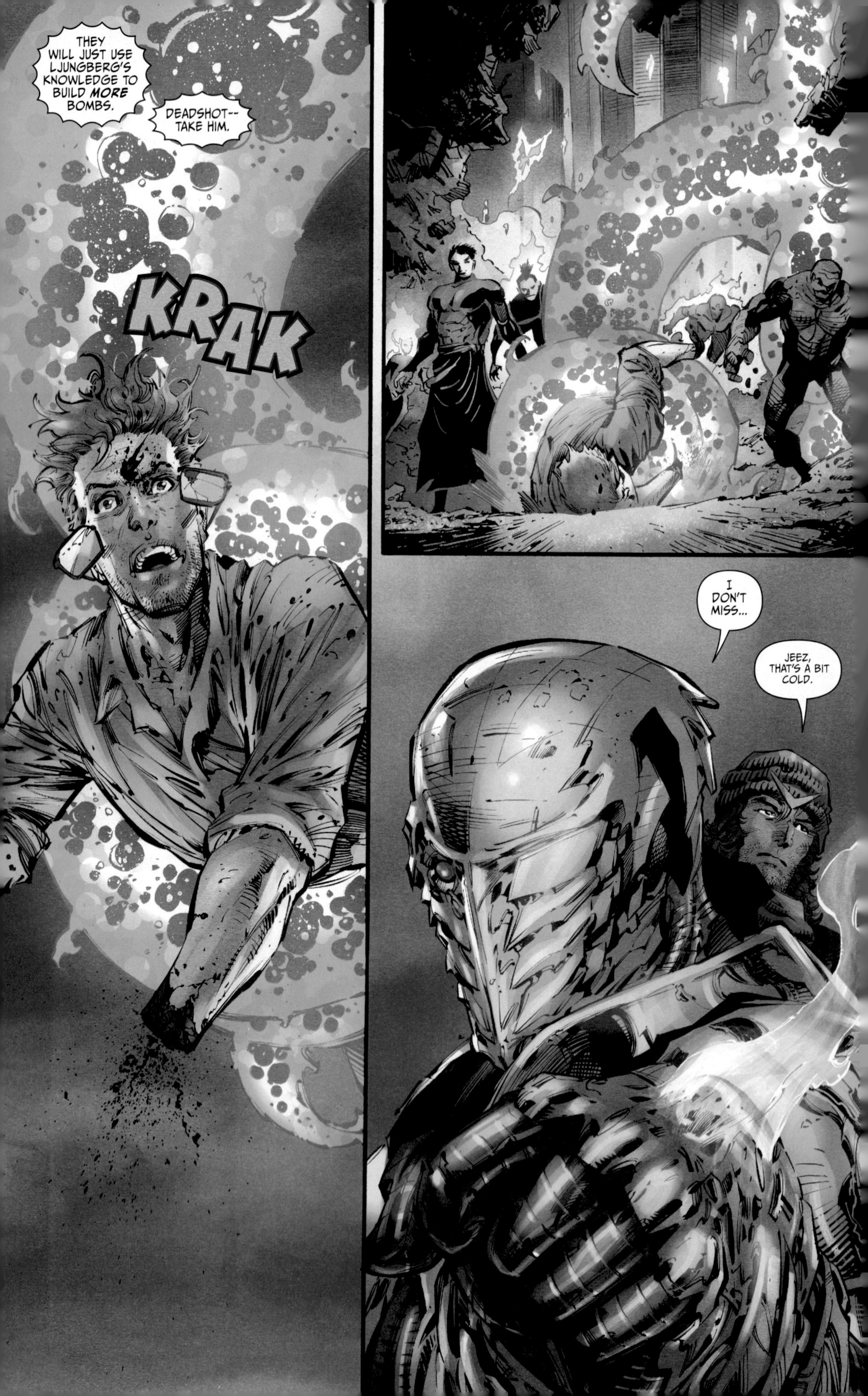
THEY WILL JUST USE LJUNGBERG'S KNOWLEDGE TO BUILD *MORE* BOMBS.
DEADSHOT-- TAKE HIM.
KRAK
I DON'T MISS...
JEEZ, THAT'S A BIT COLD.

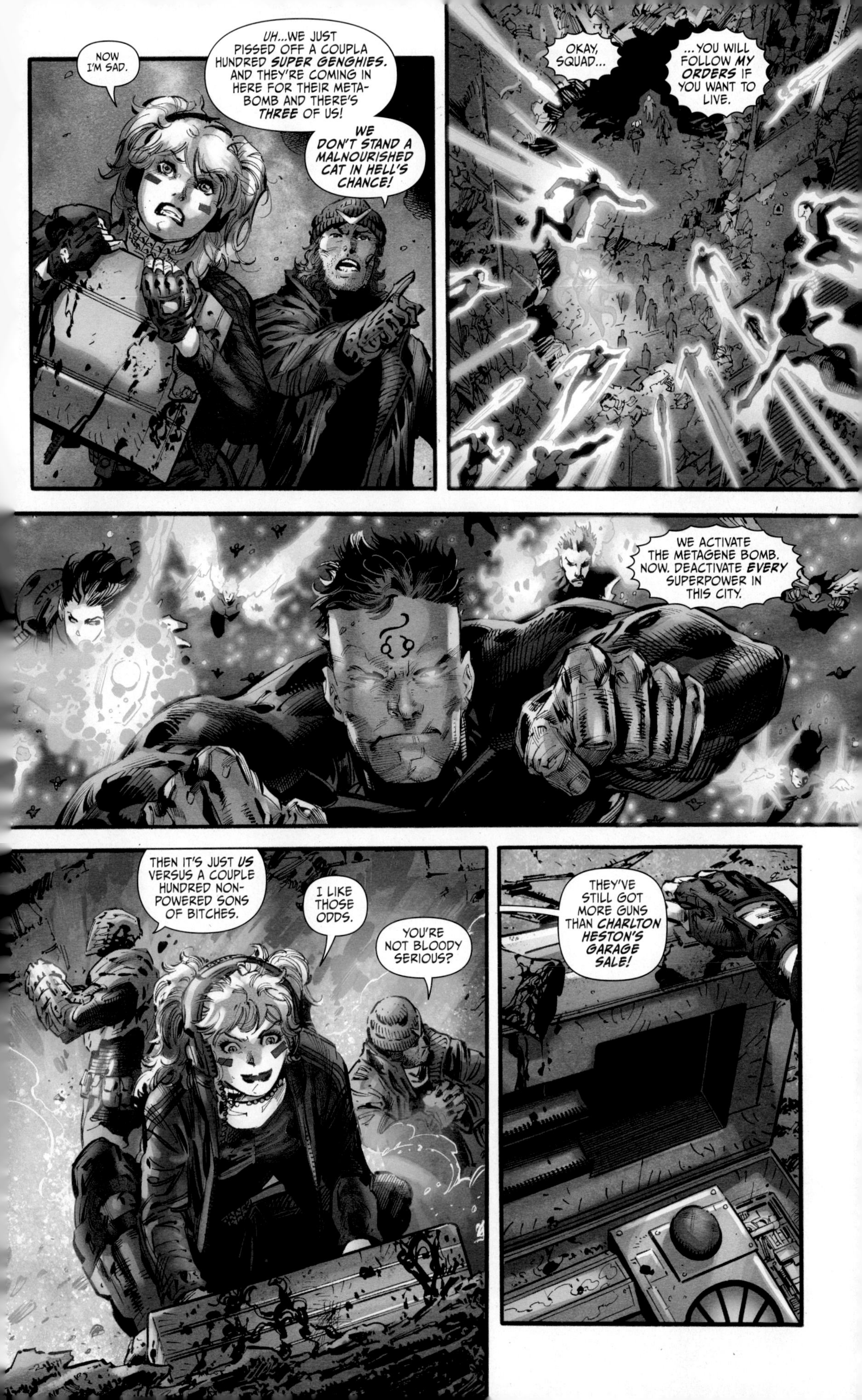
NOW I'M SAD.
UH...WE JUST PISSED OFF A COUPLA HUNDRED SUPER GENGHIES. AND THEY'RE COMING IN HERE FOR THEIR META-BOMB AND THERE'S THREE OF US!
WE DON'T STAND A MALNOURISHED CAT IN HELL'S CHANCE!
OKAY, SQUAD...
...YOU WILL FOLLOW MY ORDERS IF YOU WANT TO LIVE.
WE ACTIVATE THE METAGENE BOMB. NOW. DEACTIVATE EVERY SUPERPOWER IN THIS CITY.
THEN IT'S JUST US VERSUS A COUPLE HUNDRED NON-POWERED SONS OF BITCHES.
I LIKE THOSE ODDS.
YOU'RE NOT BLOODY SERIOUS?
THEY'VE STILL GOT MORE GUNS THAN CHARLTON HESTON'S GARAGE SALE!

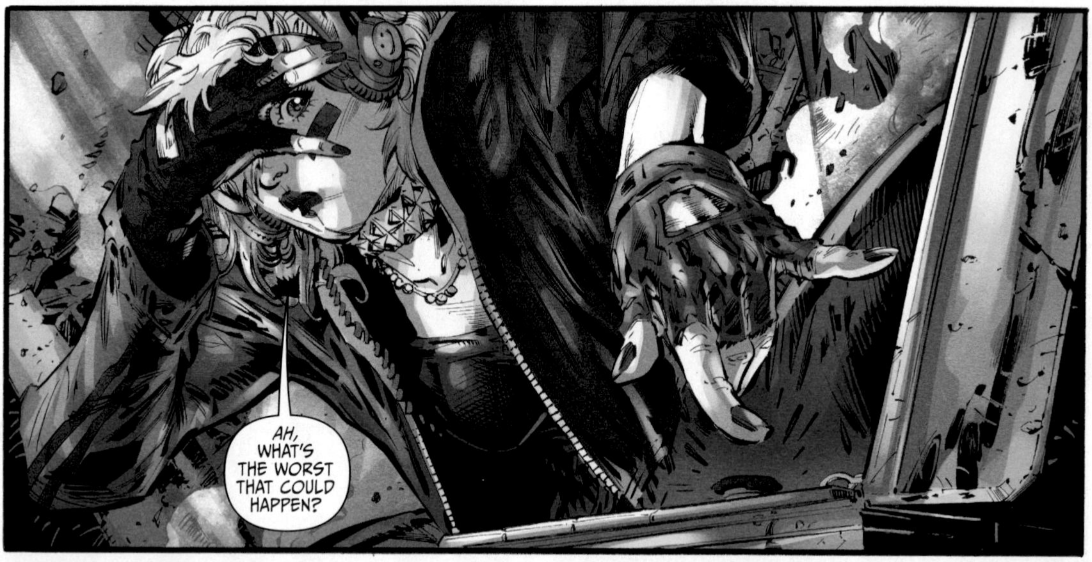
AH, WHAT'S THE WORST THAT COULD HAPPEN?

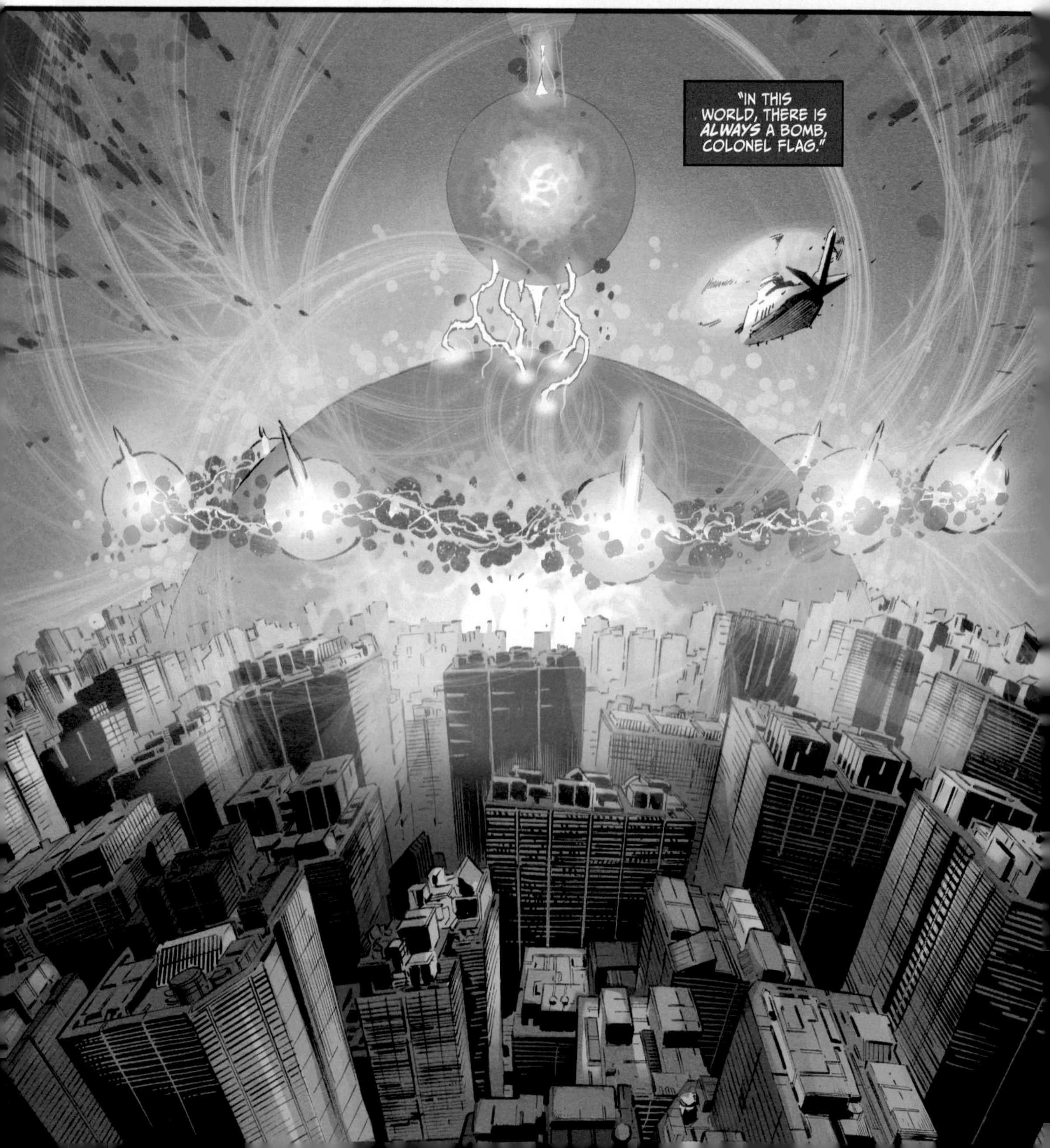
"IN THIS WORLD, THERE IS ALWAYS A BOMB, COLONEL FLAG."

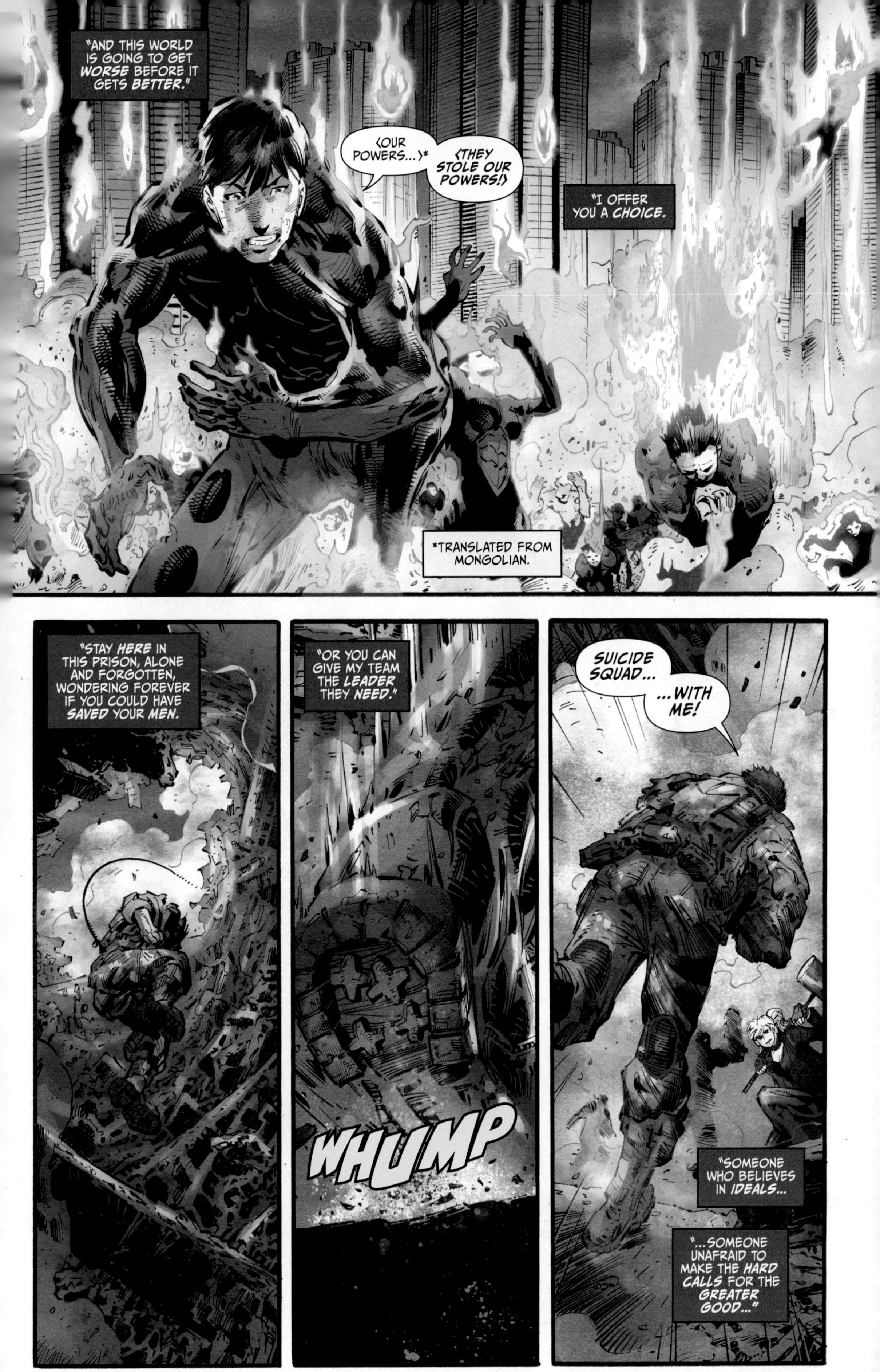
"AND THIS WORLD IS GOING TO GET WORSE BEFORE IT GETS BETTER."
‹OUR POWERS...›*
‹THEY STOLE OUR POWERS!›
"I OFFER YOU A CHOICE.
*TRANSLATED FROM MONGOLIAN.
"STAY HERE IN THIS PRISON, ALONE AND FORGOTTEN, WONDERING FOREVER IF YOU COULD HAVE SAVED YOUR MEN.
"OR YOU CAN GIVE MY TEAM THE LEADER THEY NEED."
WHUMP
SUICIDE SQUAD...
...WITH ME!
"SOMEONE WHO BELIEVES IN IDEALS...
"...SOMEONE UNAFRAID TO MAKE THE HARD CALLS FOR THE GREATER GOOD..."

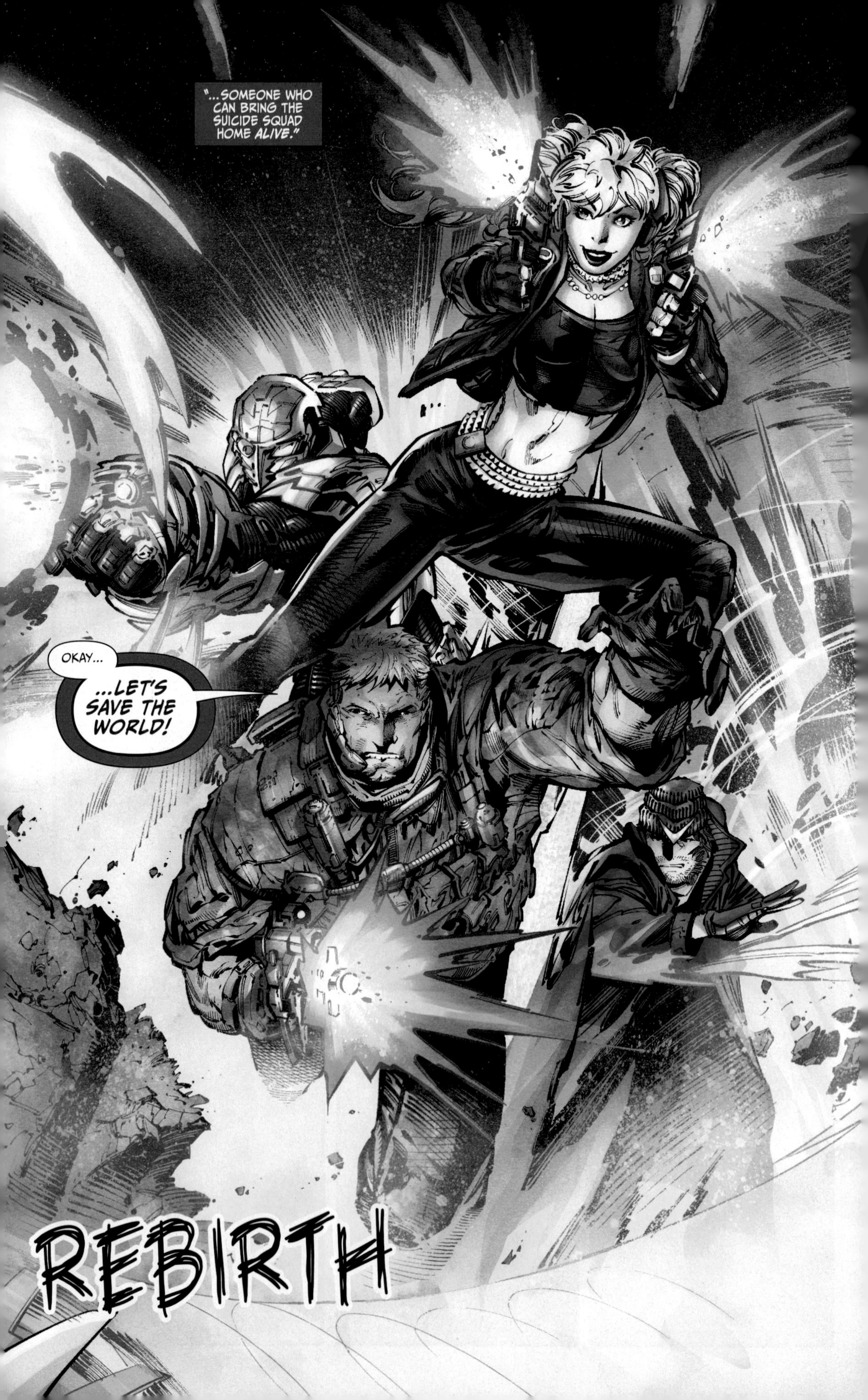
"...SOMEONE WHO CAN BRING THE SUICIDE SQUAD HOME ALIVE."
OKAY...
...LET'S SAVE THE WORLD!
REBIRTH

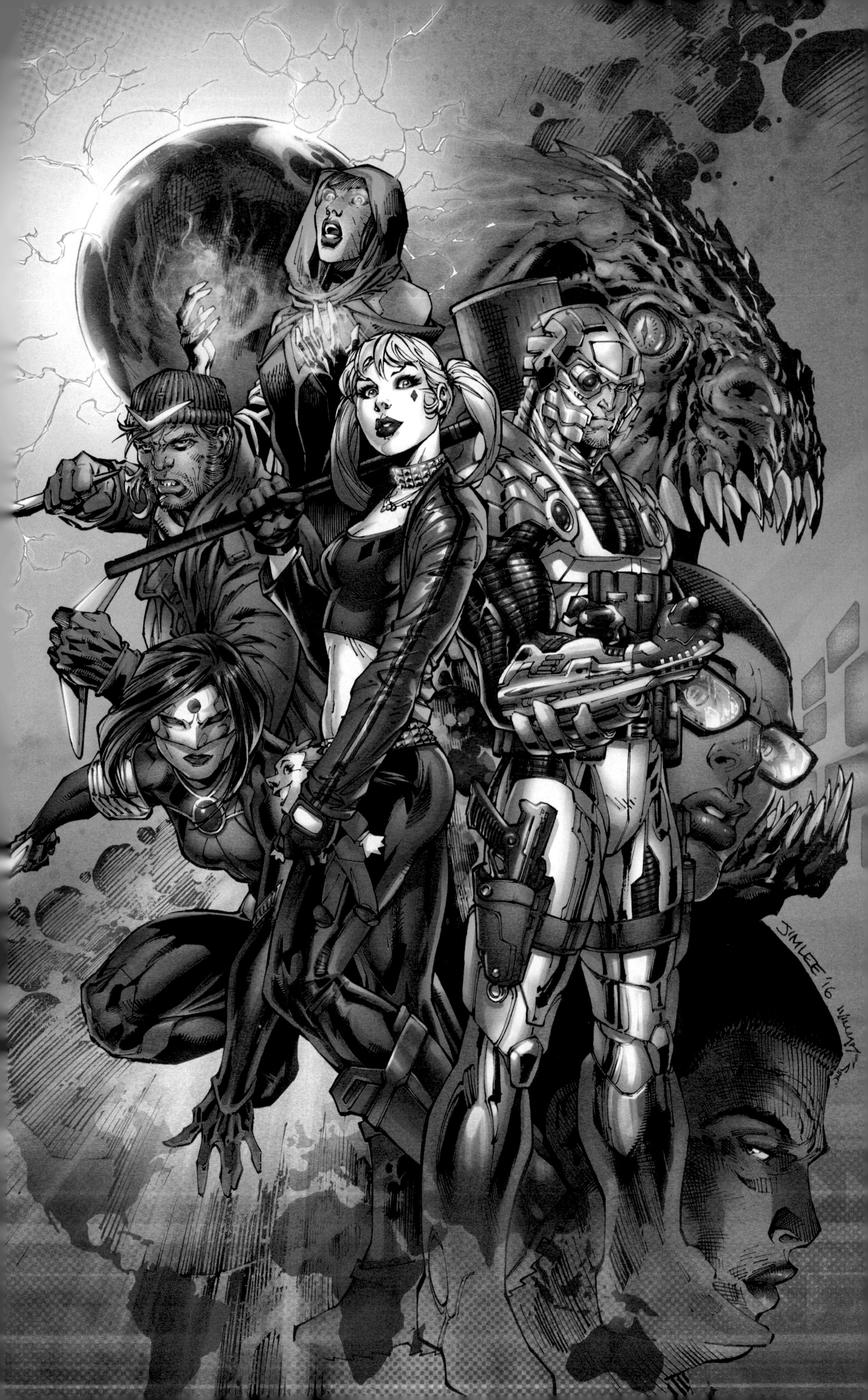
JIMLEE '16

THE BLACK VAULT

ROB WILLIAMS writer * JIM LEE penciller
SCOTT WILLIAMS (parts 1-3) SCOTT WILLIAMS, SANDRA HOPE, JONATHAN GLAPION and TREVOR SCOTT (part 4) inkers
ALEX SINCLAIR (parts 1-3) ALEX SINCLAIR and HI-FI (part 4) colorists * NATE PIEKOS OF BLAMBOT® (parts 1-3) ROB LEIGH (part 4) letterers
Cover by JIM LEE, SCOTT WILLIAMS and ALEX SINCLAIR

HARVEY RICHARDS associate editor * ANDY KHOURI editor * BRIAN CUNNINGHAM group editor

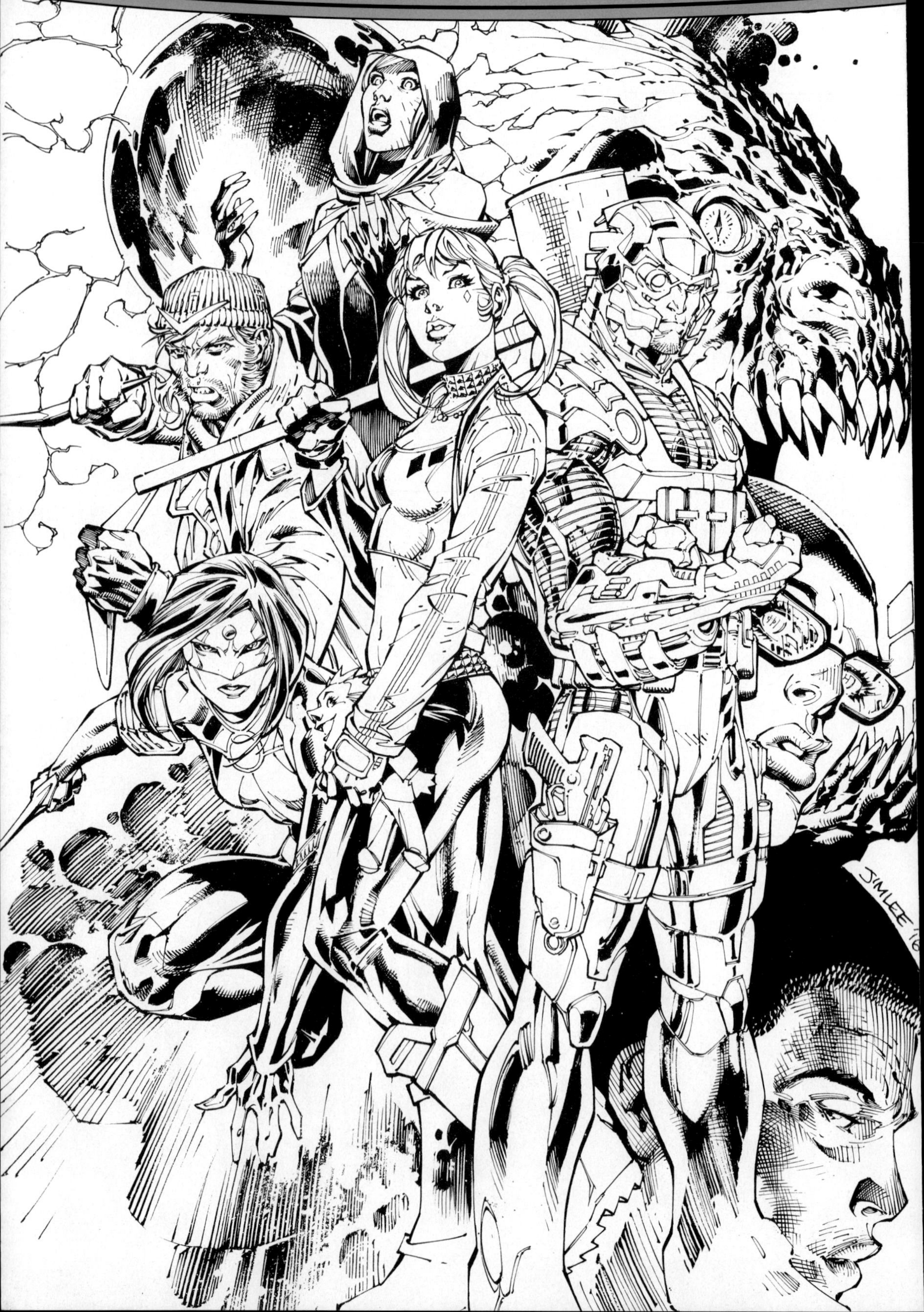
JIM LEE '16

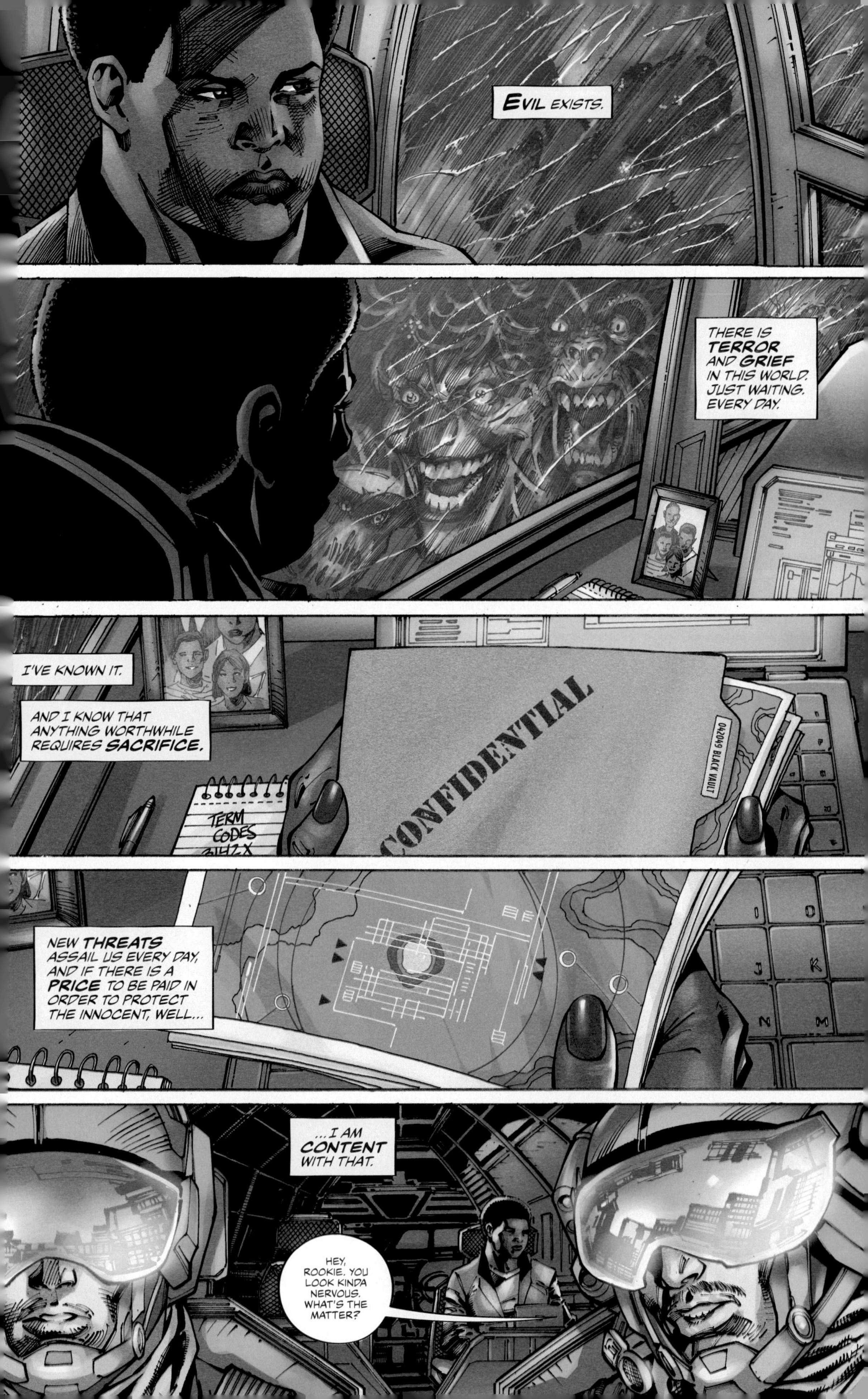
EVIL EXISTS.
THERE IS TERROR AND GRIEF IN THIS WORLD. JUST WAITING. EVERY DAY.
I'VE KNOWN IT.
AND I KNOW THAT ANYTHING WORTHWHILE REQUIRES SACRIFICE.
TERM CODES 3142X
CONFIDENTIAL
042049 BLACK VAULT
NEW THREATS ASSAIL US EVERY DAY, AND IF THERE IS A PRICE TO BE PAID IN ORDER TO PROTECT THE INNOCENT, WELL...
...I AM CONTENT WITH THAT.
HEY, ROOKIE. YOU LOOK KINDA NERVOUS. WHAT'S THE MATTER?

YOU'VE NEVER DELIVERED THE DEVIL TO HELL BEFORE?
THE BLACK VAULT
PART ONE: I WANNA BE SEDATED

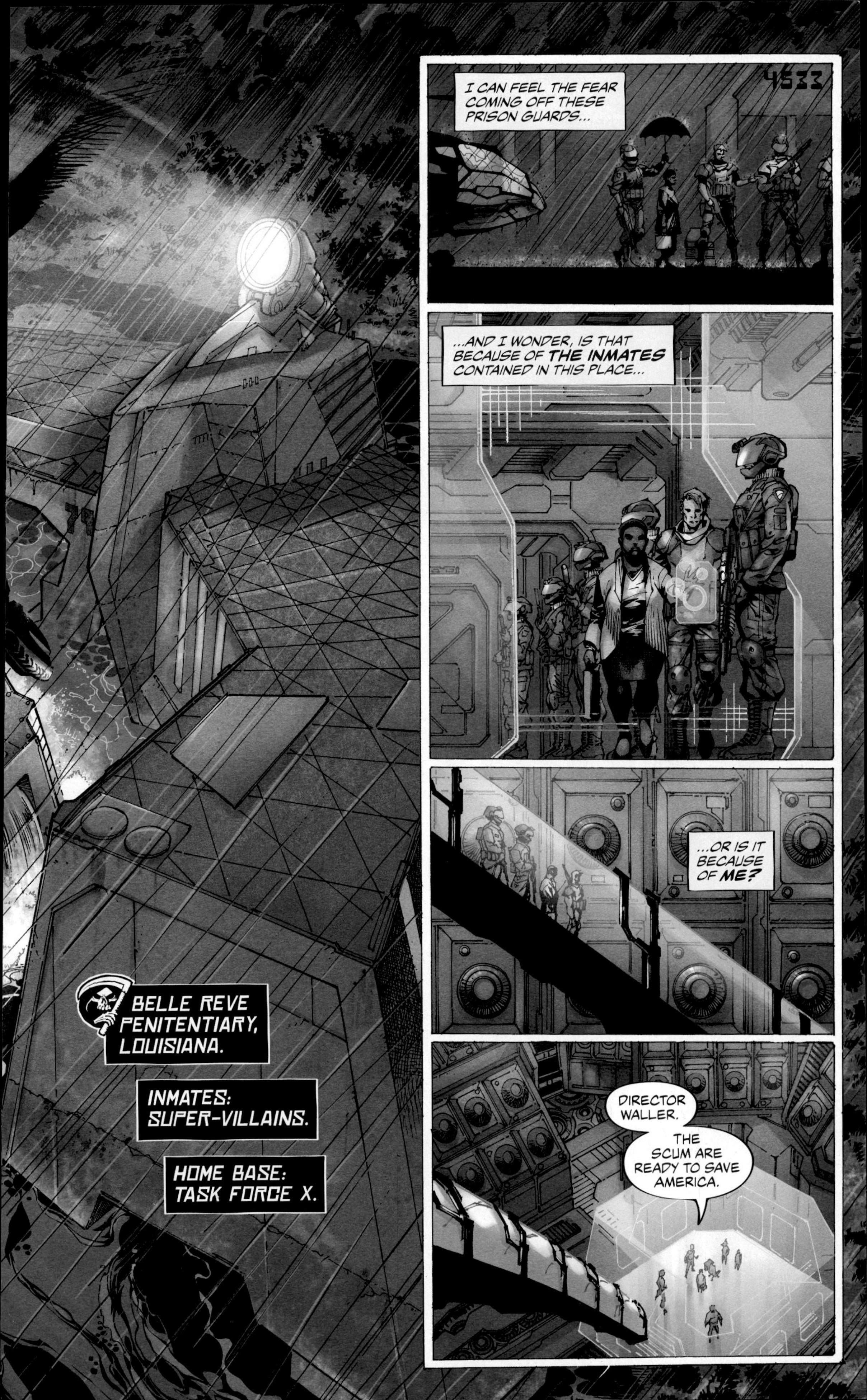
4533
I CAN FEEL THE FEAR COMING OFF THESE PRISON GUARDS...
...AND I WONDER, IS THAT BECAUSE OF THE INMATES CONTAINED IN THIS PLACE...
...OR IS IT BECAUSE OF ME?
DIRECTOR WALLER.
THE SCUM ARE READY TO SAVE AMERICA.
BELLE REVE PENITENTIARY, LOUISIANA.
INMATES: SUPER-VILLAINS.
HOME BASE: TASK FORCE X.

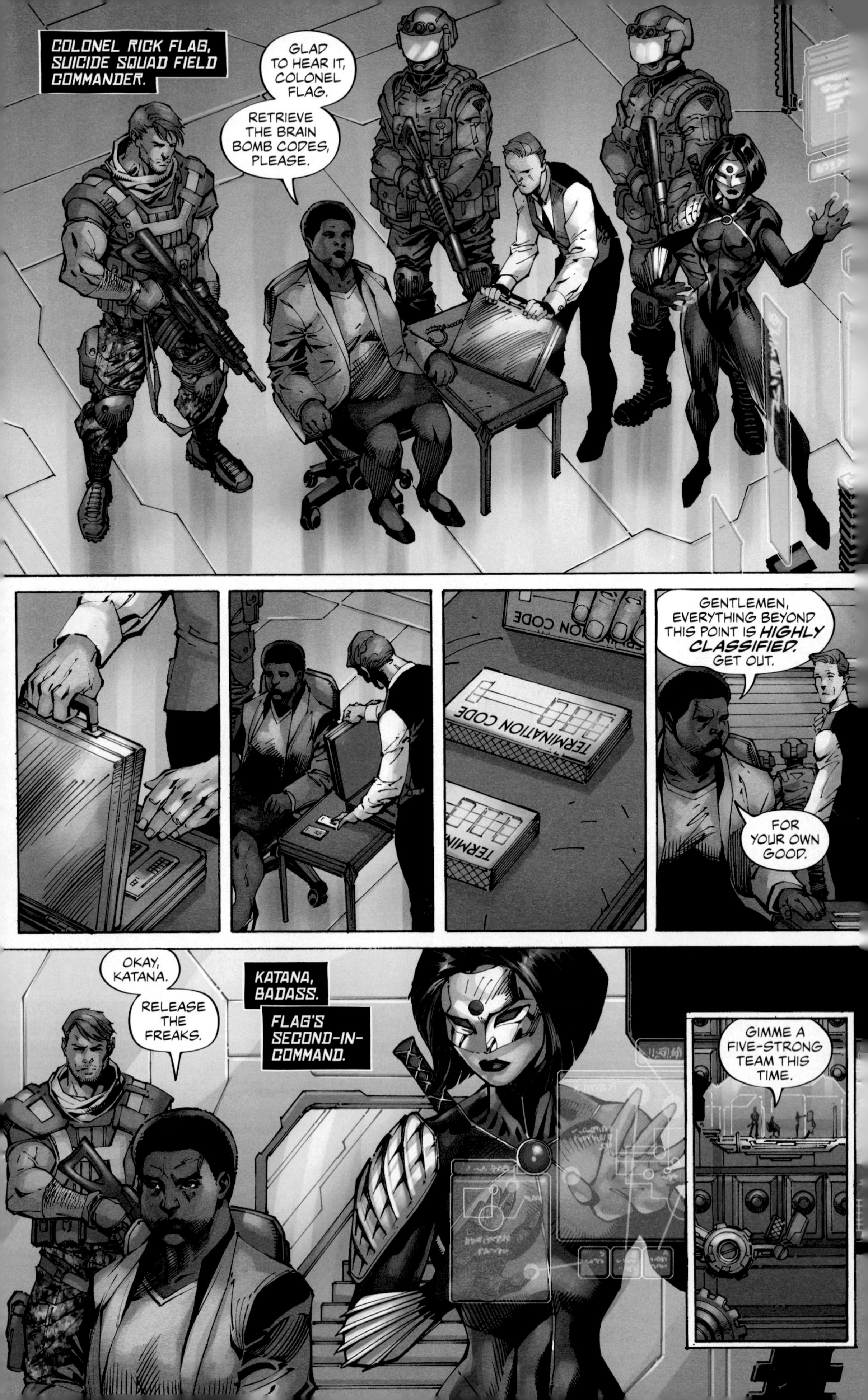
COLONEL RICK FLAG, SUICIDE SQUAD FIELD COMMANDER.
GLAD TO HEAR IT, COLONEL FLAG.
RETRIEVE THE BRAIN BOMB CODES, PLEASE.
TERMINATION CODE
GENTLEMEN, EVERYTHING BEYOND THIS POINT IS HIGHLY CLASSIFIED. GET OUT.
FOR YOUR OWN GOOD.
OKAY, KATANA.
RELEASE THE FREAKS.
KATANA, BADASS.
FLAG'S SECOND-IN-COMMAND.
GIMME A FIVE-STRONG TEAM THIS TIME.

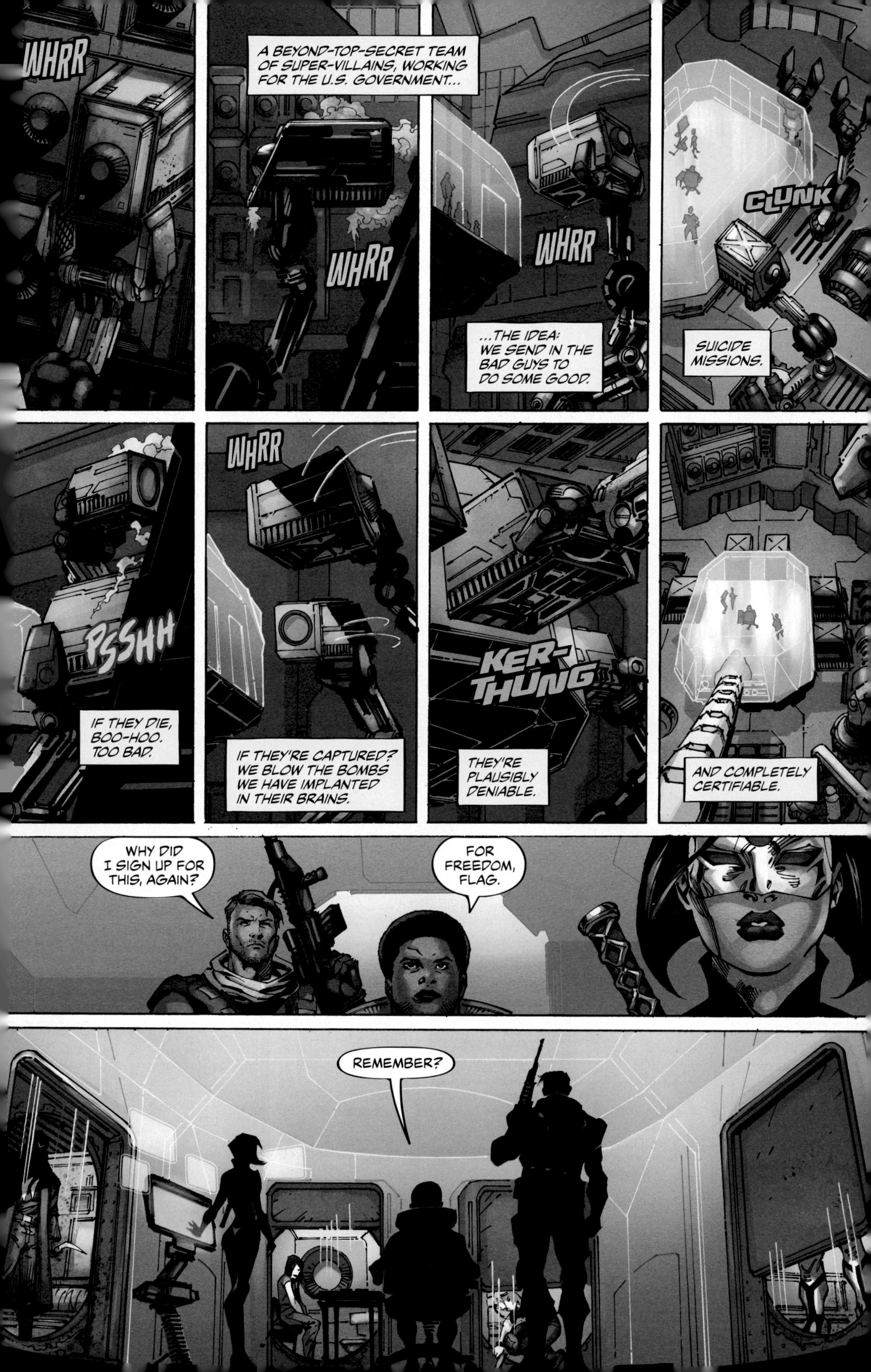
WHRR
A BEYOND-TOP-SECRET TEAM OF SUPER-VILLAINS, WORKING FOR THE U.S. GOVERNMENT...
WHRR
WHRR
...THE IDEA: WE SEND IN THE BAD GUYS TO DO SOME GOOD.
CLUNK
SUICIDE MISSIONS.
PSSHH
IF THEY DIE, BOO-HOO. TOO BAD.
WHRR
IF THEY'RE CAPTURED? WE BLOW THE BOMBS WE HAVE IMPLANTED IN THEIR BRAINS.
KER-THUNG
THEY'RE PLAUSIBLY DENIABLE.
AND COMPLETELY CERTIFIABLE.
WHY DID I SIGN UP FOR THIS, AGAIN?
FOR FREEDOM, FLAG.
REMEMBER?

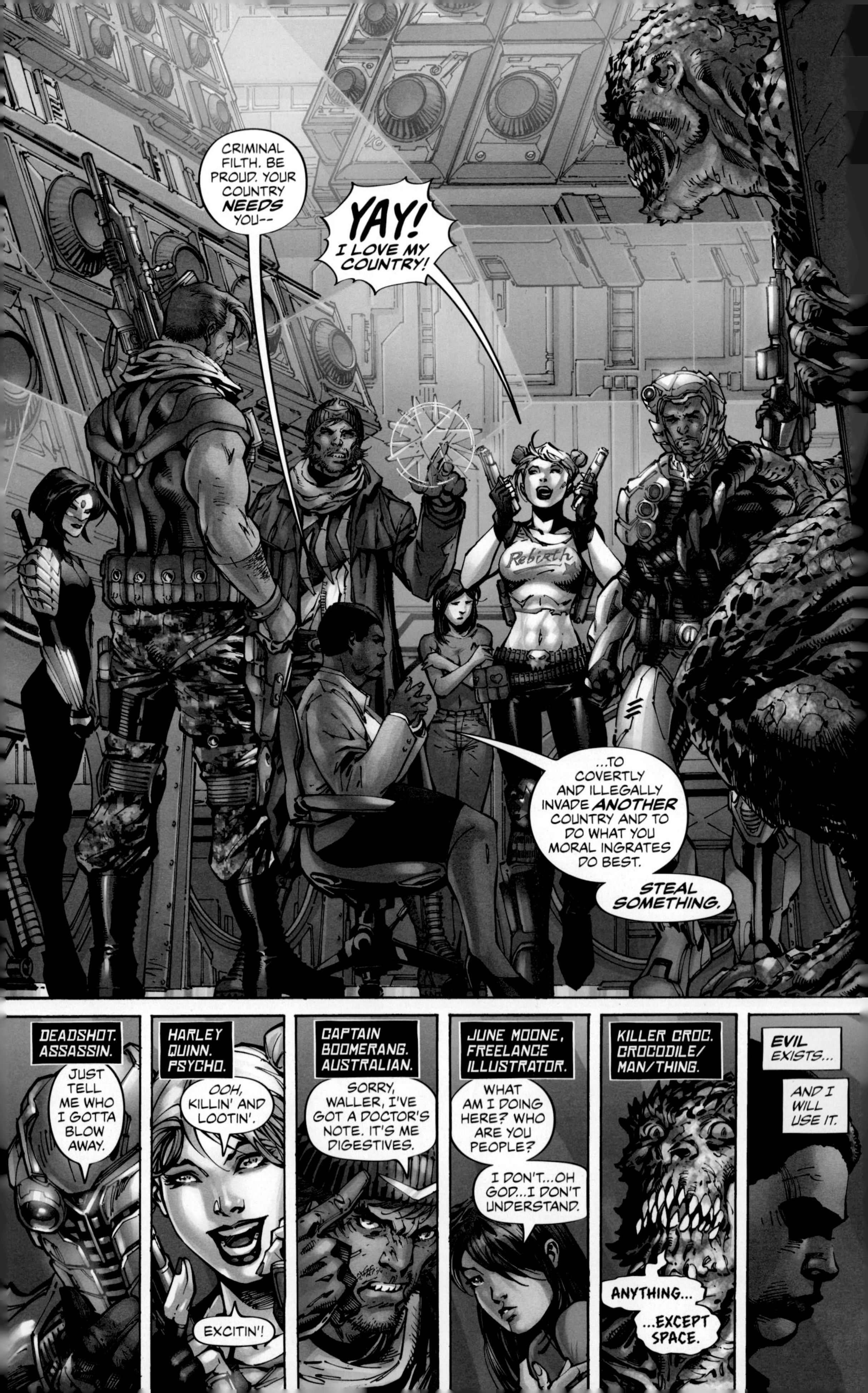
CRIMINAL FILTH. BE PROUD. YOUR COUNTRY NEEDS YOU--
YAY! I LOVE MY COUNTRY!
...TO COVERTLY AND ILLEGALLY INVADE ANOTHER COUNTRY AND TO DO WHAT YOU MORAL INGRATES DO BEST.
STEAL SOMETHING.
Rebirth
DEADSHOT. ASSASSIN.
JUST TELL ME WHO I GOTTA BLOW AWAY.
HARLEY QUINN. PSYCHO.
OOH, KILLIN' AND LOOTIN'.
EXCITIN'!
CAPTAIN BOOMERANG. AUSTRALIAN.
SORRY, WALLER, I'VE GOT A DOCTOR'S NOTE. IT'S ME DIGESTIVES.
JUNE MOONE, FREELANCE ILLUSTRATOR.
WHAT AM I DOING HERE? WHO ARE YOU PEOPLE?
I DON'T...OH GOD...I DON'T UNDERSTAND.
KILLER CROC. CROCODILE/ MAN/THING.
ANYTHING...
...EXCEPT SPACE.
EVIL EXISTS...
AND I WILL USE IT.

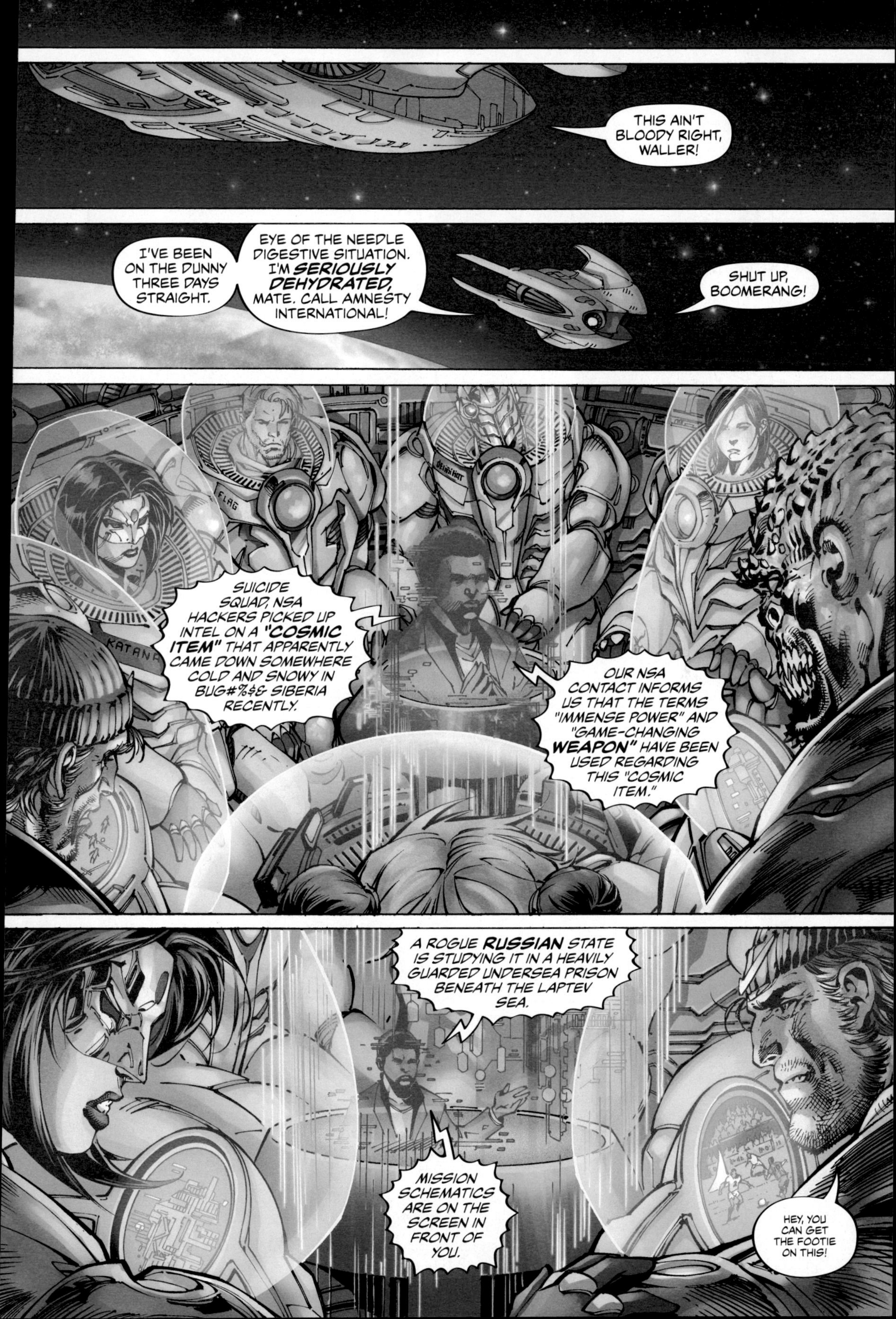
THIS AIN'T BLOODY RIGHT, WALLER!
I'VE BEEN ON THE DUNNY THREE DAYS STRAIGHT.
EYE OF THE NEEDLE DIGESTIVE SITUATION. I'M SERIOUSLY DEHYDRATED, MATE. CALL AMNESTY INTERNATIONAL!
SHUT UP, BOOMERANG!
SUICIDE SQUAD, NSA HACKERS PICKED UP INTEL ON A "COSMIC ITEM" THAT APPARENTLY CAME DOWN SOMEWHERE COLD AND SNOWY IN BUG#%$& SIBERIA RECENTLY.
OUR NSA CONTACT INFORMS US THAT THE TERMS "IMMENSE POWER" AND "GAME-CHANGING WEAPON" HAVE BEEN USED REGARDING THIS "COSMIC ITEM."
A ROGUE RUSSIAN STATE IS STUDYING IT IN A HEAVILY GUARDED UNDERSEA PRISON BENEATH THE LAPTEV SEA.
MISSION SCHEMATICS ARE ON THE SCREEN IN FRONT OF YOU.
HEY, YOU CAN GET THE FOOTIE ON THIS!

ANY ASSAULT VIA AIR OR SEA WOULD BE PICKED UP BY THEIR SENTRIES WAY BEFORE WE GOT WITHIN MILES. AND, BESIDES, THAT WOULD BE AN "ACT OF WAR," WHICH THE U.S. WOULD *NEVER* SANCTION.

ZZZZZ

DEADSHOT

BUT WE HAVE A WAY TO GET US ON-SITE *FAST* BEFORE THEY EVEN KNOW WE'RE THERE.

OH GOD. I SHOULDN'T BE HERE. I...THERE'S *TOO MUCH DARKNESS.* *SHE'S* INSIDE ME. I CAN FEEL IT. *SHE'S* INSIDE ME AND SHE WANTS TO *EMERGE!* TO *TRANSCEND!*

I FEEL A BIT... UNWELL.

I'LL SAY THIS IN TWO-SYLLABLE WORDS, FOR *BOOMERANG...*

OI!

OOOH, THERE'S A POKÉCUTEY UP HERE!

GET IN, *STEAL* OR *DESTROY* THIS COSMIC ITEM. ENSURE THIS RUSSIAN ROGUE STATE DOESN'T HAVE IT.

AND REMEMBER THAT IF YOU GET ANY IDEAS ABOUT *RUNNING* FOR IT...

...I WILL NOT HESITATE TO *BLOW YOUR MINDS.*

IN THE MOST *LITERAL* SENSE.

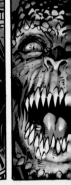

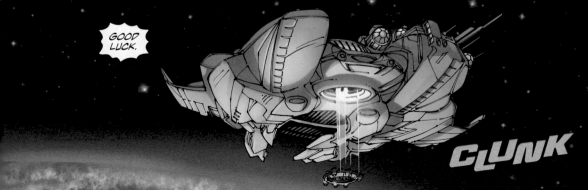

GOOD LUCK.

CLUNK

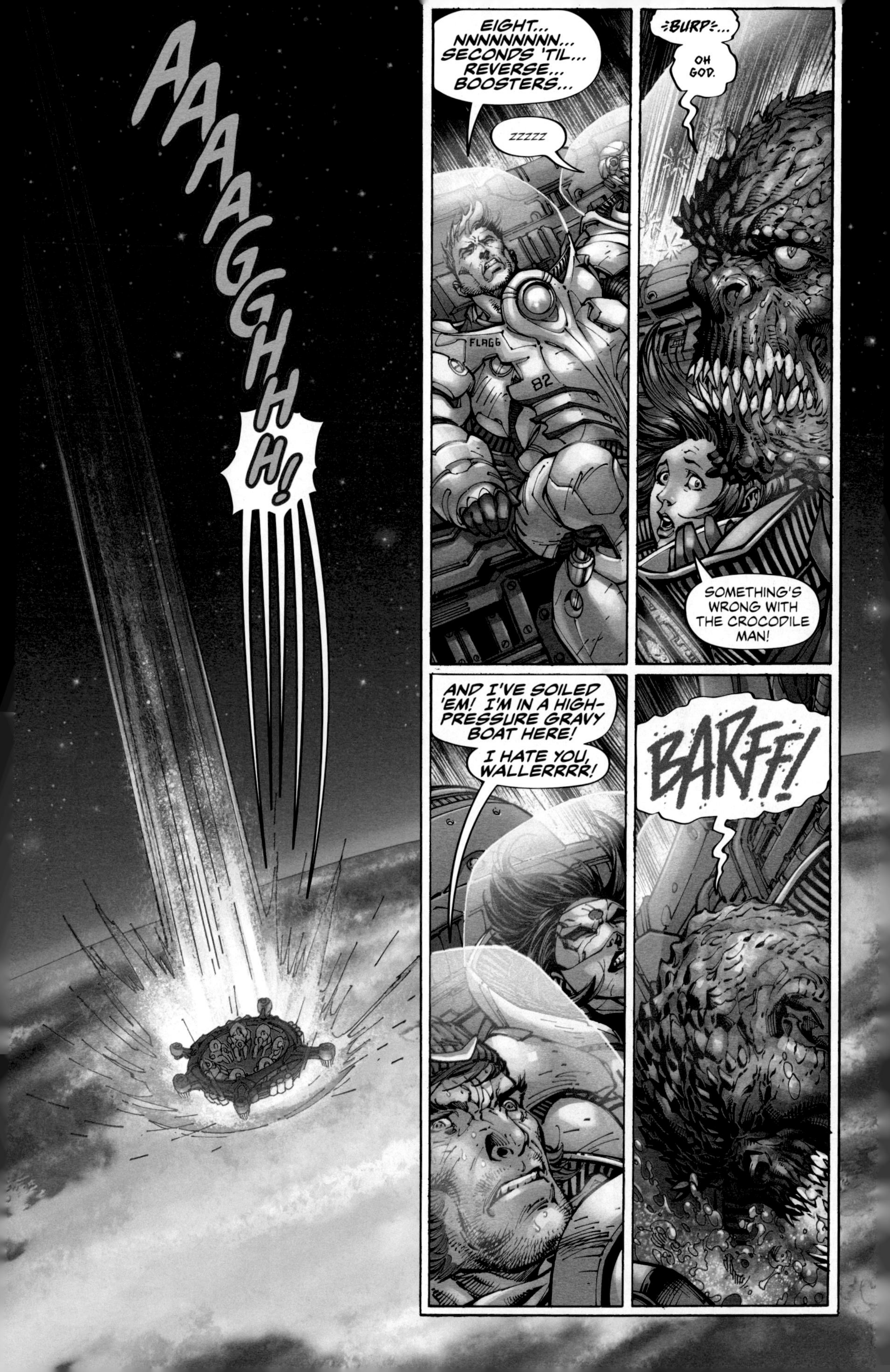
AAAAGGHHHH!
EIGHT... NNNNNNNNN... SECONDS 'TIL... REVERSE... BOOSTERS...
ZZZZZ
FLAGG
B2
BURP...
OH GOD.
SOMETHING'S WRONG WITH THE CROCODILE MAN!
AND I'VE SOILED 'EM! I'M IN A HIGH-PRESSURE GRAVY BOAT HERE!
I HATE YOU, WALLERRRR!
BARFF!

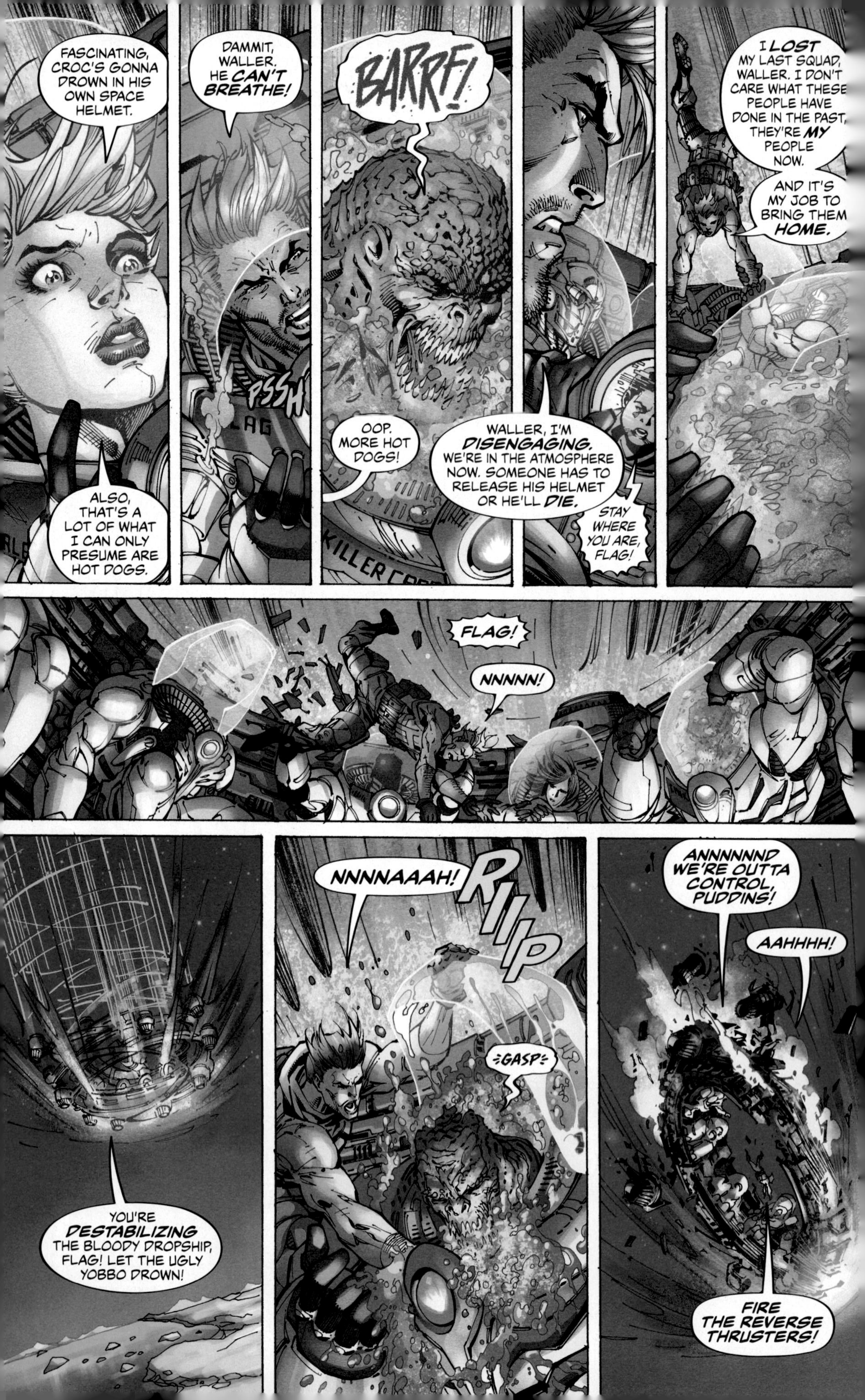
FASCINATING, CROC'S GONNA DROWN IN HIS OWN SPACE HELMET.
ALSO, THAT'S A LOT OF WHAT I CAN ONLY PRESUME ARE HOT DOGS.
DAMMIT, WALLER. HE CAN'T BREATHE!
PSSH
BARRF!
OOP. MORE HOT DOGS!
KILLER CROC
WALLER, I'M DISENGAGING. WE'RE IN THE ATMOSPHERE NOW. SOMEONE HAS TO RELEASE HIS HELMET OR HE'LL DIE.
STAY WHERE YOU ARE, FLAG!
I LOST MY LAST SQUAD, WALLER. I DON'T CARE WHAT THESE PEOPLE HAVE DONE IN THE PAST, THEY'RE MY PEOPLE NOW.
AND IT'S MY JOB TO BRING THEM HOME.
FLAG!
NNNNN!
YOU'RE DESTABILIZING THE BLOODY DROPSHIP, FLAG! LET THE UGLY YOBBO DROWN!
NNNNAAAH!
RIIIP
GASP
ANNNNNND WE'RE OUTTA CONTROL, PUDDINS!
AAHHHH!
FIRE THE REVERSE THRUSTERS!

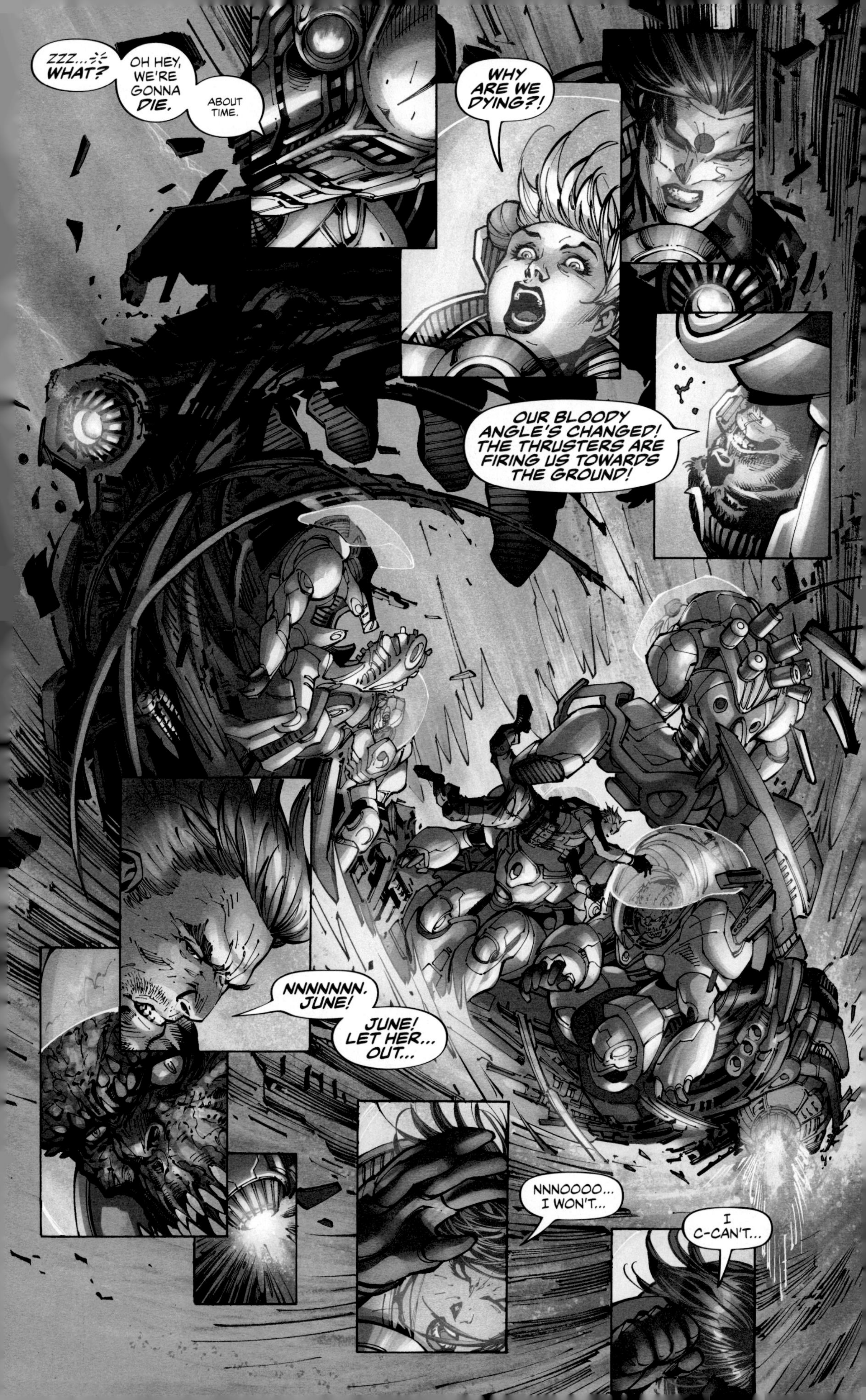
ZZZ... WHAT?
OH HEY, WE'RE GONNA DIE.
ABOUT TIME.
WHY ARE WE DYING?!
OUR BLOODY ANGLE'S CHANGED! THE THRUSTERS ARE FIRING US TOWARDS THE GROUND!
NNNNNNN. JUNE!
JUNE! LET HER... OUT...
NNNOOOO... I WON'T...
I C-CAN'T...

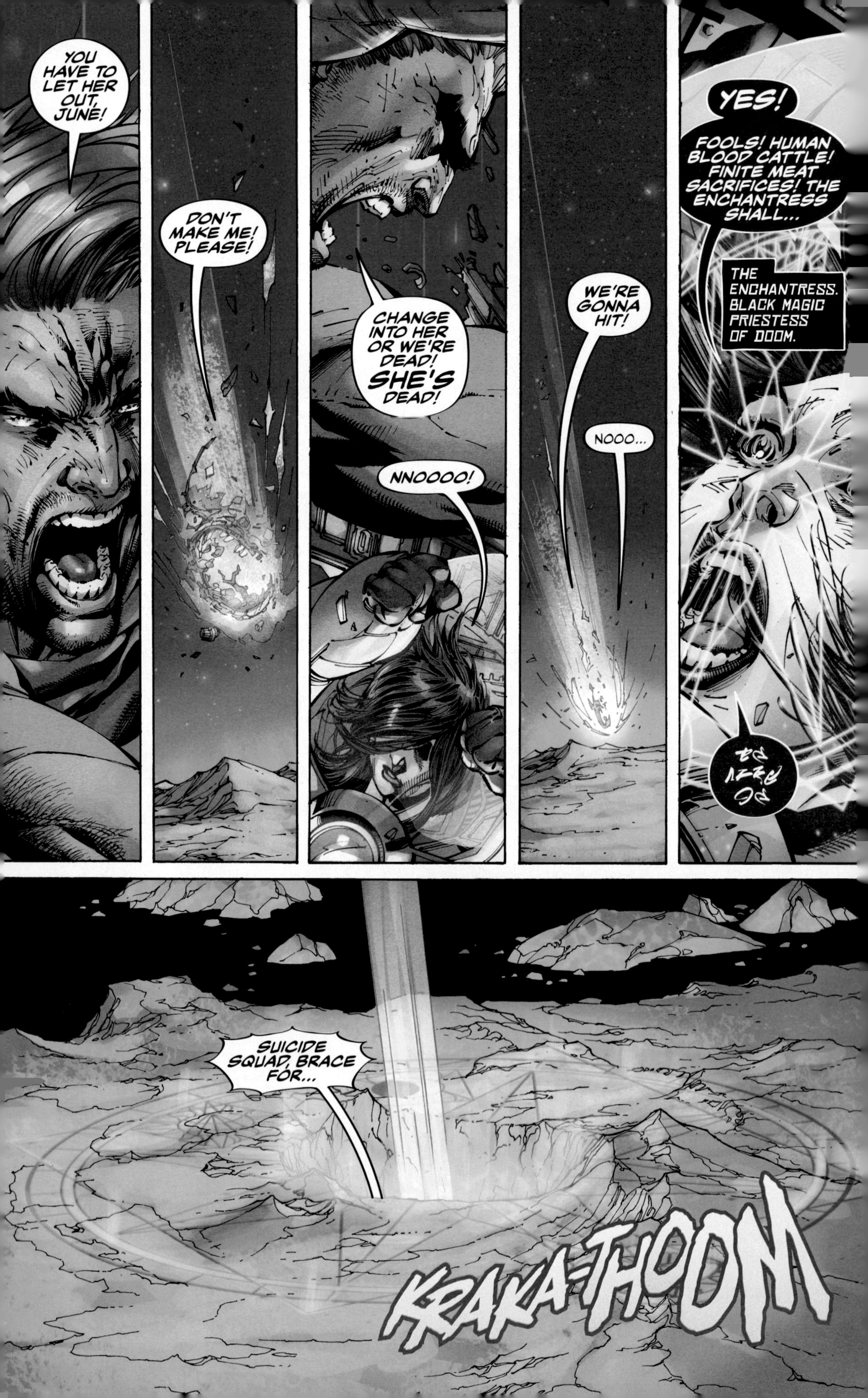

YOU HAVE TO LET HER OUT, JUNE!
DON'T MAKE ME! PLEASE!
CHANGE INTO HER OR WE'RE DEAD! SHE'S DEAD!
NNOOOO!
WE'RE GONNA HIT!
NOOO...
YES!
FOOLS! HUMAN BLOOD CATTLE! FINITE MEAT SACRIFICES! THE ENCHANTRESS SHALL...
THE ENCHANTRESS. BLACK MAGIC PRIESTESS OF DOOM.
SUICIDE SQUAD, BRACE FOR...
KRAKA-THOOM

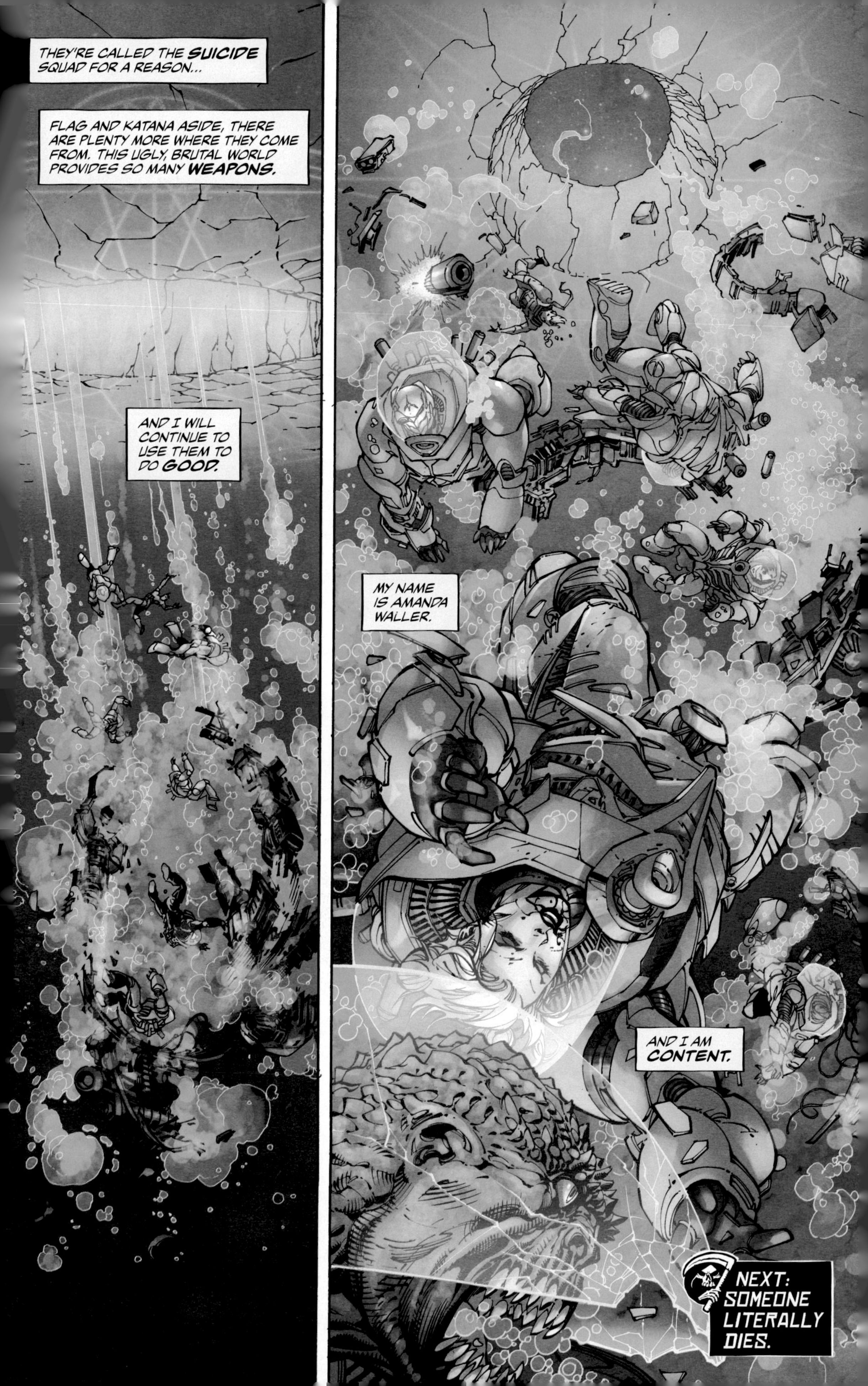
THEY'RE CALLED THE SUICIDE SQUAD FOR A REASON...
FLAG AND KATANA ASIDE, THERE ARE PLENTY MORE WHERE THEY COME FROM. THIS UGLY, BRUTAL WORLD PROVIDES SO MANY WEAPONS.
AND I WILL CONTINUE TO USE THEM TO DO GOOD.
MY NAME IS AMANDA WALLER.
AND I AM CONTENT.
NEXT: SOMEONE LITERALLY DIES.

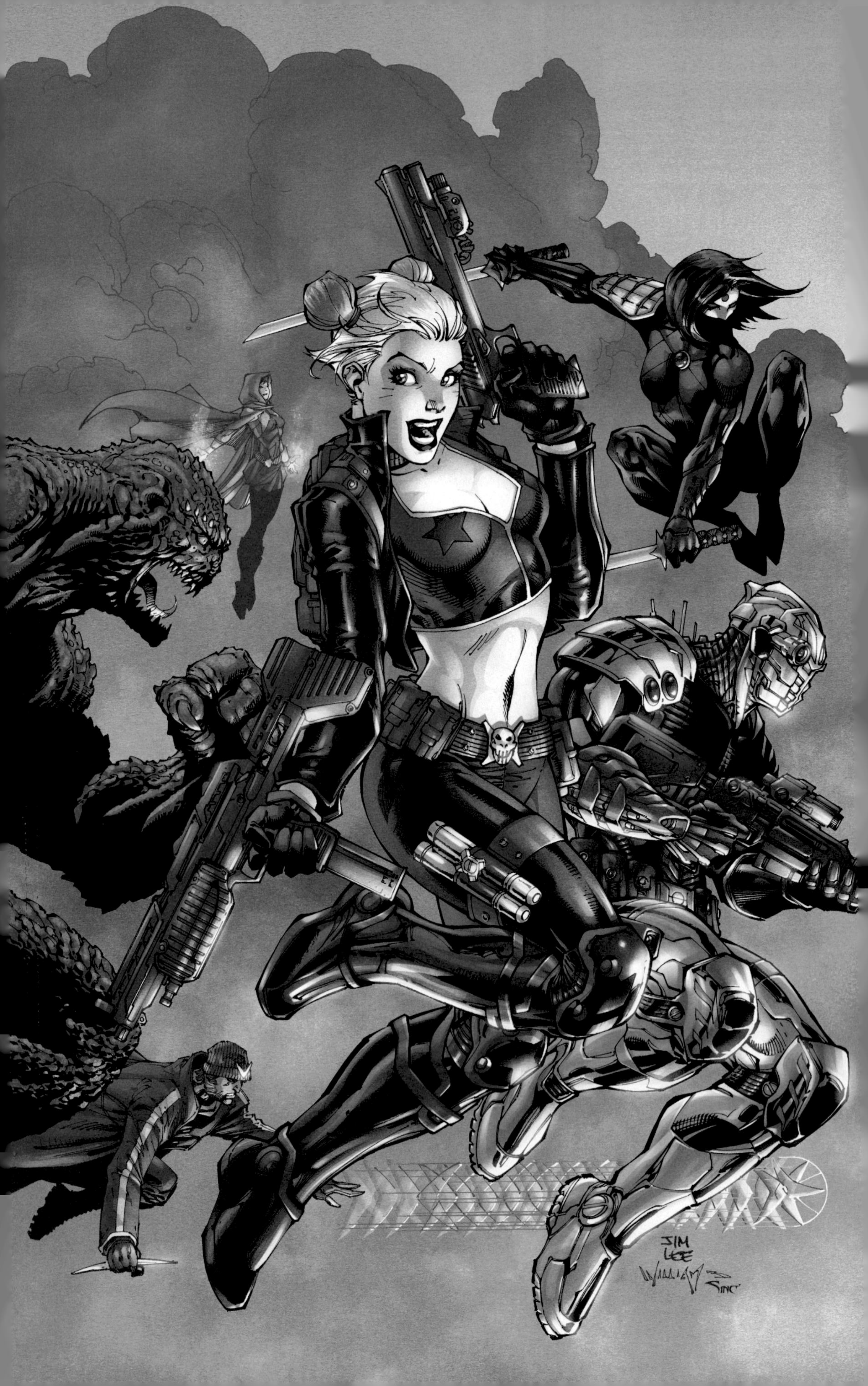
JIM LEE

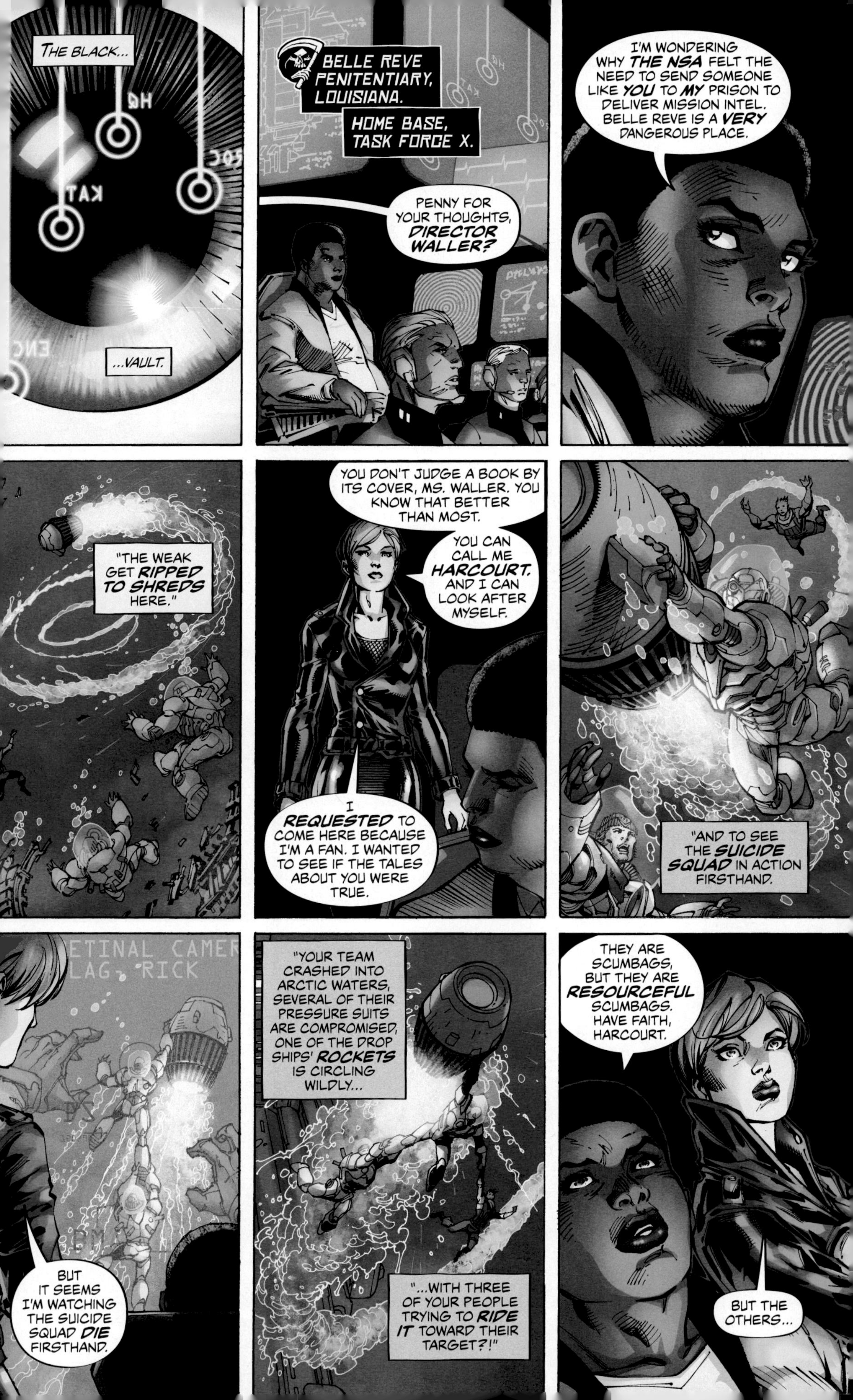
THE BLACK...
...VAULT.
BELLE REVE PENITENTIARY, LOUISIANA.
HOME BASE, TASK FORCE X.
PENNY FOR YOUR THOUGHTS, DIRECTOR WALLER?
I'M WONDERING WHY THE NSA FELT THE NEED TO SEND SOMEONE LIKE YOU TO MY PRISON TO DELIVER MISSION INTEL. BELLE REVE IS A VERY DANGEROUS PLACE.
"THE WEAK GET RIPPED TO SHREDS HERE."
YOU DON'T JUDGE A BOOK BY ITS COVER, MS. WALLER. YOU KNOW THAT BETTER THAN MOST.
YOU CAN CALL ME HARCOURT. AND I CAN LOOK AFTER MYSELF.
I REQUESTED TO COME HERE BECAUSE I'M A FAN. I WANTED TO SEE IF THE TALES ABOUT YOU WERE TRUE.
"AND TO SEE THE SUICIDE SQUAD IN ACTION FIRSTHAND.
BUT IT SEEMS I'M WATCHING THE SUICIDE SQUAD DIE FIRSTHAND.
"YOUR TEAM CRASHED INTO ARCTIC WATERS, SEVERAL OF THEIR PRESSURE SUITS ARE COMPROMISED, ONE OF THE DROP SHIPS' ROCKETS IS CIRCLING WILDLY...
"...WITH THREE OF YOUR PEOPLE TRYING TO RIDE IT TOWARD THEIR TARGET?!"
THEY ARE SCUMBAGS, BUT THEY ARE RESOURCEFUL SCUMBAGS. HAVE FAITH, HARCOURT.
BUT THE OTHERS...

"WATER HAS FILLED THEIR SUITS. THEY'RE DROWNING...

...SINKING TO THE BOTTOM OF THE LAPTEV SEA LIKE **CONCRETE COFFINS.**

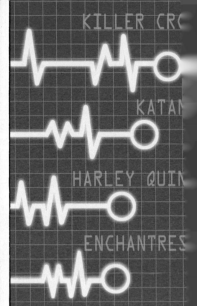

KILLER CROC

KATANA

HARLEY QUINN

ENCHANTRESS

"YOUR GIRL KATANA WILL LAST 60 SECONDS-- **TOPS**--IN THAT ICE-COLD WATER WITHOUT HER SUIT.

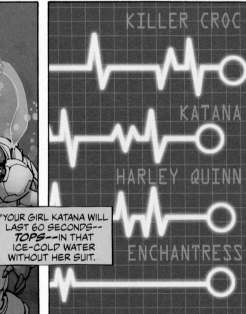

KILLER CROC

KATANA

HARLEY QUINN

ENCHANTRESS

"SELF-SACRIFICE...

"IT SEEMS EVEN VILLAINS ARE WORTH **DYING** FOR.

I THINK YOU JUST LOST OVER HALF YOUR TEAM, MS. WALLER.

THE OTHERS HAD BETTER GET THE JOB DONE.

"OUR ENEMIES **CANNOT** POSSESS THE COSMIC ITEM."

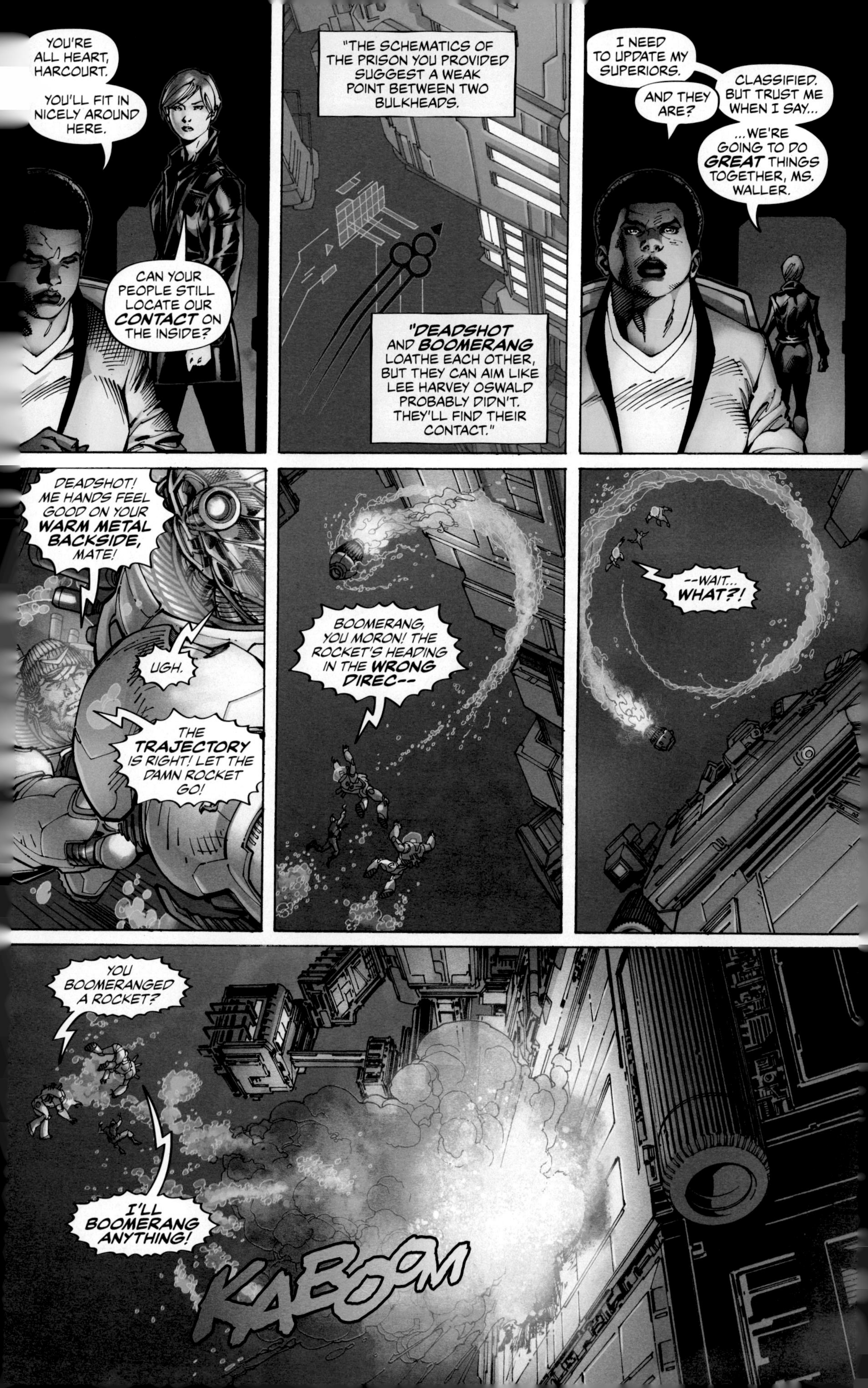

YOU'RE ALL HEART, HARCOURT.
YOU'LL FIT IN NICELY AROUND HERE.
CAN YOUR PEOPLE STILL LOCATE OUR **CONTACT** ON THE INSIDE?
"THE SCHEMATICS OF THE PRISON YOU PROVIDED SUGGEST A WEAK POINT BETWEEN TWO BULKHEADS.
"**DEADSHOT** AND **BOOMERANG** LOATHE EACH OTHER, BUT THEY CAN AIM LIKE LEE HARVEY OSWALD PROBABLY DIDN'T. THEY'LL FIND THEIR CONTACT."
I NEED TO UPDATE MY SUPERIORS.
AND THEY ARE?
CLASSIFIED. BUT TRUST ME WHEN I SAY...
...WE'RE GOING TO DO **GREAT** THINGS TOGETHER, MS. WALLER.
DEADSHOT! ME HANDS FEEL GOOD ON YOUR **WARM METAL BACKSIDE,** MATE!
UGH.
THE **TRAJECTORY** IS RIGHT! LET THE DAMN ROCKET GO!
BOOMERANG, YOU MORON! THE ROCKET'S HEADING IN THE **WRONG** DIREC--
--WAIT... **WHAT?!**
YOU BOOMERANGED A ROCKET?
I'LL BOOMERANG ANYTHING!
KABOOM

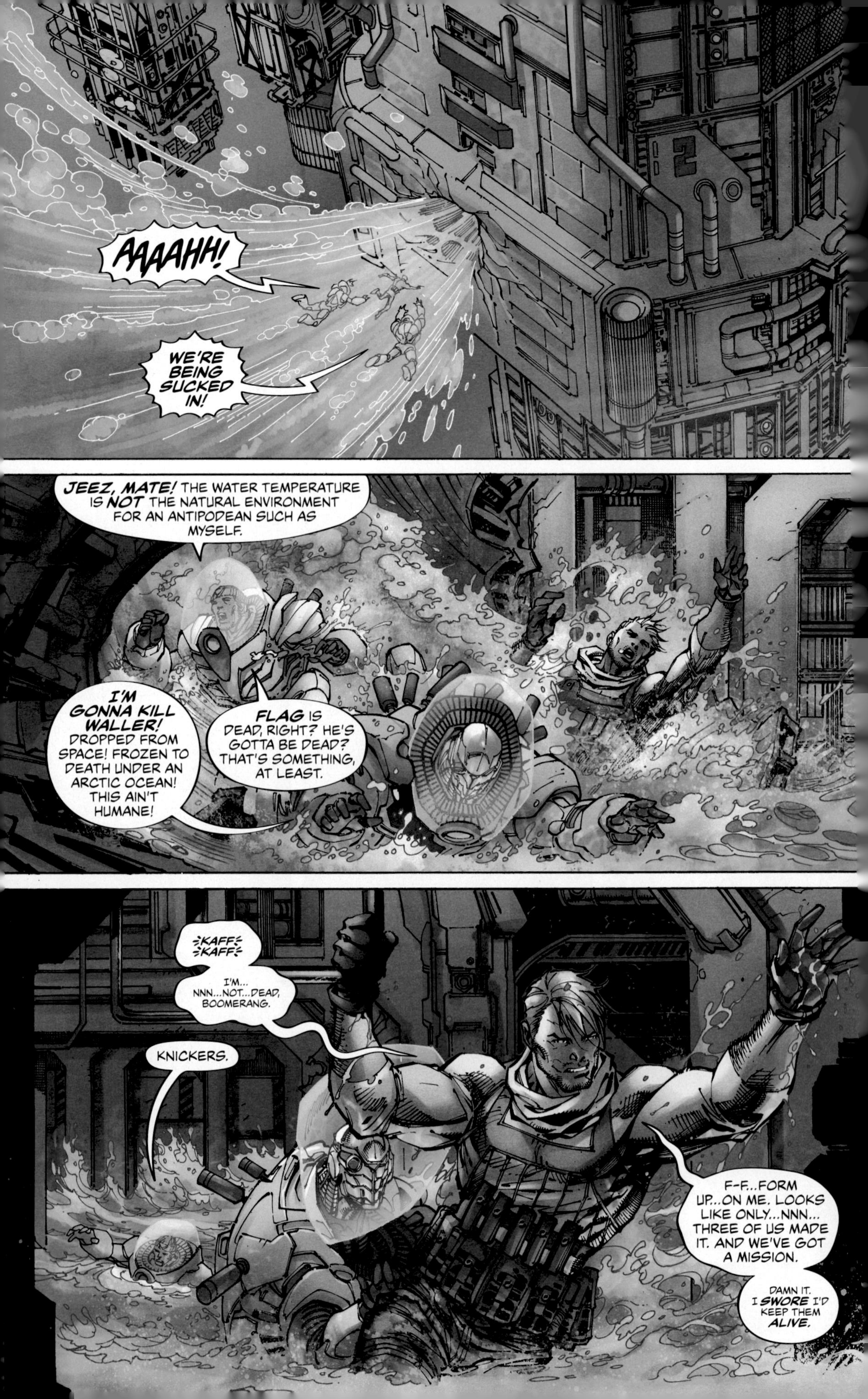
AAAAHH!
WE'RE BEING SUCKED IN!
JEEZ, MATE! THE WATER TEMPERATURE IS NOT THE NATURAL ENVIRONMENT FOR AN ANTIPODEAN SUCH AS MYSELF.
I'M GONNA KILL WALLER! DROPPED FROM SPACE! FROZEN TO DEATH UNDER AN ARCTIC OCEAN! THIS AIN'T HUMANE!
FLAG IS DEAD, RIGHT? HE'S GOTTA BE DEAD? THAT'S SOMETHING, AT LEAST.
KAFF KAFF
I'M... NNN...NOT...DEAD, BOOMERANG.
KNICKERS.
F-F...FORM UP...ON ME. LOOKS LIKE ONLY...NNN... THREE OF US MADE IT. AND WE'VE GOT A MISSION.
DAMN IT. I SWORE I'D KEEP THEM ALIVE.

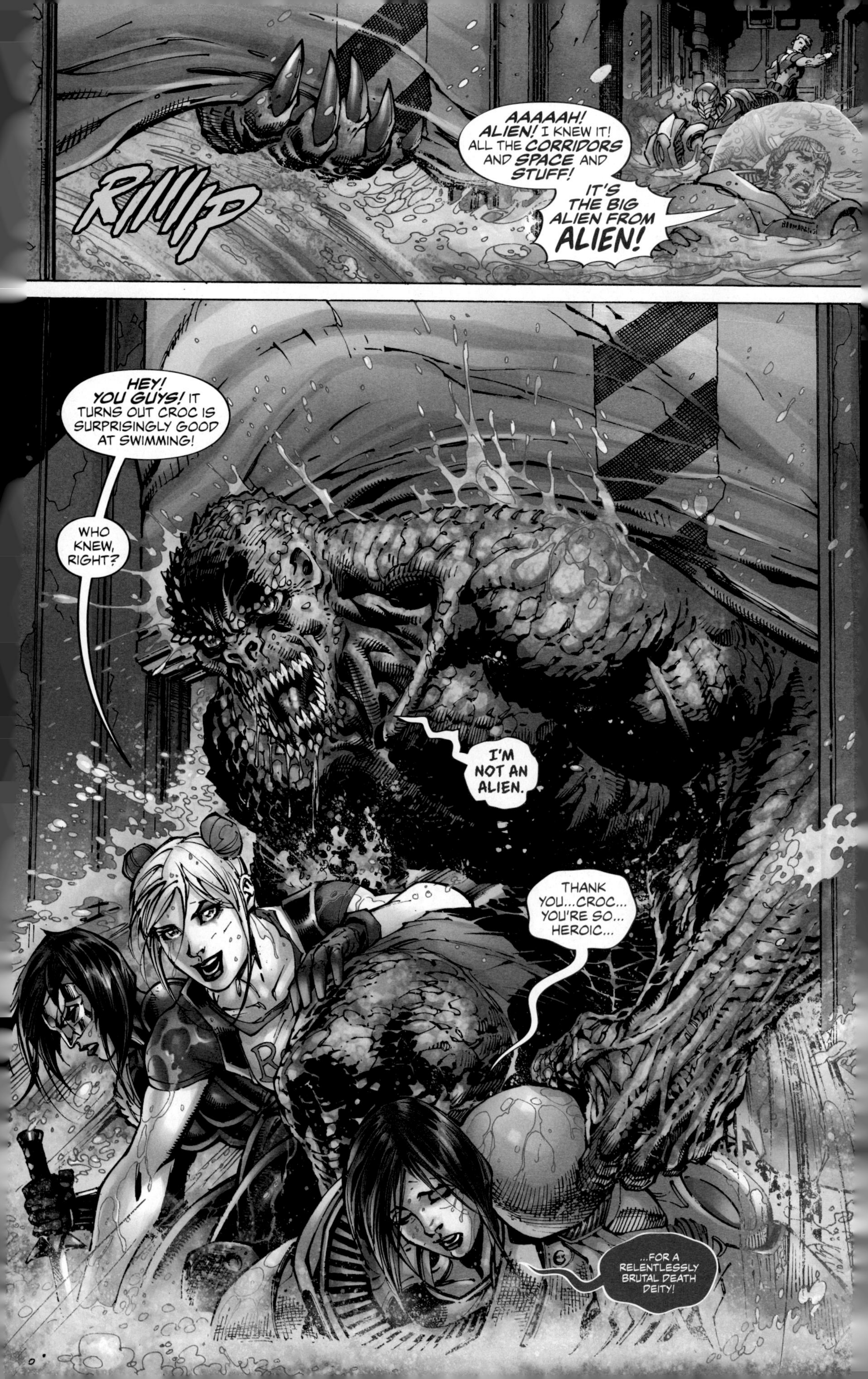
RIIIIP
AAAAAH! ALIEN! I KNEW IT! ALL THE CORRIDORS AND SPACE AND STUFF!
IT'S THE BIG ALIEN FROM ALIEN!
HEY! YOU GUYS! IT TURNS OUT CROC IS SURPRISINGLY GOOD AT SWIMMING!
WHO KNEW, RIGHT?
I'M NOT AN ALIEN.
THANK YOU...CROC... YOU'RE SO... HEROIC...
...FOR A RELENTLESSLY BRUTAL DEATH DEITY!

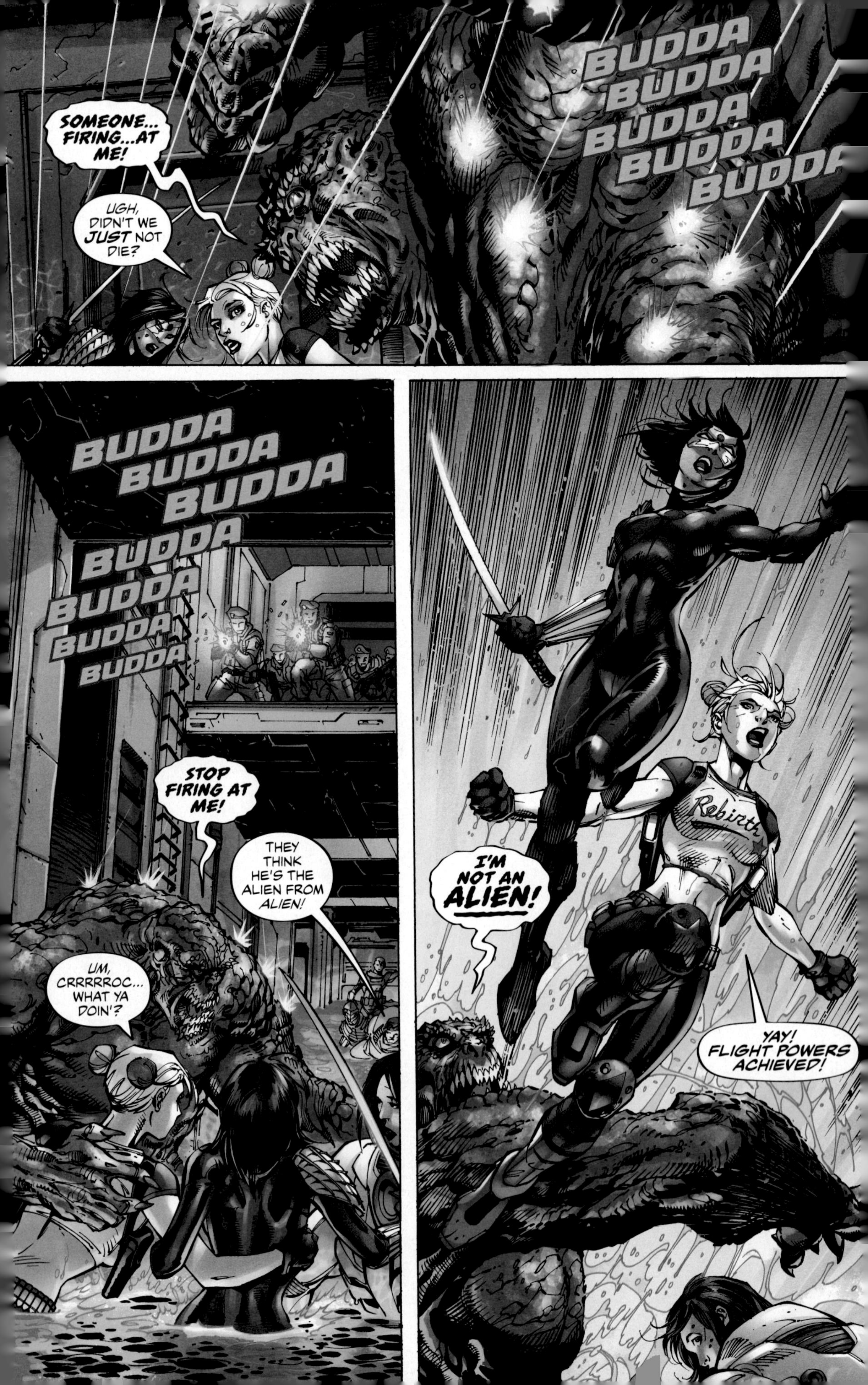
BUDDA BUDDA BUDDA BUDDA BUDDA
SOMEONE... FIRING...AT ME!
UGH, DIDN'T WE JUST NOT DIE?
BUDDA BUDDA BUDDA BUDDA BUDDA BUDDA BUDDA
STOP FIRING AT ME!
THEY THINK HE'S THE ALIEN FROM ALIEN!
UM, CRRRRROC... WHAT YA DOIN'?
I'M NOT AN ALIEN!
YAY! FLIGHT POWERS ACHIEVED!

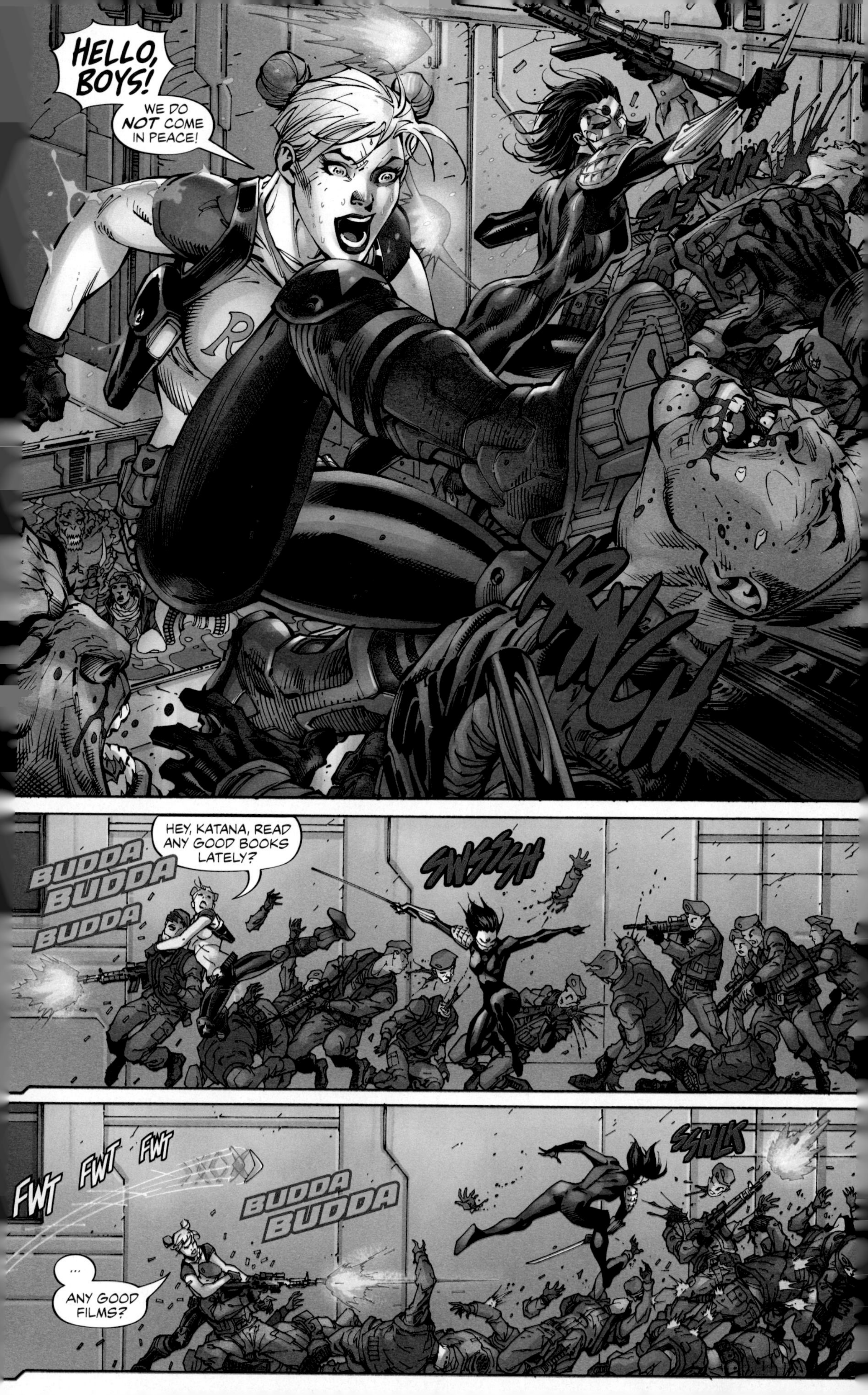
HELLO, BOYS!
WE DO NOT COME IN PEACE!
SLSSHH
KRNCH
BUDDA BUDDA BUDDA
HEY, KATANA, READ ANY GOOD BOOKS LATELY?
SWSSH
FWT FWT FWT FWT
BUDDA BUDDA
SSHLK
... ANY GOOD FILMS?

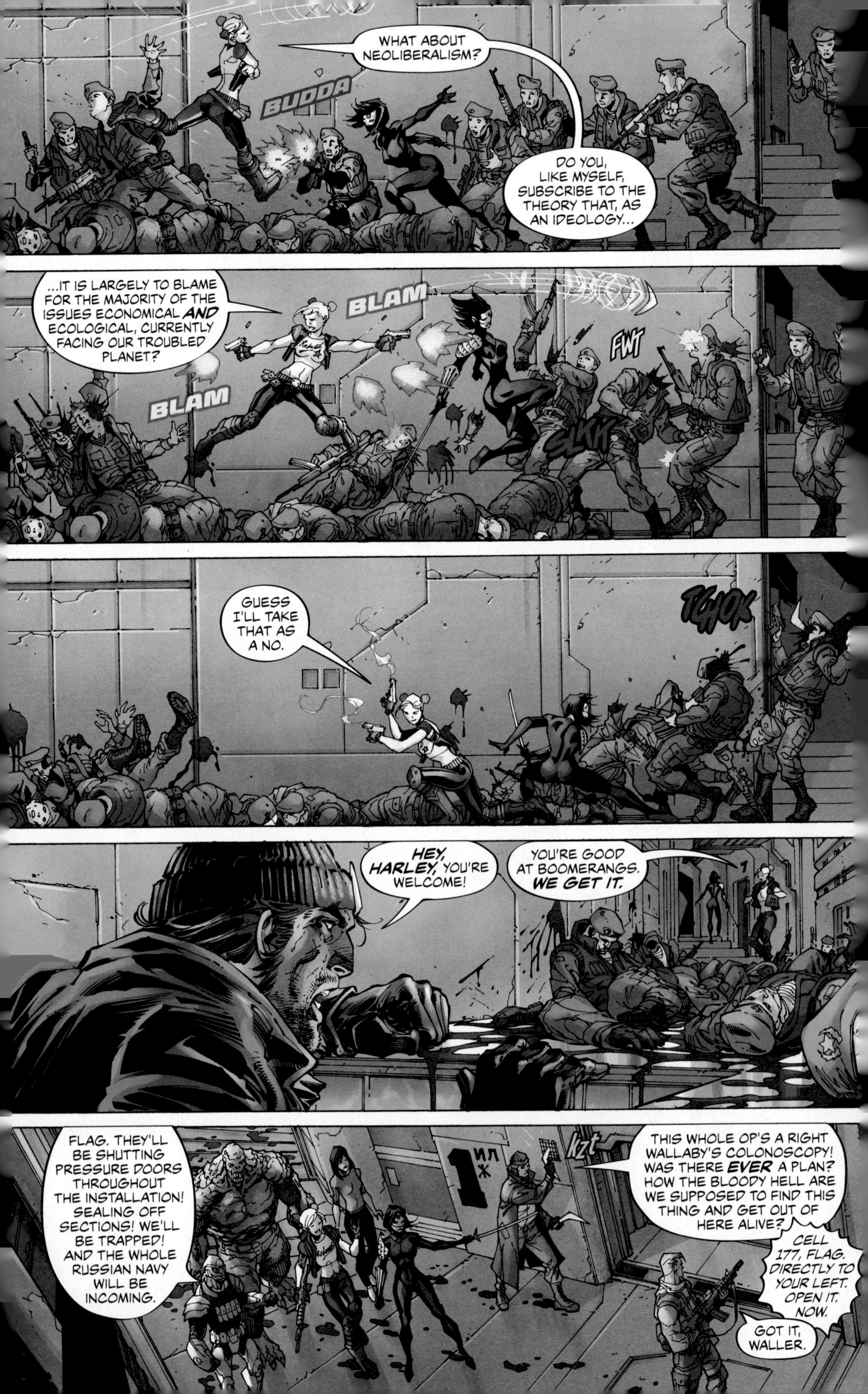
WHAT ABOUT NEOLIBERALISM?
BUDDA
DO YOU, LIKE MYSELF, SUBSCRIBE TO THE THEORY THAT, AS AN IDEOLOGY...
...IT IS LARGELY TO BLAME FOR THE MAJORITY OF THE ISSUES ECONOMICAL AND ECOLOGICAL, CURRENTLY FACING OUR TROUBLED PLANET?
BLAM
BLAM
FWT
SLKK
GUESS I'LL TAKE THAT AS A NO.
TCHOK
HEY, HARLEY, YOU'RE WELCOME!
YOU'RE GOOD AT BOOMERANGS. WE GET IT.
FLAG. THEY'LL BE SHUTTING PRESSURE DOORS THROUGHOUT THE INSTALLATION! SEALING OFF SECTIONS! WE'LL BE TRAPPED! AND THE WHOLE RUSSIAN NAVY WILL BE INCOMING.
kzt
THIS WHOLE OP'S A RIGHT WALLABY'S COLONOSCOPY! WAS THERE EVER A PLAN? HOW THE BLOODY HELL ARE WE SUPPOSED TO FIND THIS THING AND GET OUT OF HERE ALIVE?
CELL 177, FLAG. DIRECTLY TO YOUR LEFT. OPEN IT. NOW.
GOT IT, WALLER.

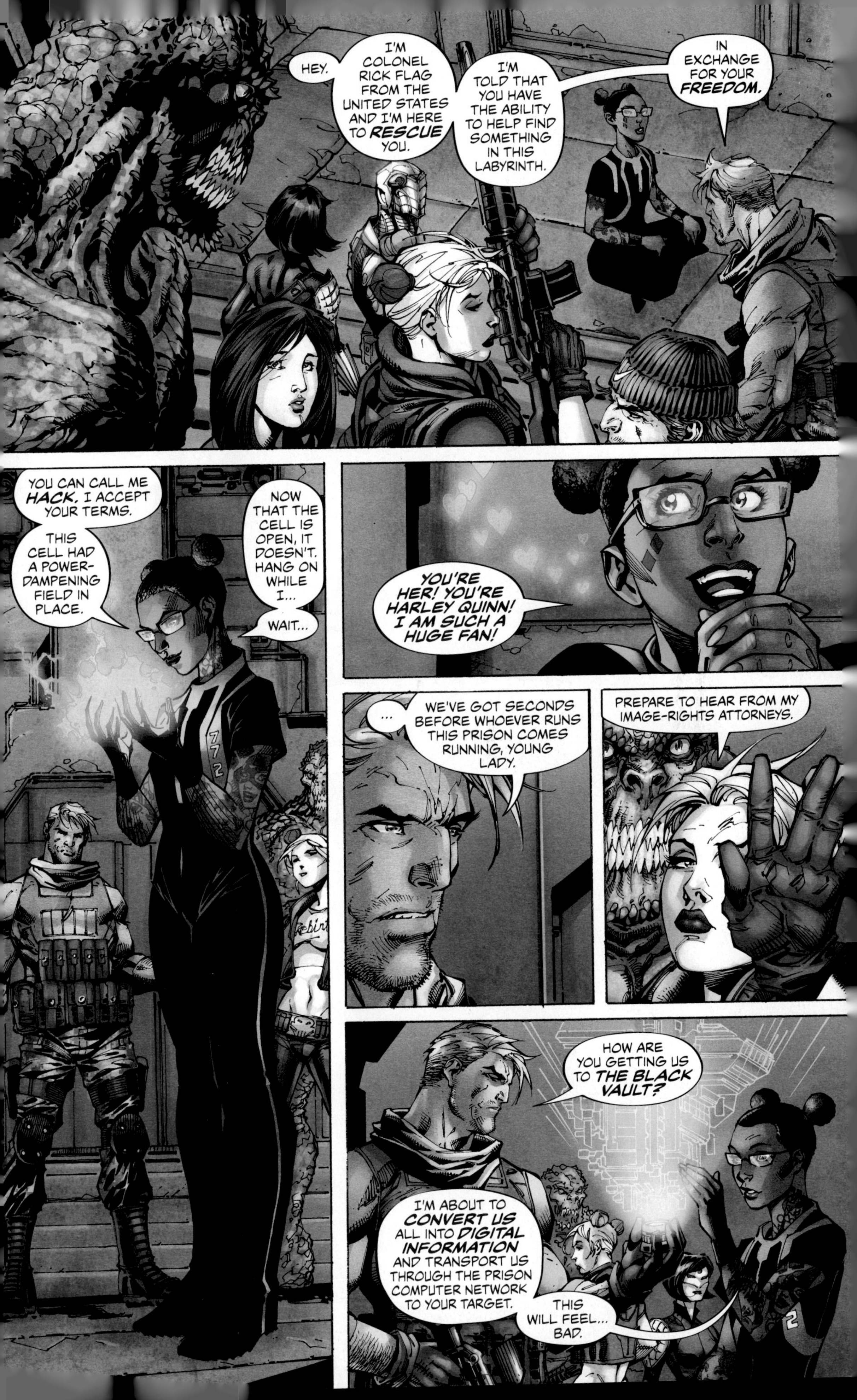
HEY.
I'M COLONEL RICK FLAG FROM THE UNITED STATES AND I'M HERE TO RESCUE YOU.
I'M TOLD THAT YOU HAVE THE ABILITY TO HELP FIND SOMETHING IN THIS LABYRINTH.
IN EXCHANGE FOR YOUR FREEDOM.
YOU CAN CALL ME HACK. I ACCEPT YOUR TERMS.
THIS CELL HAD A POWER-DAMPENING FIELD IN PLACE.
NOW THAT THE CELL IS OPEN, IT DOESN'T. HANG ON WHILE I...
WAIT...
YOU'RE HER! YOU'RE HARLEY QUINN! I AM SUCH A HUGE FAN!
...
WE'VE GOT SECONDS BEFORE WHOEVER RUNS THIS PRISON COMES RUNNING, YOUNG LADY.
PREPARE TO HEAR FROM MY IMAGE-RIGHTS ATTORNEYS.
HOW ARE YOU GETTING US TO THE BLACK VAULT?
I'M ABOUT TO CONVERT US ALL INTO DIGITAL INFORMATION AND TRANSPORT US THROUGH THE PRISON COMPUTER NETWORK TO YOUR TARGET.
THIS WILL FEEL... BAD.

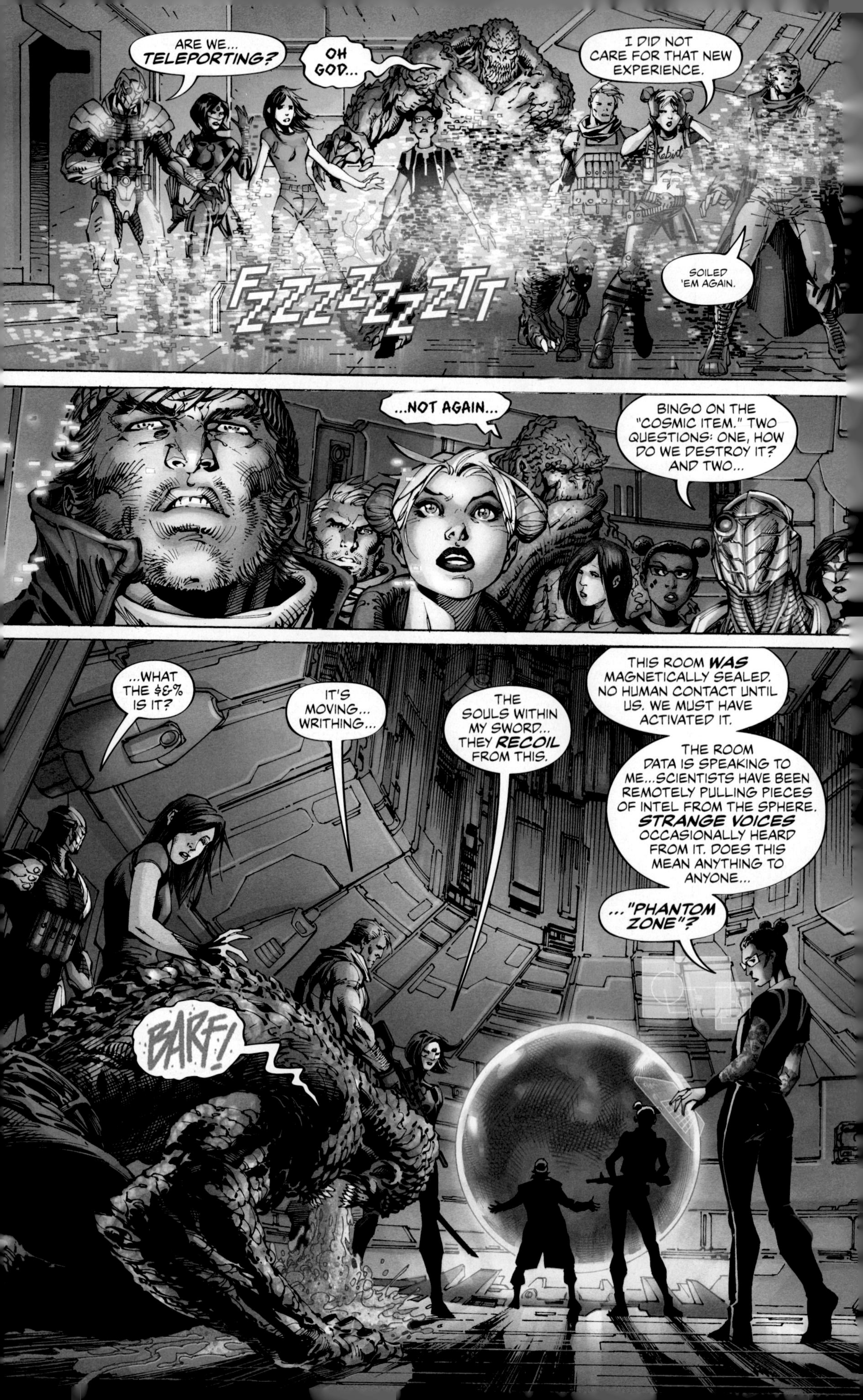
ARE WE... TELEPORTING?
OH GOD...
I DID NOT CARE FOR THAT NEW EXPERIENCE.
FZZZZZZZZTT
SOILED 'EM AGAIN.
...NOT AGAIN...
BINGO ON THE "COSMIC ITEM." TWO QUESTIONS: ONE, HOW DO WE DESTROY IT? AND TWO...
...WHAT THE $&% IS IT?
IT'S MOVING... WRITHING...
THE SOULS WITHIN MY SWORD... THEY RECOIL FROM THIS.
THIS ROOM WAS MAGNETICALLY SEALED. NO HUMAN CONTACT UNTIL US. WE MUST HAVE ACTIVATED IT.
THE ROOM DATA IS SPEAKING TO ME...SCIENTISTS HAVE BEEN REMOTELY PULLING PIECES OF INTEL FROM THE SPHERE. STRANGE VOICES OCCASIONALLY HEARD FROM IT. DOES THIS MEAN ANYTHING TO ANYONE...
..."PHANTOM ZONE"?
BARF!

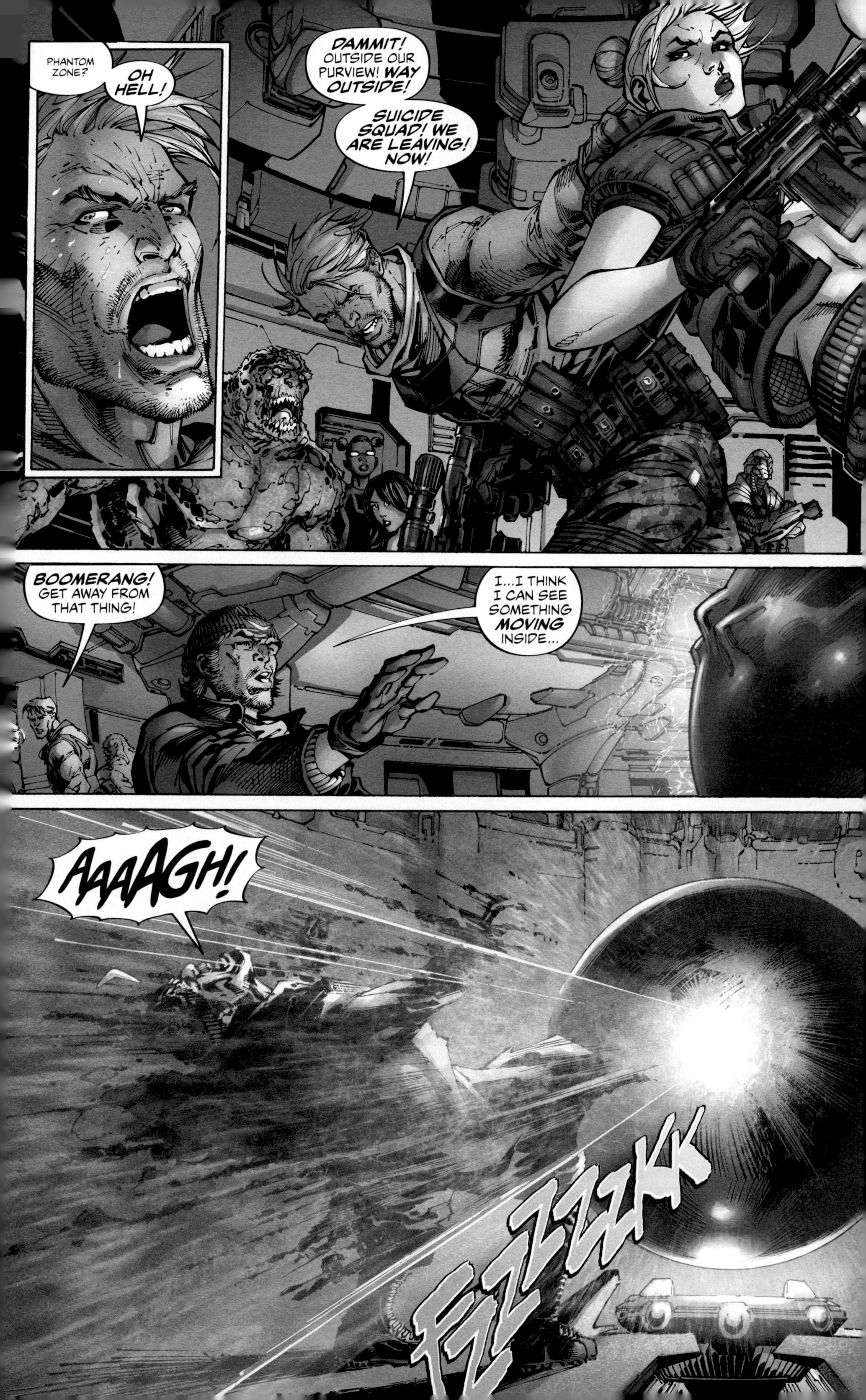
PHANTOM ZONE?
OH HELL!
DAMMIT! OUTSIDE OUR PURVIEW! WAY OUTSIDE!
SUICIDE SQUAD! WE ARE LEAVING! NOW!
BOOMERANG! GET AWAY FROM THAT THING!
I...I THINK I CAN SEE SOMETHING MOVING INSIDE...
AAAAGH!
FZZZZZKK

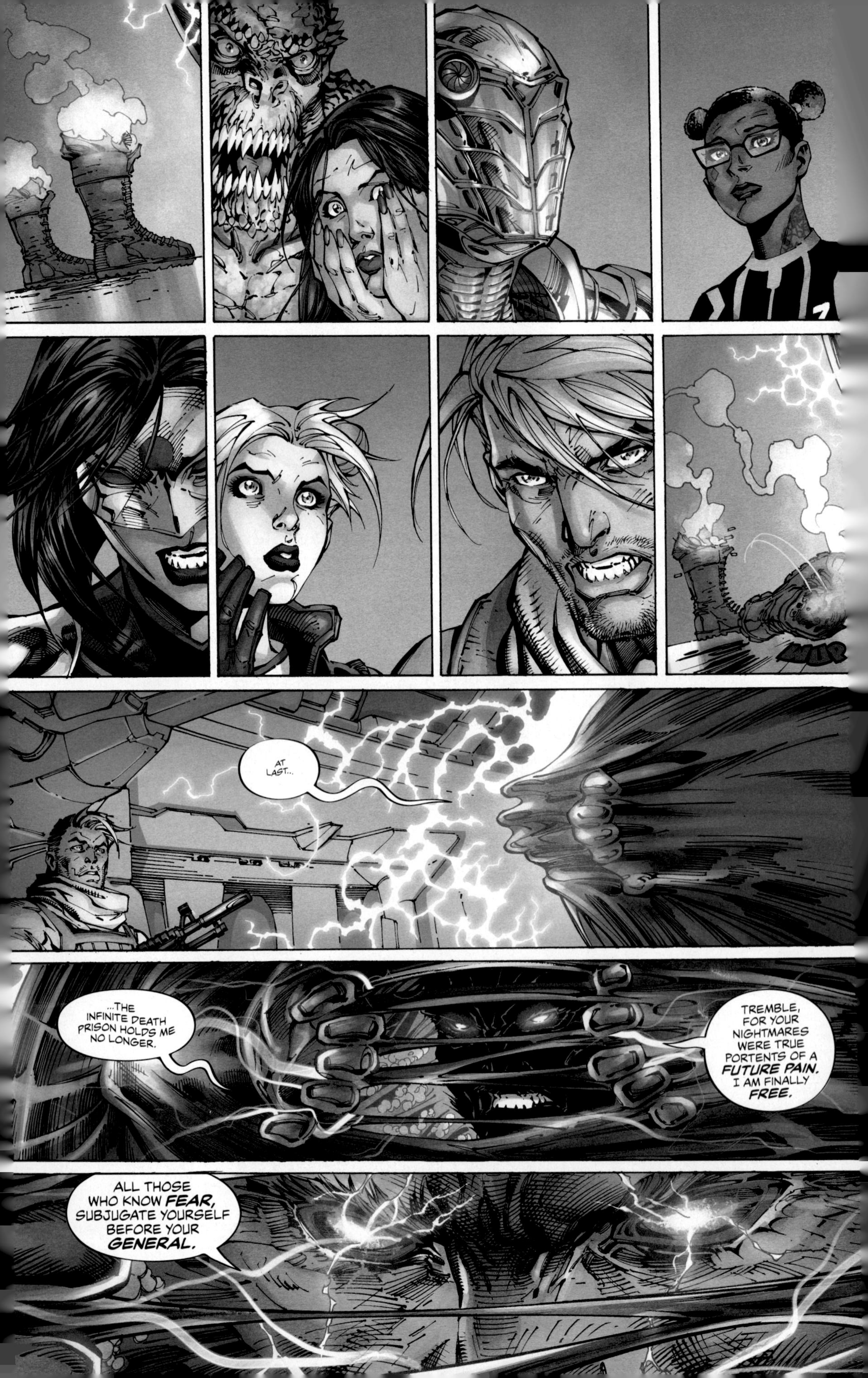
WUP
AT LAST...
...THE INFINITE DEATH PRISON HOLDS ME NO LONGER.
TREMBLE, FOR YOUR NIGHTMARES WERE TRUE PORTENTS OF A FUTURE PAIN. I AM FINALLY FREE.
ALL THOSE WHO KNOW FEAR, SUBJUGATE YOURSELF BEFORE YOUR GENERAL.

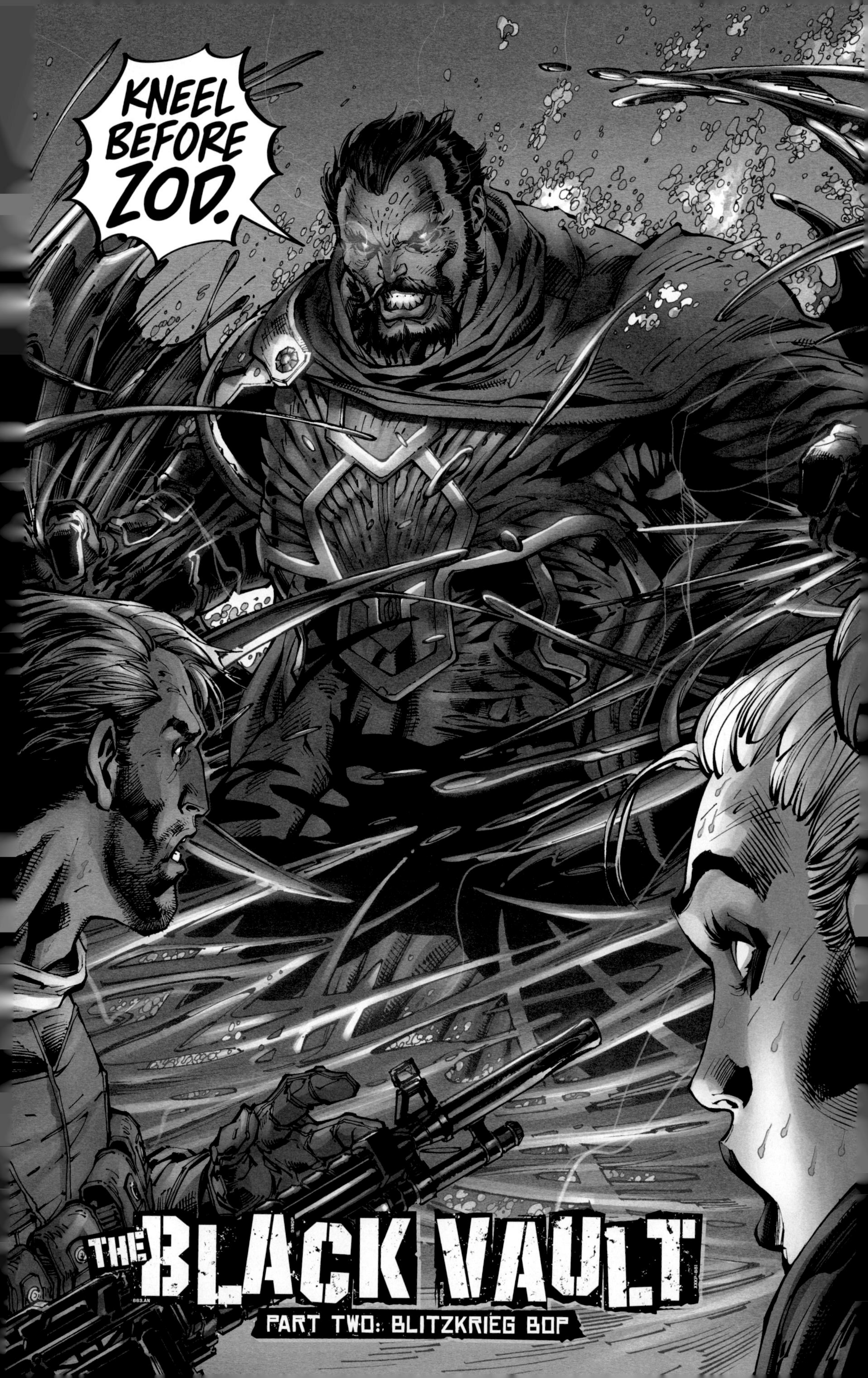
KNEEL BEFORE ZOD.
THE BLACK VAULT
PART TWO: BLITZKRIEG BOP

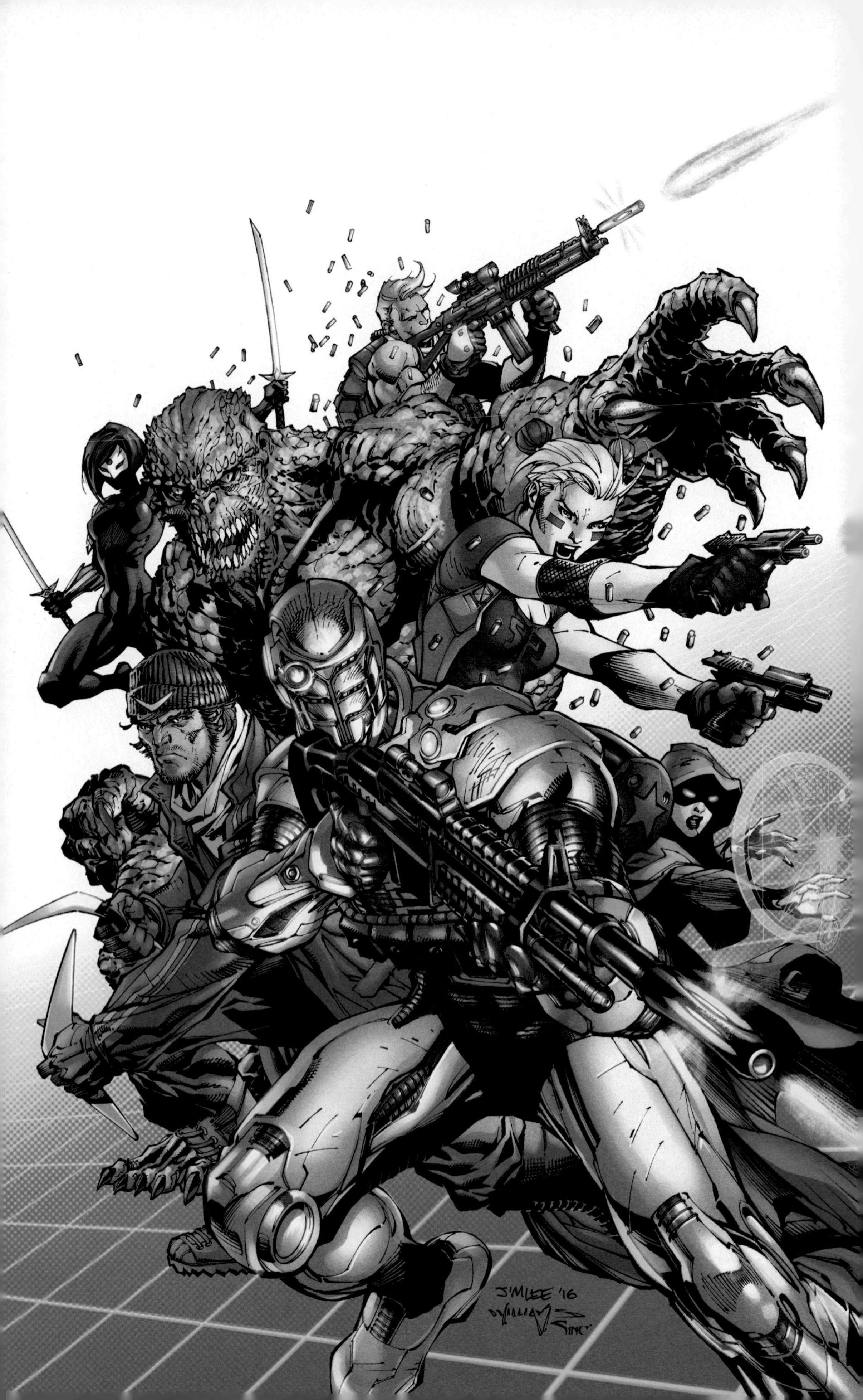

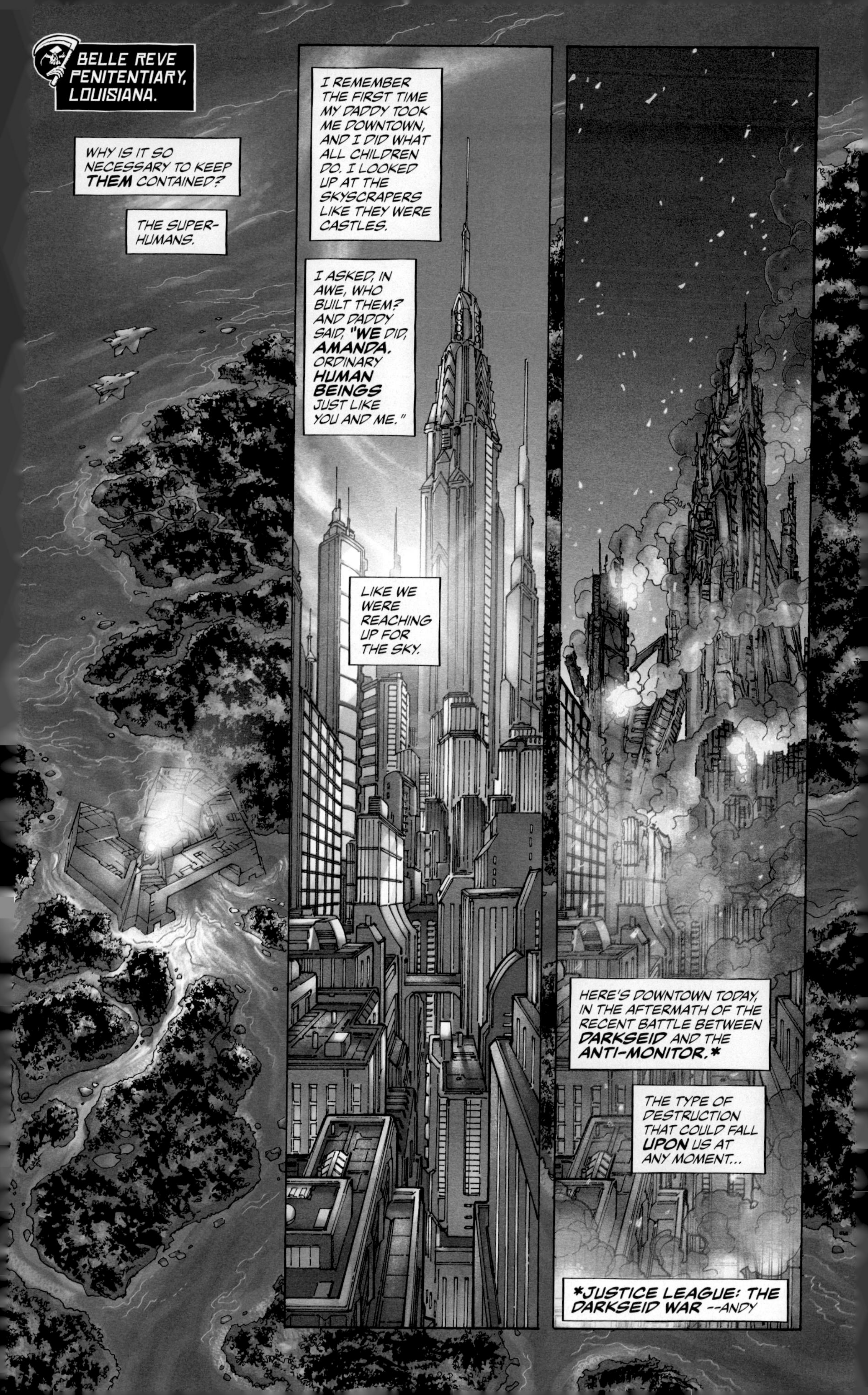
BELLE REVE PENITENTIARY, LOUISIANA.
WHY IS IT SO NECESSARY TO KEEP THEM CONTAINED?
THE SUPER-HUMANS.
I REMEMBER THE FIRST TIME MY DADDY TOOK ME DOWNTOWN, AND I DID WHAT ALL CHILDREN DO. I LOOKED UP AT THE SKYSCRAPERS LIKE THEY WERE CASTLES.
I ASKED, IN AWE, WHO BUILT THEM? AND DADDY SAID, "WE DID, AMANDA. ORDINARY HUMAN BEINGS JUST LIKE YOU AND ME."
LIKE WE WERE REACHING UP FOR THE SKY.
HERE'S DOWNTOWN TODAY, IN THE AFTERMATH OF THE RECENT BATTLE BETWEEN DARKSEID AND THE ANTI-MONITOR.*
THE TYPE OF DESTRUCTION THAT COULD FALL UPON US AT ANY MOMENT...
*JUSTICE LEAGUE: THE DARKSEID WAR --ANDY

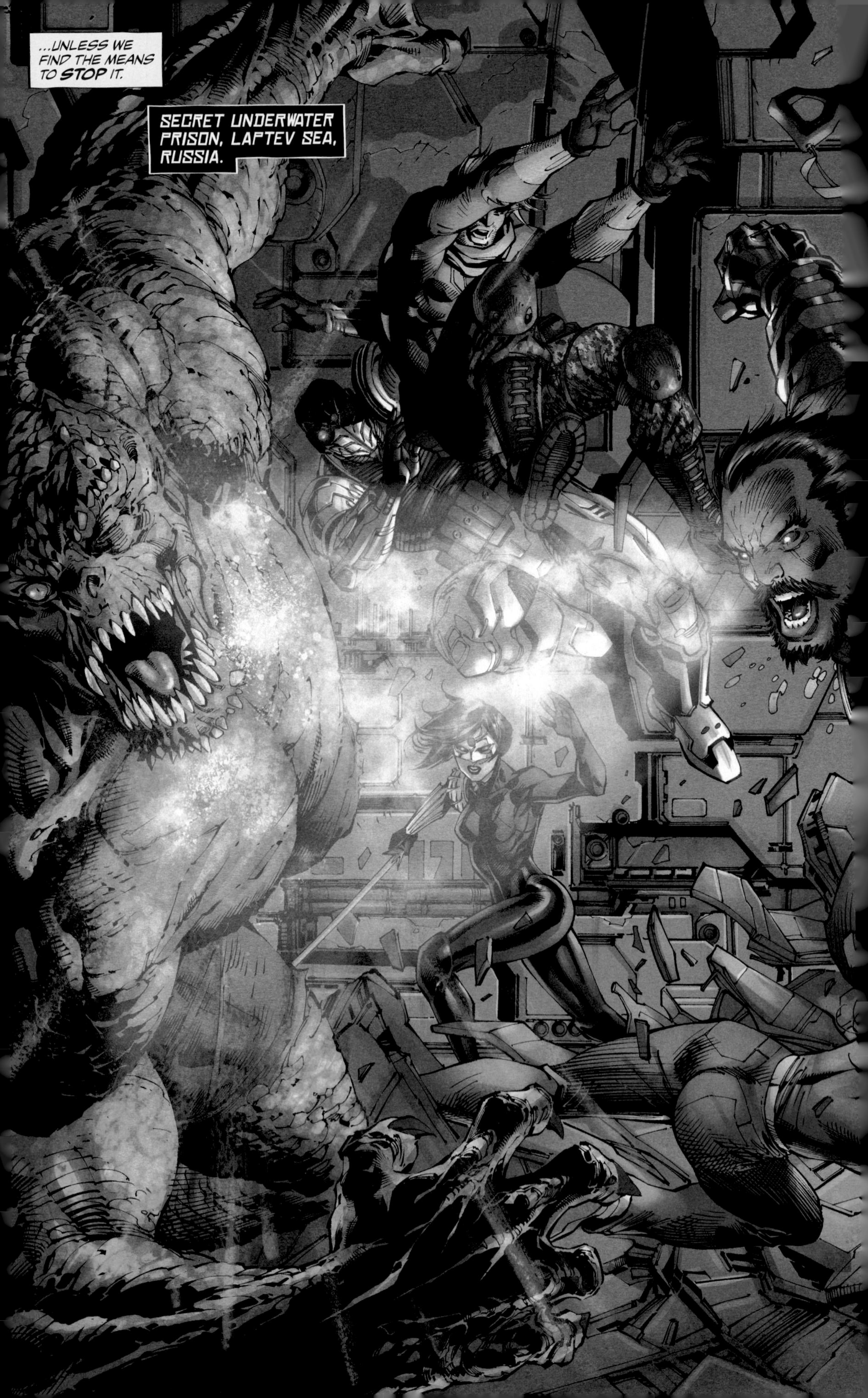
...UNLESS WE FIND THE MEANS TO STOP IT.
SECRET UNDERWATER PRISON, LAPTEV SEA, RUSSIA.

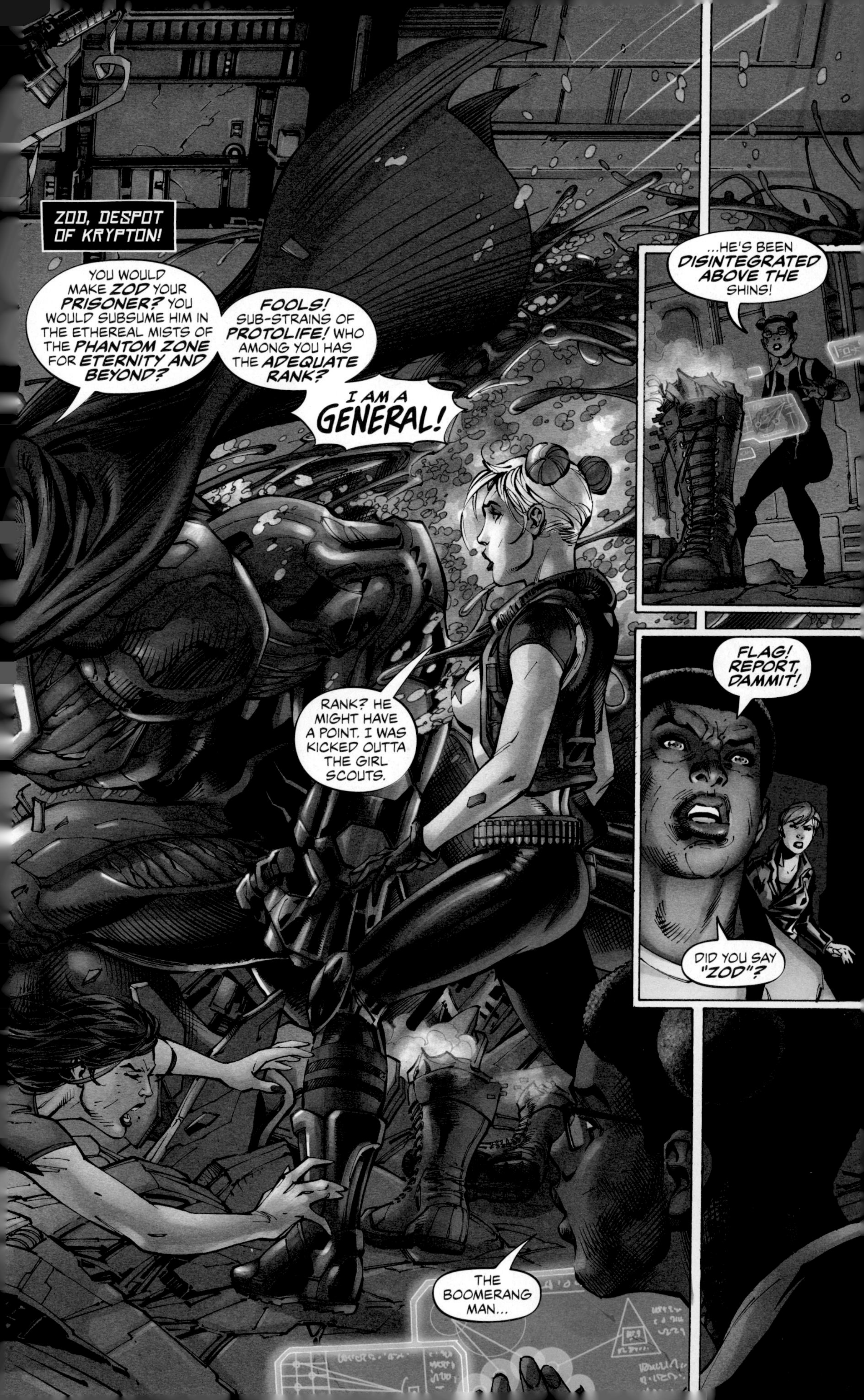
ZOD, DESPOT OF KRYPTON!
YOU WOULD MAKE ZOD YOUR PRISONER? YOU WOULD SUBSUME HIM IN THE ETHEREAL MISTS OF THE PHANTOM ZONE FOR ETERNITY AND BEYOND?
FOOLS! SUB-STRAINS OF PROTOLIFE! WHO AMONG YOU HAS THE ADEQUATE RANK?
I AM A GENERAL!
...HE'S BEEN DISINTEGRATED ABOVE THE SHINS!
RANK? HE MIGHT HAVE A POINT. I WAS KICKED OUTTA THE GIRL SCOUTS.
FLAG! REPORT, DAMMIT!
DID YOU SAY "ZOD"?
THE BOOMERANG MAN...

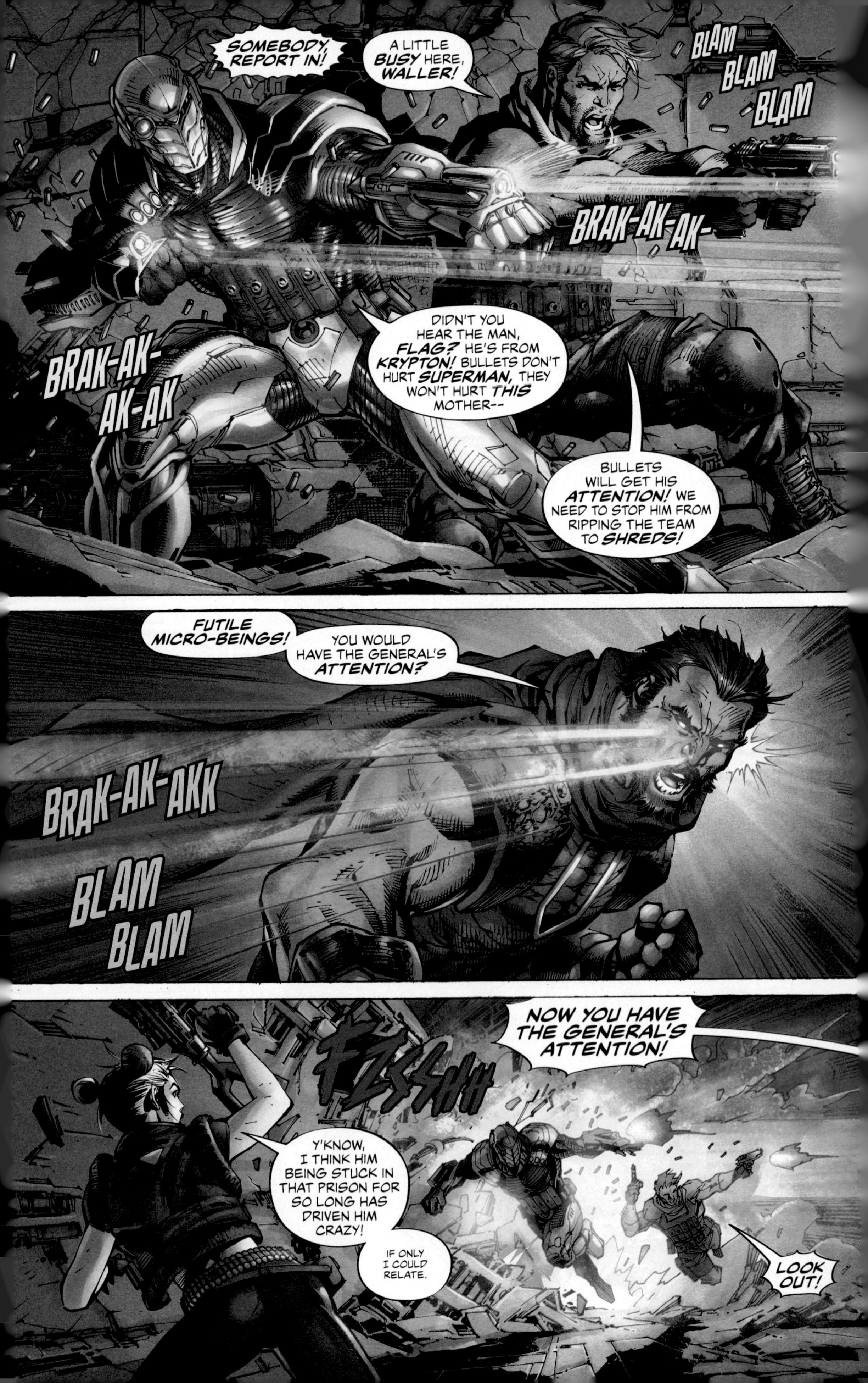
SOMEBODY, REPORT IN!
A LITTLE BUSY HERE, WALLER!
BLAM BLAM BLAM
BRAK-AK-AK-
BRAK-AK-AK-AK
DIDN'T YOU HEAR THE MAN, FLAG? HE'S FROM KRYPTON! BULLETS DON'T HURT SUPERMAN, THEY WON'T HURT THIS MOTHER--
BULLETS WILL GET HIS ATTENTION! WE NEED TO STOP HIM FROM RIPPING THE TEAM TO SHREDS!
FUTILE MICRO-BEINGS!
YOU WOULD HAVE THE GENERAL'S ATTENTION?
BRAK-AK-AKK
BLAM BLAM
NOW YOU HAVE THE GENERAL'S ATTENTION!
FZSSHH
Y'KNOW, I THINK HIM BEING STUCK IN THAT PRISON FOR SO LONG HAS DRIVEN HIM CRAZY!
IF ONLY I COULD RELATE.
LOOK OUT!

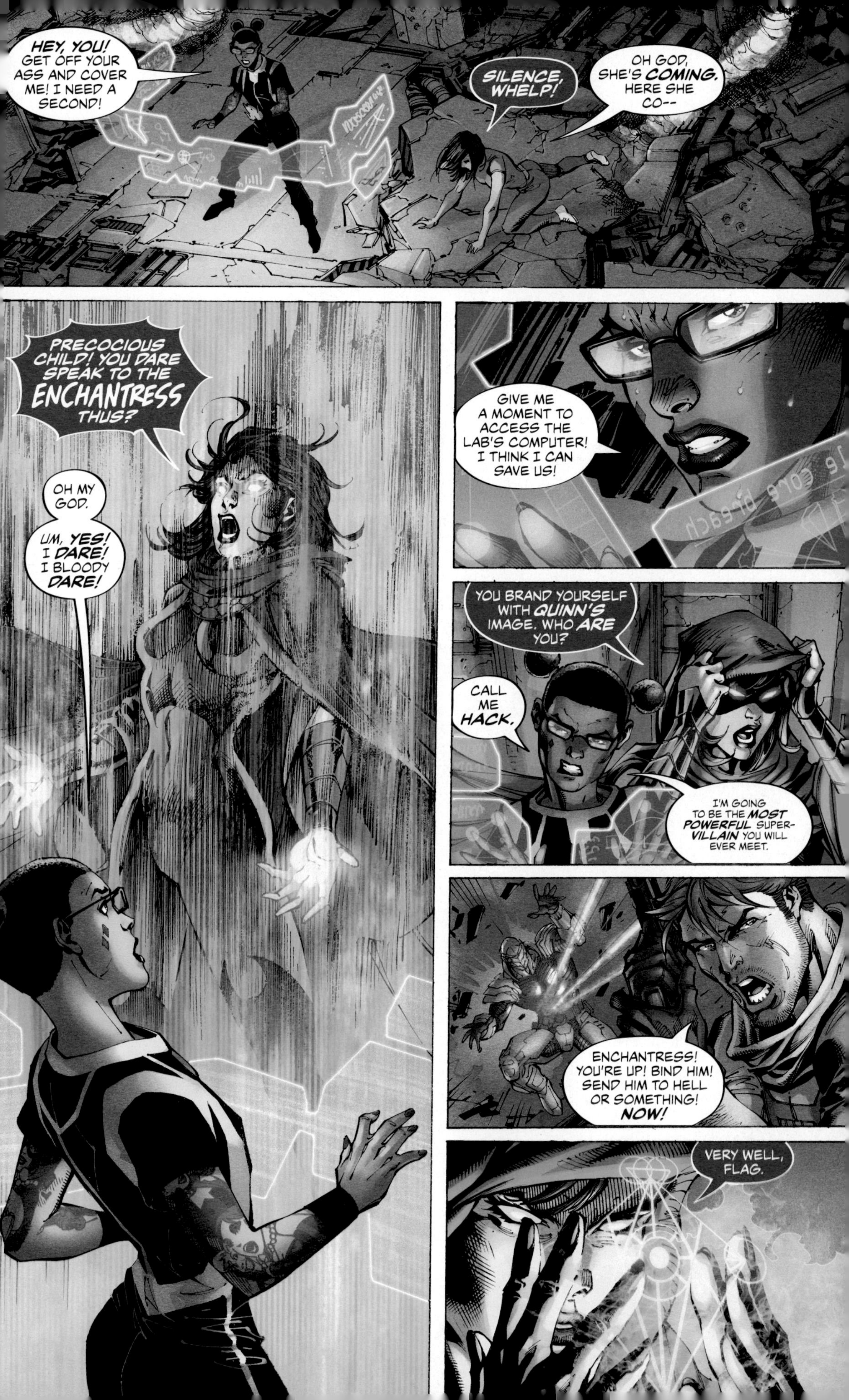
HEY, YOU! GET OFF YOUR ASS AND COVER ME! I NEED A SECOND!
SILENCE, WHELP!
OH GOD, SHE'S COMING. HERE SHE CO--
PRECOCIOUS CHILD! YOU DARE SPEAK TO THE ENCHANTRESS THUS?
OH MY GOD.
UM, YES! I DARE! I BLOODY DARE!
GIVE ME A MOMENT TO ACCESS THE LAB'S COMPUTER! I THINK I CAN SAVE US!
YOU BRAND YOURSELF WITH QUINN'S IMAGE. WHO ARE YOU?
CALL ME HACK.
I'M GOING TO BE THE MOST POWERFUL SUPER-VILLAIN YOU WILL EVER MEET.
ENCHANTRESS! YOU'RE UP! BIND HIM! SEND HIM TO HELL OR SOMETHING! NOW!
VERY WELL, FLAG.

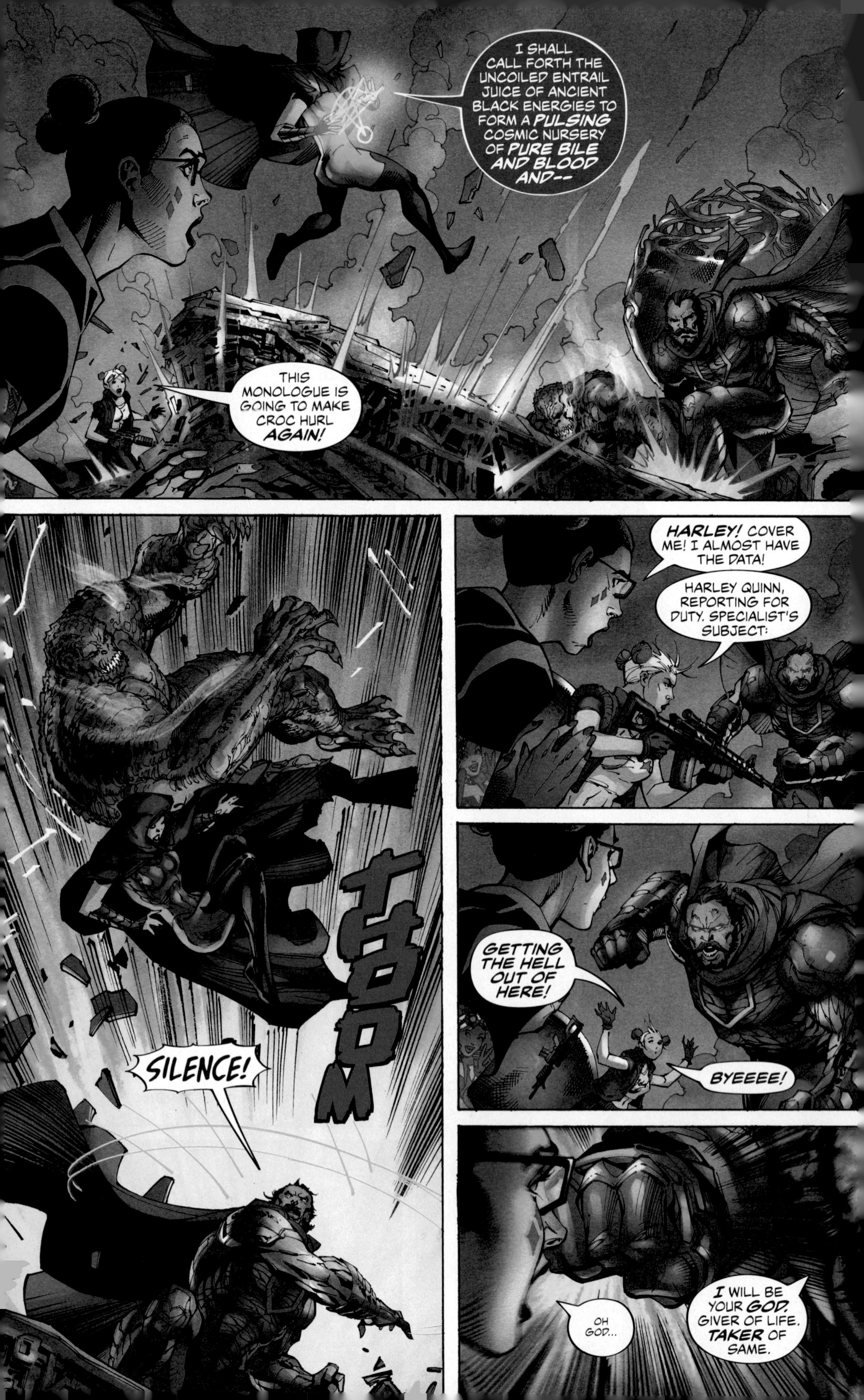

I SHALL CALL FORTH THE UNCOILED ENTRAIL JUICE OF ANCIENT BLACK ENERGIES TO FORM A PULSING COSMIC NURSERY OF PURE BILE AND BLOOD AND--
THIS MONOLOGUE IS GOING TO MAKE CROC HURL AGAIN!
THOOM
SILENCE!
HARLEY! COVER ME! I ALMOST HAVE THE DATA!
HARLEY QUINN, REPORTING FOR DUTY. SPECIALIST'S SUBJECT:
GETTING THE HELL OUT OF HERE!
BYEEEE!
OH GOD...
I WILL BE YOUR GOD. GIVER OF LIFE. TAKER OF SAME.

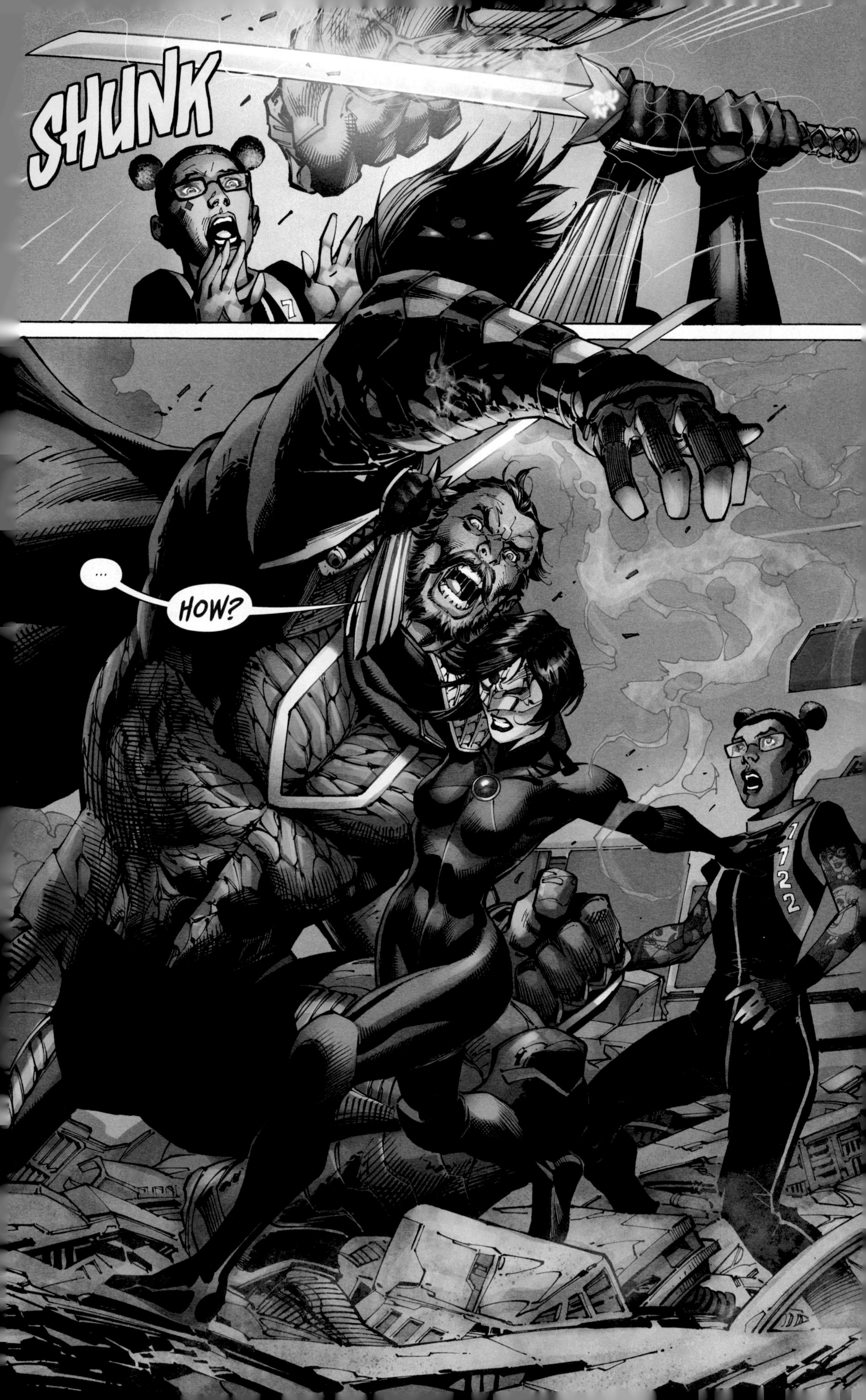
SHUNK
...
HOW?

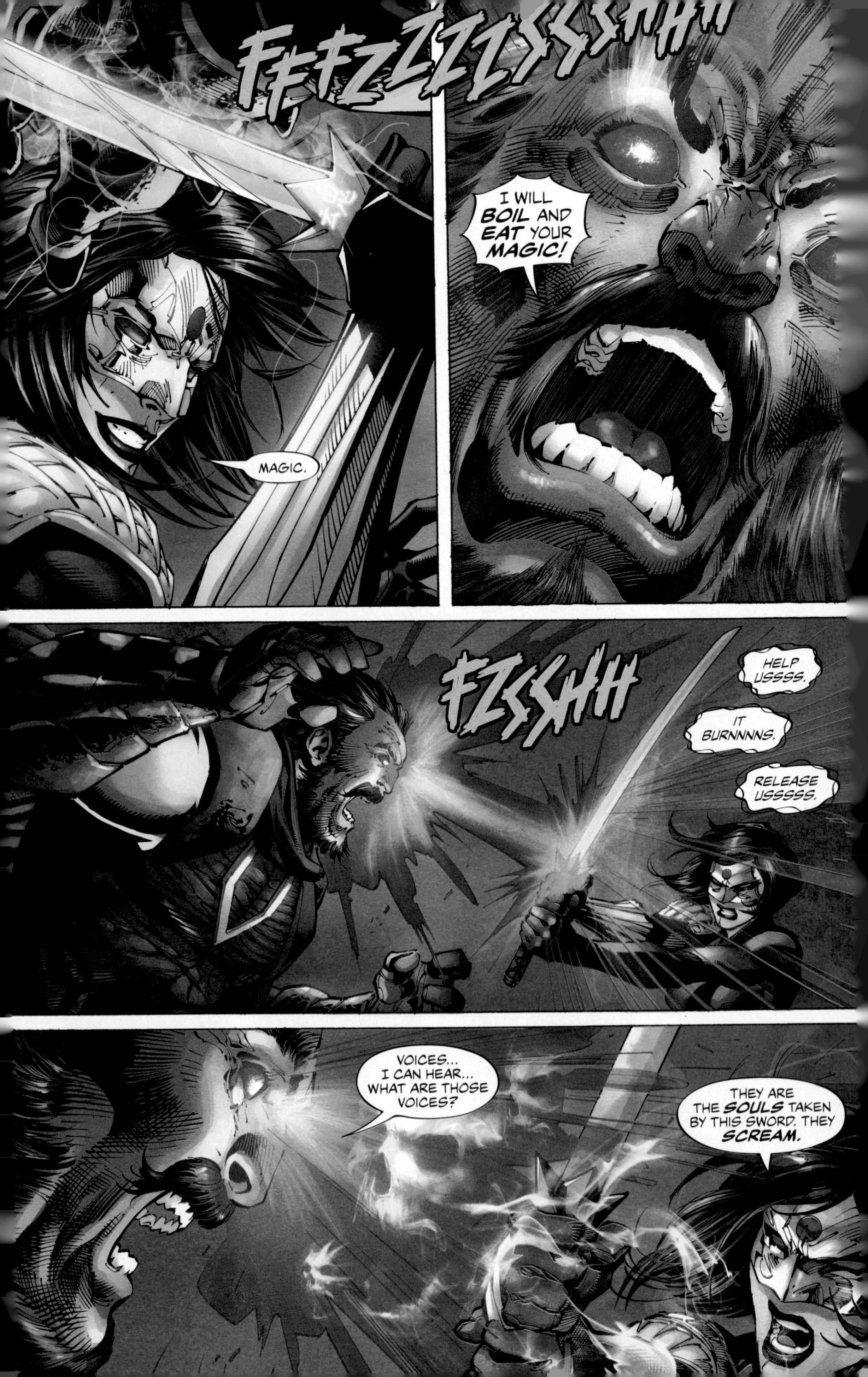

FFFZZZZSSSHH
MAGIC.
I WILL BOIL AND EAT YOUR MAGIC!
FZSSHH
HELP USSSS.
IT BURNNNNS.
RELEASE USSSSS.
VOICES... I CAN HEAR... WHAT ARE THOSE VOICES?
THEY ARE THE SOULS TAKEN BY THIS SWORD. THEY SCREAM.

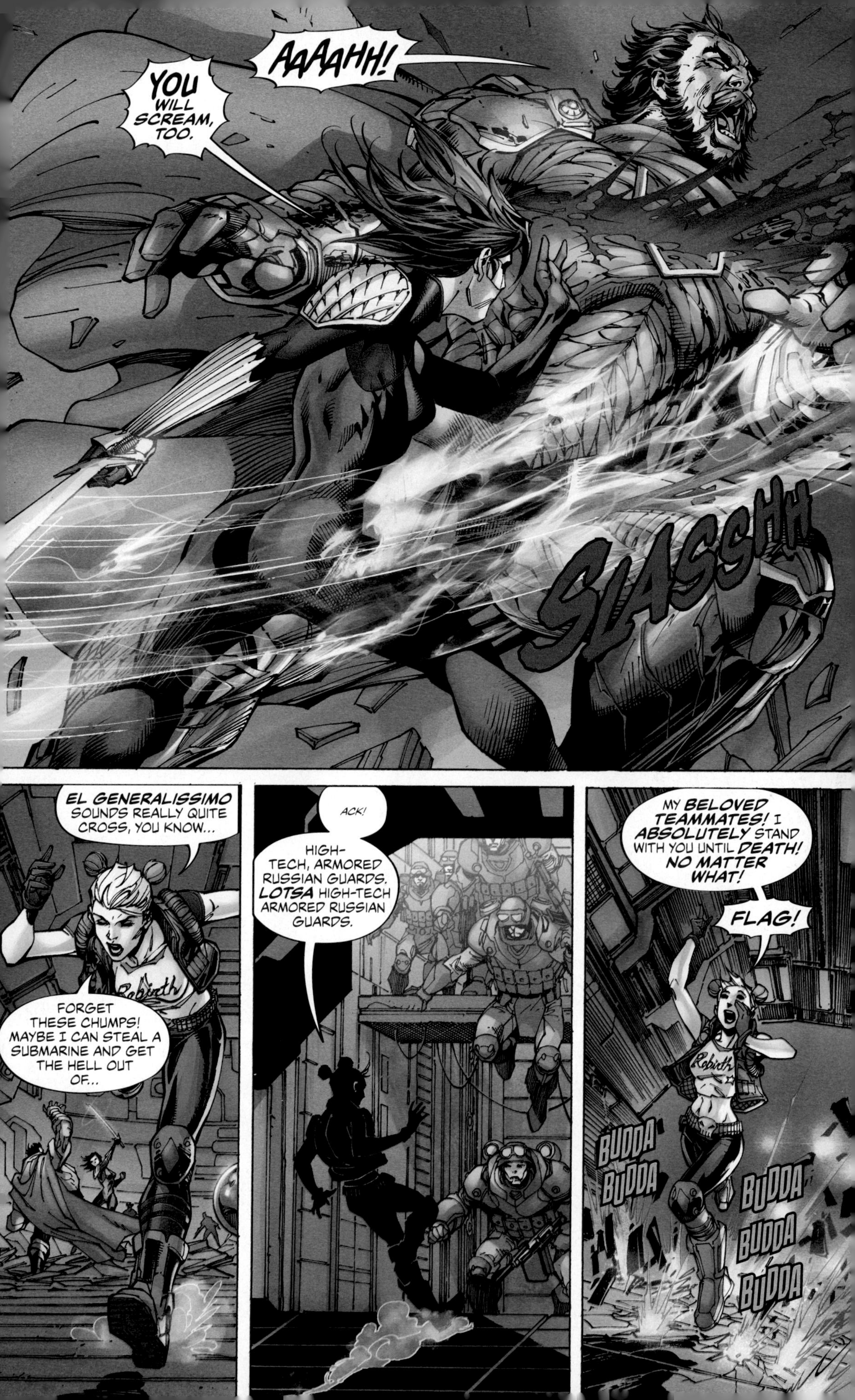
AAAAHH!
YOU WILL SCREAM, TOO.
SLASSHH
EL GENERALISSIMO SOUNDS REALLY QUITE CROSS, YOU KNOW...
FORGET THESE CHUMPS! MAYBE I CAN STEAL A SUBMARINE AND GET THE HELL OUT OF...
ACK!
HIGH-TECH, ARMORED RUSSIAN GUARDS. LOTSA HIGH-TECH ARMORED RUSSIAN GUARDS.
MY BELOVED TEAMMATES! I ABSOLUTELY STAND WITH YOU UNTIL DEATH! NO MATTER WHAT!
FLAG!
BUDDA BUDDA
BUDDA BUDDA BUDDA

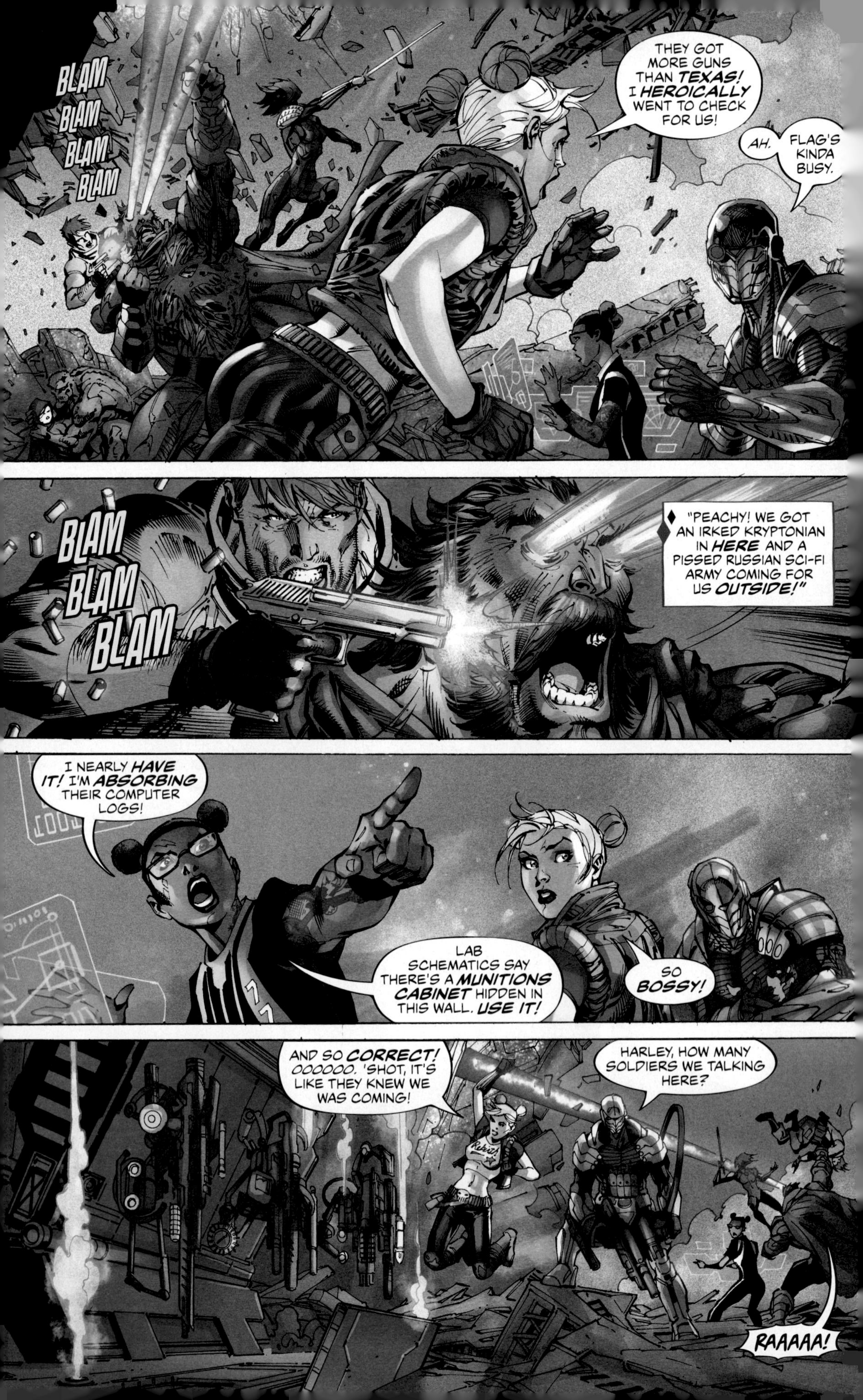
BLAM
BLAM
BLAM
BLAM
THEY GOT MORE GUNS THAN TEXAS! I HEROICALLY WENT TO CHECK FOR US!
AH.
FLAG'S KINDA BUSY.
BLAM
BLAM
BLAM
"PEACHY! WE GOT AN IRKED KRYPTONIAN IN HERE AND A PISSED RUSSIAN SCI-FI ARMY COMING FOR US OUTSIDE!"
I NEARLY HAVE IT! I'M ABSORBING THEIR COMPUTER LOGS!
LAB SCHEMATICS SAY THERE'S A MUNITIONS CABINET HIDDEN IN THIS WALL. USE IT!
SO BOSSY!
AND SO CORRECT! OOOOOOO. 'SHOT, IT'S LIKE THEY KNEW WE WAS COMING!
HARLEY, HOW MANY SOLDIERS WE TALKING HERE?
RAAAAA!

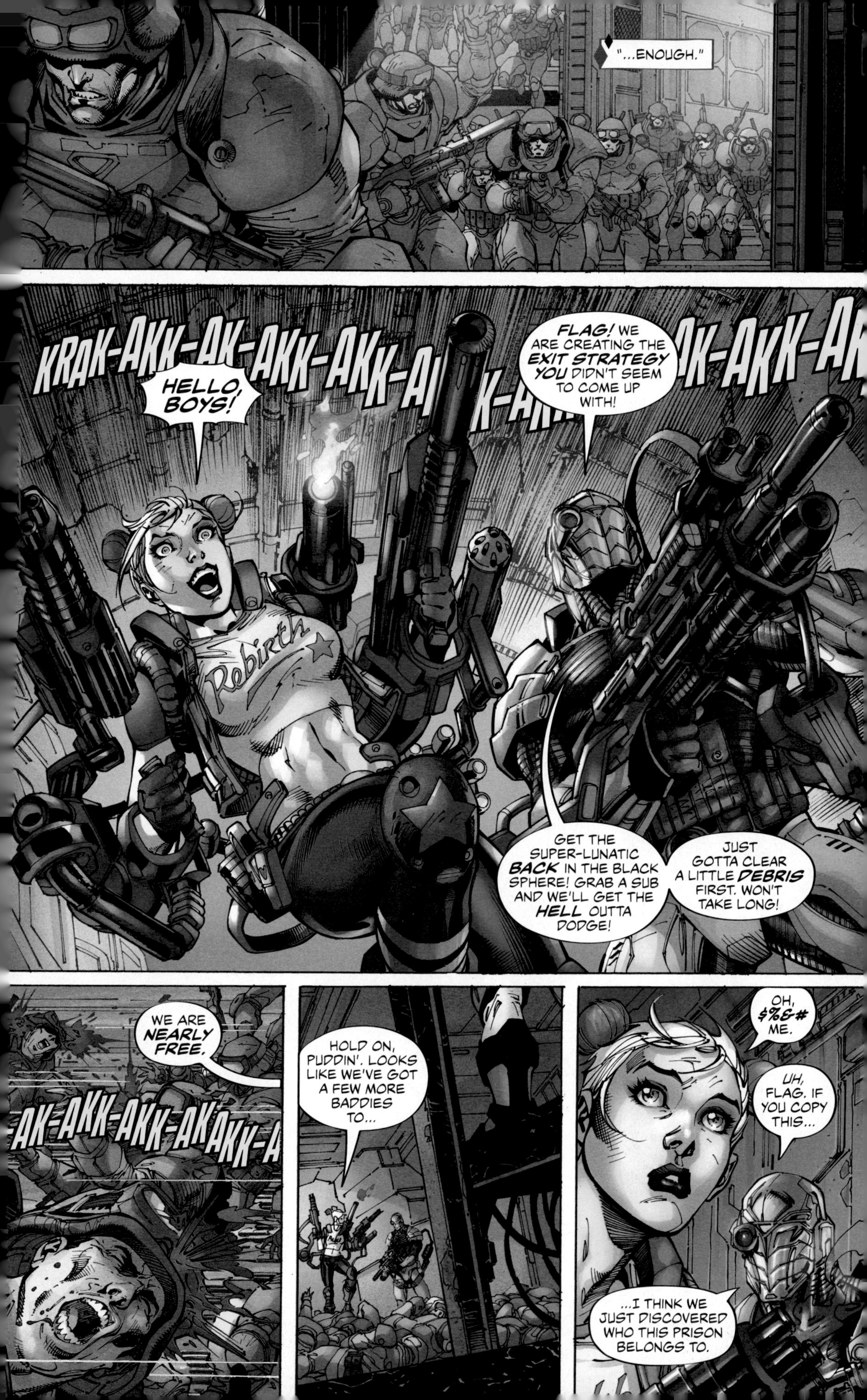
"...ENOUGH."
KRAK-AKK-AK-AKK-AKK-AKK-AKK-AKK-AK-AKK-AK
HELLO, BOYS!
FLAG! WE ARE CREATING THE EXIT STRATEGY YOU DIDN'T SEEM TO COME UP WITH!
GET THE SUPER-LUNATIC BACK IN THE BLACK SPHERE! GRAB A SUB AND WE'LL GET THE HELL OUTTA DODGE!
JUST GOTTA CLEAR A LITTLE DEBRIS FIRST. WON'T TAKE LONG!
WE ARE NEARLY FREE.
AK-AKK-AKK-AKAKK-A
HOLD ON, PUDDIN'. LOOKS LIKE WE'VE GOT A FEW MORE BADDIES TO...
OH, $%&# ME.
UH, FLAG. IF YOU COPY THIS...
...I THINK WE JUST DISCOVERED WHO THIS PRISON BELONGS TO.

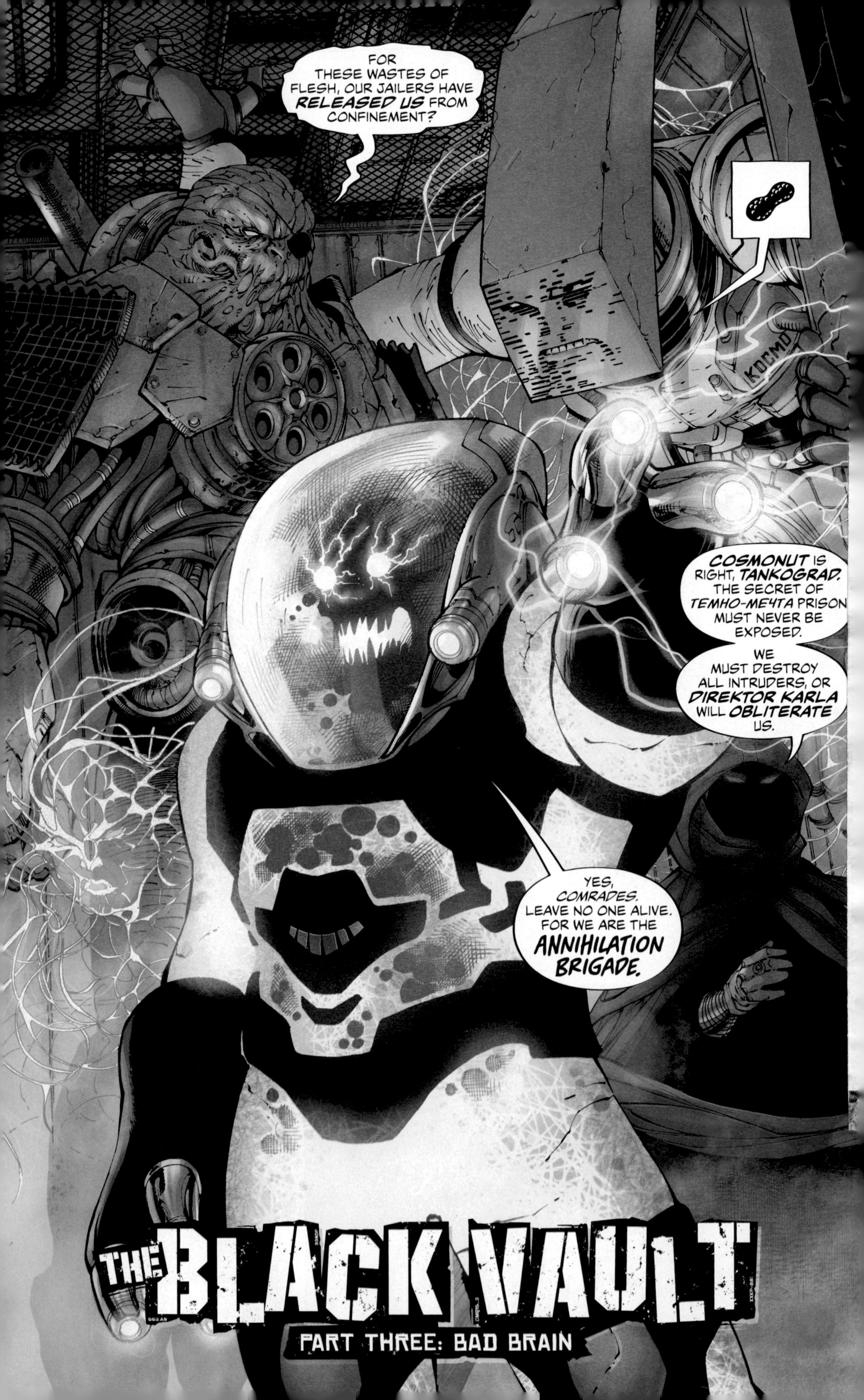
FOR THESE WASTES OF FLESH, OUR JAILERS HAVE RELEASED US FROM CONFINEMENT?
COSMONUT IS RIGHT, TANKOGRAD. THE SECRET OF TEMHO-MEЧTA PRISON MUST NEVER BE EXPOSED.
WE MUST DESTROY ALL INTRUDERS, OR DIREKTOR KARLA WILL OBLITERATE US.
YES, COMRADES. LEAVE NO ONE ALIVE. FOR WE ARE THE ANNIHILATION BRIGADE.
THE BLACK VAULT
PART THREE: BAD BRAIN

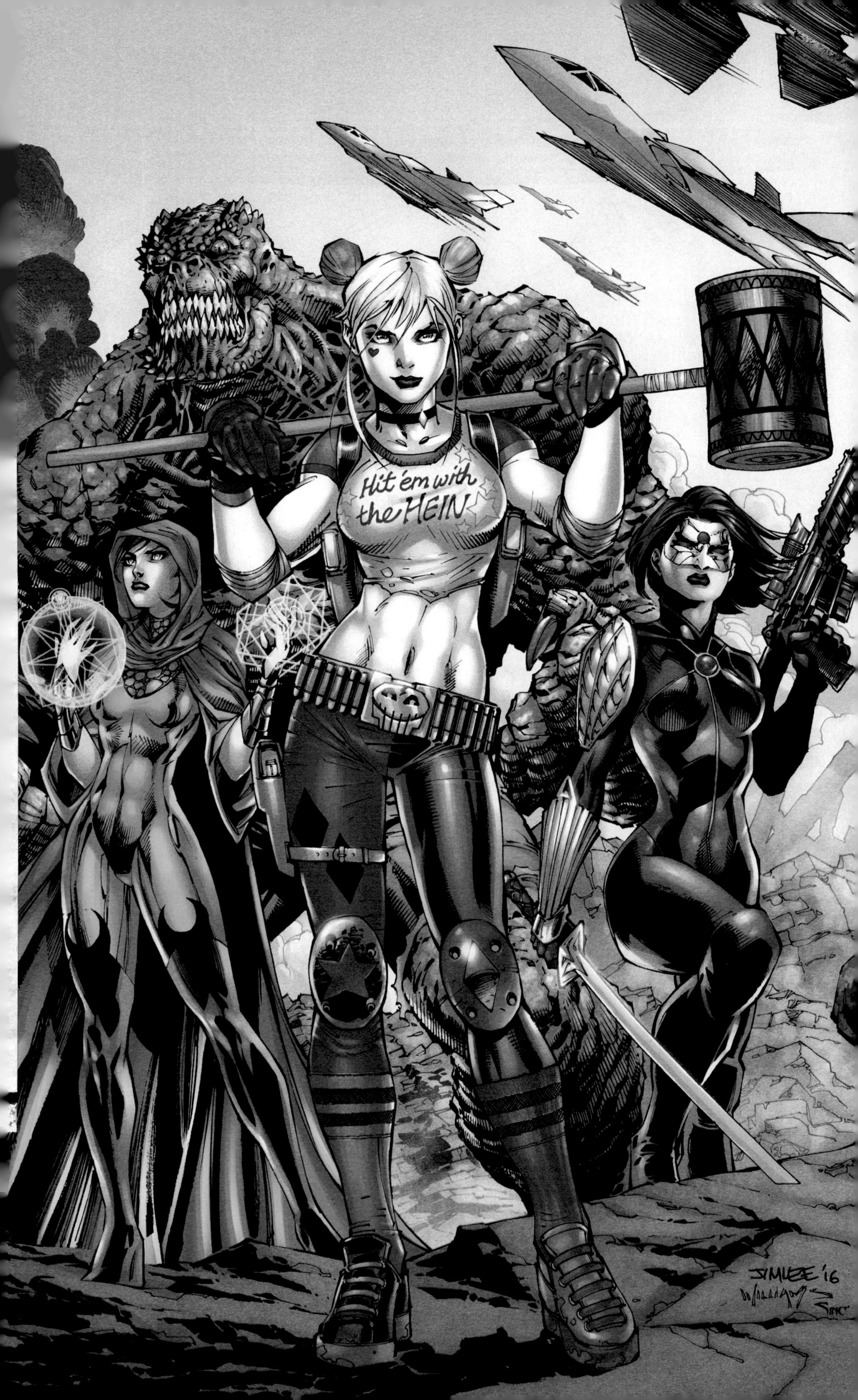
Hit 'em with the HEIN
JIM LEE '16

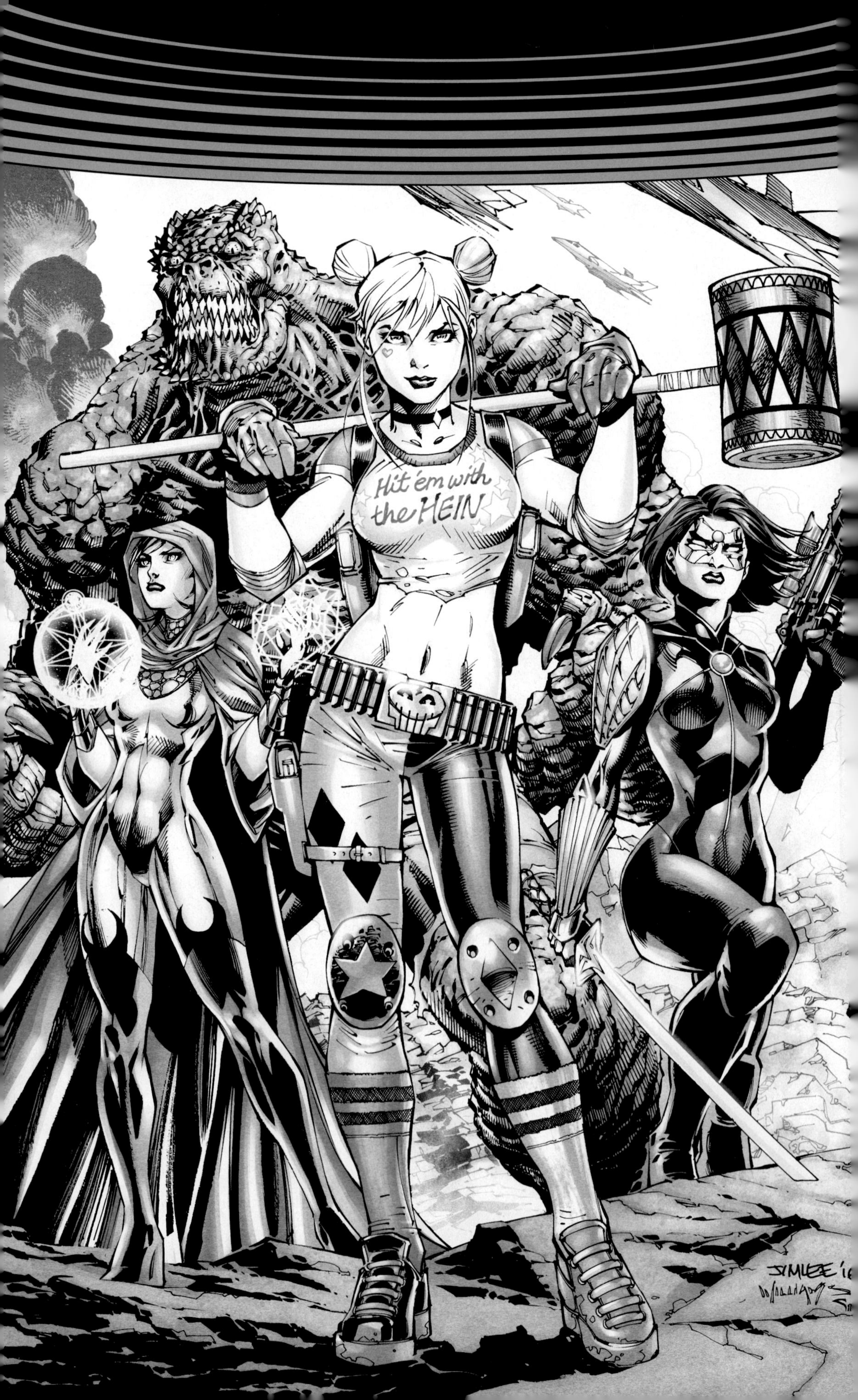
Hit 'em with the HEIN

LAPTEV SEA, SIBERIA.

MY NAME IS AMANDA WALLER, AND THE DEFINITION OF A SUICIDE MISSION IS:

A LOCATION THAT DOES NOT SUSTAIN HUMAN LIFE.

UNIDENTIFIED UNDERSEA PRISON.

NO POSSIBLE ESCAPE.

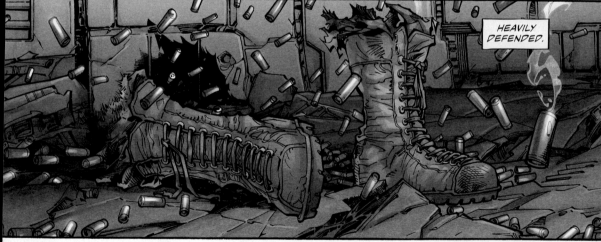

HEAVILY DEFENDED.

HIGHLY ERRATIC TARGET.

PROSTRATE YOURSELF BEFORE YOUR GENERAL, SUB-CREATURES!

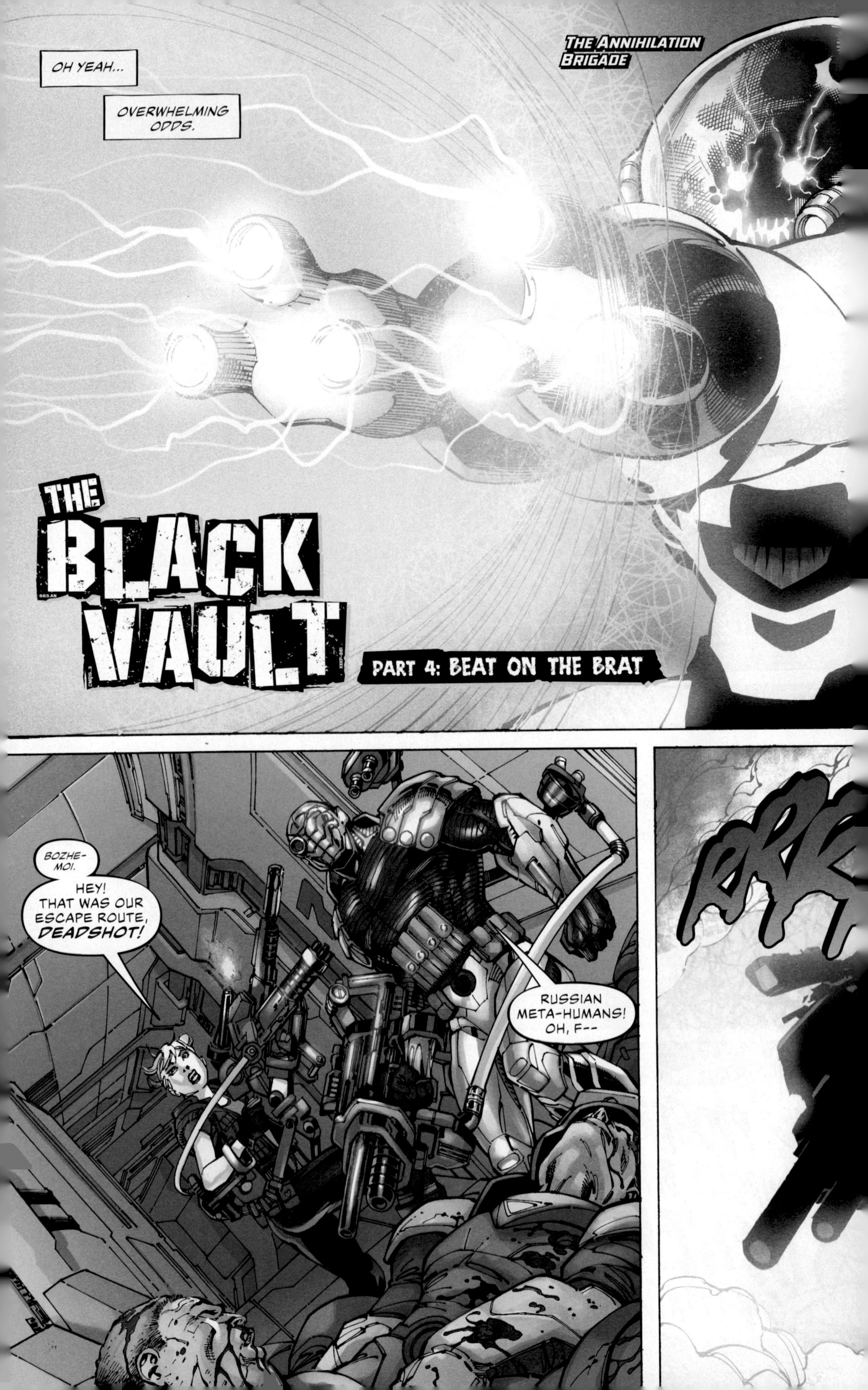
OH YEAH...
OVERWHELMING ODDS.
THE ANNIHILATION BRIGADE
THE BLACK VAULT
PART 4: BEAT ON THE BRAT
BOZHE-MOI.
HEY! THAT WAS OUR ESCAPE ROUTE, DEADSHOT!
RUSSIAN META-HUMANS! OH, F--

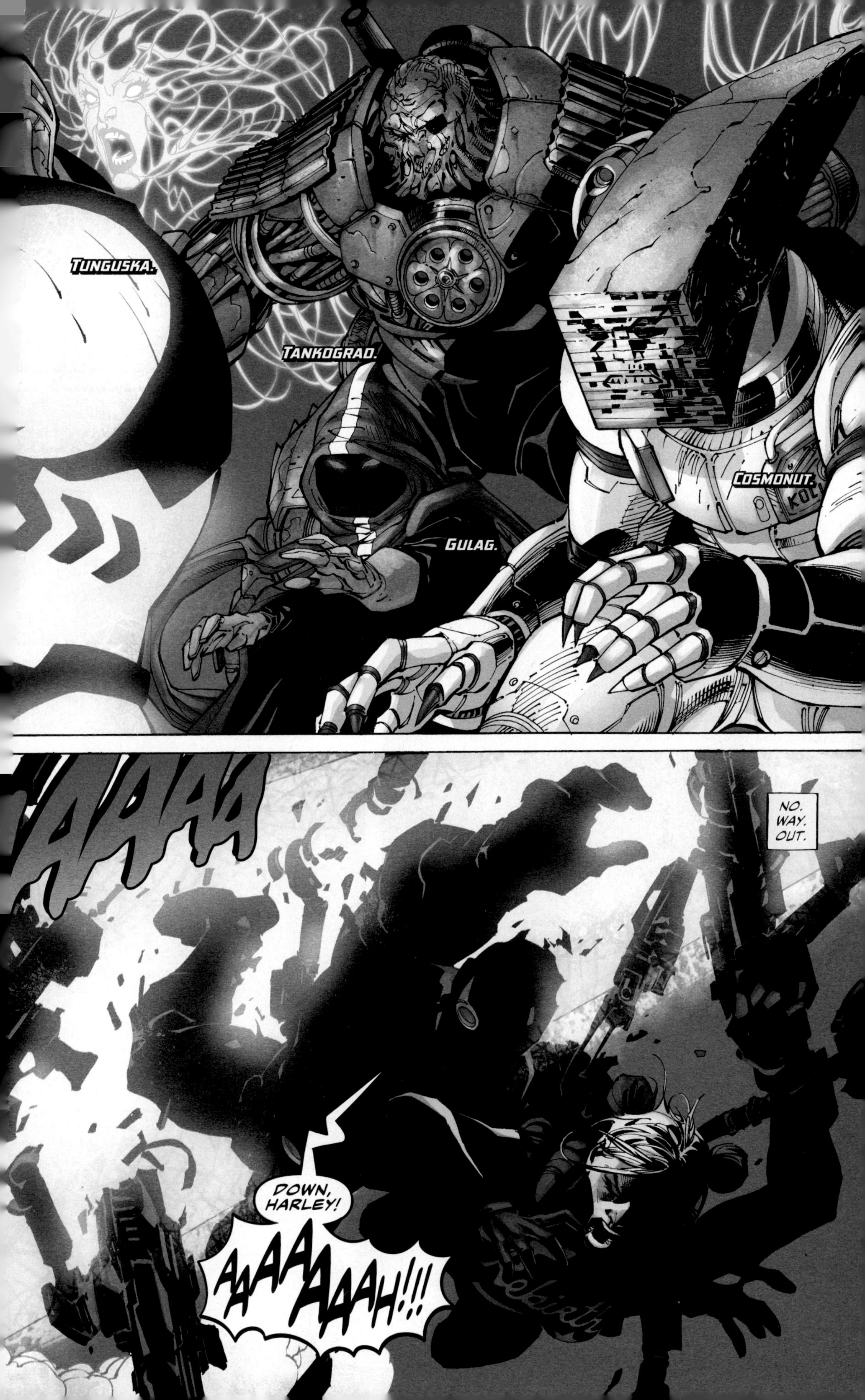
TUNGUSKA.
TANKOGRAD.
COSMONUT.
GULAG.
NO. WAY. OUT.
DOWN, HARLEY!
AAAAAAAAH!!!

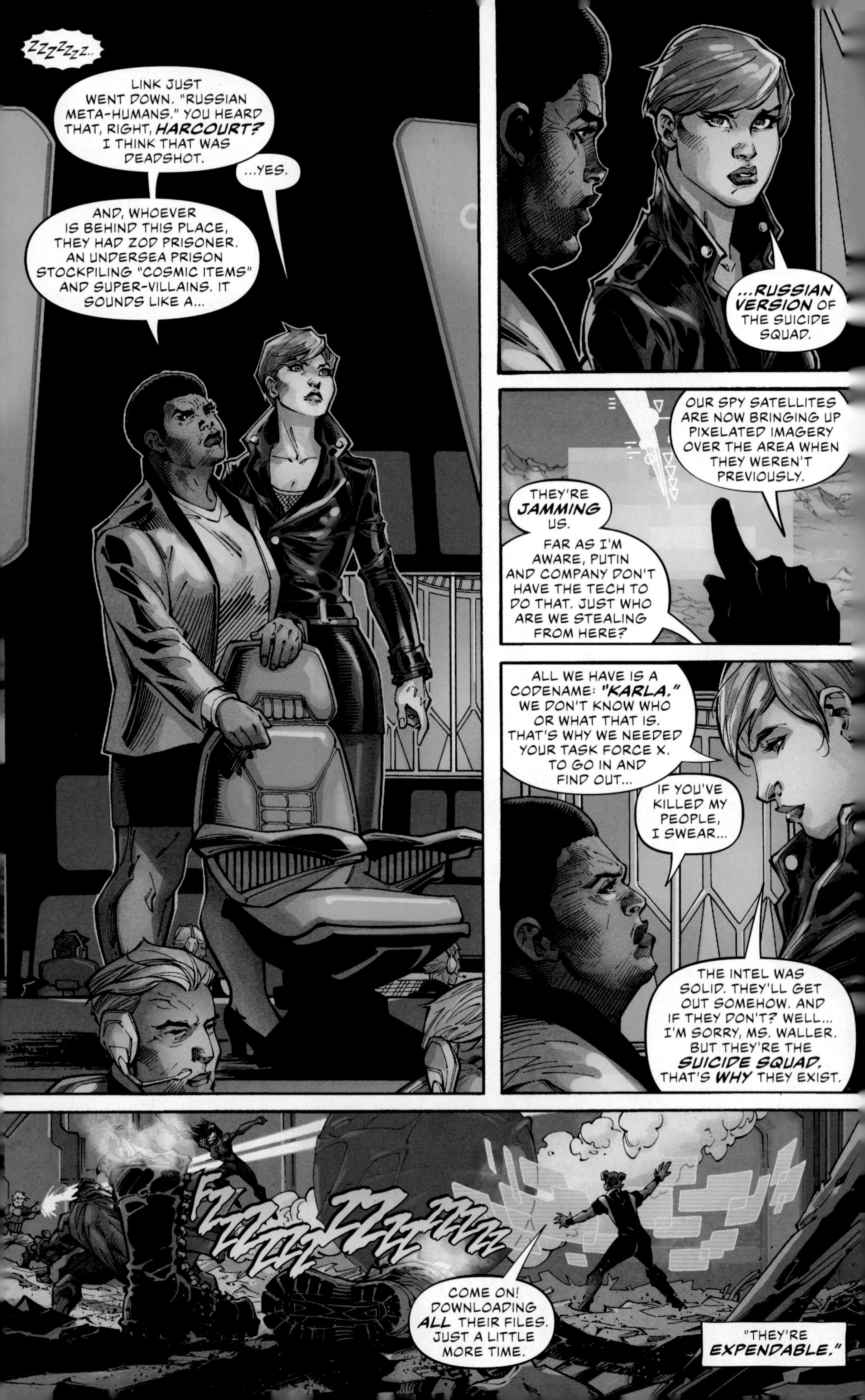
ZZZZZZZ..
LINK JUST WENT DOWN. "RUSSIAN META-HUMANS." YOU HEARD THAT, RIGHT, HARCOURT? I THINK THAT WAS DEADSHOT.
...YES.
AND, WHOEVER IS BEHIND THIS PLACE, THEY HAD ZOD PRISONER. AN UNDERSEA PRISON STOCKPILING "COSMIC ITEMS" AND SUPER-VILLAINS. IT SOUNDS LIKE A...
...RUSSIAN VERSION OF THE SUICIDE SQUAD.
OUR SPY SATELLITES ARE NOW BRINGING UP PIXELATED IMAGERY OVER THE AREA WHEN THEY WEREN'T PREVIOUSLY.
THEY'RE JAMMING US.
FAR AS I'M AWARE, PUTIN AND COMPANY DON'T HAVE THE TECH TO DO THAT. JUST WHO ARE WE STEALING FROM HERE?
ALL WE HAVE IS A CODENAME: "KARLA." WE DON'T KNOW WHO OR WHAT THAT IS. THAT'S WHY WE NEEDED YOUR TASK FORCE X. TO GO IN AND FIND OUT...
IF YOU'VE KILLED MY PEOPLE, I SWEAR...
THE INTEL WAS SOLID. THEY'LL GET OUT SOMEHOW. AND IF THEY DON'T? WELL... I'M SORRY, MS. WALLER. BUT THEY'RE THE SUICIDE SQUAD. THAT'S WHY THEY EXIST.
ZZZZZZZZZZZZ
COME ON! DOWNLOADING ALL THEIR FILES. JUST A LITTLE MORE TIME.
"THEY'RE EXPENDABLE."

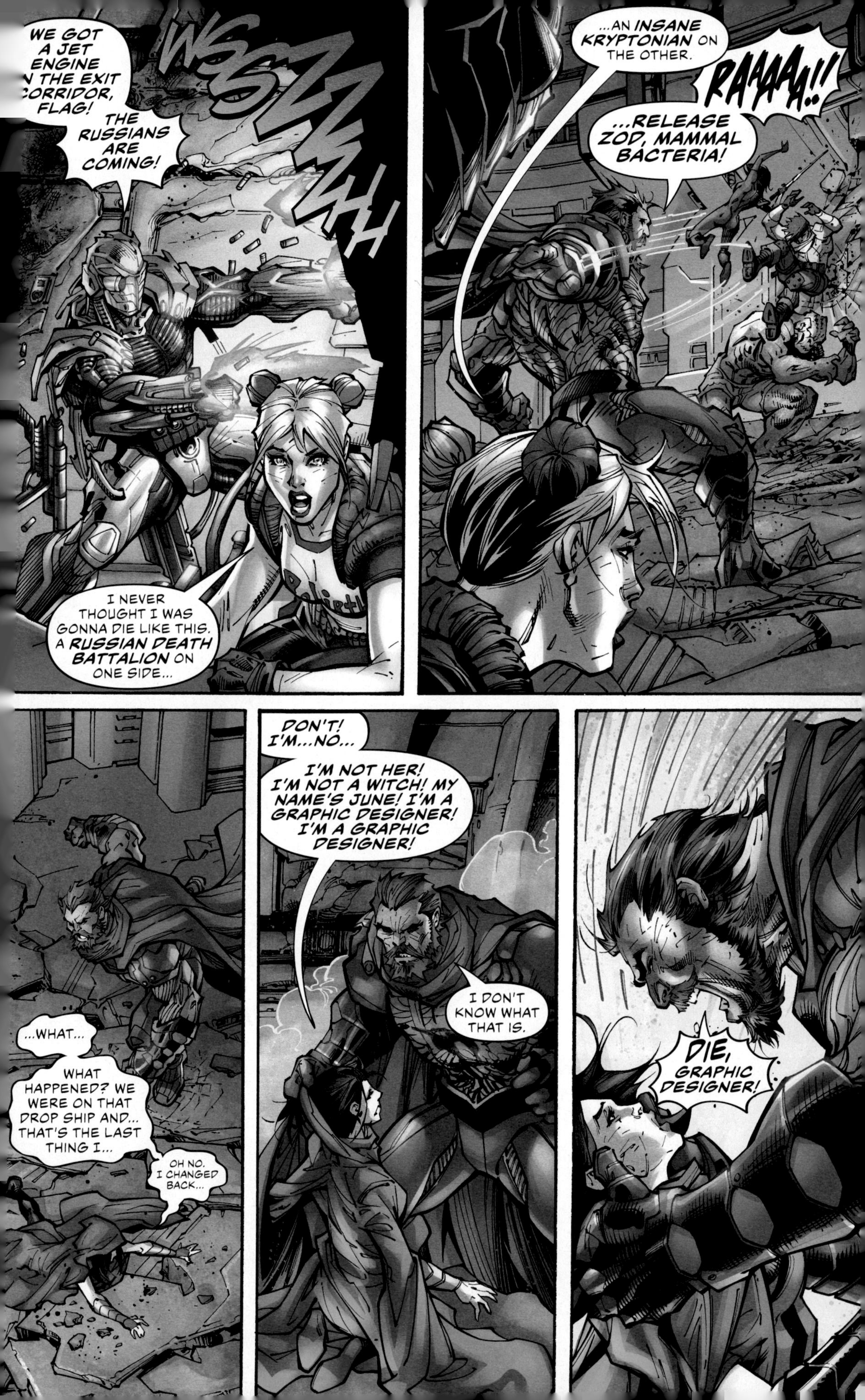

WE GOT A JET ENGINE N THE EXIT CORRIDOR, FLAG!
THE RUSSIANS ARE COMING!
I NEVER THOUGHT I WAS GONNA DIE LIKE THIS. A RUSSIAN DEATH BATTALION ON ONE SIDE...
...AN INSANE KRYPTONIAN ON THE OTHER.
RAAAAA!!
...RELEASE ZOD, MAMMAL BACTERIA!
...WHAT...
WHAT HAPPENED? WE WERE ON THAT DROP SHIP AND... THAT'S THE LAST THING I...
OH NO. I CHANGED BACK...
DON'T! I'M...NO...
I'M NOT HER! I'M NOT A WITCH! MY NAME'S JUNE! I'M A GRAPHIC DESIGNER! I'M A GRAPHIC DESIGNER!
I DON'T KNOW WHAT THAT IS.
DIE, GRAPHIC DESIGNER!

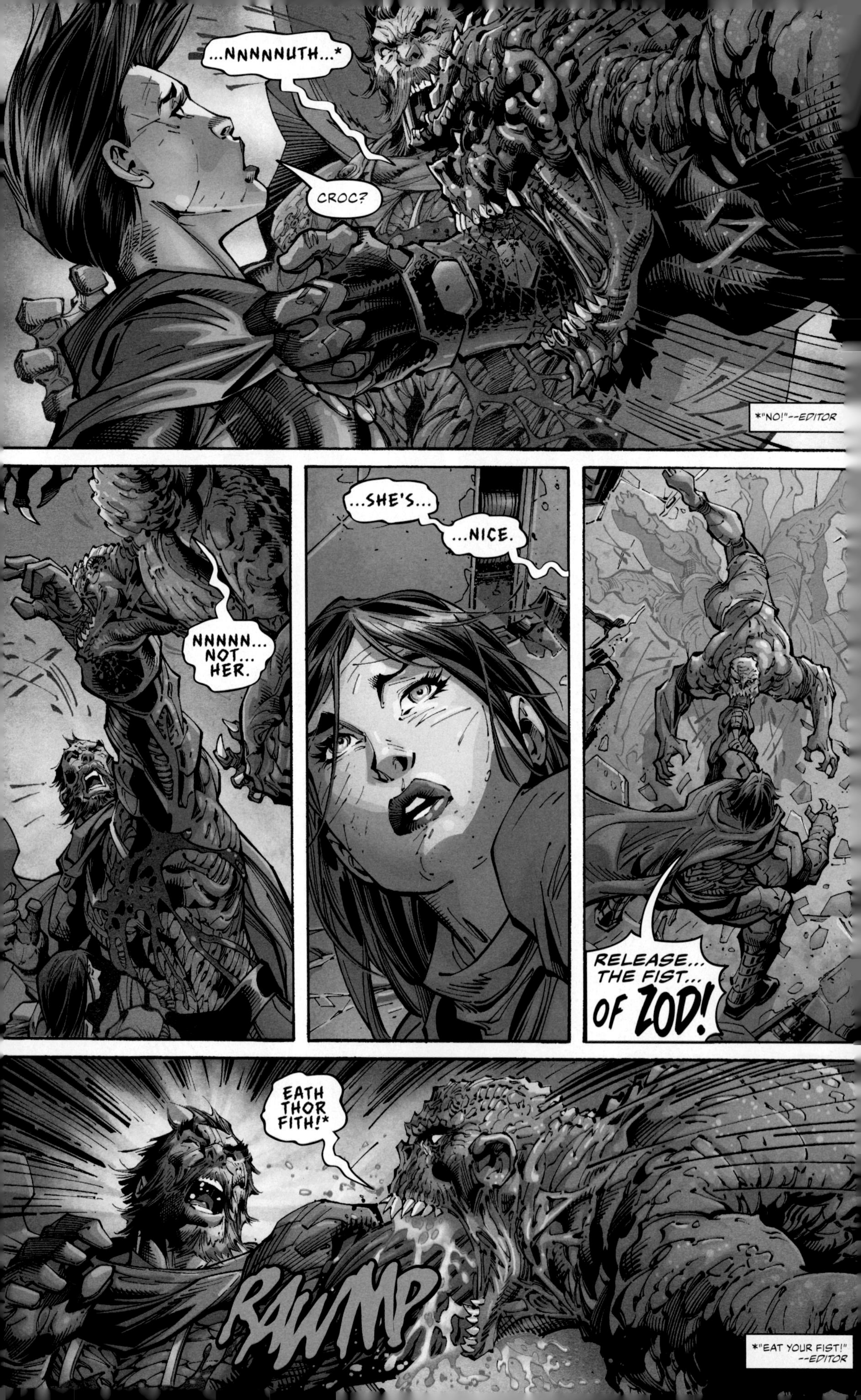
...NNNNNUTH...*
CROC?
*"NO!"--EDITOR
NNNNN... NOT... HER.
...SHE'S...
...NICE.
RELEASE... THE FIST... OF ZOD!
EATH THOR FITH!*
RAWMP
*"EAT YOUR FIST!" --EDITOR

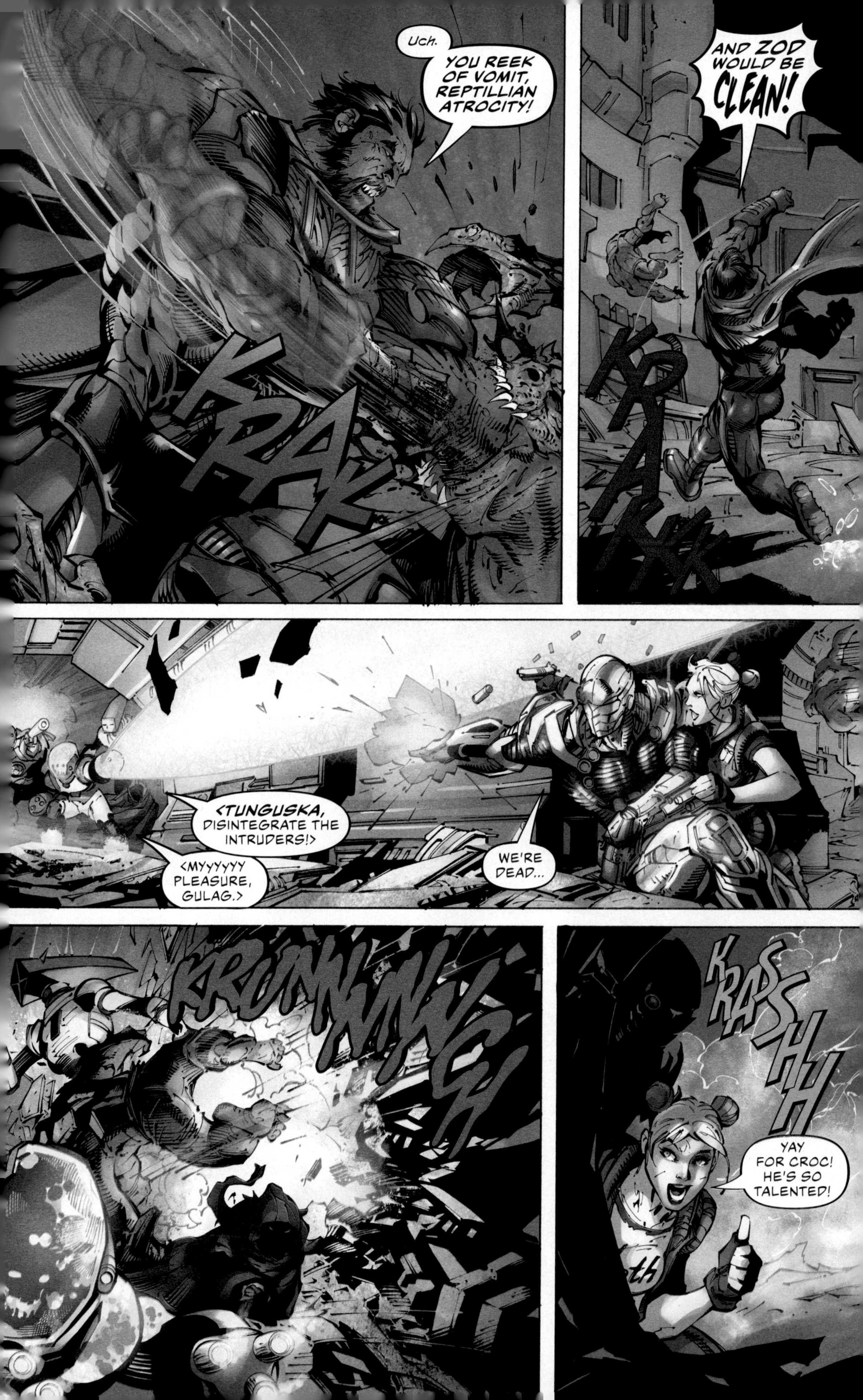
Uch.
YOU REEK OF VOMIT, REPTILLIAN ATROCITY!
KRAK
AND ZOD WOULD BE CLEAN!
KRAKKK
<TUNGUSKA, DISINTEGRATE THE INTRUDERS!>
<MYYYYYY PLEASURE, GULAG.>
WE'RE DEAD...
KRONNNNNGH
KRASHH
YAY FOR CROC! HE'S SO TALENTED!

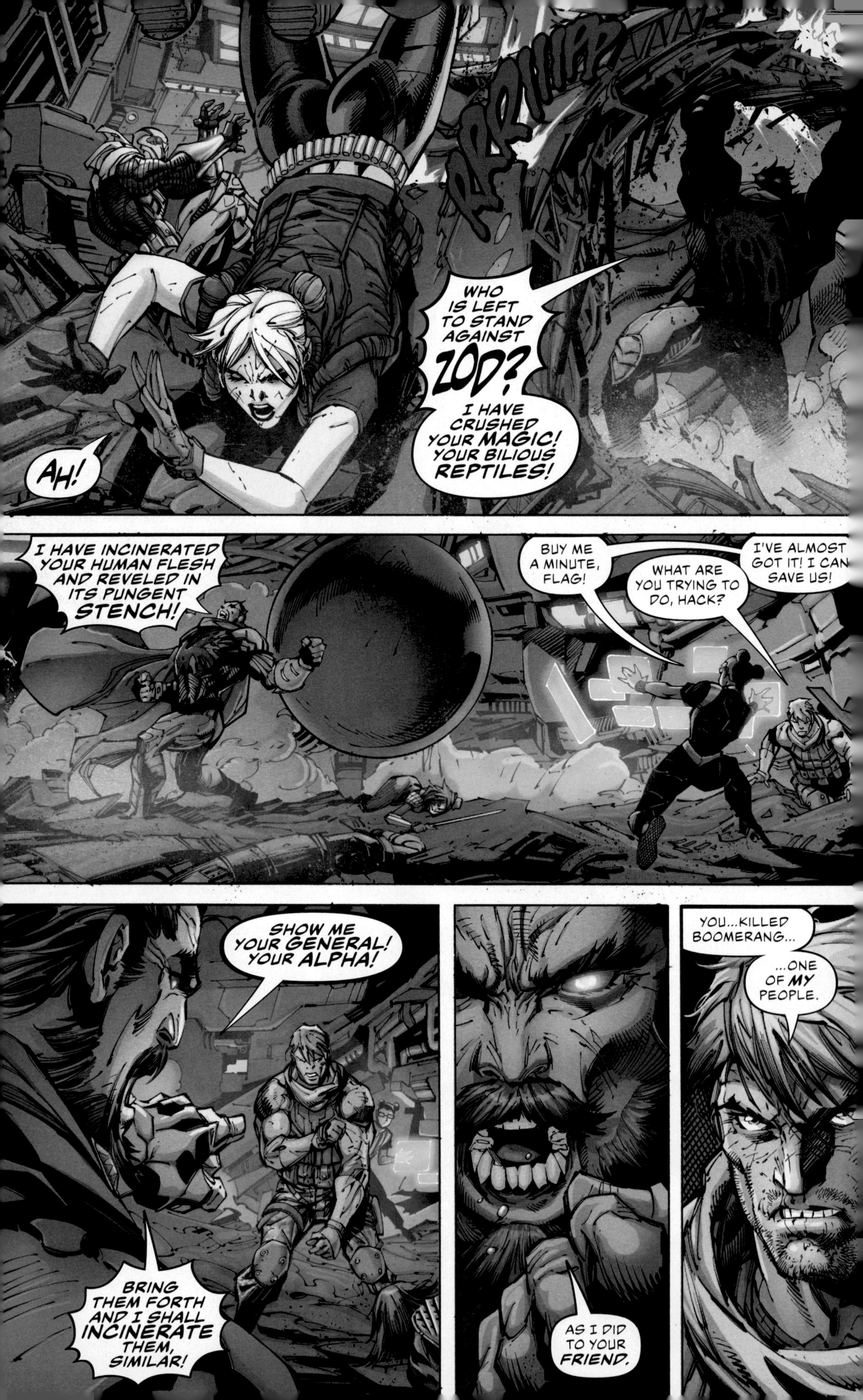
RRRWHAP
WHO IS LEFT TO STAND AGAINST ZOD?
I HAVE CRUSHED YOUR MAGIC! YOUR BILIOUS REPTILES!
AH!
I HAVE INCINERATED YOUR HUMAN FLESH AND REVELED IN ITS PUNGENT STENCH!
BUY ME A MINUTE, FLAG!
WHAT ARE YOU TRYING TO DO, HACK?
I'VE ALMOST GOT IT! I CAN SAVE US!
SHOW ME YOUR GENERAL! YOUR ALPHA!
BRING THEM FORTH AND I SHALL INCINERATE THEM, SIMILAR!
AS I DID TO YOUR FRIEND.
YOU...KILLED BOOMERANG...
...ONE OF MY PEOPLE.

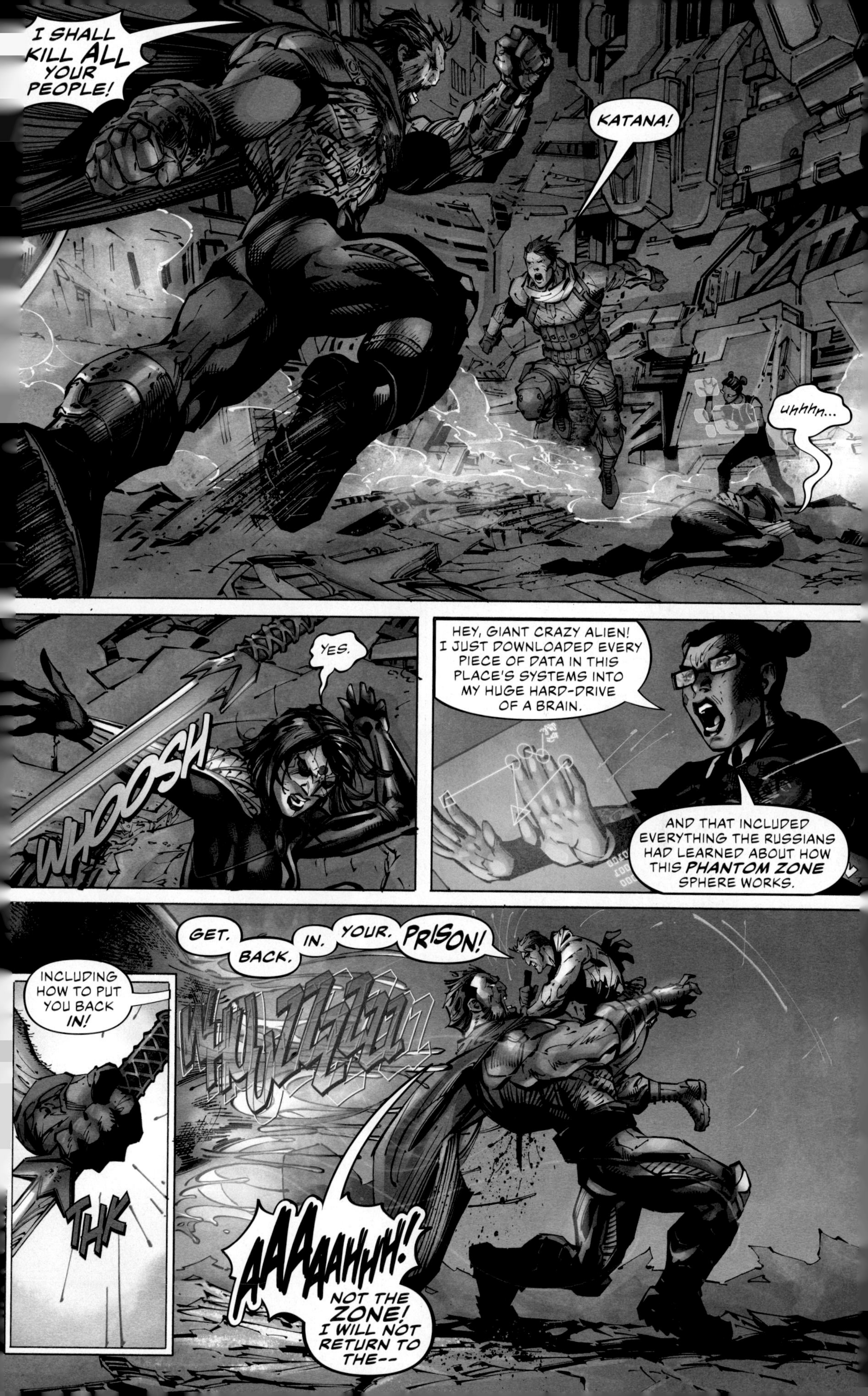
I SHALL KILL ALL YOUR PEOPLE!
KATANA!
uhhhn...
YES.
WHOOSH
HEY, GIANT CRAZY ALIEN! I JUST DOWNLOADED EVERY PIECE OF DATA IN THIS PLACE'S SYSTEMS INTO MY HUGE HARD-DRIVE OF A BRAIN.
AND THAT INCLUDED EVERYTHING THE RUSSIANS HAD LEARNED ABOUT HOW THIS PHANTOM ZONE SPHERE WORKS.
GET. BACK. IN. YOUR. PRISON!
INCLUDING HOW TO PUT YOU BACK IN!
THK
AAAAAHHH! NOT THE ZONE! I WILL NOT RETURN TO THE--

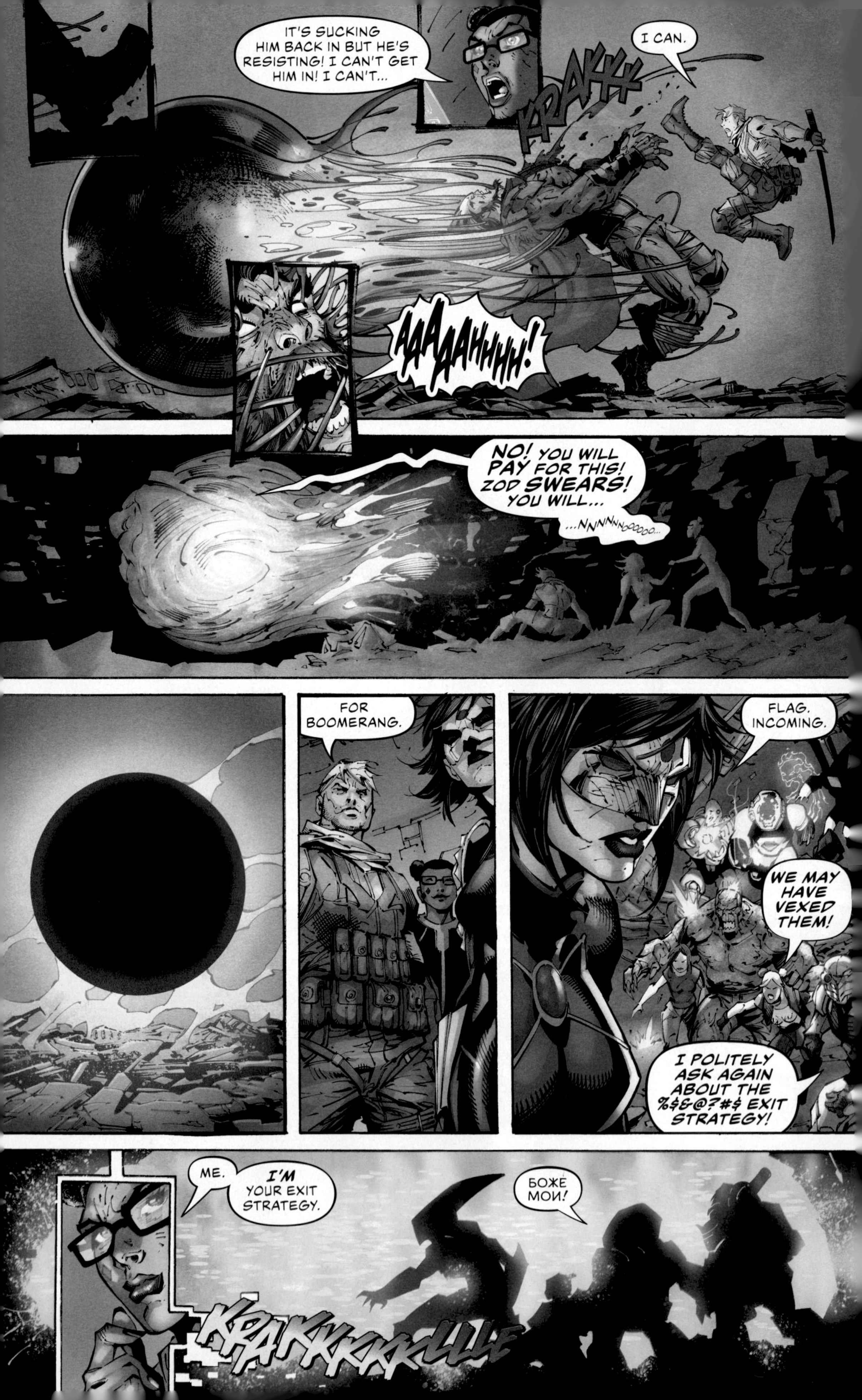
IT'S SUCKING HIM BACK IN BUT HE'S RESISTING! I CAN'T GET HIM IN! I CAN'T...
I CAN.
KRAKK
AAAAAHHHHH!
NO! YOU WILL PAY FOR THIS! ZOD SWEARS! YOU WILL...
...NNNNNNooooo...
FOR BOOMERANG.
FLAG. INCOMING.
WE MAY HAVE VEXED THEM!
I POLITELY ASK AGAIN ABOUT THE %$&@?#$ EXIT STRATEGY!
ME.
I'M YOUR EXIT STRATEGY.
БОЖЕ МОИ!
KRAKKKKKKLLLE

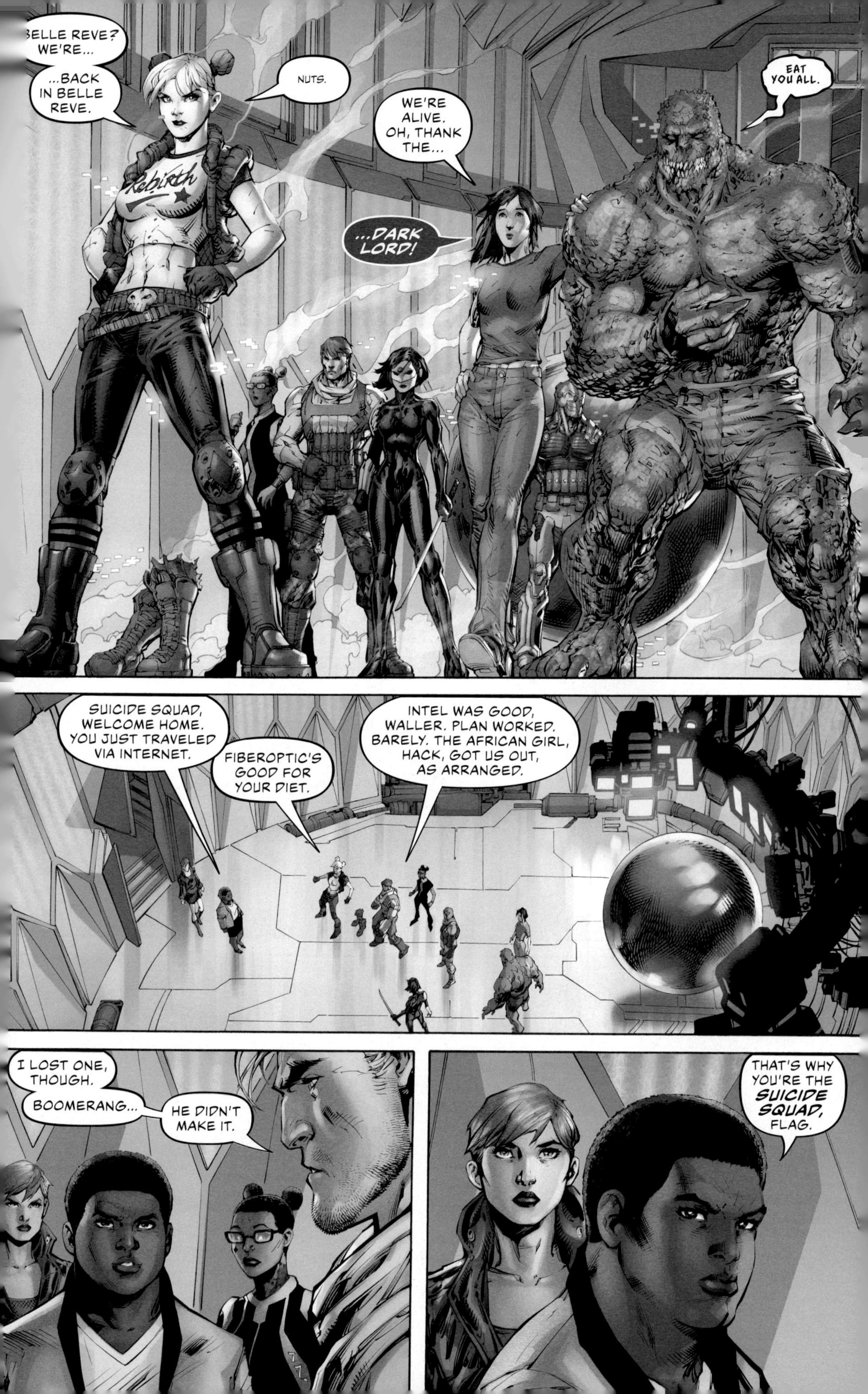
BELLE REVE? WE'RE...
...BACK IN BELLE REVE.
NUTS.
WE'RE ALIVE. OH, THANK THE...
...DARK LORD!
EAT YOU ALL.
SUICIDE SQUAD, WELCOME HOME. YOU JUST TRAVELED VIA INTERNET.
FIBEROPTIC'S GOOD FOR YOUR DIET.
INTEL WAS GOOD, WALLER. PLAN WORKED. BARELY. THE AFRICAN GIRL, HACK, GOT US OUT, AS ARRANGED.
I LOST ONE, THOUGH.
BOOMERANG...
HE DIDN'T MAKE IT.
THAT'S WHY YOU'RE THE SUICIDE SQUAD, FLAG.

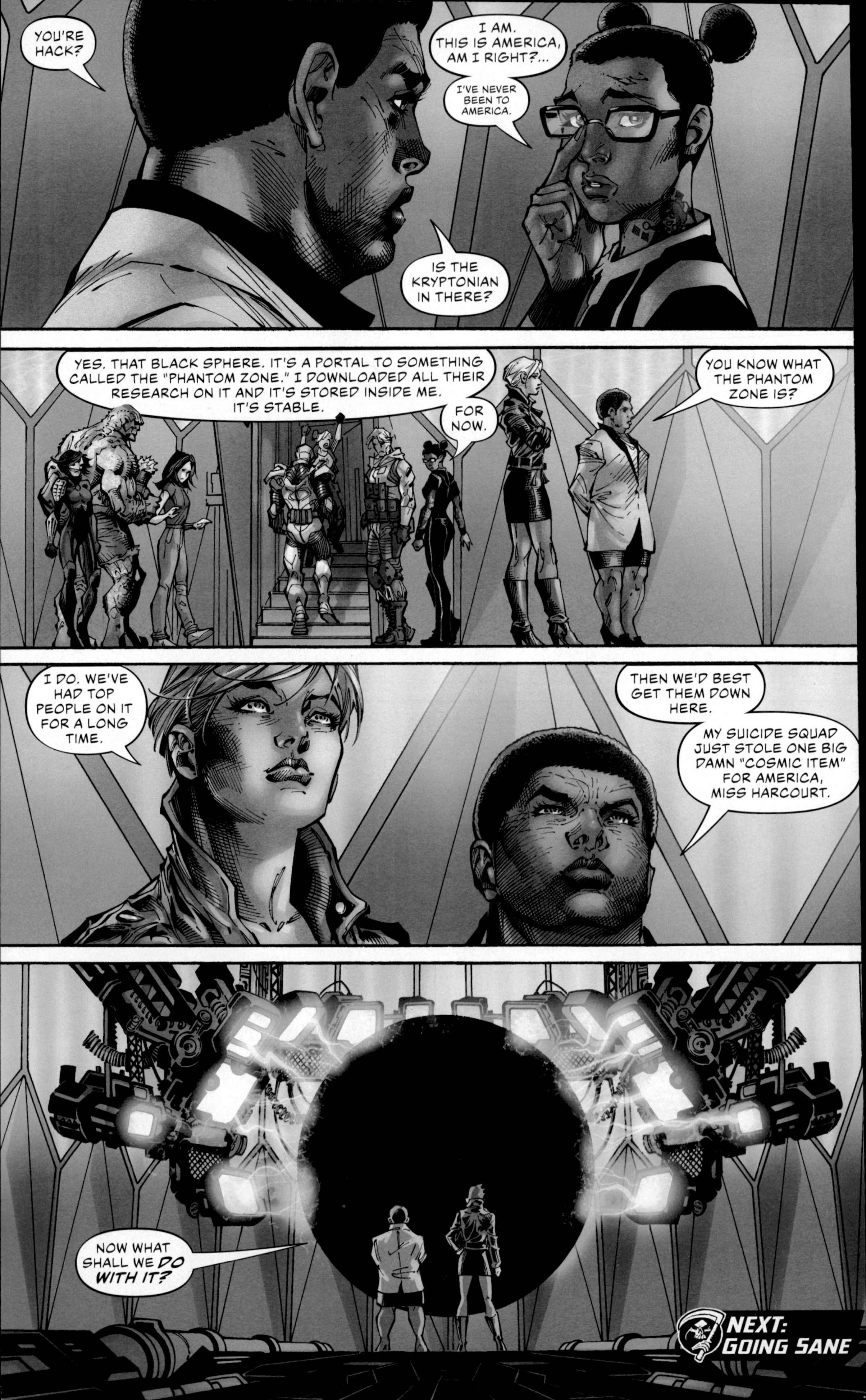
YOU'RE HACK?
I AM. THIS IS AMERICA, AM I RIGHT?...
I'VE NEVER BEEN TO AMERICA.
IS THE KRYPTONIAN IN THERE?
YES. THAT BLACK SPHERE. IT'S A PORTAL TO SOMETHING CALLED THE "PHANTOM ZONE." I DOWNLOADED ALL THEIR RESEARCH ON IT AND IT'S STORED INSIDE ME. IT'S STABLE.
FOR NOW.
YOU KNOW WHAT THE PHANTOM ZONE IS?
I DO. WE'VE HAD TOP PEOPLE ON IT FOR A LONG TIME.
THEN WE'D BEST GET THEM DOWN HERE.
MY SUICIDE SQUAD JUST STOLE ONE BIG DAMN "COSMIC ITEM" FOR AMERICA, MISS HARCOURT.
NOW WHAT SHALL WE DO WITH IT?
NEXT: GOING SANE

TASK FORCE X
PERSONNEL FILES

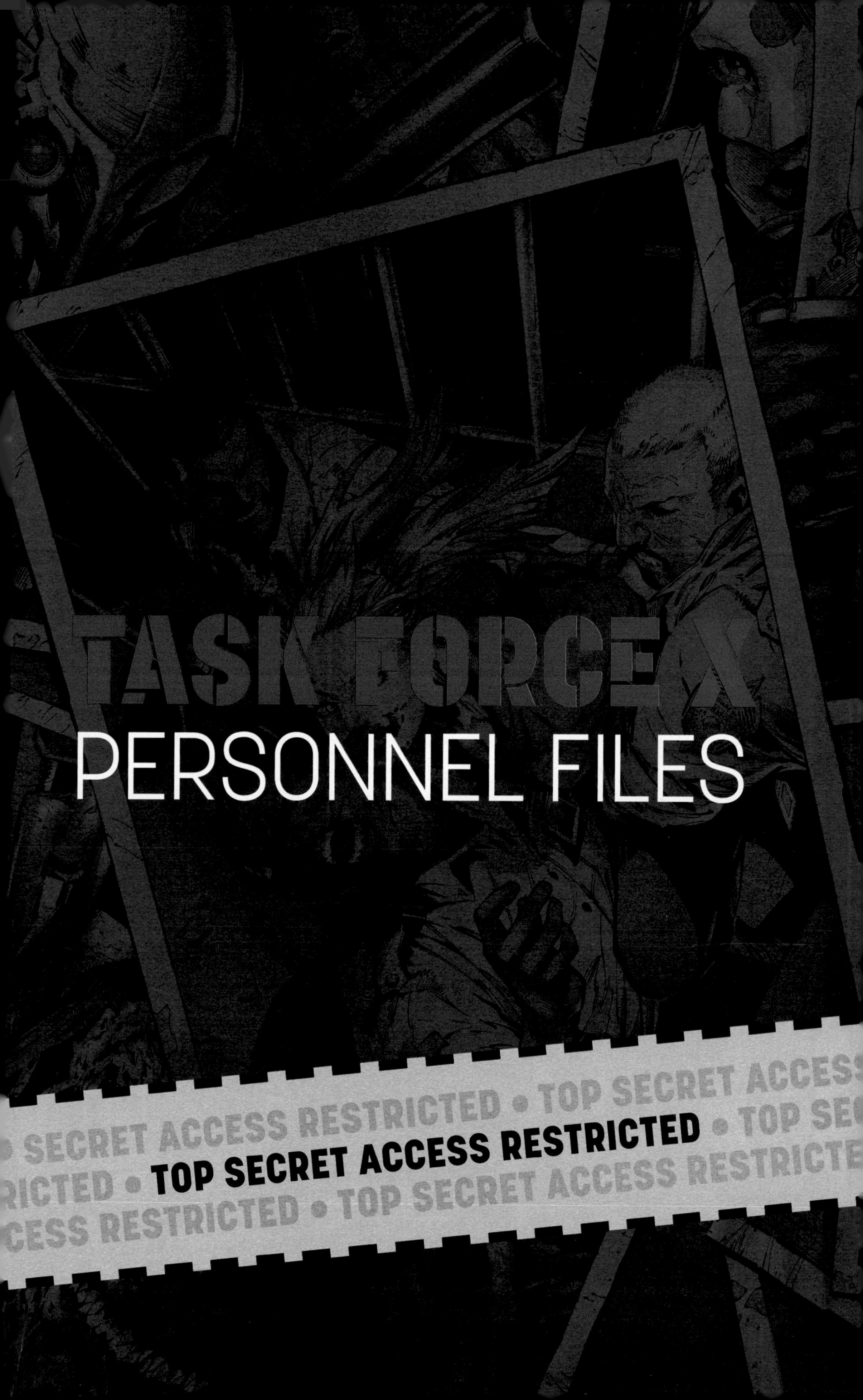
TOP SECRET ACCESS RESTRICTED

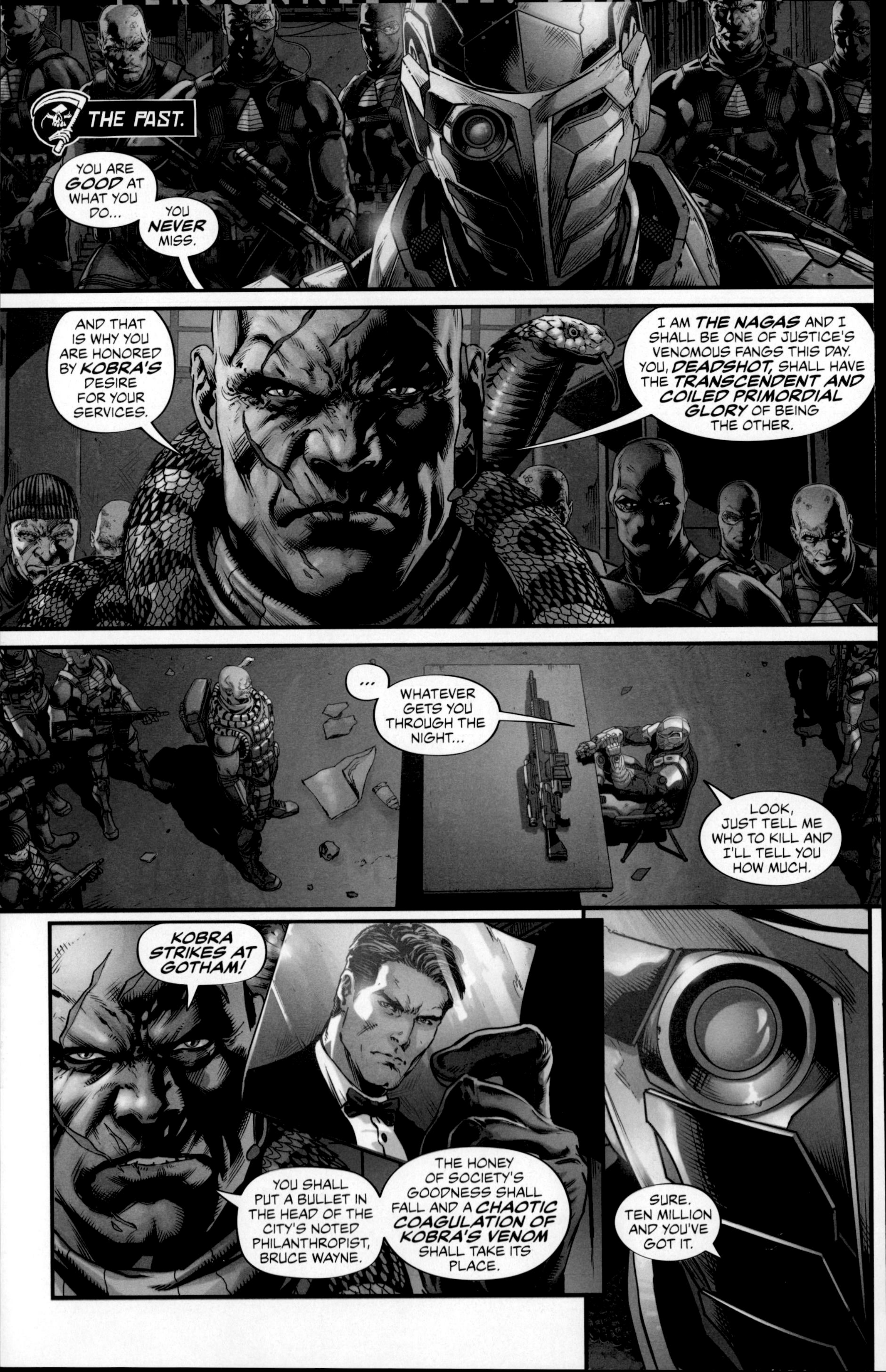
THE PAST.
YOU ARE GOOD AT WHAT YOU DO...
YOU NEVER MISS.
AND THAT IS WHY YOU ARE HONORED BY KOBRA'S DESIRE FOR YOUR SERVICES.
I AM THE NAGAS AND I SHALL BE ONE OF JUSTICE'S VENOMOUS FANGS THIS DAY. YOU, DEADSHOT, SHALL HAVE THE TRANSCENDENT AND COILED PRIMORDIAL GLORY OF BEING THE OTHER.
...
WHATEVER GETS YOU THROUGH THE NIGHT...
LOOK, JUST TELL ME WHO TO KILL AND I'LL TELL YOU HOW MUCH.
KOBRA STRIKES AT GOTHAM!
YOU SHALL PUT A BULLET IN THE HEAD OF THE CITY'S NOTED PHILANTHROPIST, BRUCE WAYNE.
THE HONEY OF SOCIETY'S GOODNESS SHALL FALL AND A CHAOTIC COAGULATION OF KOBRA'S VENOM SHALL TAKE ITS PLACE.
SURE. TEN MILLION AND YOU'VE GOT IT.

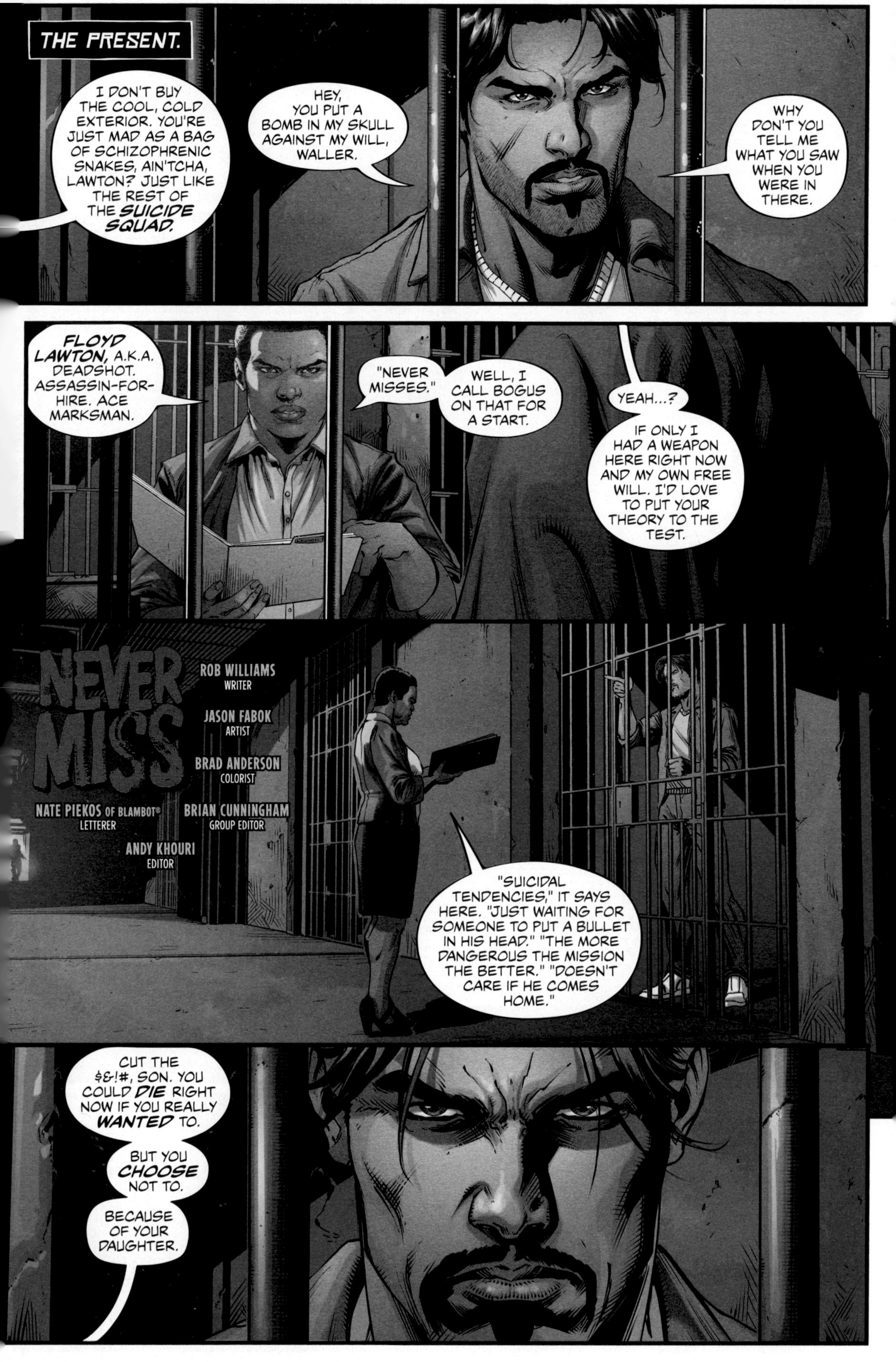
THE PRESENT.
I DON'T BUY THE COOL, COLD EXTERIOR. YOU'RE JUST MAD AS A BAG OF SCHIZOPHRENIC SNAKES, AIN'TCHA, LAWTON? JUST LIKE THE REST OF THE SUICIDE SQUAD.
HEY, YOU PUT A BOMB IN MY SKULL AGAINST MY WILL, WALLER.
WHY DON'T YOU TELL ME WHAT YOU SAW WHEN YOU WERE IN THERE.
FLOYD LAWTON, A.K.A. DEADSHOT. ASSASSIN-FOR-HIRE. ACE MARKSMAN.
"NEVER MISSES."
WELL, I CALL BOGUS ON THAT FOR A START.
YEAH...?
IF ONLY I HAD A WEAPON HERE RIGHT NOW AND MY OWN FREE WILL. I'D LOVE TO PUT YOUR THEORY TO THE TEST.
NEVER MISS
ROB WILLIAMS WRITER
JASON FABOK ARTIST
BRAD ANDERSON COLORIST
NATE PIEKOS OF BLAMBOT® LETTERER
BRIAN CUNNINGHAM GROUP EDITOR
ANDY KHOURI EDITOR
"SUICIDAL TENDENCIES," IT SAYS HERE. "JUST WAITING FOR SOMEONE TO PUT A BULLET IN HIS HEAD." "THE MORE DANGEROUS THE MISSION THE BETTER." "DOESN'T CARE IF HE COMES HOME."
CUT THE $&!#, SON. YOU COULD DIE RIGHT NOW IF YOU REALLY WANTED TO.
BUT YOU CHOOSE NOT TO.
BECAUSE OF YOUR DAUGHTER.

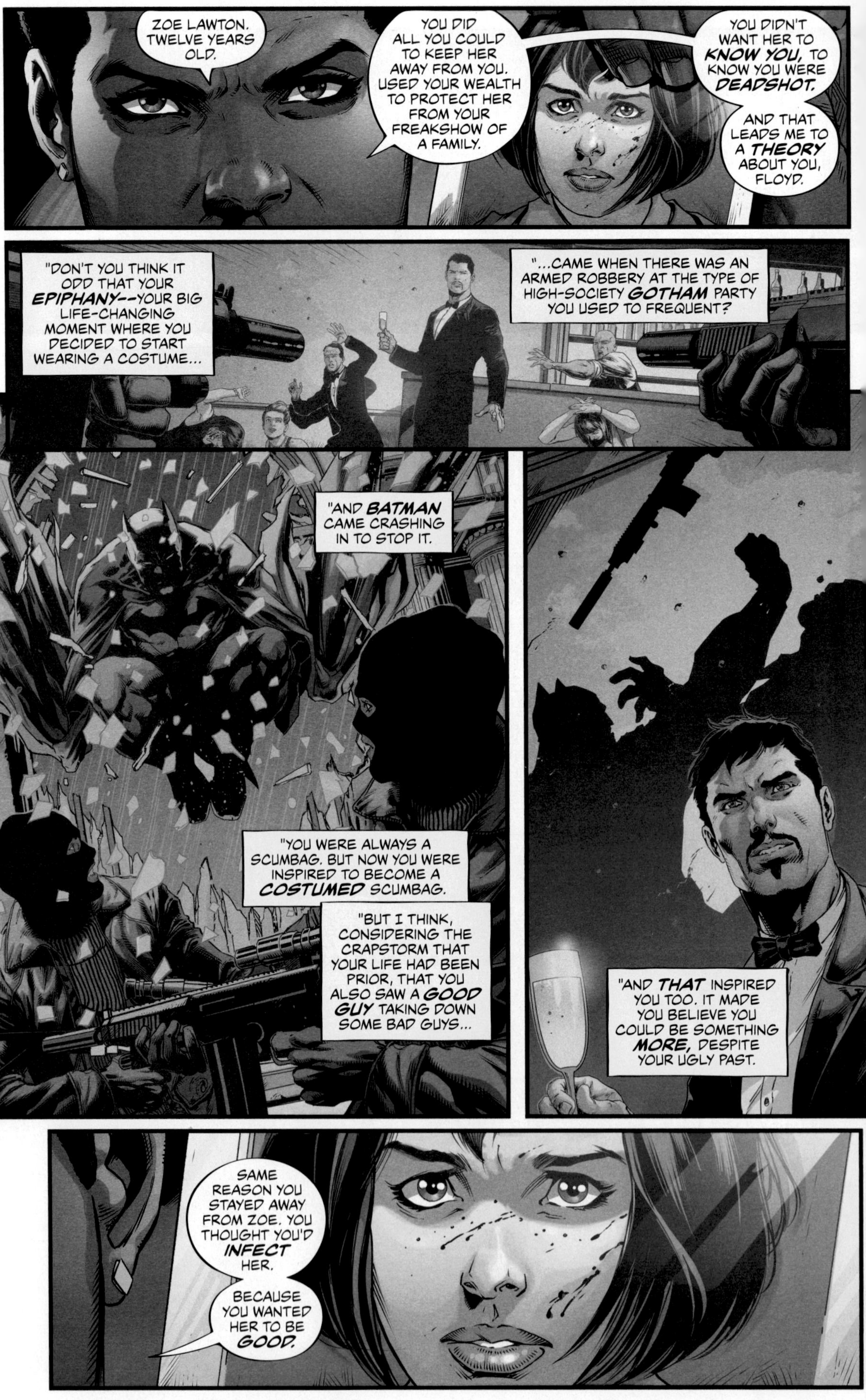
ZOE LAWTON. TWELVE YEARS OLD.
YOU DID ALL YOU COULD TO KEEP HER AWAY FROM YOU. USED YOUR WEALTH TO PROTECT HER FROM YOUR FREAKSHOW OF A FAMILY.
YOU DIDN'T WANT HER TO KNOW YOU, TO KNOW YOU WERE DEADSHOT.
AND THAT LEADS ME TO A THEORY ABOUT YOU, FLOYD.
"DON'T YOU THINK IT ODD THAT YOUR EPIPHANY--YOUR BIG LIFE-CHANGING MOMENT WHERE YOU DECIDED TO START WEARING A COSTUME...
"...CAME WHEN THERE WAS AN ARMED ROBBERY AT THE TYPE OF HIGH-SOCIETY GOTHAM PARTY YOU USED TO FREQUENT?
"AND BATMAN CAME CRASHING IN TO STOP IT.
"YOU WERE ALWAYS A SCUMBAG. BUT NOW YOU WERE INSPIRED TO BECOME A COSTUMED SCUMBAG.
"BUT I THINK, CONSIDERING THE CRAPSTORM THAT YOUR LIFE HAD BEEN PRIOR, THAT YOU ALSO SAW A GOOD GUY TAKING DOWN SOME BAD GUYS...
"AND THAT INSPIRED YOU TOO. IT MADE YOU BELIEVE YOU COULD BE SOMETHING MORE, DESPITE YOUR UGLY PAST.
SAME REASON YOU STAYED AWAY FROM ZOE. YOU THOUGHT YOU'D INFECT HER.
BECAUSE YOU WANTED HER TO BE GOOD.

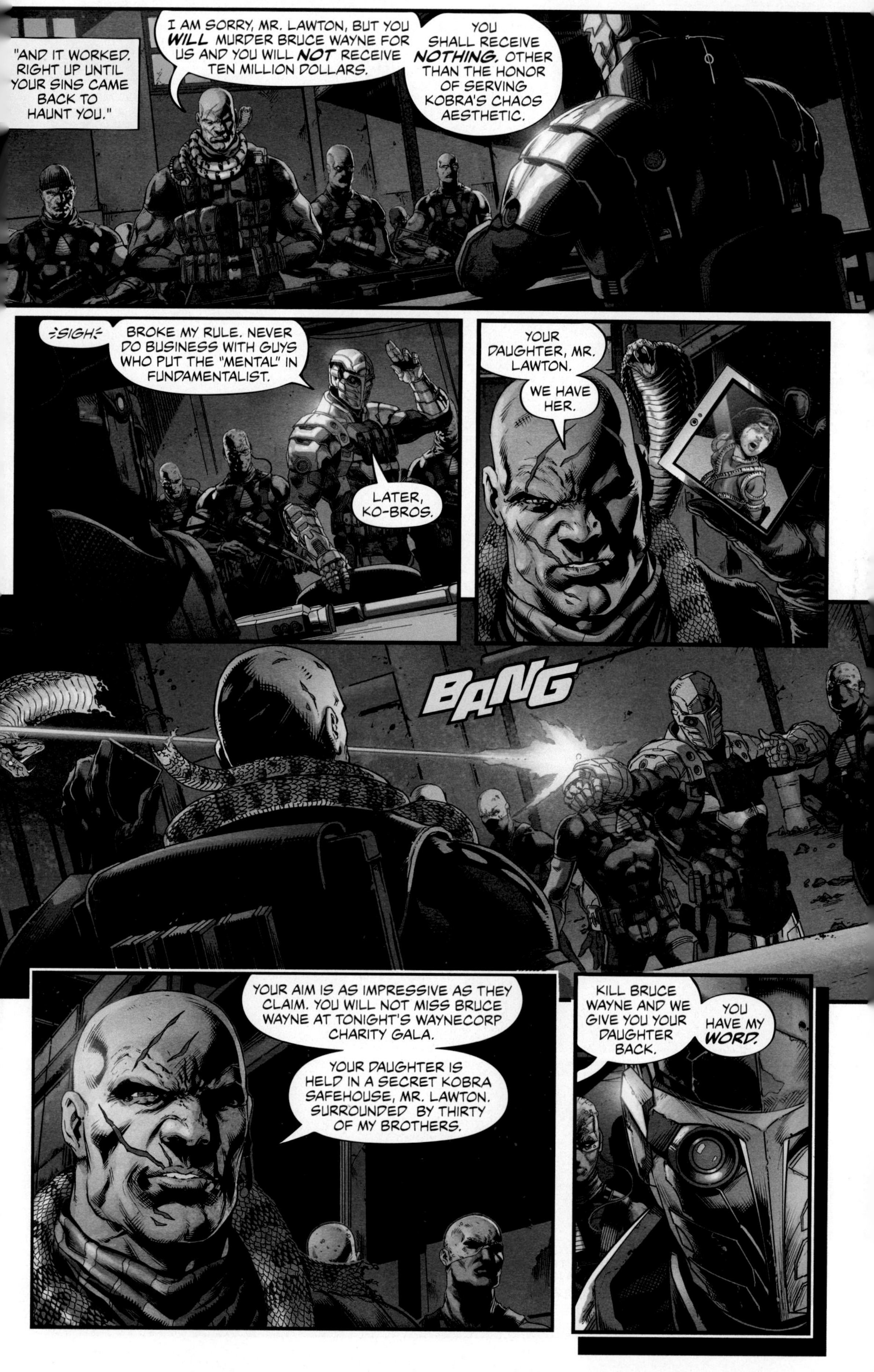
"AND IT WORKED. RIGHT UP UNTIL YOUR SINS CAME BACK TO HAUNT YOU."
I AM SORRY, MR. LAWTON, BUT YOU WILL MURDER BRUCE WAYNE FOR US AND YOU WILL NOT RECEIVE TEN MILLION DOLLARS.
YOU SHALL RECEIVE NOTHING, OTHER THAN THE HONOR OF SERVING KOBRA'S CHAOS AESTHETIC.
=SIGH=
BROKE MY RULE. NEVER DO BUSINESS WITH GUYS WHO PUT THE "MENTAL" IN FUNDAMENTALIST.
LATER, KO-BROS.
YOUR DAUGHTER, MR. LAWTON.
WE HAVE HER.
BANG
YOUR AIM IS AS IMPRESSIVE AS THEY CLAIM. YOU WILL NOT MISS BRUCE WAYNE AT TONIGHT'S WAYNECORP CHARITY GALA.
YOUR DAUGHTER IS HELD IN A SECRET KOBRA SAFEHOUSE, MR. LAWTON. SURROUNDED BY THIRTY OF MY BROTHERS.
KILL BRUCE WAYNE AND WE GIVE YOU YOUR DAUGHTER BACK.
YOU HAVE MY WORD.

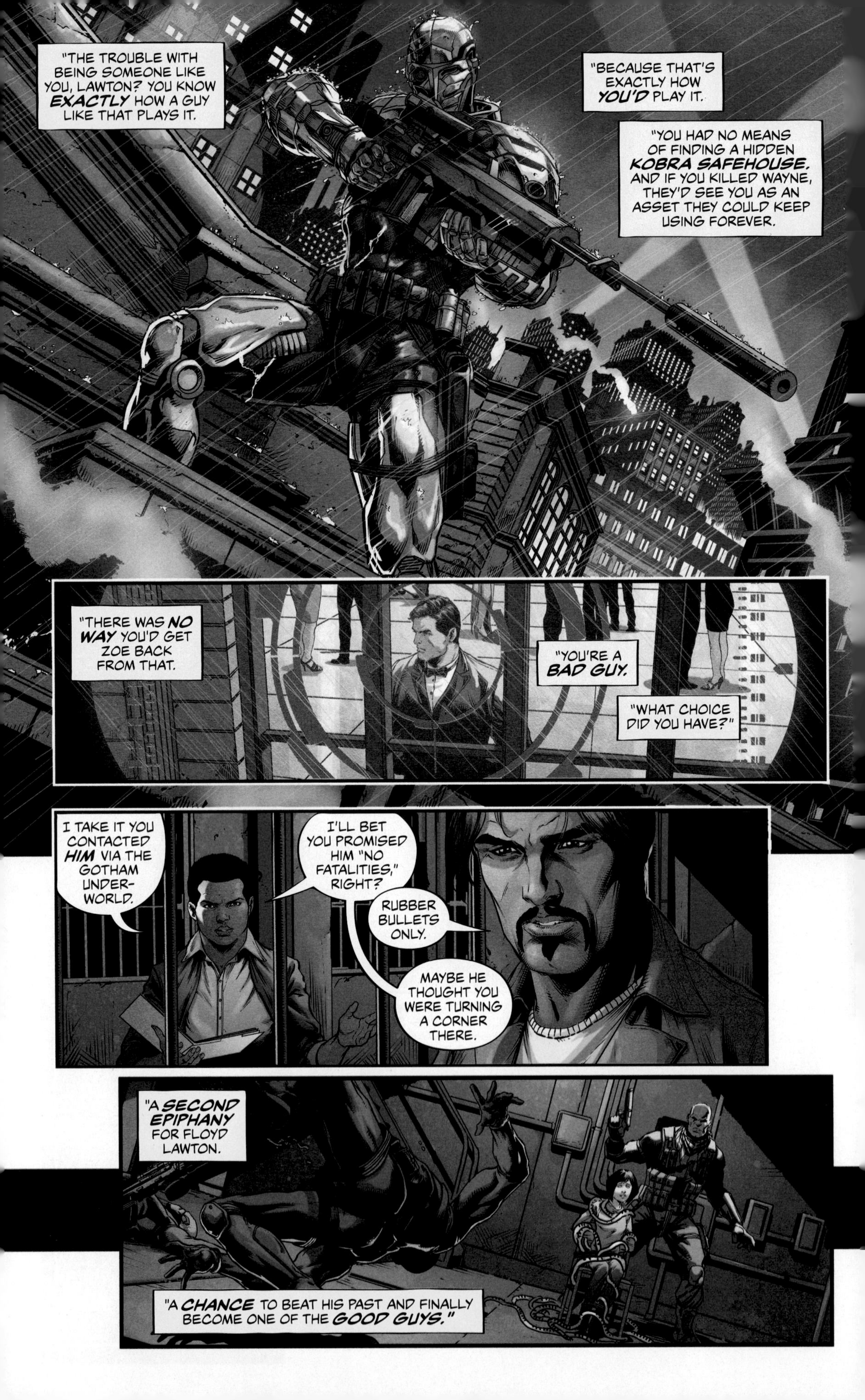
"THE TROUBLE WITH BEING SOMEONE LIKE YOU, LAWTON? YOU KNOW EXACTLY HOW A GUY LIKE THAT PLAYS IT.
"BECAUSE THAT'S EXACTLY HOW YOU'D PLAY IT.
"YOU HAD NO MEANS OF FINDING A HIDDEN KOBRA SAFEHOUSE. AND IF YOU KILLED WAYNE, THEY'D SEE YOU AS AN ASSET THEY COULD KEEP USING FOREVER.
"THERE WAS NO WAY YOU'D GET ZOE BACK FROM THAT.
"YOU'RE A BAD GUY.
"WHAT CHOICE DID YOU HAVE?"
I TAKE IT YOU CONTACTED HIM VIA THE GOTHAM UNDER-WORLD.
I'LL BET YOU PROMISED HIM "NO FATALITIES," RIGHT?
RUBBER BULLETS ONLY.
MAYBE HE THOUGHT YOU WERE TURNING A CORNER THERE.
"A SECOND EPIPHANY FOR FLOYD LAWTON.
"A CHANCE TO BEAT HIS PAST AND FINALLY BECOME ONE OF THE GOOD GUYS."

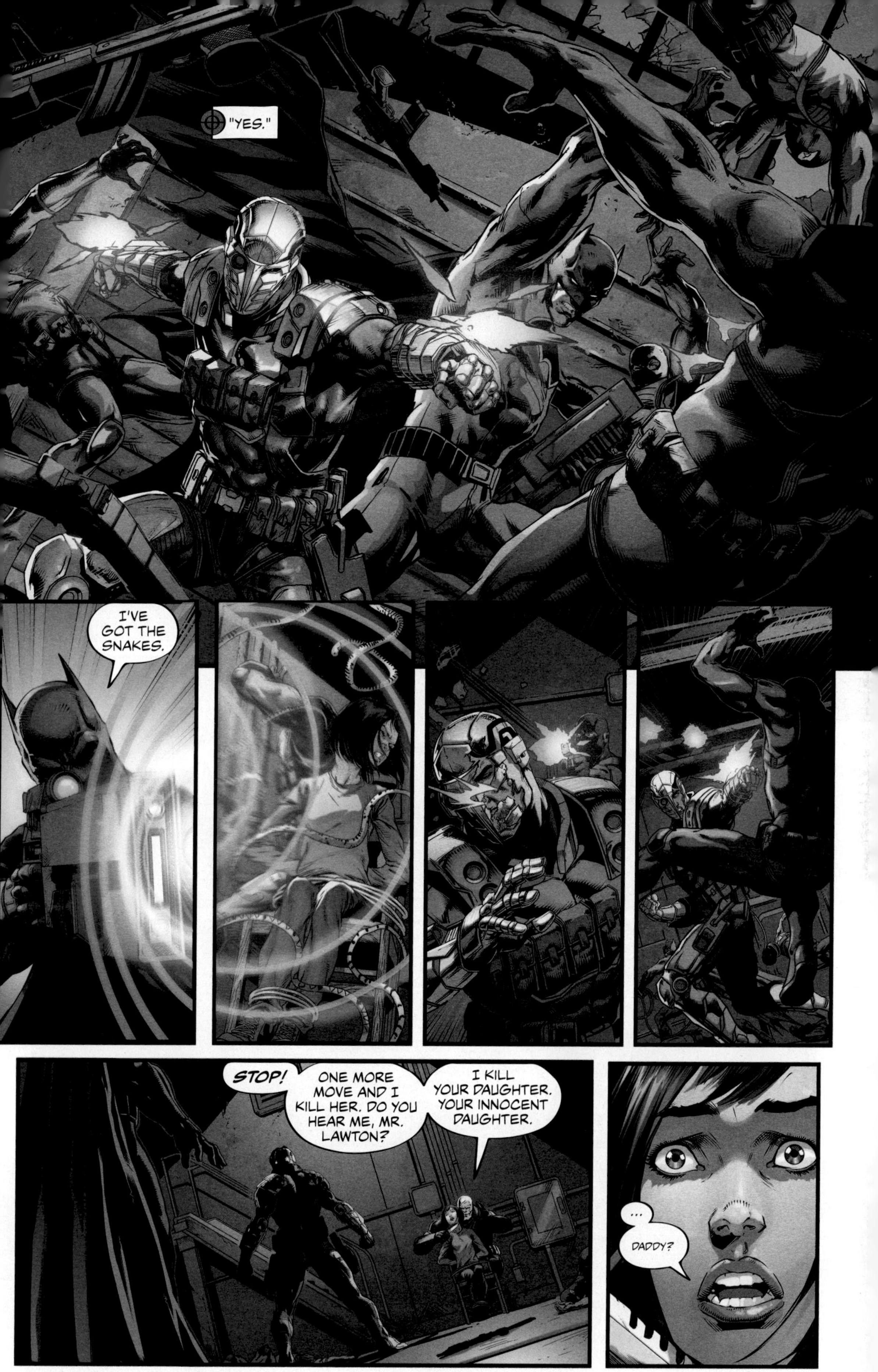
"YES."
I'VE GOT THE SNAKES.
STOP!
ONE MORE MOVE AND I KILL HER. DO YOU HEAR ME, MR. LAWTON?
I KILL YOUR DAUGHTER. YOUR INNOCENT DAUGHTER.
...
DADDY?

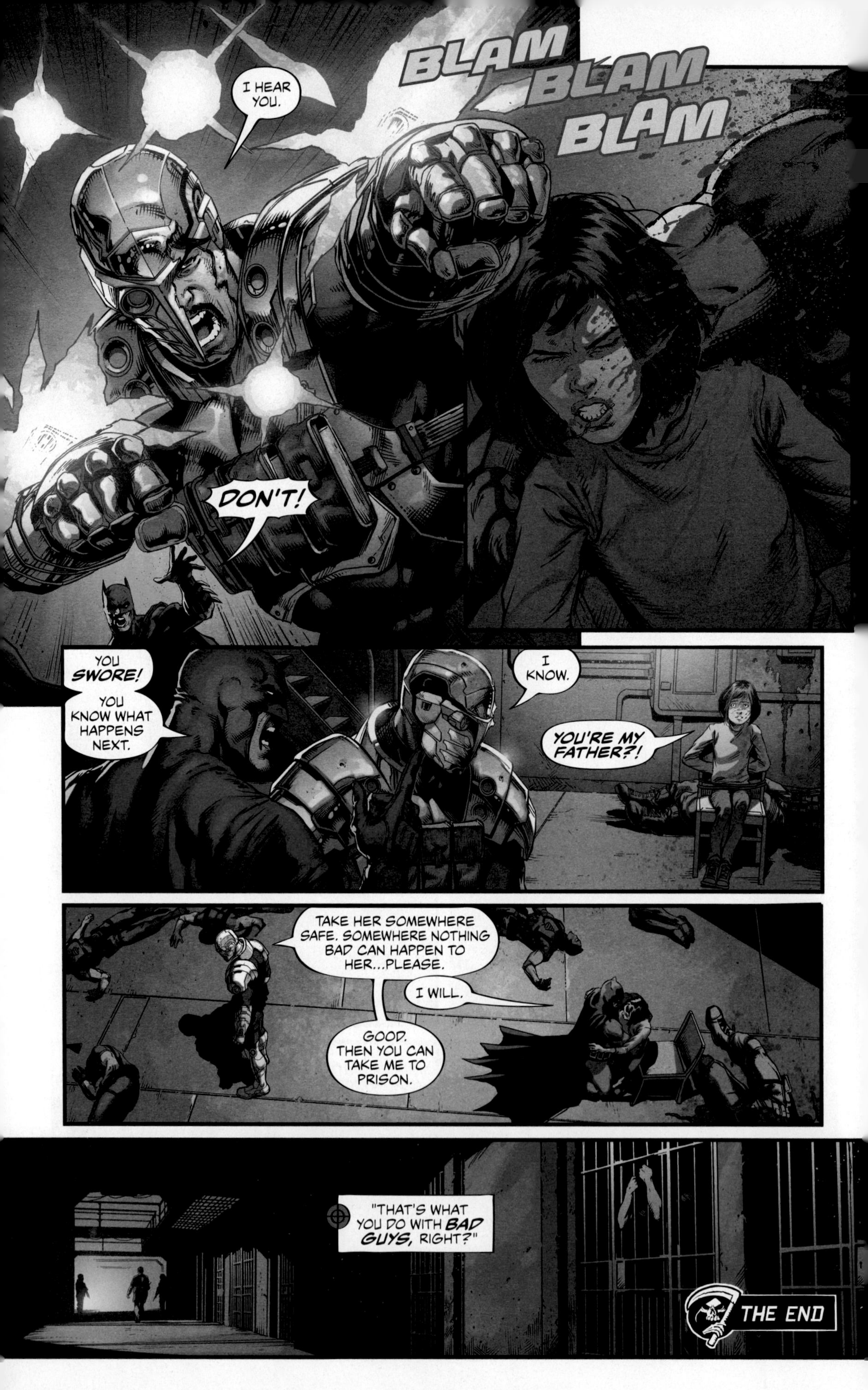
BLAM
BLAM
BLAM
I HEAR YOU.
DON'T!
YOU SWORE! YOU KNOW WHAT HAPPENS NEXT.
I KNOW.
YOU'RE MY FATHER?!
TAKE HER SOMEWHERE SAFE. SOMEWHERE NOTHING BAD CAN HAPPEN TO HER...PLEASE.
I WILL.
GOOD. THEN YOU CAN TAKE ME TO PRISON.
"THAT'S WHAT YOU DO WITH BAD GUYS, RIGHT?"
THE END

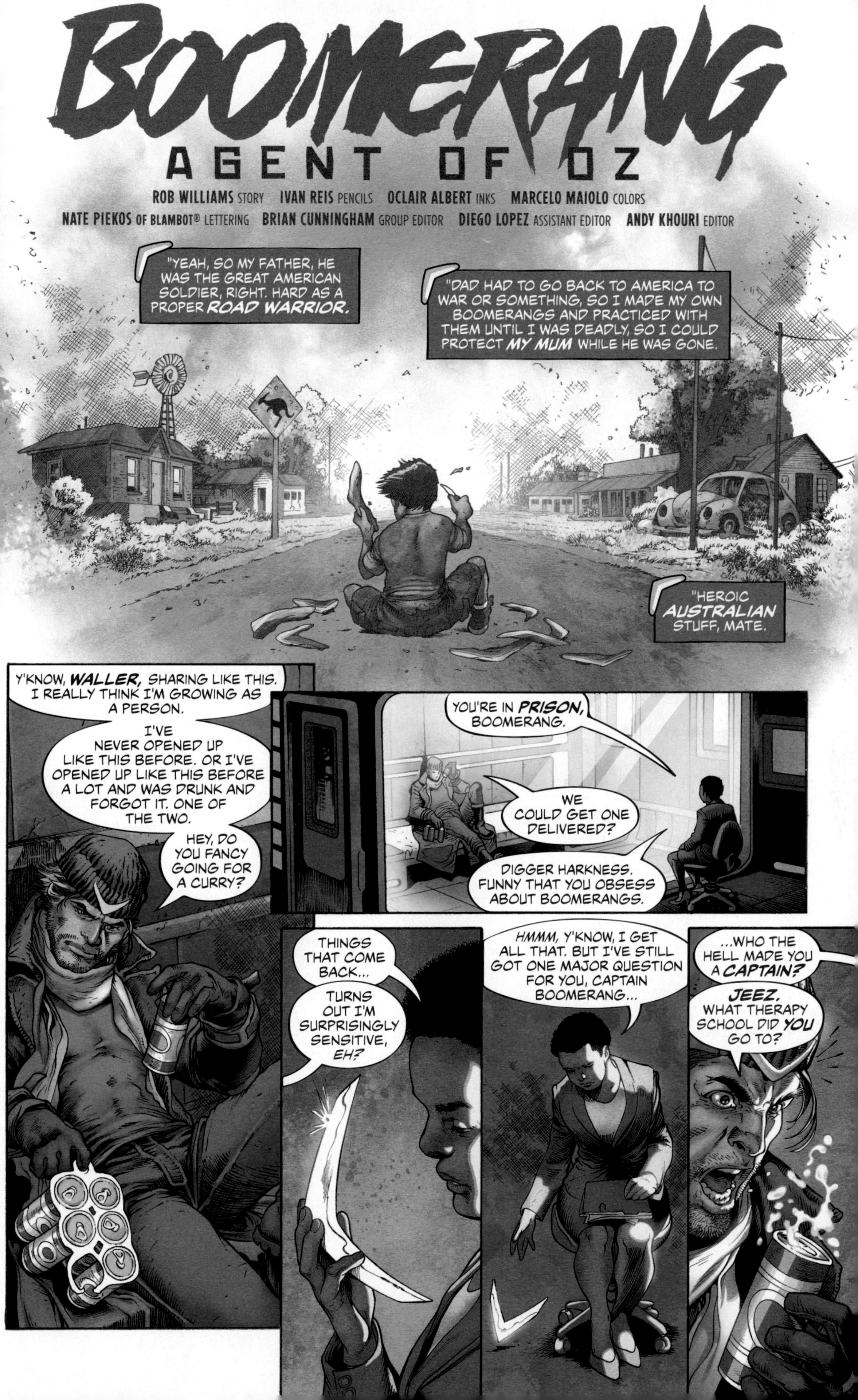
BOOMERANG
AGENT OF OZ
ROB WILLIAMS STORY IVAN REIS PENCILS OCLAIR ALBERT INKS MARCELO MAIOLO COLORS
NATE PIEKOS OF BLAMBOT® LETTERING BRIAN CUNNINGHAM GROUP EDITOR DIEGO LOPEZ ASSISTANT EDITOR ANDY KHOURI EDITOR
"YEAH, SO MY FATHER, HE WAS THE GREAT AMERICAN SOLDIER, RIGHT. HARD AS A PROPER ROAD WARRIOR.
"DAD HAD TO GO BACK TO AMERICA TO WAR OR SOMETHING, SO I MADE MY OWN BOOMERANGS AND PRACTICED WITH THEM UNTIL I WAS DEADLY, SO I COULD PROTECT MY MUM WHILE HE WAS GONE.
"HEROIC AUSTRALIAN STUFF, MATE.
Y'KNOW, WALLER, SHARING LIKE THIS. I REALLY THINK I'M GROWING AS A PERSON.
I'VE NEVER OPENED UP LIKE THIS BEFORE. OR I'VE OPENED UP LIKE THIS BEFORE A LOT AND WAS DRUNK AND FORGOT IT. ONE OF THE TWO.
HEY, DO YOU FANCY GOING FOR A CURRY?
YOU'RE IN PRISON, BOOMERANG.
WE COULD GET ONE DELIVERED?
DIGGER HARKNESS. FUNNY THAT YOU OBSESS ABOUT BOOMERANGS.
THINGS THAT COME BACK...
TURNS OUT I'M SURPRISINGLY SENSITIVE, EH?
HMMM, Y'KNOW, I GET ALL THAT. BUT I'VE STILL GOT ONE MAJOR QUESTION FOR YOU, CAPTAIN BOOMERANG...
...WHO THE HELL MADE YOU A CAPTAIN?
JEEZ. WHAT THERAPY SCHOOL DID YOU GO TO?

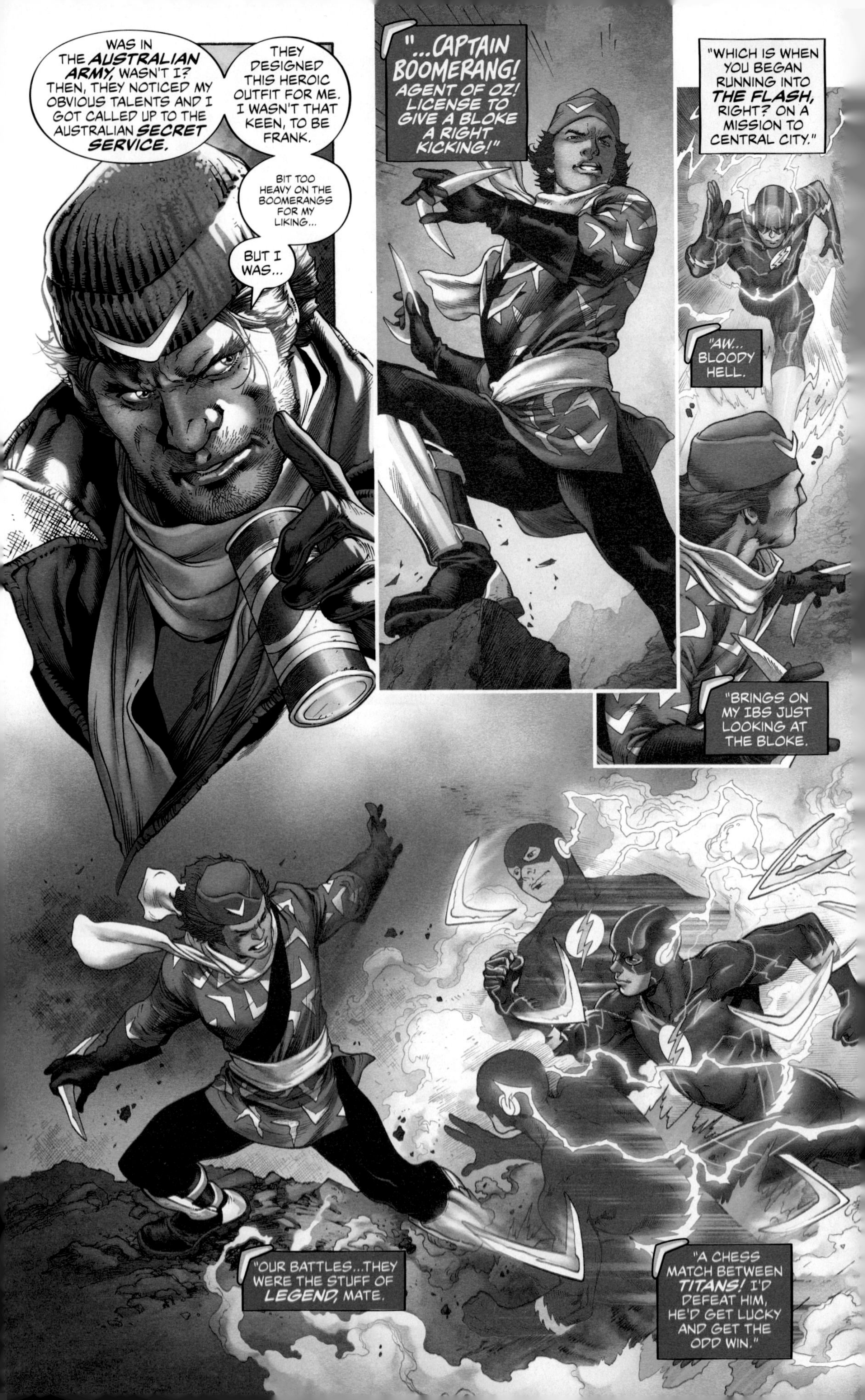

WAS IN THE AUSTRALIAN ARMY, WASN'T I? THEN, THEY NOTICED MY OBVIOUS TALENTS AND I GOT CALLED UP TO THE AUSTRALIAN SECRET SERVICE.
THEY DESIGNED THIS HEROIC OUTFIT FOR ME. I WASN'T THAT KEEN, TO BE FRANK.
BIT TOO HEAVY ON THE BOOMERANGS FOR MY LIKING...
BUT I WAS...
"...CAPTAIN BOOMERANG! AGENT OF OZ! LICENSE TO GIVE A BLOKE A RIGHT KICKING!"
"WHICH IS WHEN YOU BEGAN RUNNING INTO THE FLASH, RIGHT? ON A MISSION TO CENTRAL CITY."
"AW... BLOODY HELL.
"BRINGS ON MY IBS JUST LOOKING AT THE BLOKE.
"OUR BATTLES...THEY WERE THE STUFF OF LEGEND, MATE.
"A CHESS MATCH BETWEEN TITANS! I'D DEFEAT HIM, HE'D GET LUCKY AND GET THE ODD WIN."

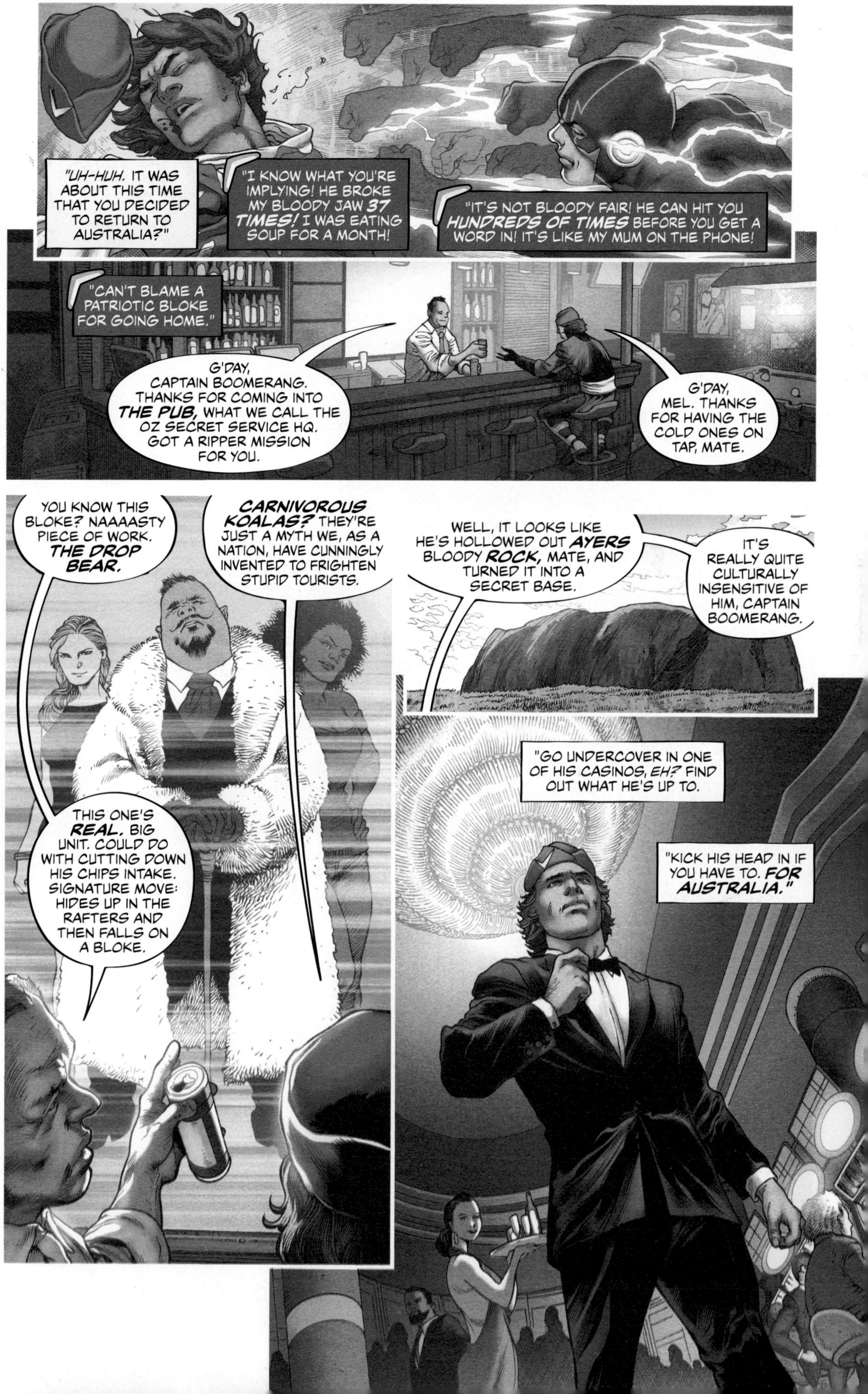
"UH-HUH. IT WAS ABOUT THIS TIME THAT YOU DECIDED TO RETURN TO AUSTRALIA?"
"I KNOW WHAT YOU'RE IMPLYING! HE BROKE MY BLOODY JAW 37 TIMES! I WAS EATING SOUP FOR A MONTH!
"IT'S NOT BLOODY FAIR! HE CAN HIT YOU HUNDREDS OF TIMES BEFORE YOU GET A WORD IN! IT'S LIKE MY MUM ON THE PHONE!
"CAN'T BLAME A PATRIOTIC BLOKE FOR GOING HOME."
G'DAY, CAPTAIN BOOMERANG. THANKS FOR COMING INTO THE PUB, WHAT WE CALL THE OZ SECRET SERVICE HQ. GOT A RIPPER MISSION FOR YOU.
G'DAY, MEL. THANKS FOR HAVING THE COLD ONES ON TAP, MATE.
YOU KNOW THIS BLOKE? NAAAASTY PIECE OF WORK. THE DROP BEAR.
CARNIVOROUS KOALAS? THEY'RE JUST A MYTH WE, AS A NATION, HAVE CUNNINGLY INVENTED TO FRIGHTEN STUPID TOURISTS.
THIS ONE'S REAL. BIG UNIT. COULD DO WITH CUTTING DOWN HIS CHIPS INTAKE. SIGNATURE MOVE: HIDES UP IN THE RAFTERS AND THEN FALLS ON A BLOKE.
WELL, IT LOOKS LIKE HE'S HOLLOWED OUT AYERS BLOODY ROCK, MATE, AND TURNED IT INTO A SECRET BASE.
IT'S REALLY QUITE CULTURALLY INSENSITIVE OF HIM, CAPTAIN BOOMERANG.
"GO UNDERCOVER IN ONE OF HIS CASINOS, EH? FIND OUT WHAT HE'S UP TO.
"KICK HIS HEAD IN IF YOU HAVE TO. FOR AUSTRALIA."

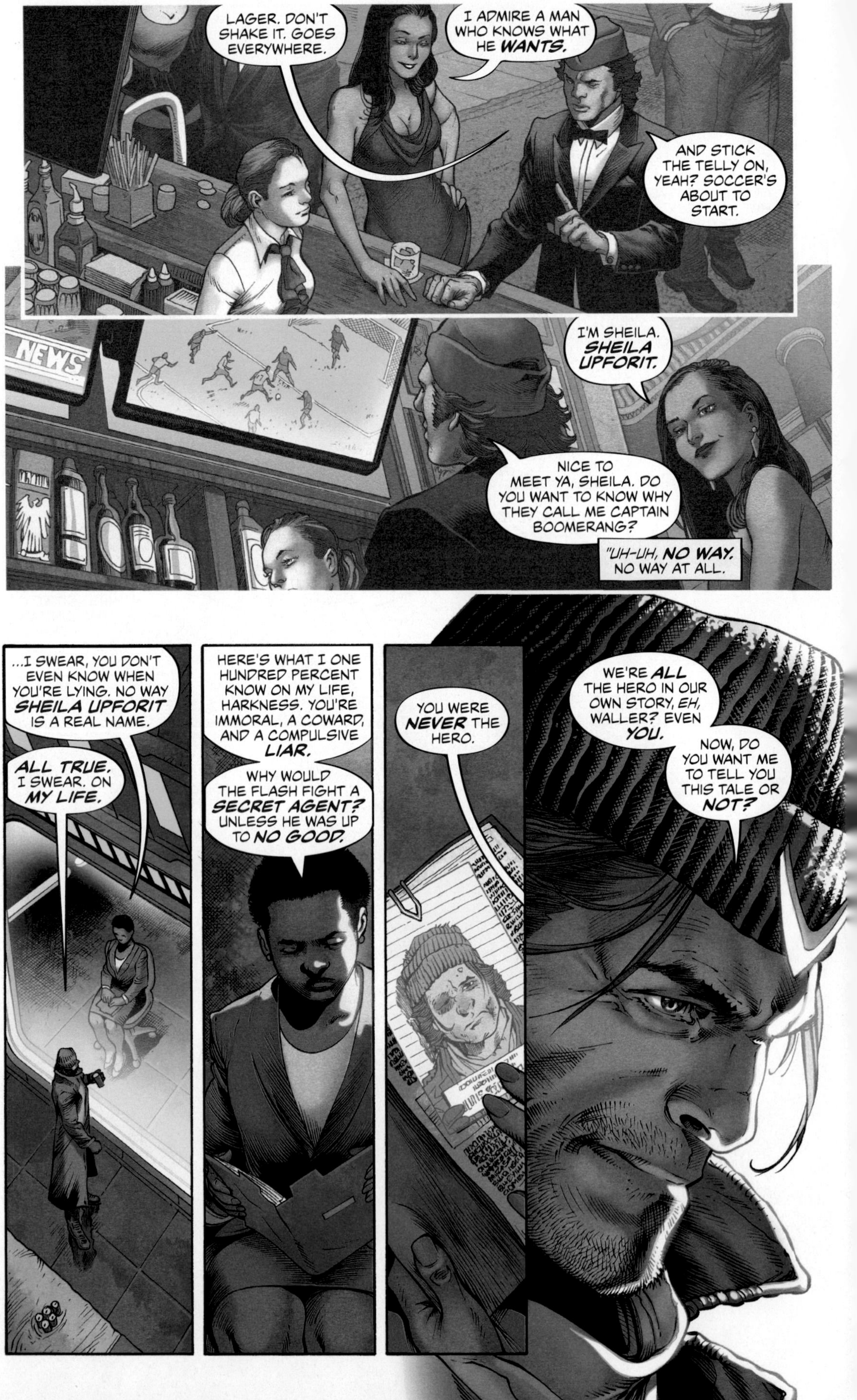
LAGER. DON'T SHAKE IT. GOES EVERYWHERE.
I ADMIRE A MAN WHO KNOWS WHAT HE WANTS.
AND STICK THE TELLY ON, YEAH? SOCCER'S ABOUT TO START.
NEWS
I'M SHEILA. SHEILA UPFORIT.
NICE TO MEET YA, SHEILA. DO YOU WANT TO KNOW WHY THEY CALL ME CAPTAIN BOOMERANG?
"UH-UH, NO WAY. NO WAY AT ALL.
...I SWEAR, YOU DON'T EVEN KNOW WHEN YOU'RE LYING. NO WAY SHEILA UPFORIT IS A REAL NAME.
ALL TRUE. I SWEAR. ON MY LIFE.
HERE'S WHAT I ONE HUNDRED PERCENT KNOW ON MY LIFE, HARKNESS. YOU'RE IMMORAL, A COWARD, AND A COMPULSIVE LIAR.
WHY WOULD THE FLASH FIGHT A SECRET AGENT? UNLESS HE WAS UP TO NO GOOD.
YOU WERE NEVER THE HERO.
WE'RE ALL THE HERO IN OUR OWN STORY, EH, WALLER? EVEN YOU.
NOW, DO YOU WANT ME TO TELL YOU THIS TALE OR NOT?

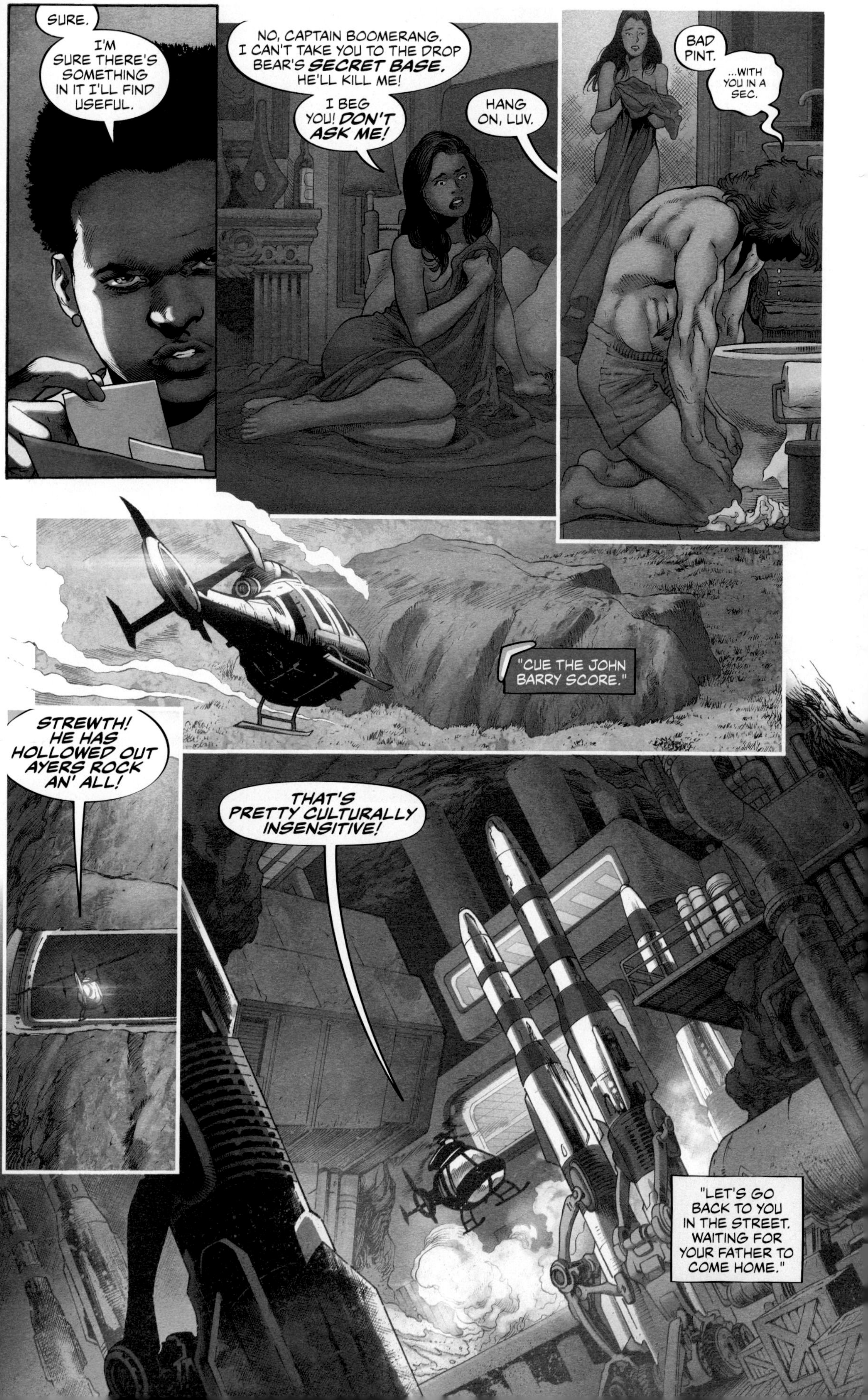
SURE.
I'M SURE THERE'S SOMETHING IN IT I'LL FIND USEFUL.
NO, CAPTAIN BOOMERANG. I CAN'T TAKE YOU TO THE DROP BEAR'S SECRET BASE. HE'LL KILL ME!
I BEG YOU! DON'T ASK ME!
HANG ON, LUV.
BAD PINT.
...WITH YOU IN A SEC.
"CUE THE JOHN BARRY SCORE."
STREWTH! HE HAS HOLLOWED OUT AYERS ROCK AN' ALL!
THAT'S PRETTY CULTURALLY INSENSITIVE!
"LET'S GO BACK TO YOU IN THE STREET. WAITING FOR YOUR FATHER TO COME HOME."

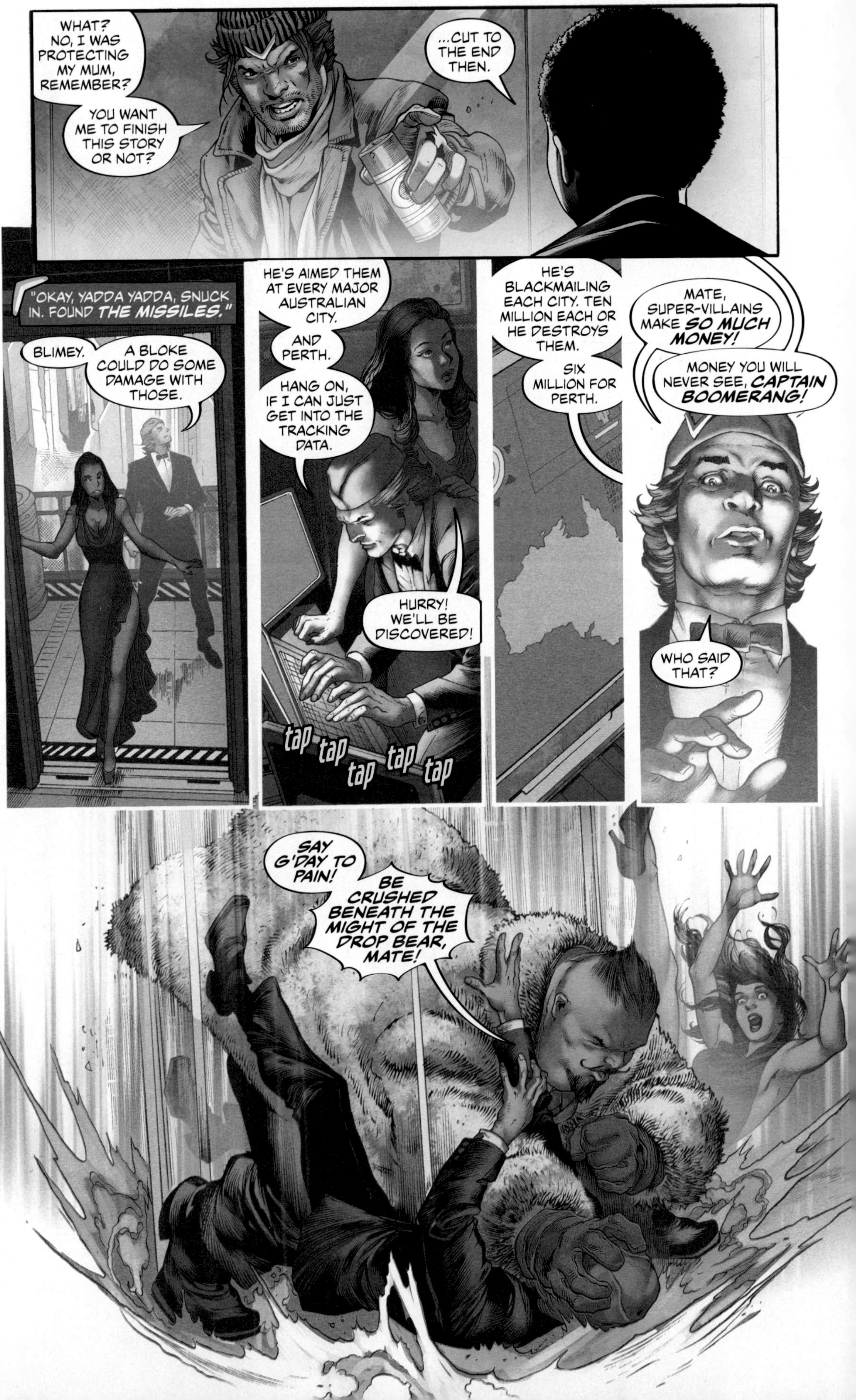
WHAT? NO, I WAS PROTECTING MY MUM, REMEMBER?
YOU WANT ME TO FINISH THIS STORY OR NOT?
...CUT TO THE END THEN.
"OKAY, YADDA YADDA, SNUCK IN. FOUND THE MISSILES."
BLIMEY.
A BLOKE COULD DO SOME DAMAGE WITH THOSE.
HE'S AIMED THEM AT EVERY MAJOR AUSTRALIAN CITY.
AND PERTH.
HANG ON, IF I CAN JUST GET INTO THE TRACKING DATA.
HURRY! WE'LL BE DISCOVERED!
tap tap tap tap tap
HE'S BLACKMAILING EACH CITY. TEN MILLION EACH OR HE DESTROYS THEM.
SIX MILLION FOR PERTH.
MATE, SUPER-VILLAINS MAKE SO MUCH MONEY!
MONEY YOU WILL NEVER SEE, CAPTAIN BOOMERANG!
WHO SAID THAT?
SAY G'DAY TO PAIN!
BE CRUSHED BENEATH THE MIGHT OF THE DROP BEAR, MATE!

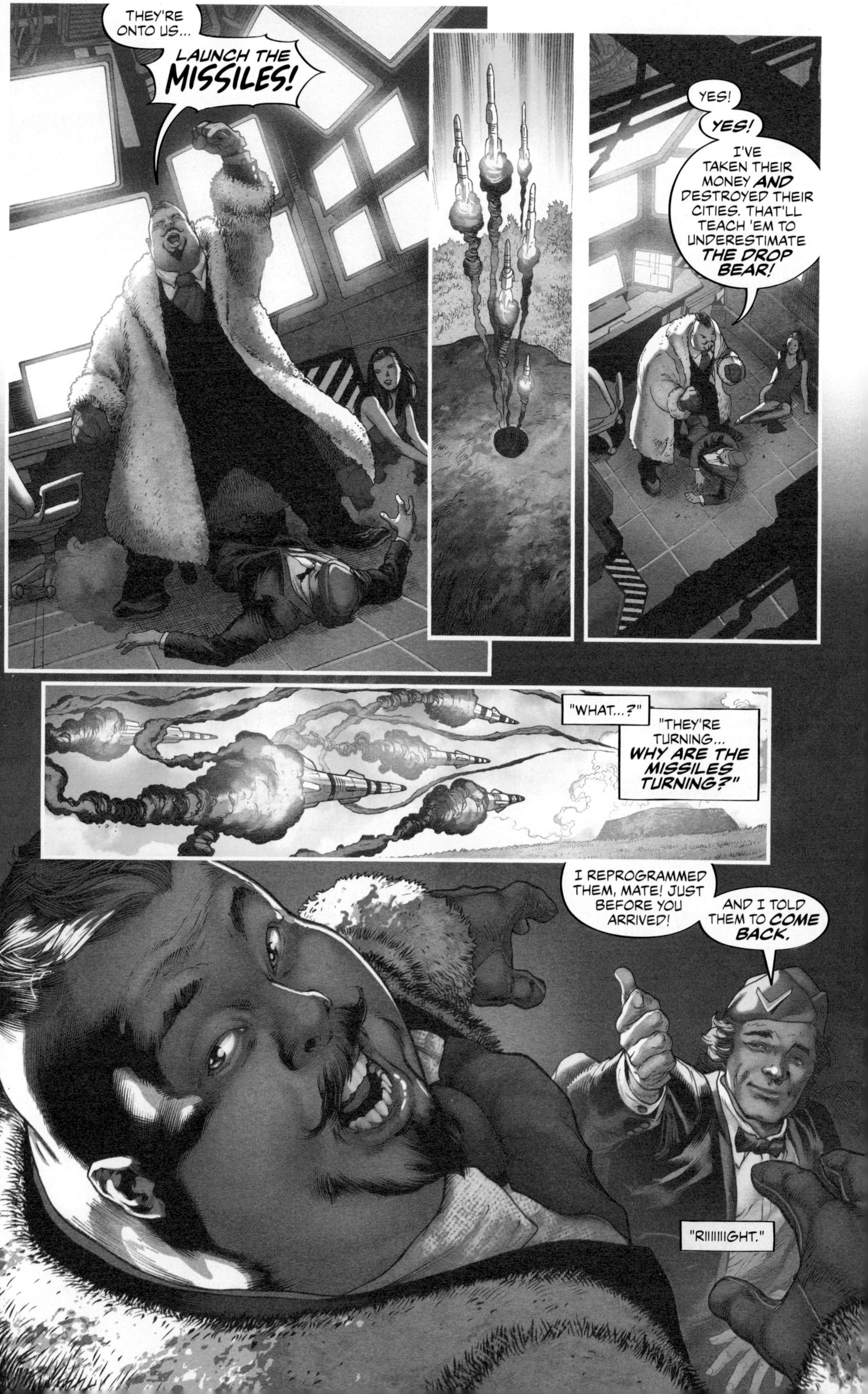
THEY'RE ONTO US... LAUNCH THE MISSILES!
YES!
YES!
I'VE TAKEN THEIR MONEY AND DESTROYED THEIR CITIES. THAT'LL TEACH 'EM TO UNDERESTIMATE THE DROP BEAR!
"WHAT...?"
"THEY'RE TURNING... WHY ARE THE MISSILES TURNING?"
I REPROGRAMMED THEM, MATE! JUST BEFORE YOU ARRIVED!
AND I TOLD THEM TO COME BACK.
"RIIIIIIGHT."

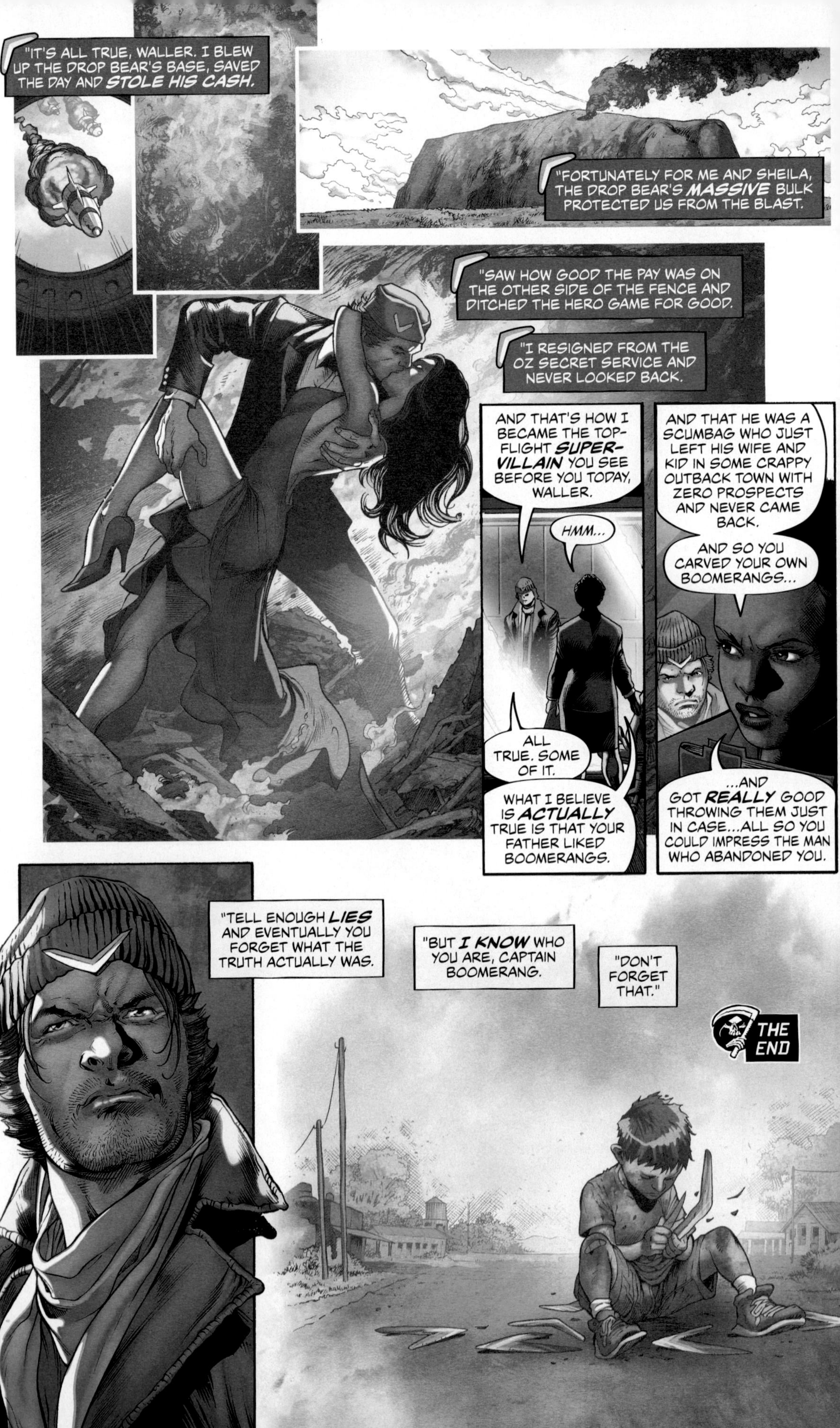
"IT'S ALL TRUE, WALLER. I BLEW UP THE DROP BEAR'S BASE, SAVED THE DAY AND STOLE HIS CASH.
"FORTUNATELY FOR ME AND SHEILA, THE DROP BEAR'S MASSIVE BULK PROTECTED US FROM THE BLAST.
"SAW HOW GOOD THE PAY WAS ON THE OTHER SIDE OF THE FENCE AND DITCHED THE HERO GAME FOR GOOD.
"I RESIGNED FROM THE OZ SECRET SERVICE AND NEVER LOOKED BACK.
AND THAT'S HOW I BECAME THE TOP-FLIGHT SUPER-VILLAIN YOU SEE BEFORE YOU TODAY, WALLER.
HMM...
ALL TRUE. SOME OF IT.
WHAT I BELIEVE IS ACTUALLY TRUE IS THAT YOUR FATHER LIKED BOOMERANGS.
AND THAT HE WAS A SCUMBAG WHO JUST LEFT HIS WIFE AND KID IN SOME CRAPPY OUTBACK TOWN WITH ZERO PROSPECTS AND NEVER CAME BACK.
AND SO YOU CARVED YOUR OWN BOOMERANGS...
...AND GOT REALLY GOOD THROWING THEM JUST IN CASE...ALL SO YOU COULD IMPRESS THE MAN WHO ABANDONED YOU.
"TELL ENOUGH LIES AND EVENTUALLY YOU FORGET WHAT THE TRUTH ACTUALLY WAS.
"BUT I KNOW WHO YOU ARE, CAPTAIN BOOMERANG.
"DON'T FORGET THAT."
THE END

"KATANA.

CHOOSE

ROB WILLIAMS WRITER • **PHILIP TAN** ARTIST • **ELMER SANTOS** COLORIST • **NATE PIEKOS** OF BLAMBOT® LETTERER
BRIAN CUNNINGHAM GROUP EDITOR • **HARVEY RICHARDS** ASSOC. EDITOR • **ANDY KHOURI** EDITOR

"YOU NEVER SAY A WORD.

"WHY IS THAT, DO YOU THINK?"

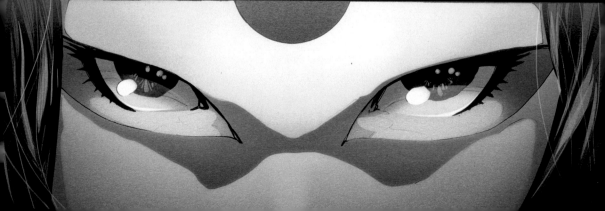

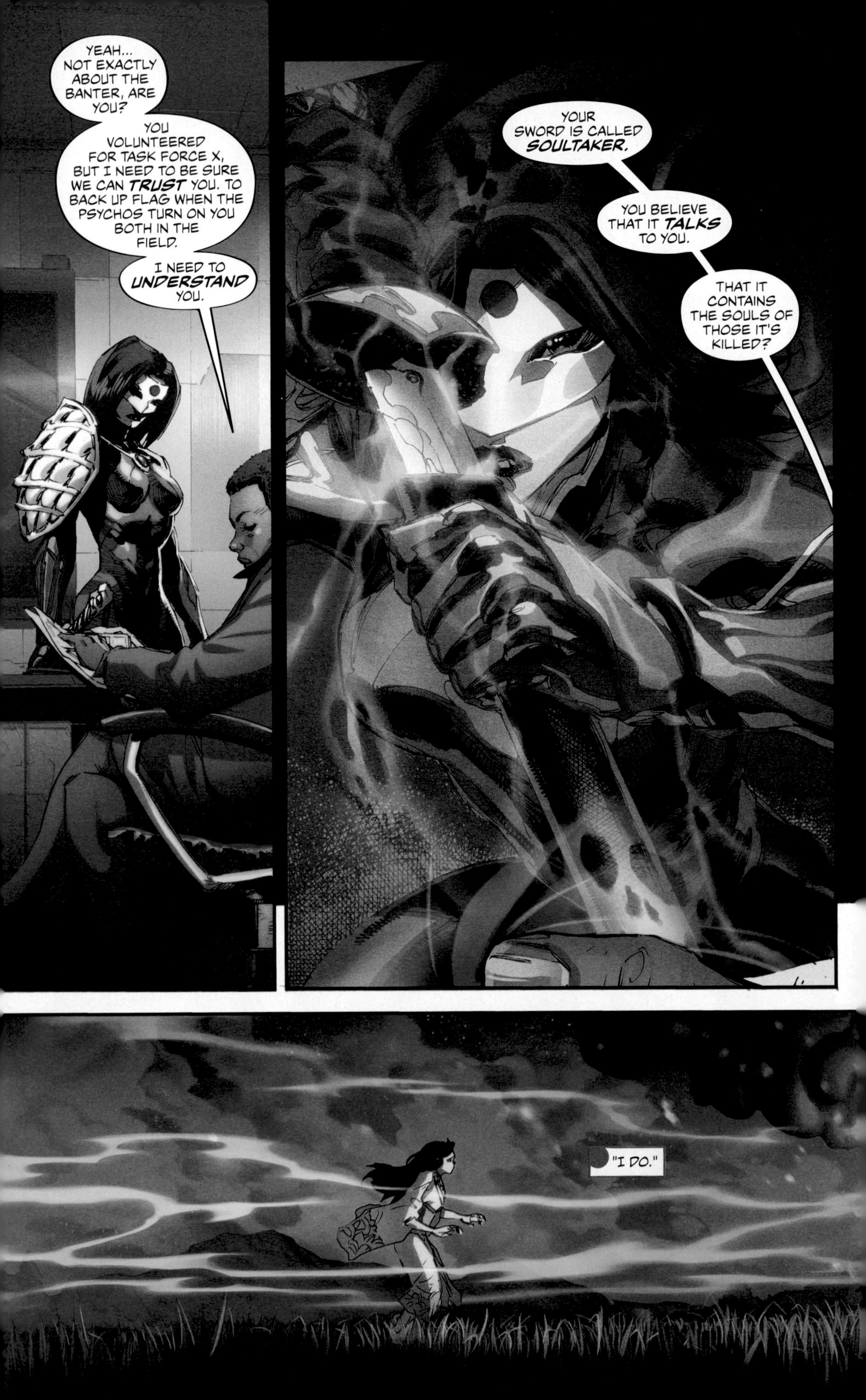
YEAH... NOT EXACTLY ABOUT THE BANTER, ARE YOU?
YOU VOLUNTEERED FOR TASK FORCE X, BUT I NEED TO BE SURE WE CAN TRUST YOU. TO BACK UP FLAG WHEN THE PSYCHOS TURN ON YOU BOTH IN THE FIELD.
I NEED TO UNDERSTAND YOU.
YOUR SWORD IS CALLED SOULTAKER.
YOU BELIEVE THAT IT TALKS TO YOU.
THAT IT CONTAINS THE SOULS OF THOSE IT'S KILLED?
"I DO."

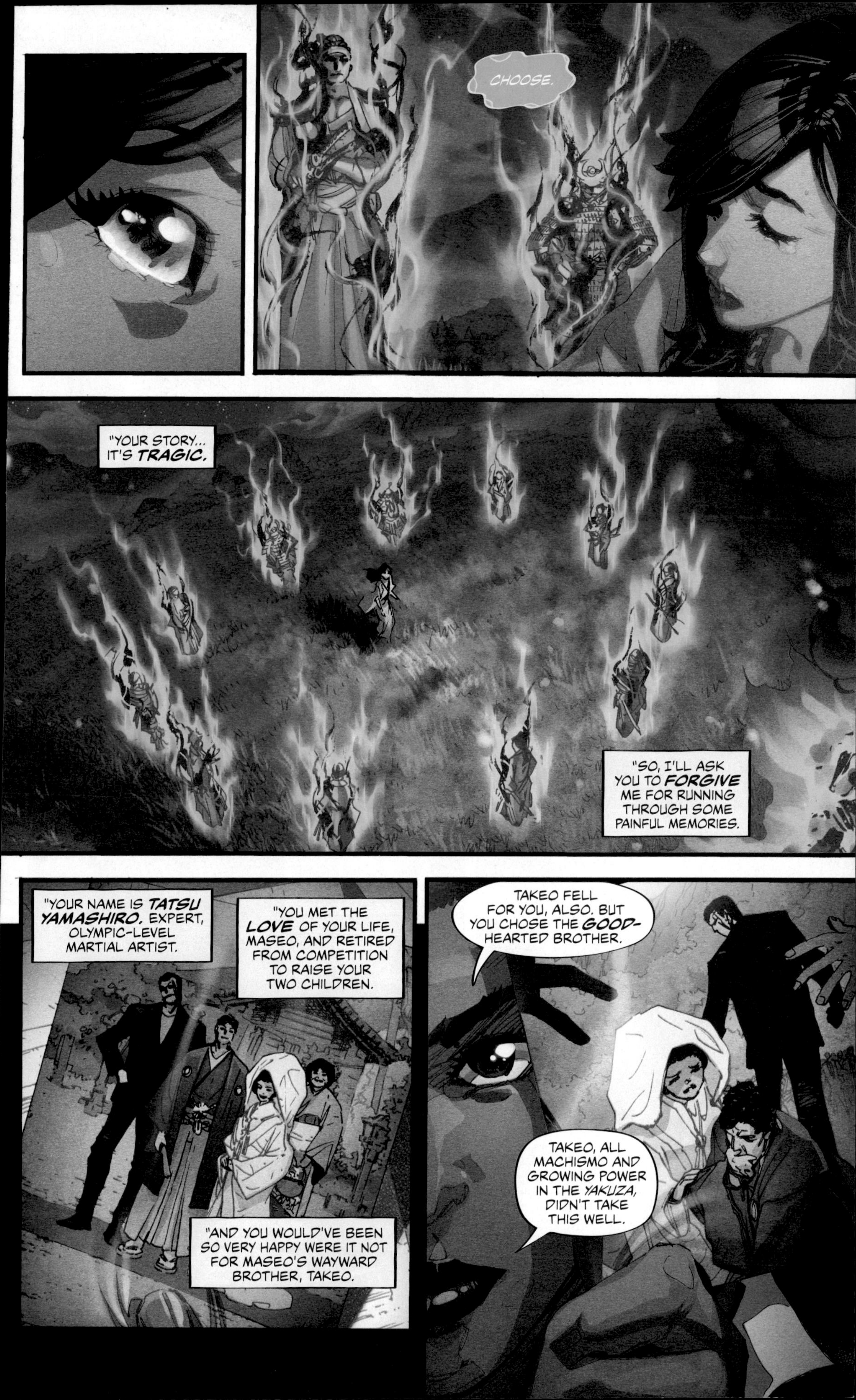
CHOOSE.
"YOUR STORY... IT'S TRAGIC.
"SO, I'LL ASK YOU TO FORGIVE ME FOR RUNNING THROUGH SOME PAINFUL MEMORIES.
"YOUR NAME IS TATSU YAMASHIRO. EXPERT, OLYMPIC-LEVEL MARTIAL ARTIST.
"YOU MET THE LOVE OF YOUR LIFE, MASEO, AND RETIRED FROM COMPETITION TO RAISE YOUR TWO CHILDREN.
"AND YOU WOULD'VE BEEN SO VERY HAPPY WERE IT NOT FOR MASEO'S WAYWARD BROTHER, TAKEO.
TAKEO FELL FOR YOU, ALSO. BUT YOU CHOSE THE GOOD-HEARTED BROTHER.
TAKEO, ALL MACHISMO AND GROWING POWER IN THE YAKUZA, DIDN'T TAKE THIS WELL.

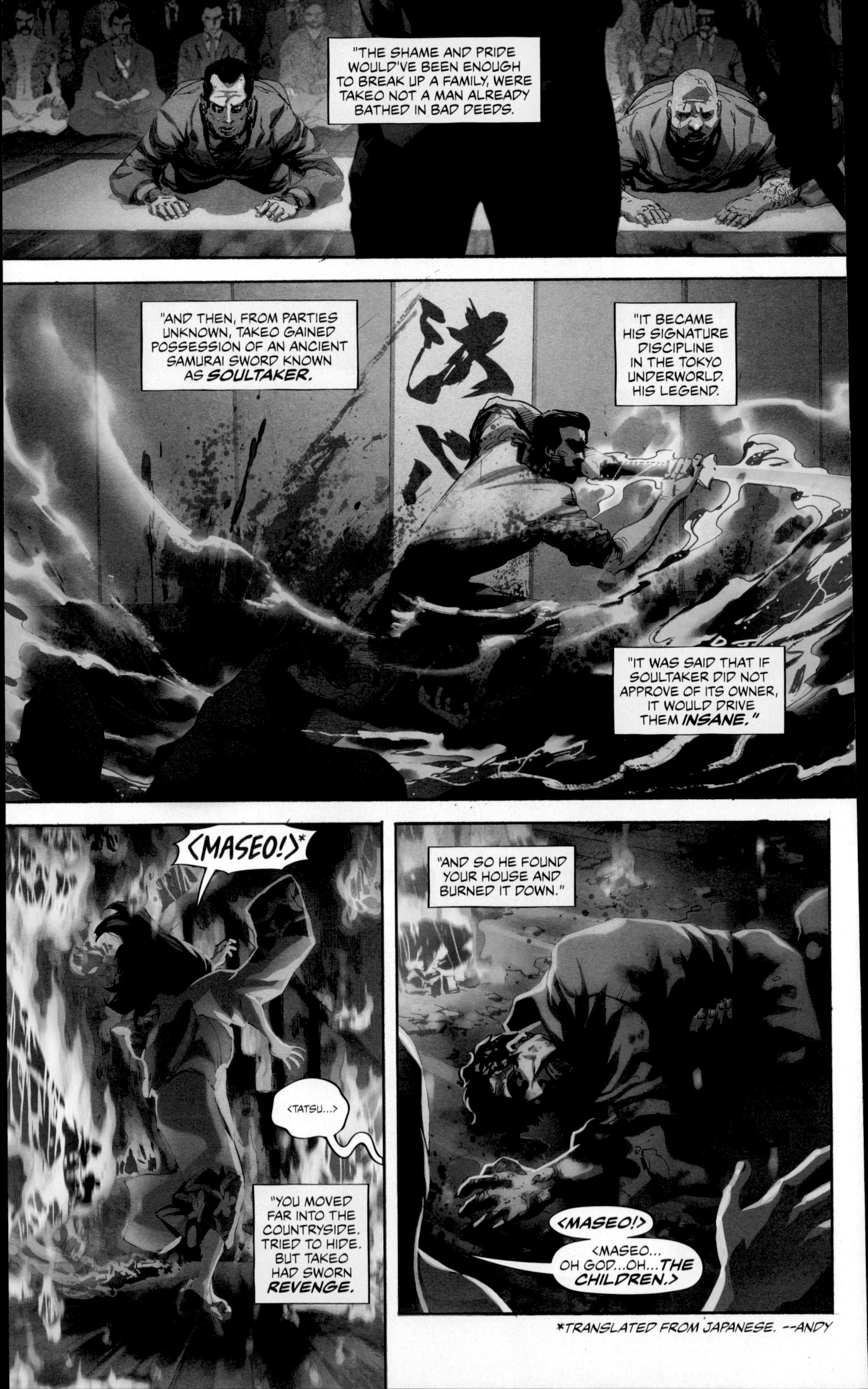
"THE SHAME AND PRIDE WOULD'VE BEEN ENOUGH TO BREAK UP A FAMILY, WERE TAKEO NOT A MAN ALREADY BATHED IN BAD DEEDS.
"AND THEN, FROM PARTIES UNKNOWN, TAKEO GAINED POSSESSION OF AN ANCIENT SAMURAI SWORD KNOWN AS ***SOULTAKER.***
"IT BECAME HIS SIGNATURE DISCIPLINE IN THE TOKYO UNDERWORLD. HIS LEGEND.
"IT WAS SAID THAT IF SOULTAKER DID NOT APPROVE OF ITS OWNER, IT WOULD DRIVE THEM ***INSANE."***
<MASEO!>*
<TATSU...>
"YOU MOVED FAR INTO THE COUNTRYSIDE. TRIED TO HIDE. BUT TAKEO HAD SWORN ***REVENGE.***
"AND SO HE FOUND YOUR HOUSE AND BURNED IT DOWN."
<MASEO!>
<MASEO... OH GOD...OH...***THE CHILDREN.>***
**TRANSLATED FROM JAPANESE. --ANDY*

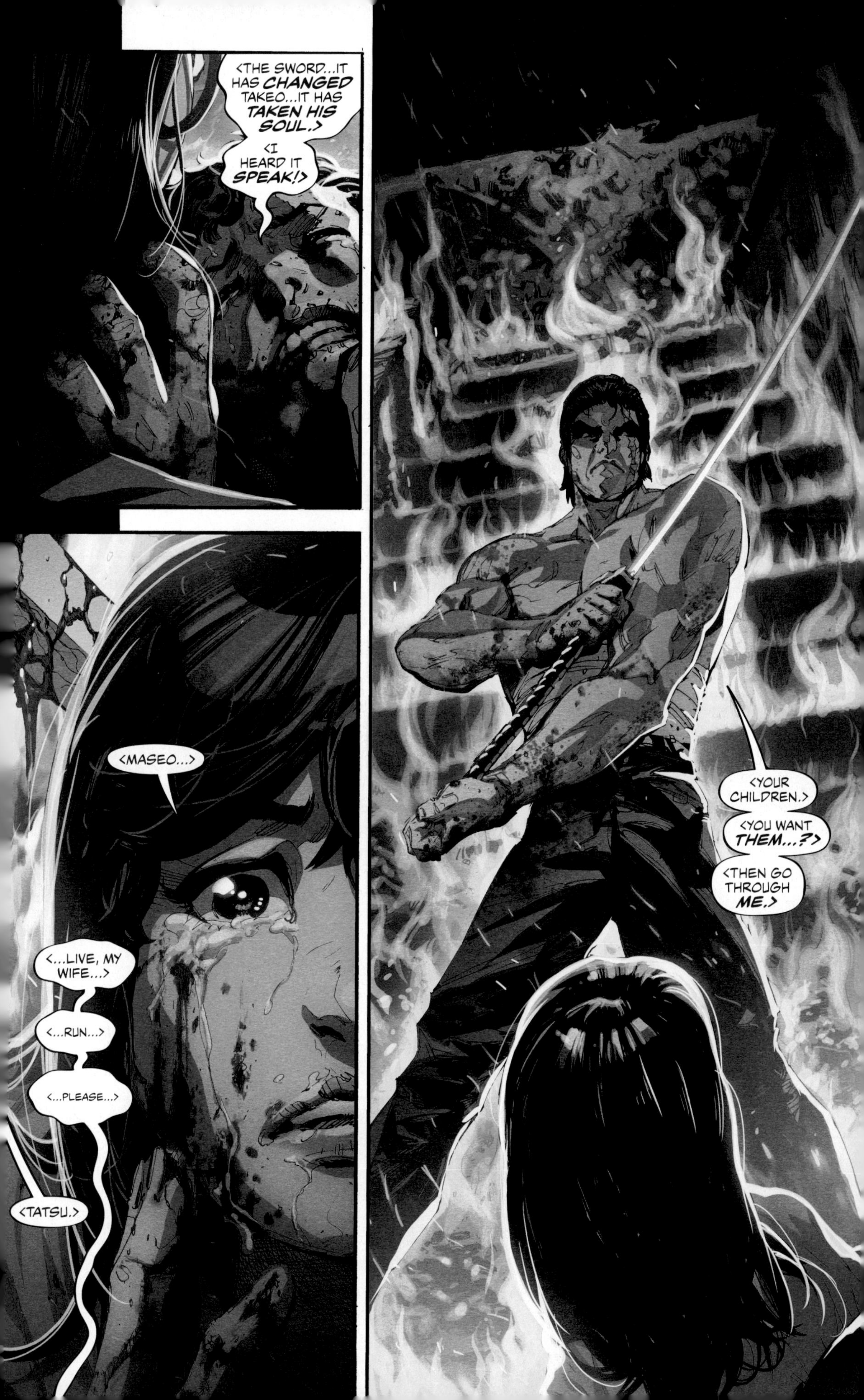
<THE SWORD...IT HAS CHANGED TAKEO...IT HAS TAKEN HIS SOUL.>
<I HEARD IT SPEAK!>
<MASEO...>
<...LIVE, MY WIFE...>
<...RUN...>
<...PLEASE...>
<TATSU.>
<YOUR CHILDREN.>
<YOU WANT THEM...?>
<THEN GO THROUGH ME.>

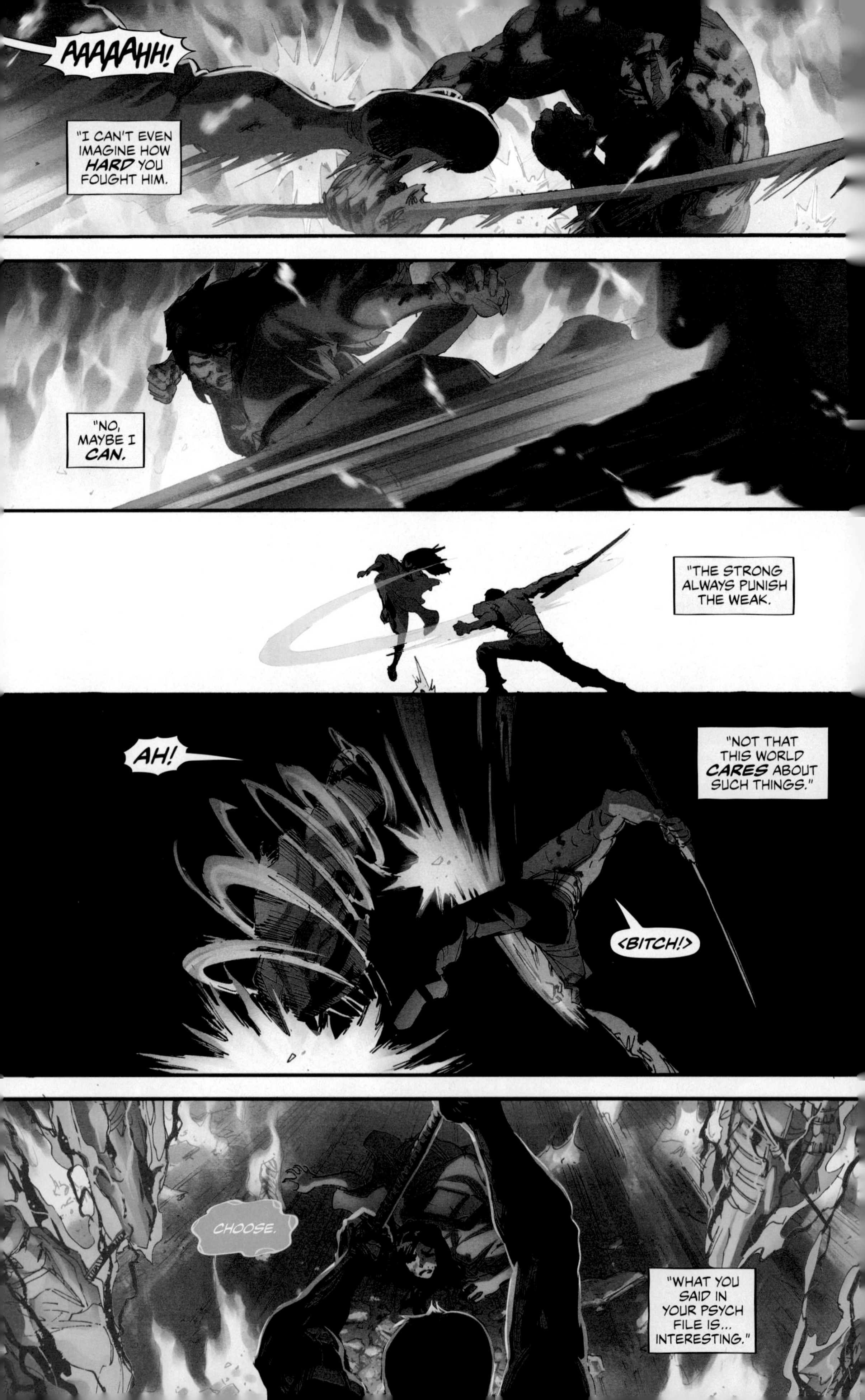

AAAAAHH!
"I CAN'T EVEN IMAGINE HOW HARD YOU FOUGHT HIM.
"NO, MAYBE I CAN.
"THE STRONG ALWAYS PUNISH THE WEAK.
AH!
"NOT THAT THIS WORLD CARES ABOUT SUCH THINGS."
<BITCH!>
CHOOSE.
"WHAT YOU SAID IN YOUR PSYCH FILE IS... INTERESTING."

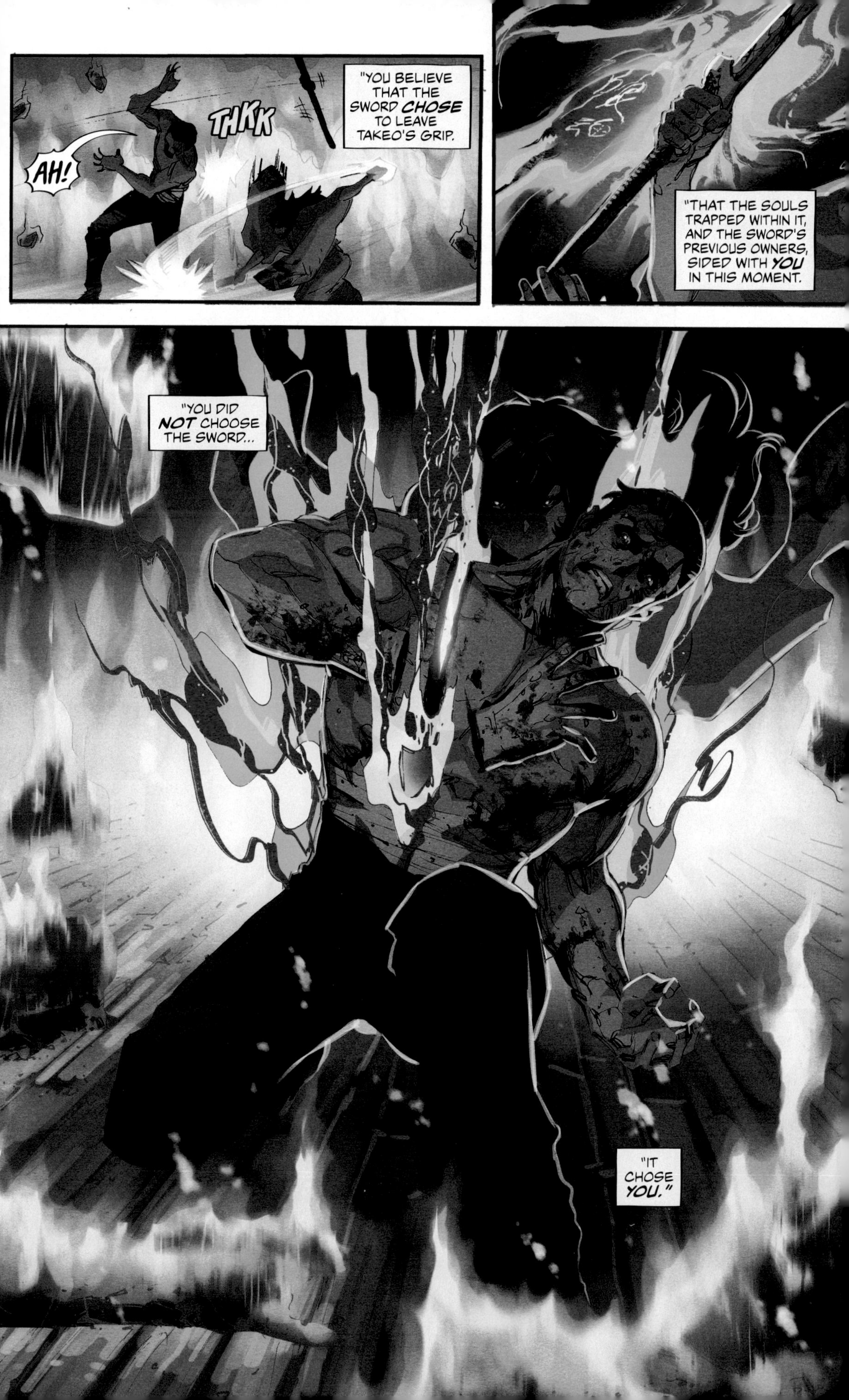
"YOU BELIEVE THAT THE SWORD CHOSE TO LEAVE TAKEO'S GRIP.
THKK
AH!
"THAT THE SOULS TRAPPED WITHIN IT, AND THE SWORD'S PREVIOUS OWNERS, SIDED WITH YOU IN THIS MOMENT.
"YOU DID NOT CHOOSE THE SWORD...
"IT CHOSE YOU."

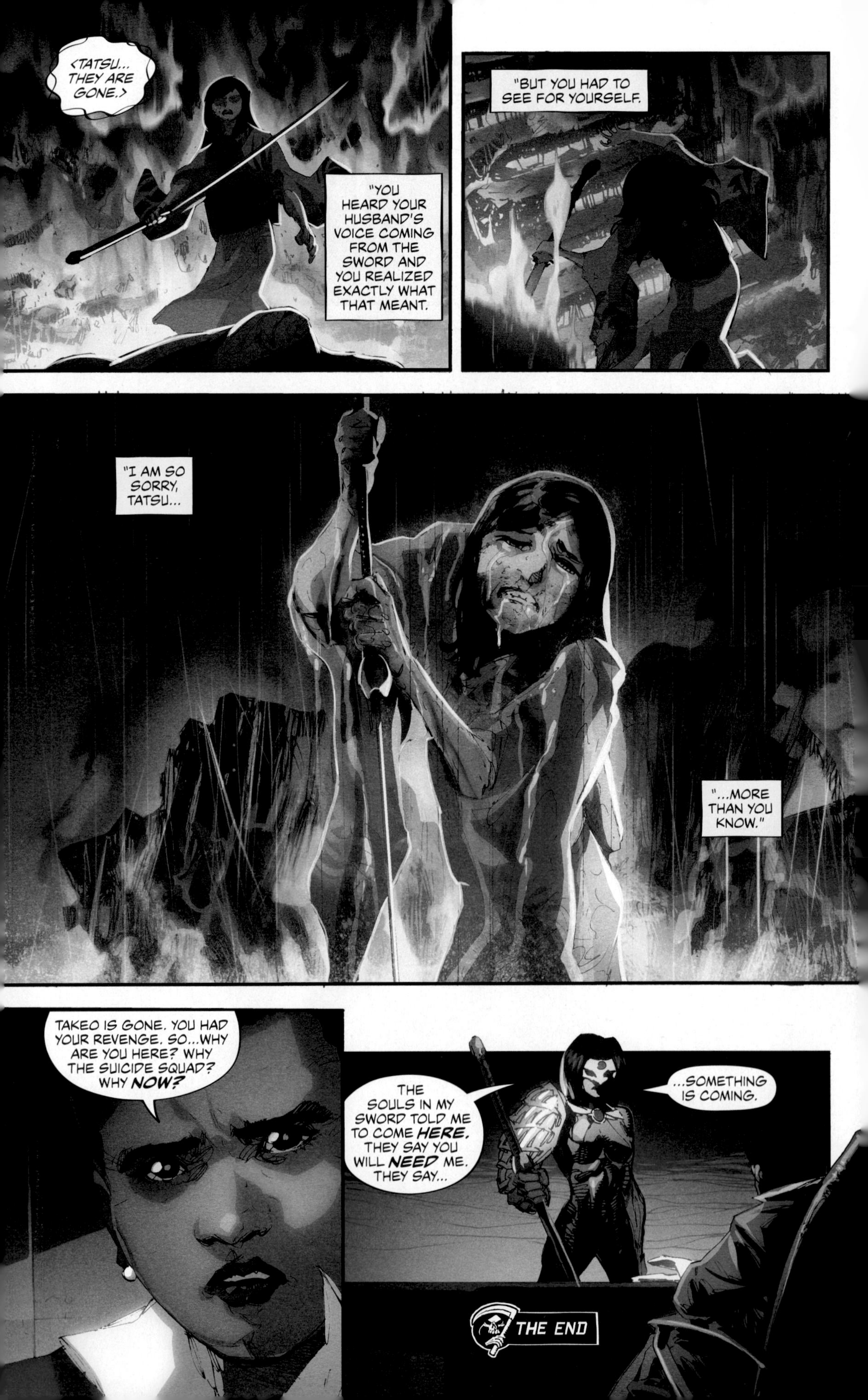
<TATSU... THEY ARE GONE.>
"YOU HEARD YOUR HUSBAND'S VOICE COMING FROM THE SWORD AND YOU REALIZED EXACTLY WHAT THAT MEANT.
"BUT YOU HAD TO SEE FOR YOURSELF.
"I AM SO SORRY, TATSU...
"...MORE THAN YOU KNOW."
TAKEO IS GONE. YOU HAD YOUR REVENGE. SO...WHY ARE YOU HERE? WHY THE SUICIDE SQUAD? WHY NOW?
THE SOULS IN MY SWORD TOLD ME TO COME HERE. THEY SAY YOU WILL NEED ME. THEY SAY...
...SOMETHING IS COMING.
THE END

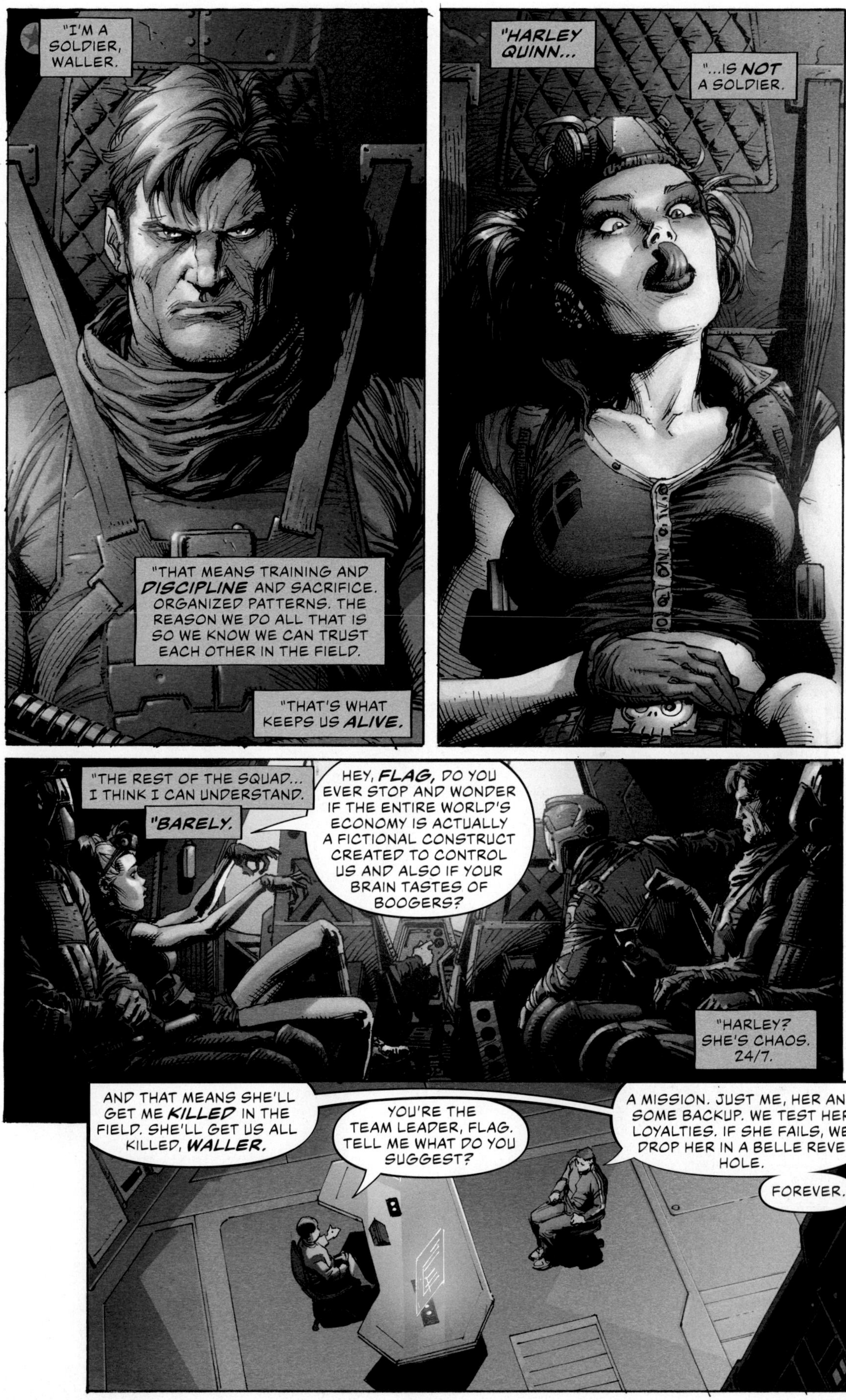
"I'M A SOLDIER, WALLER.
"THAT MEANS TRAINING AND DISCIPLINE AND SACRIFICE. ORGANIZED PATTERNS. THE REASON WE DO ALL THAT IS SO WE KNOW WE CAN TRUST EACH OTHER IN THE FIELD.
"THAT'S WHAT KEEPS US ALIVE.
"HARLEY QUINN...
"...IS NOT A SOLDIER.
"THE REST OF THE SQUAD... I THINK I CAN UNDERSTAND.
"BARELY.
HEY, FLAG, DO YOU EVER STOP AND WONDER IF THE ENTIRE WORLD'S ECONOMY IS ACTUALLY A FICTIONAL CONSTRUCT CREATED TO CONTROL US AND ALSO IF YOUR BRAIN TASTES OF BOOGERS?
"HARLEY? SHE'S CHAOS. 24/7.
AND THAT MEANS SHE'LL GET ME KILLED IN THE FIELD. SHE'LL GET US ALL KILLED, WALLER.
YOU'RE THE TEAM LEADER, FLAG. TELL ME WHAT DO YOU SUGGEST?
A MISSION. JUST ME, HER AND SOME BACKUP. WE TEST HER LOYALTIES. IF SHE FAILS, WE DROP HER IN A BELLE REVE HOLE.
FOREVER.

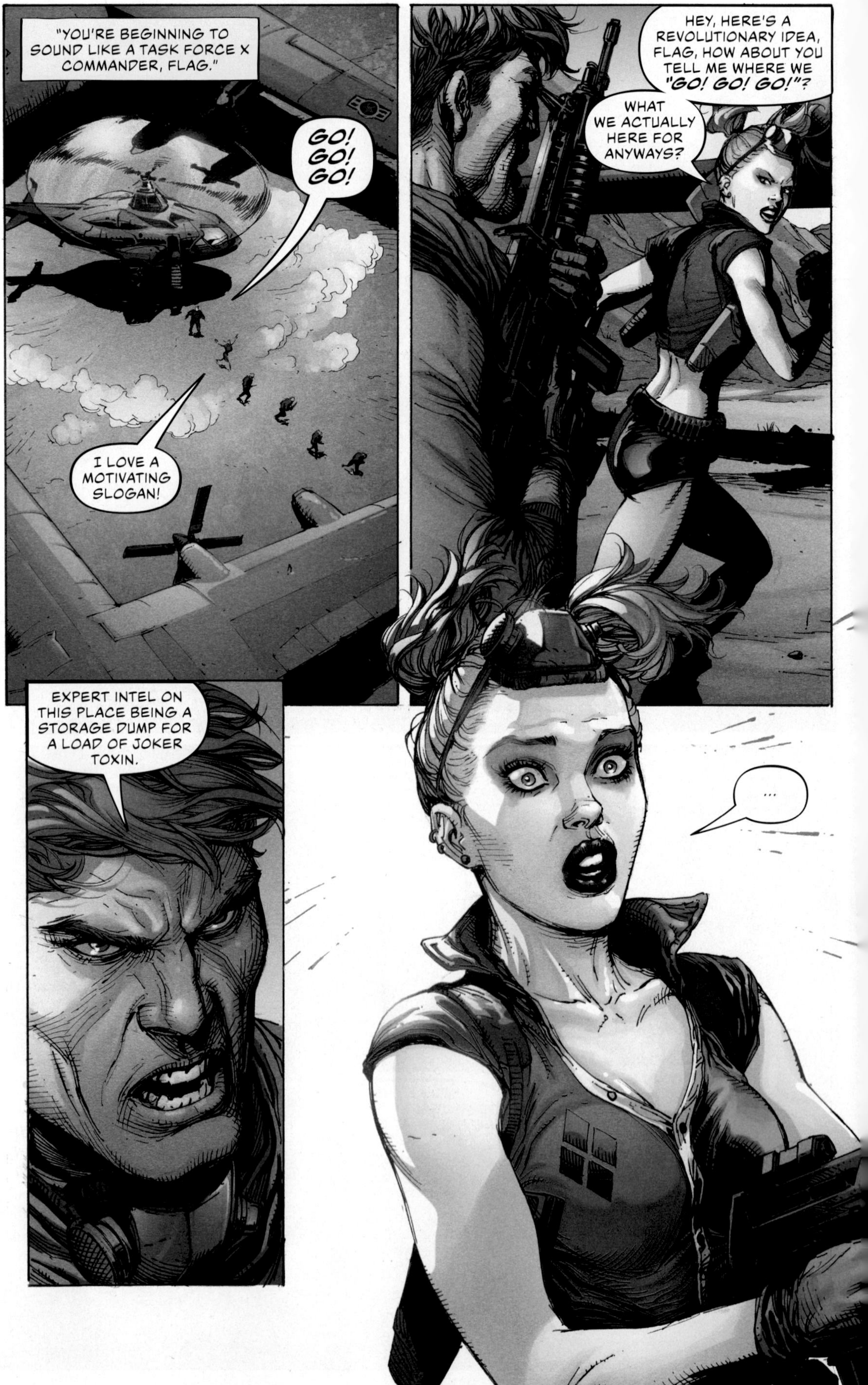

"YOU'RE BEGINNING TO SOUND LIKE A TASK FORCE X COMMANDER, FLAG."
GO! GO! GO!
I LOVE A MOTIVATING SLOGAN!
HEY, HERE'S A REVOLUTIONARY IDEA, FLAG, HOW ABOUT YOU TELL ME WHERE WE "GO! GO! GO!"?
WHAT WE ACTUALLY HERE FOR ANYWAYS?
EXPERT INTEL ON THIS PLACE BEING A STORAGE DUMP FOR A LOAD OF JOKER TOXIN.
...

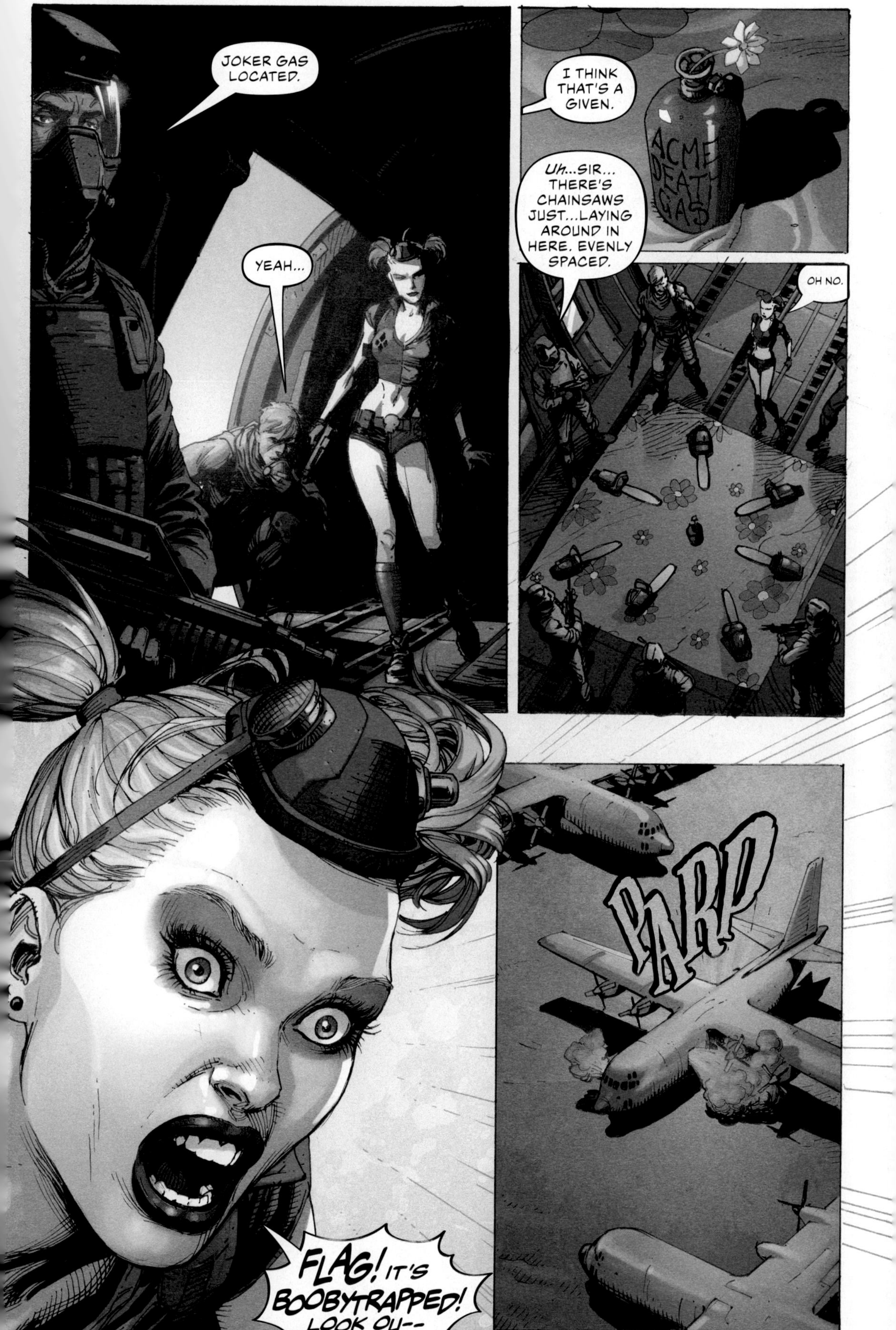
JOKER GAS LOCATED.
YEAH...
I THINK THAT'S A GIVEN.
ACME DEATH GAS
Uh...SIR... THERE'S CHAINSAWS JUST...LAYING AROUND IN HERE. EVENLY SPACED.
OH NO.
FLAG! IT'S BOOBYTRAPPED! LOOK OU--
PARP

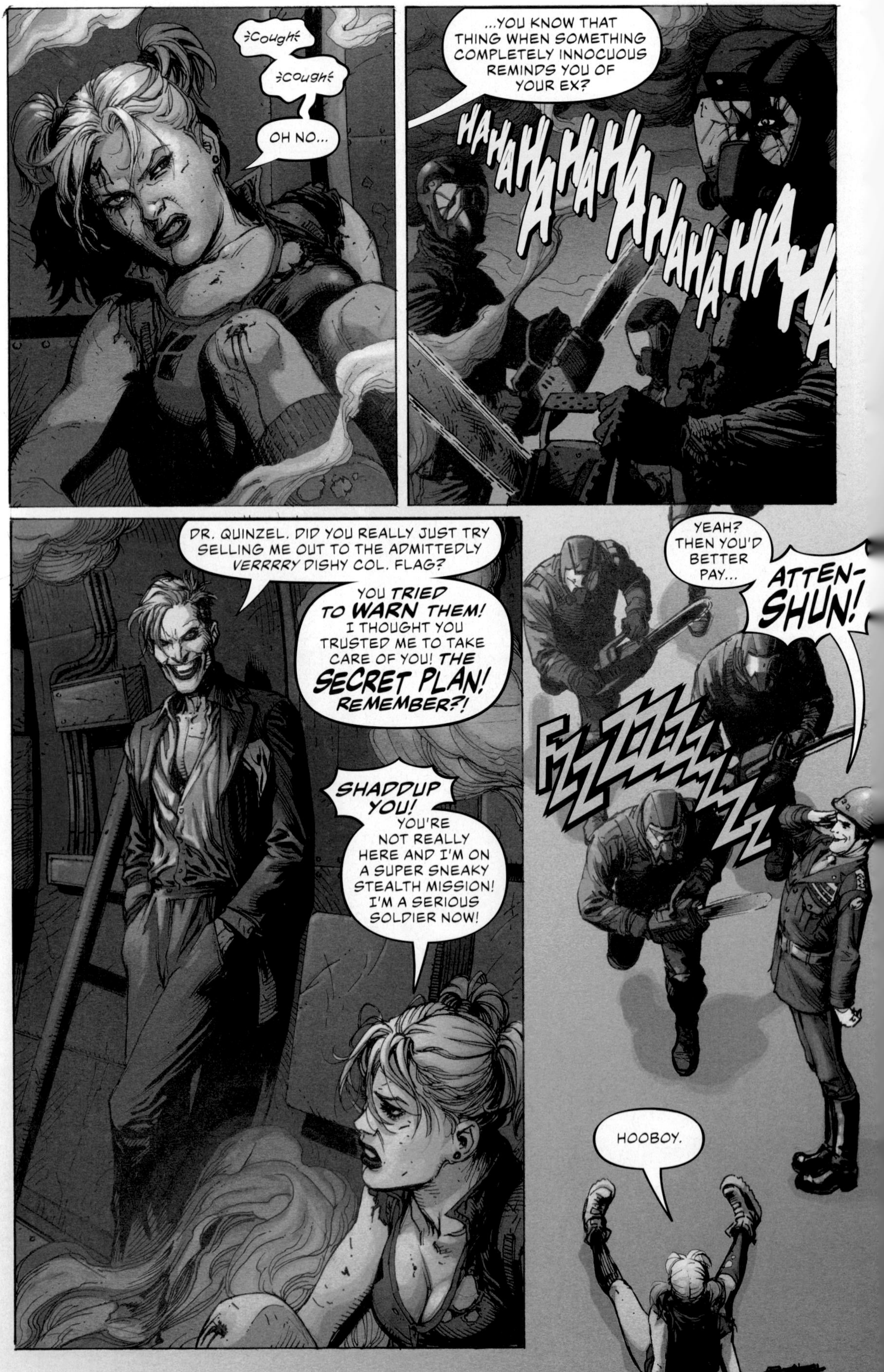

COUGH
COUGH
OH NO...
...YOU KNOW THAT THING WHEN SOMETHING COMPLETELY INNOCUOUS REMINDS YOU OF YOUR EX?
HAHAHAHAHAHAHAHAHAHAHAHAHAHAHAHA
DR. QUINZEL. DID YOU REALLY JUST TRY SELLING ME OUT TO THE ADMITTEDLY *VERRRRY* DISHY COL. FLAG?
YOU **TRIED** TO **WARN** THEM! I THOUGHT YOU TRUSTED ME TO TAKE CARE OF YOU! **THE SECRET PLAN! REMEMBER?!**
SHADDUP YOU! YOU'RE NOT REALLY HERE AND I'M ON A SUPER SNEAKY STEALTH MISSION! I'M A SERIOUS SOLDIER NOW!
YEAH? THEN YOU'D BETTER PAY...
ATTEN-SHUN!
FZZZZZZZZZZ
HOOBOY.

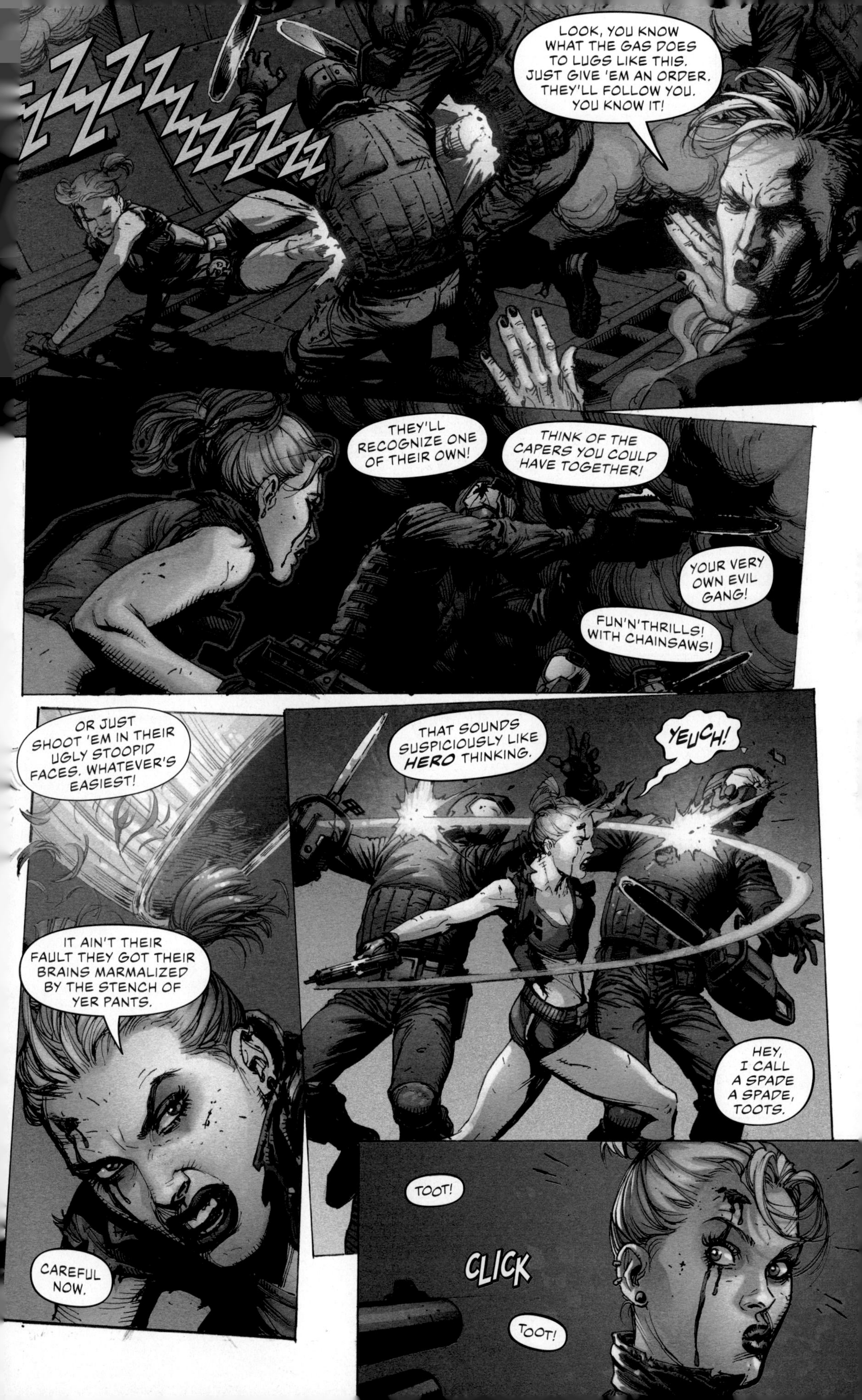
ZZZZZZZZZZZZ
LOOK, YOU KNOW WHAT THE GAS DOES TO LUGS LIKE THIS. JUST GIVE 'EM AN ORDER. THEY'LL FOLLOW YOU. YOU KNOW IT!
THEY'LL RECOGNIZE ONE OF THEIR OWN!
THINK OF THE CAPERS YOU COULD HAVE TOGETHER!
YOUR VERY OWN EVIL GANG!
FUN'N'THRILLS! WITH CHAINSAWS!
OR JUST SHOOT 'EM IN THEIR UGLY STOOPID FACES. WHATEVER'S EASIEST!
IT AIN'T THEIR FAULT THEY GOT THEIR BRAINS MARMALIZED BY THE STENCH OF YER PANTS.
THAT SOUNDS SUSPICIOUSLY LIKE HERO THINKING.
YEUCH!
HEY, I CALL A SPADE A SPADE, TOOTS.
CAREFUL NOW.
TOOT!
CLICK
TOOT!

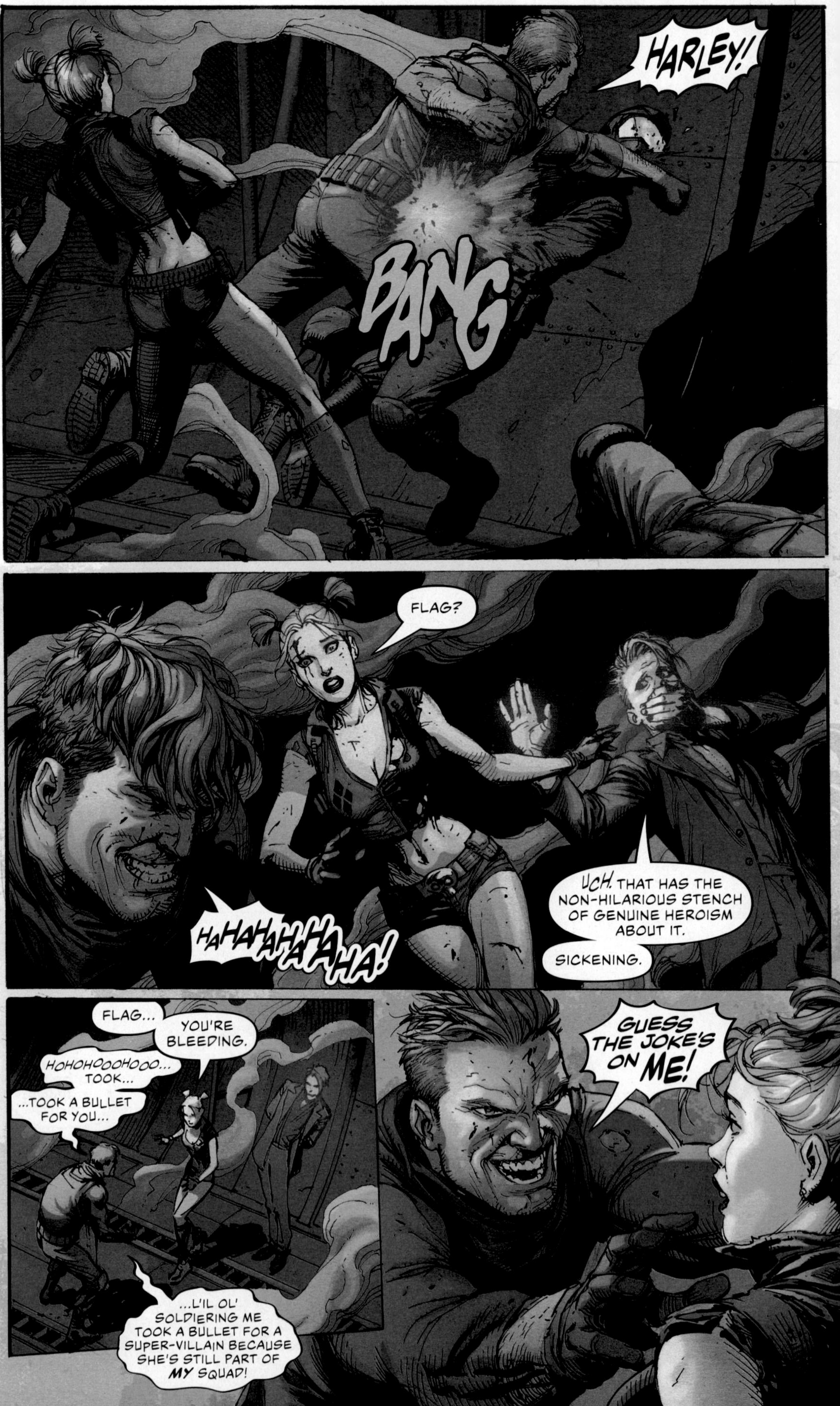
HARLEY!
BANG
FLAG?
HAHAHAHAHAHAHA!
UCH. THAT HAS THE NON-HILARIOUS STENCH OF GENUINE HEROISM ABOUT IT.
SICKENING.
FLAG...
YOU'RE BLEEDING.
HOHOHOOOHOOO... TOOK...
...TOOK A BULLET FOR YOU...
...L'IL OL' SOLDIERING ME TOOK A BULLET FOR A SUPER-VILLAIN BECAUSE SHE'S STILL PART OF MY SQUAD!
GUESS THE JOKE'S ON ME!

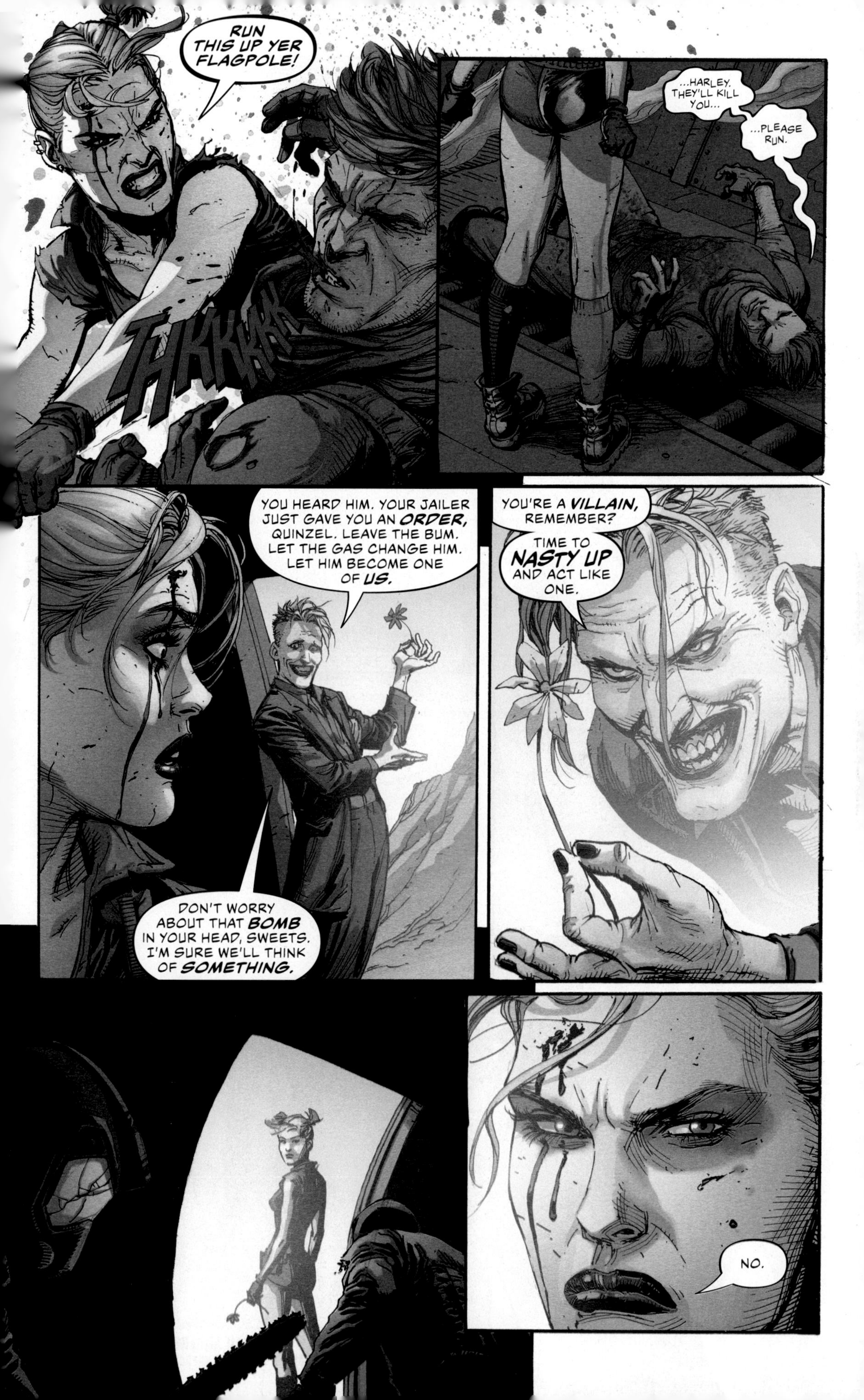
RUN THIS UP YER FLAGPOLE!
THKKKK
...HARLEY. THEY'LL KILL YOU...
...PLEASE RUN.
YOU HEARD HIM. YOUR JAILER JUST GAVE YOU AN ORDER, QUINZEL. LEAVE THE BUM. LET THE GAS CHANGE HIM. LET HIM BECOME ONE OF US.
DON'T WORRY ABOUT THAT BOMB IN YOUR HEAD, SWEETS. I'M SURE WE'LL THINK OF SOMETHING.
YOU'RE A VILLAIN, REMEMBER?
TIME TO NASTY UP AND ACT LIKE ONE.
NO.

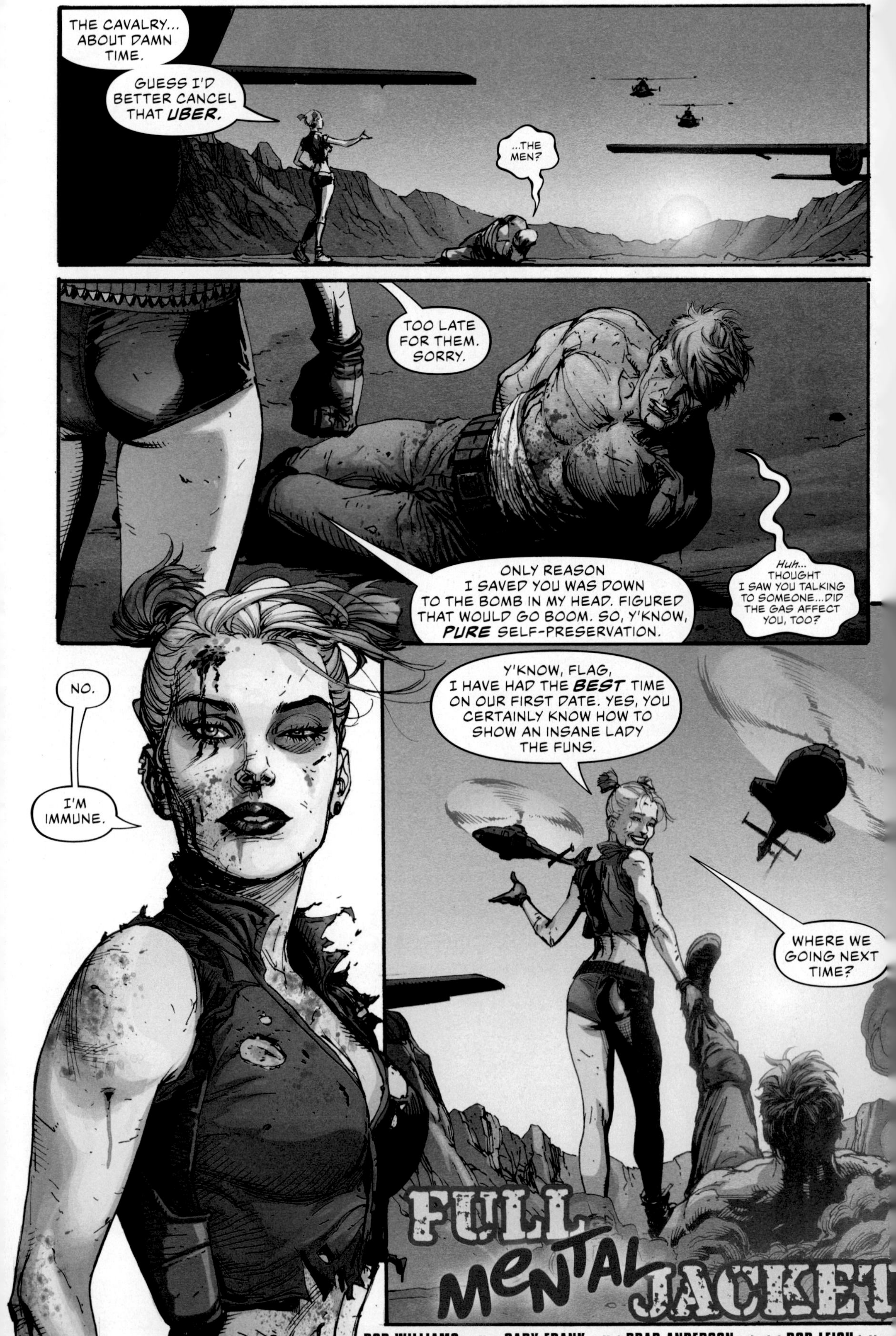

THE CAVALRY... ABOUT DAMN TIME.
GUESS I'D BETTER CANCEL THAT UBER.
...THE MEN?
TOO LATE FOR THEM. SORRY.
ONLY REASON I SAVED YOU WAS DOWN TO THE BOMB IN MY HEAD. FIGURED THAT WOULD GO BOOM. SO, Y'KNOW, PURE SELF-PRESERVATION.
Huh... THOUGHT I SAW YOU TALKING TO SOMEONE...DID THE GAS AFFECT YOU, TOO?
NO.
I'M IMMUNE.
Y'KNOW, FLAG, I HAVE HAD THE BEST TIME ON OUR FIRST DATE. YES, YOU CERTAINLY KNOW HOW TO SHOW AN INSANE LADY THE FUNS.
WHERE WE GOING NEXT TIME?
FULL MENTAL JACKET
ROB WILLIAMS writer GARY FRANK artist BRAD ANDERSON colorist ROB LEIGH letterer
BRIAN CUNNINGHAM group editor HARVEY RICHARDS associate editor ANDY KHOURI editor

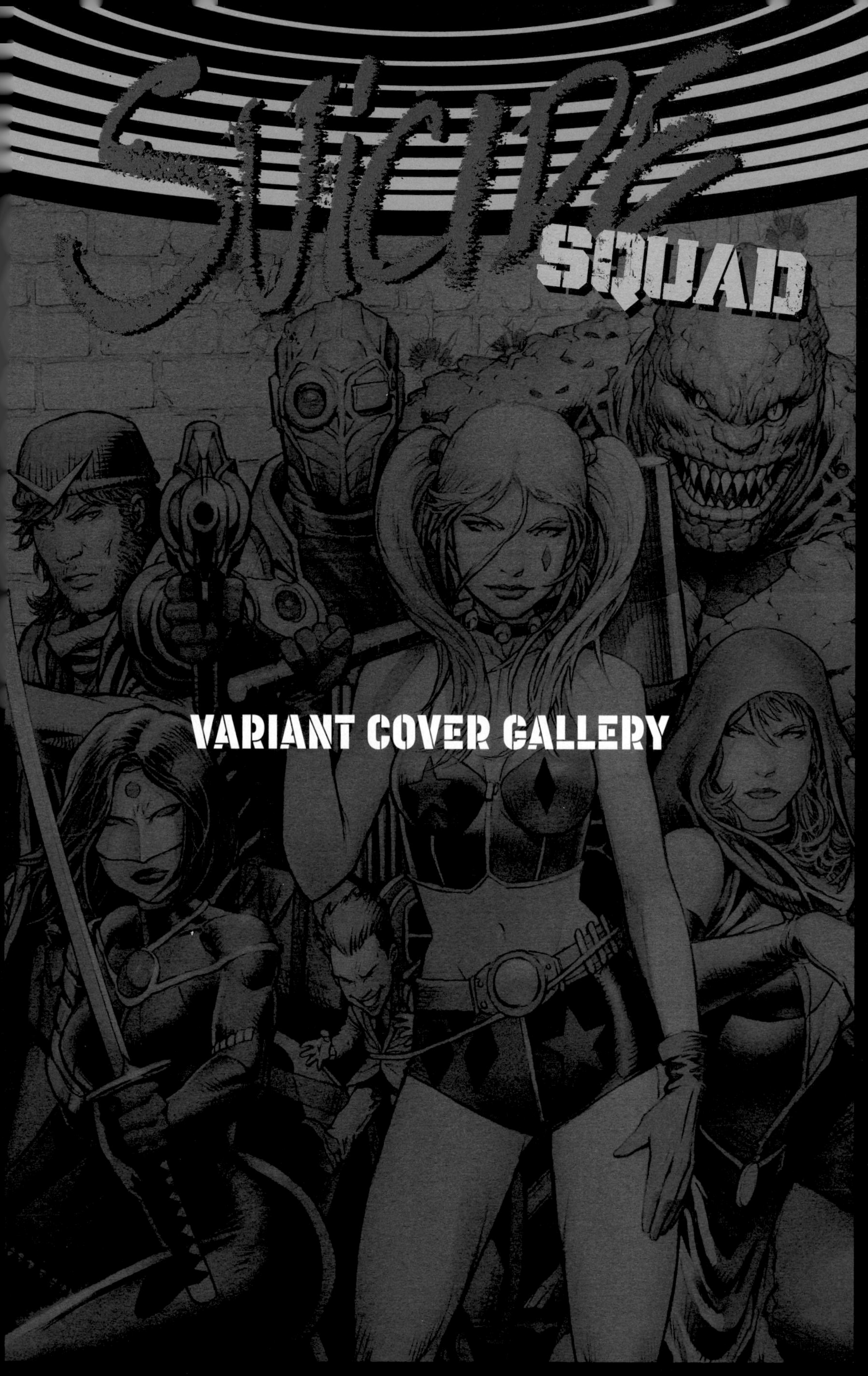
SUICIDE SQUAD

VARIANT COVER GALLERY

Variant cover art for SUICIDE SQUAD: REBIRTH #1
by Amanda Conner and Paul Mounts

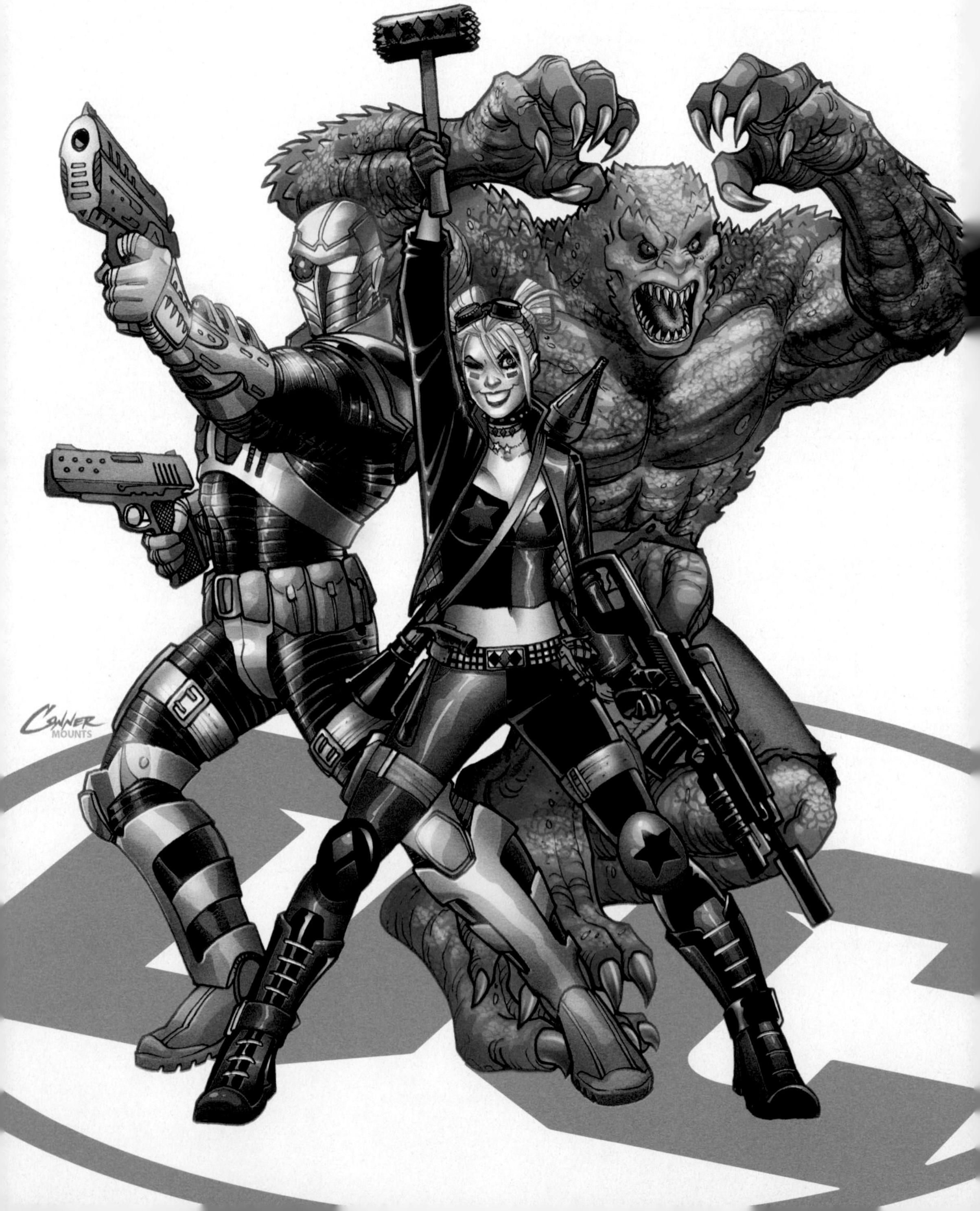
CONNER
MOUNTS

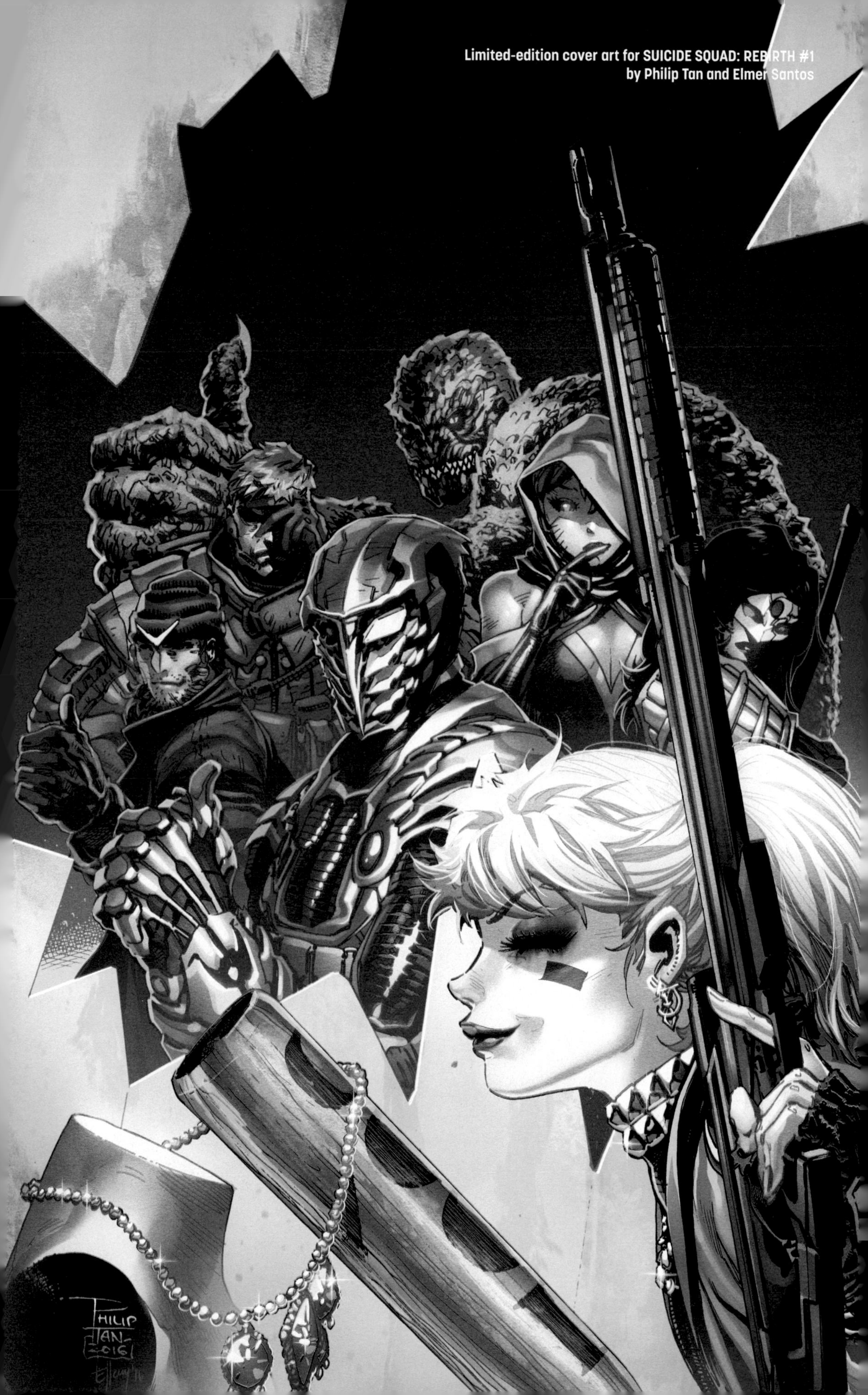
PHILIP TAN 2016

Limited-edition cover art for SUICIDE SQUAD: REBIRTH #1
by Philip Tan and Elmer Santos

Variant cover art for SUICIDE SQUAD #1 by Lee Bermejo

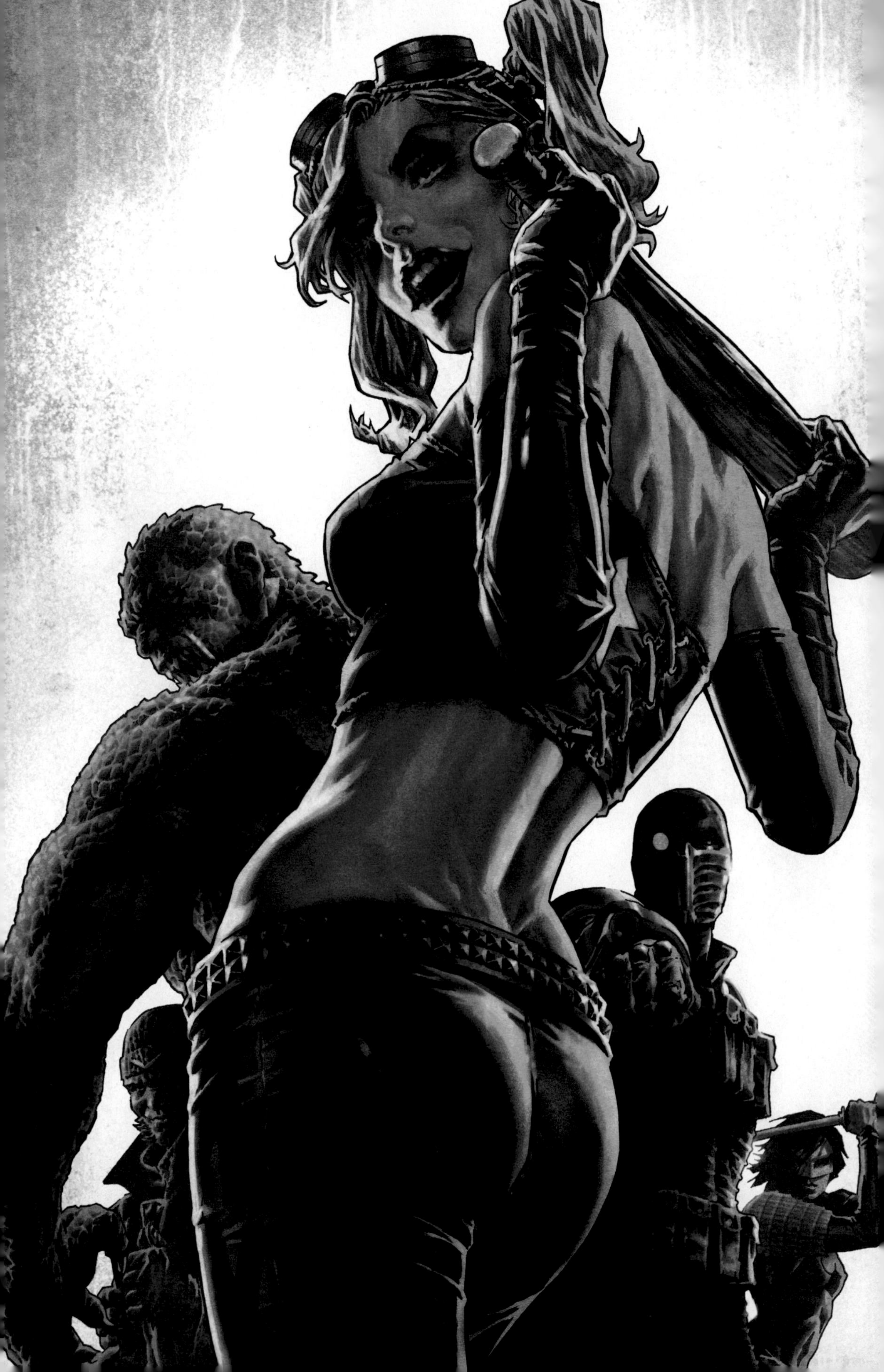

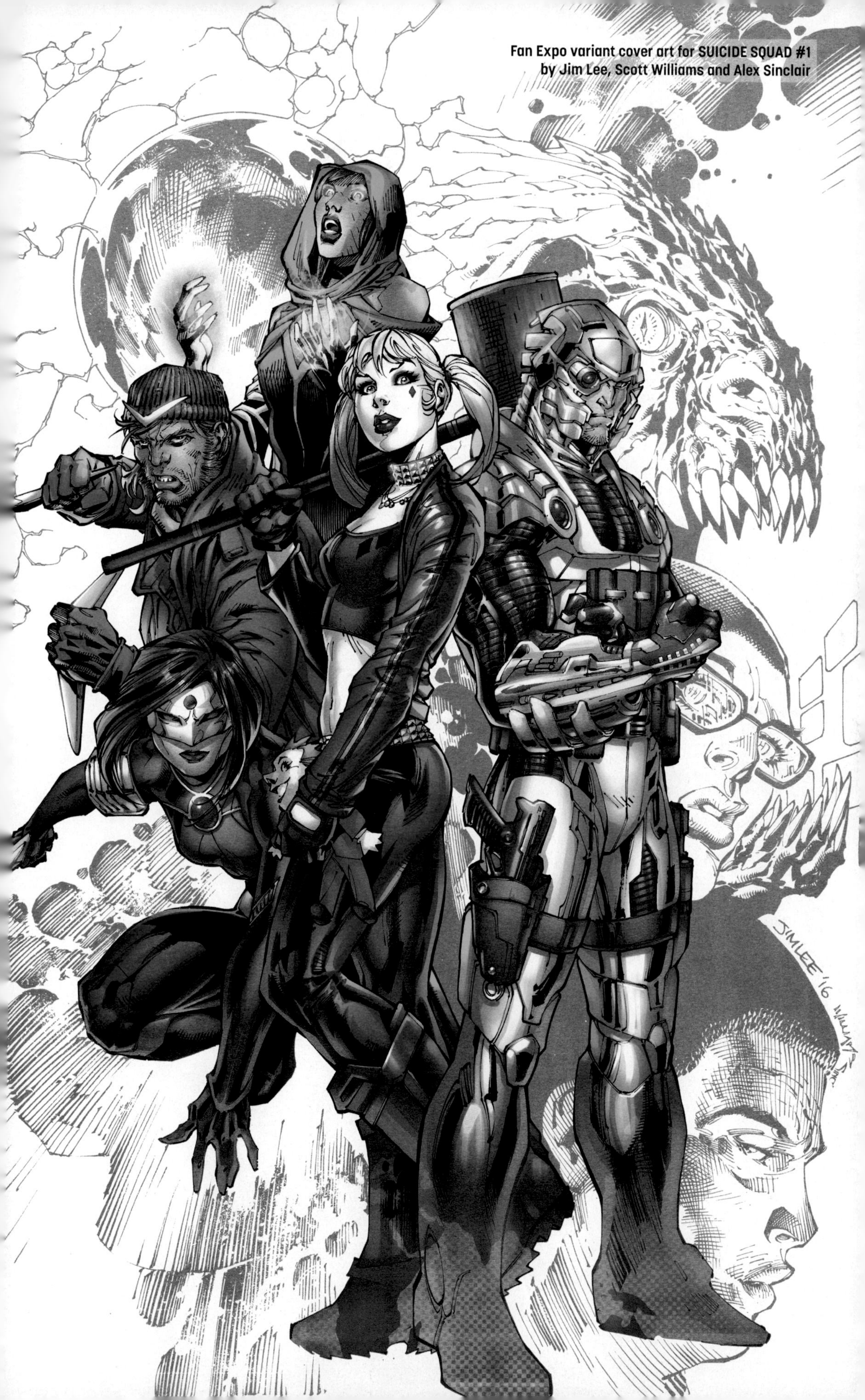
JIMLEE '16

Fan Expo variant cover art for SUICIDE SQUAD #1
by Jim Lee, Scott Williams and Alex Sinclair

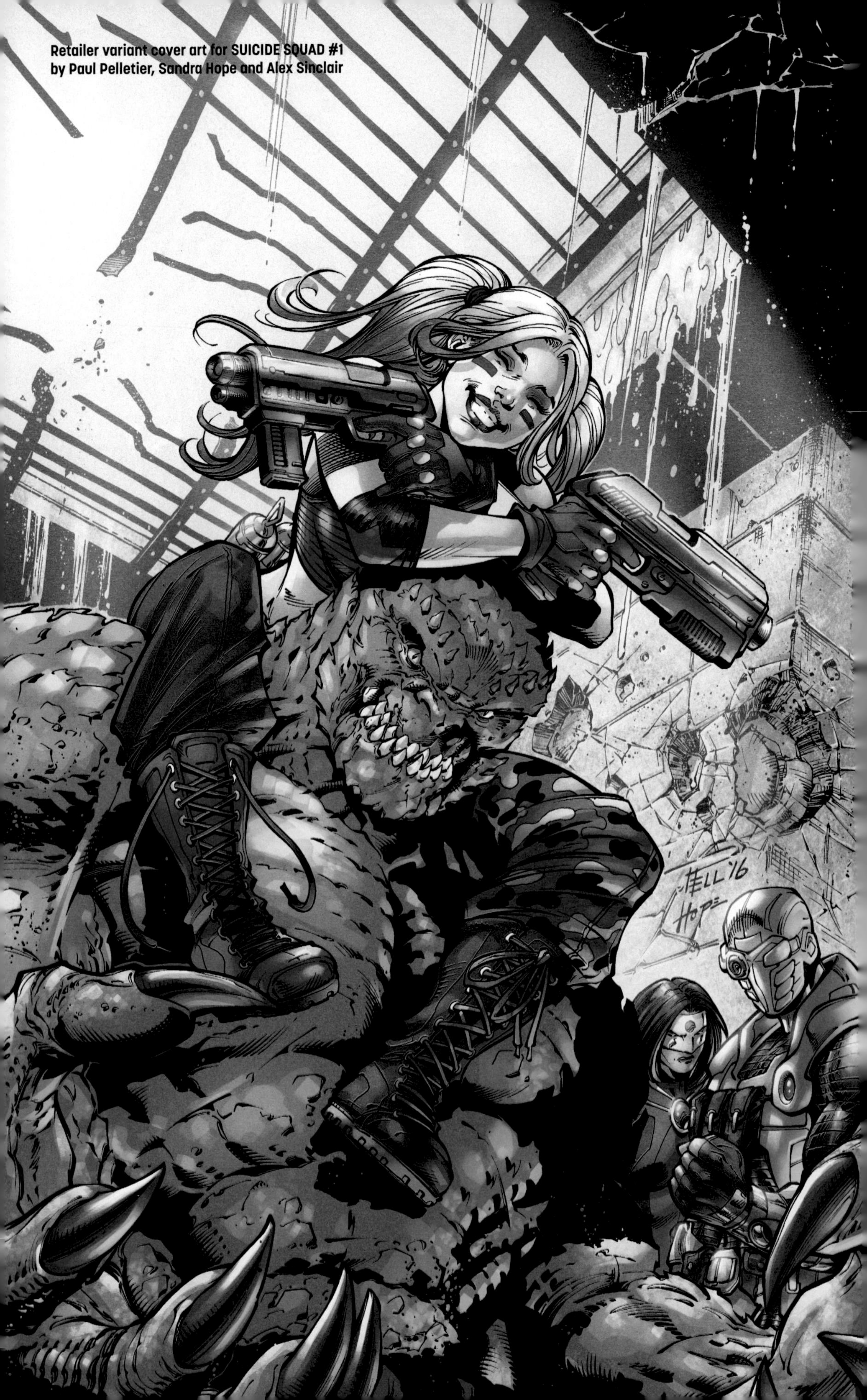

Retailer variant cover art for SUICIDE SQUAD #1
by Paul Pelletier, Sandra Hope and Alex Sinclair

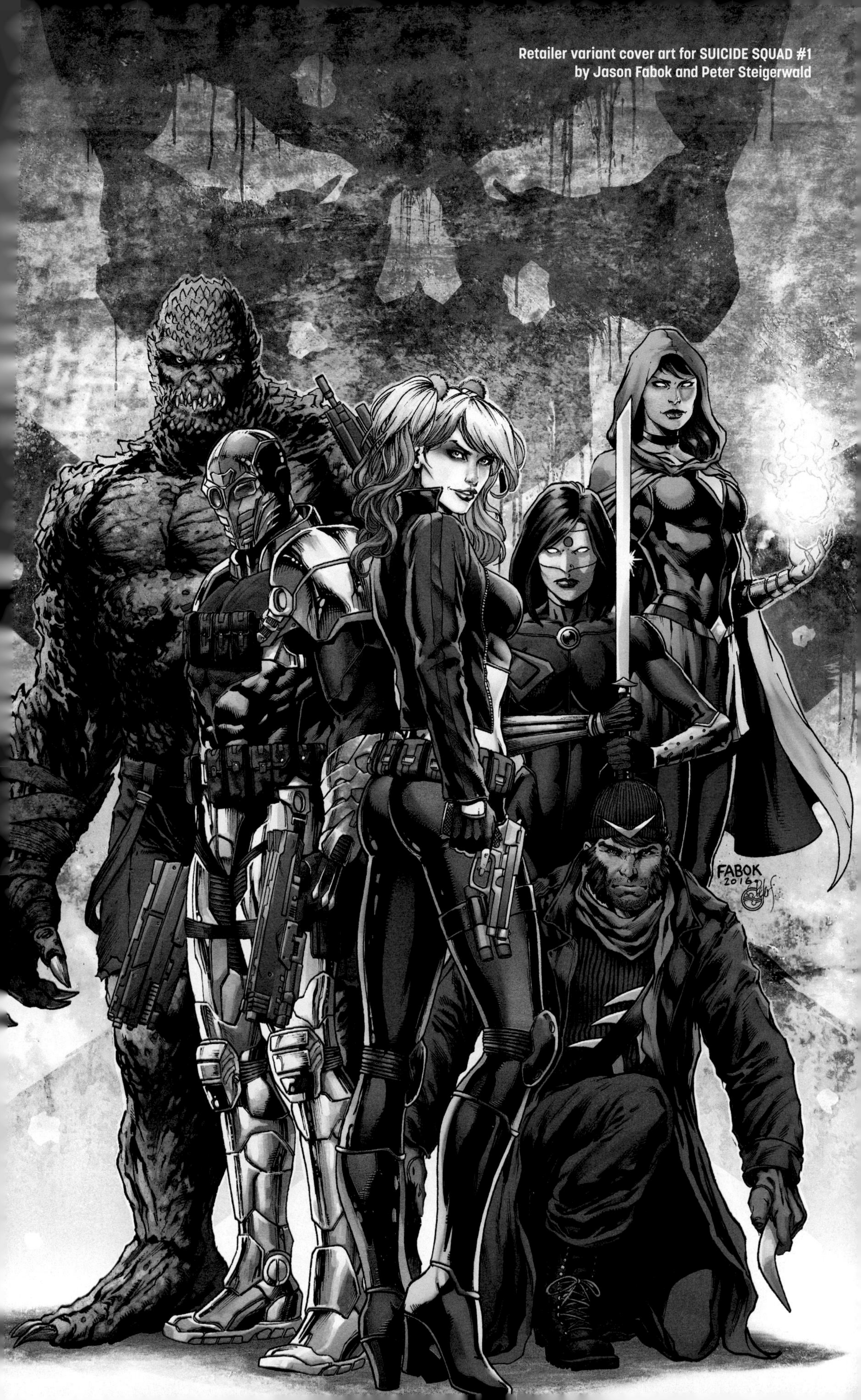
FABOK
2016

Retailer variant cover art for SUICIDE SQUAD #1
by Jason Fabok and Peter Steigerwald

Retailer variant cover art for SUICIDE SQUAD #1 by Joshua Middleton

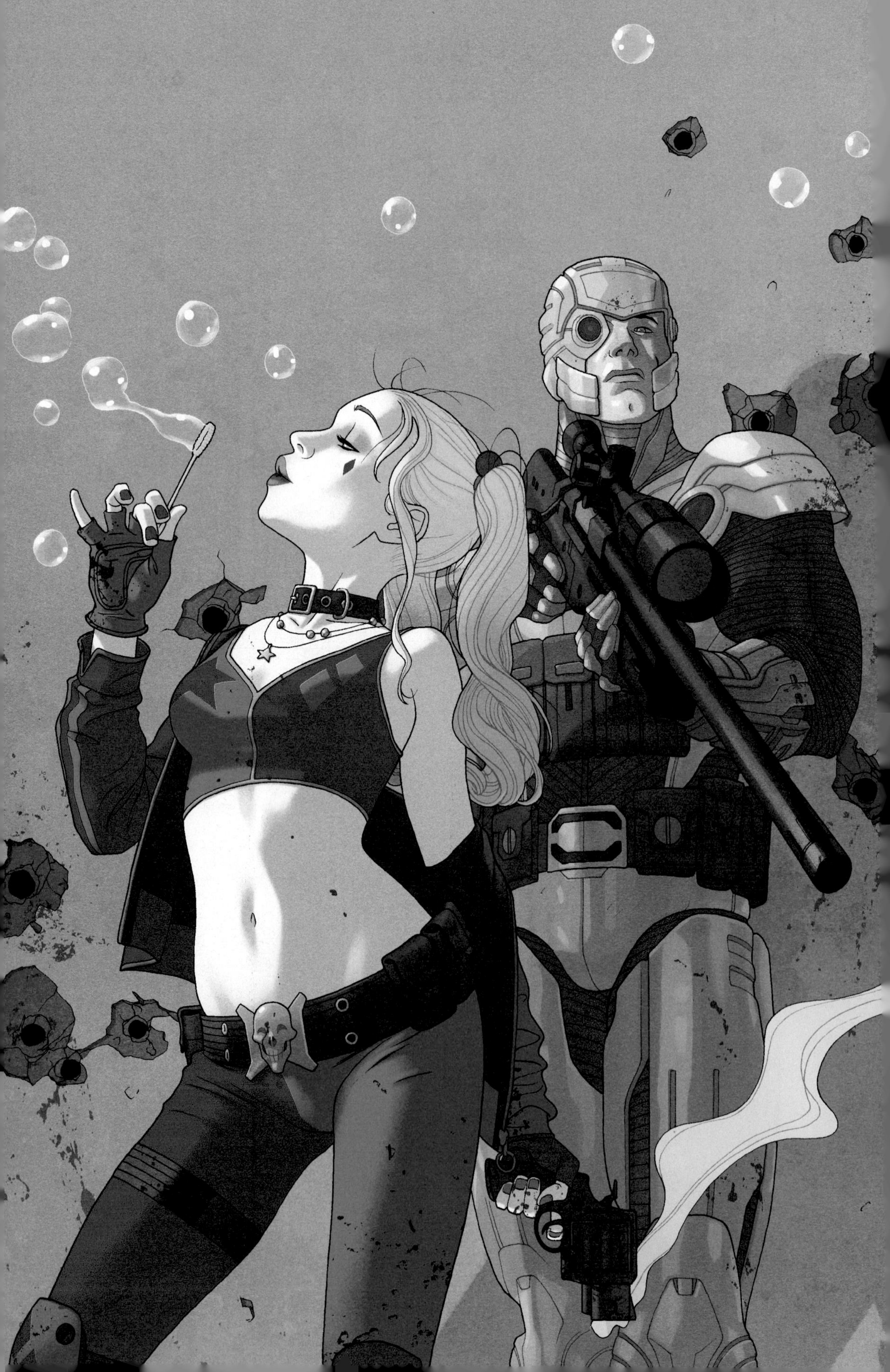

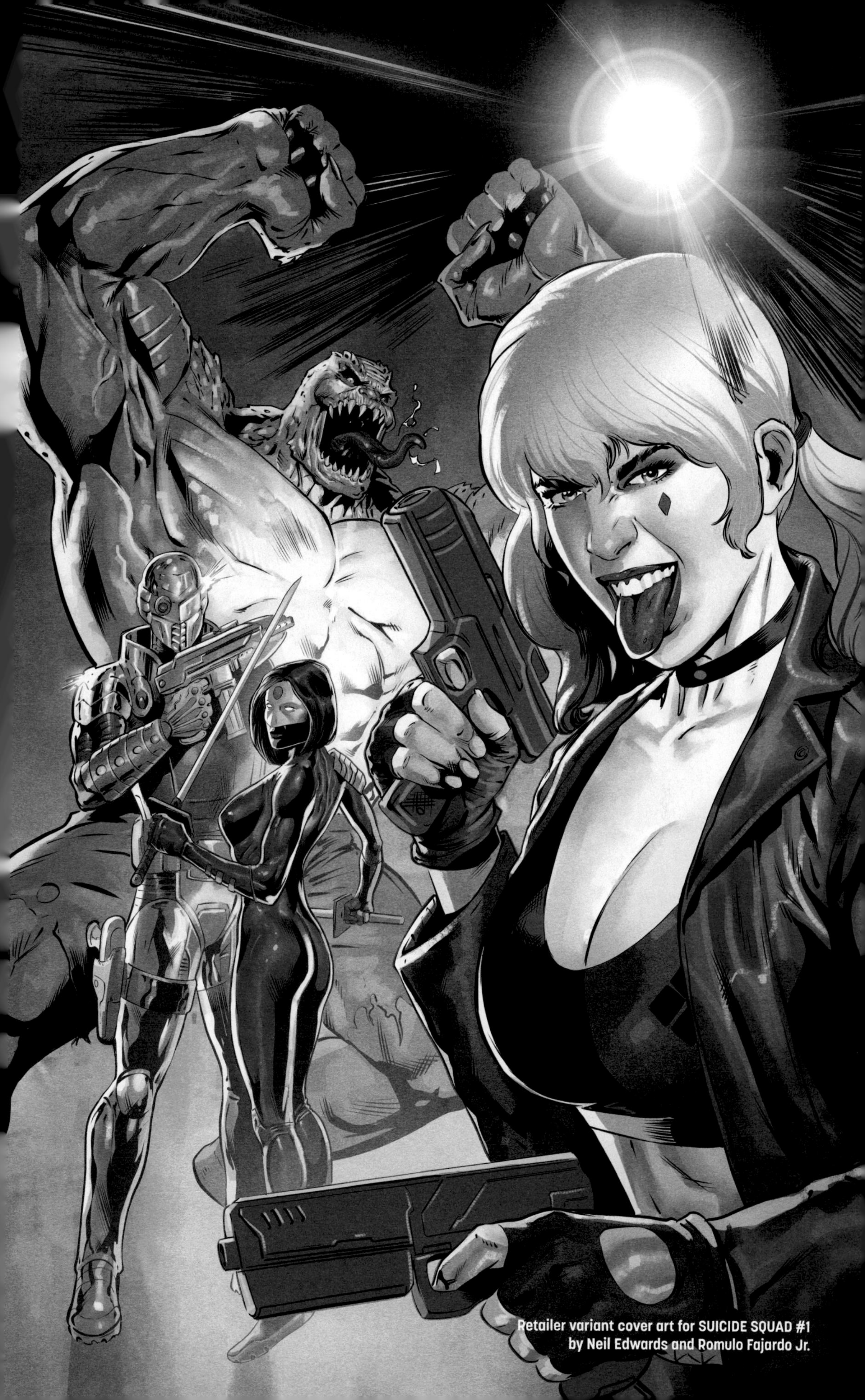

Retailer variant cover art for SUICIDE SQUAD #1
by Neil Edwards and Romulo Fajardo Jr.

Retailer variant cover art for SUICIDE SQUAD #1
by Liam Sharp and Alex Sinclair

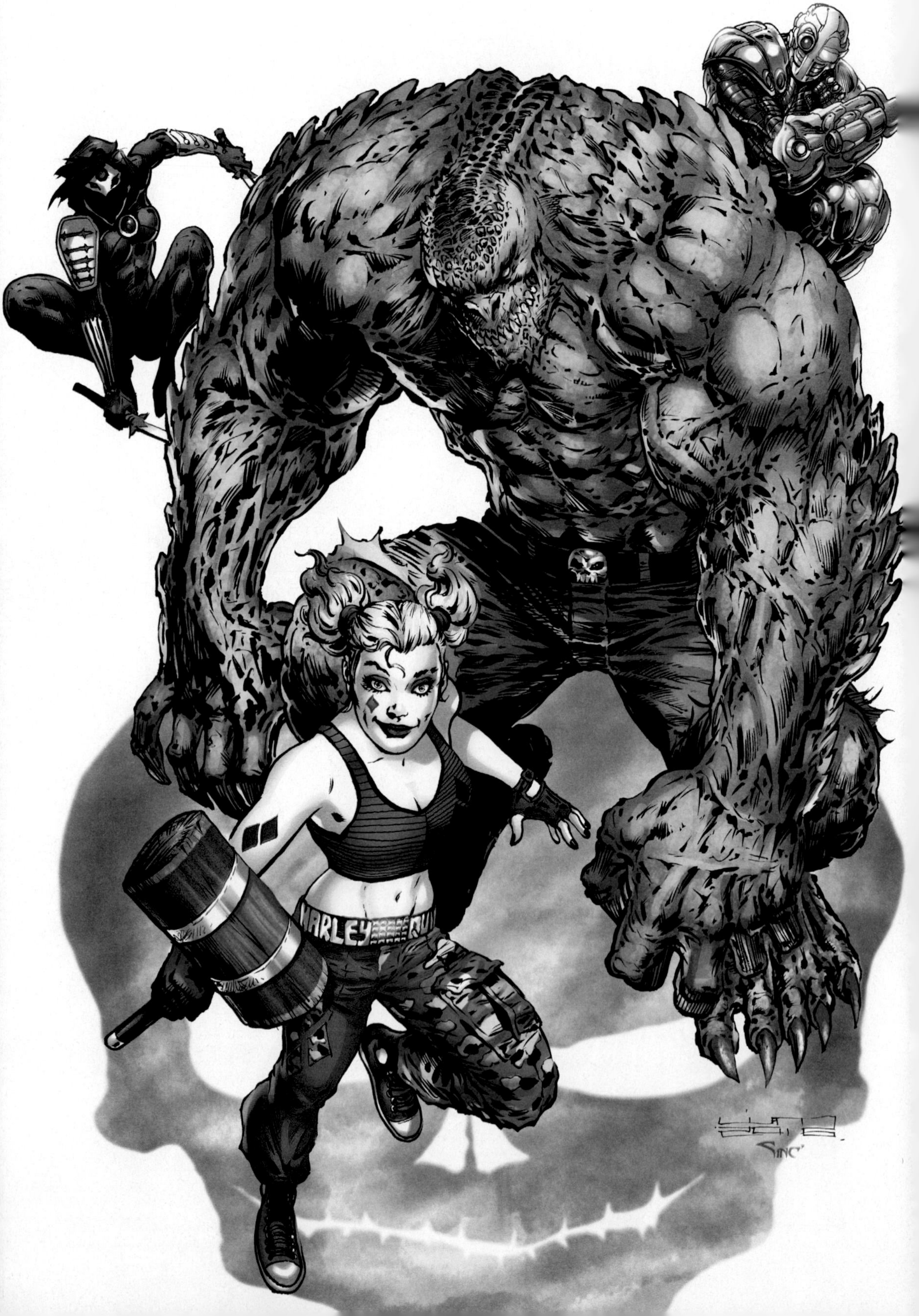
HARLEY

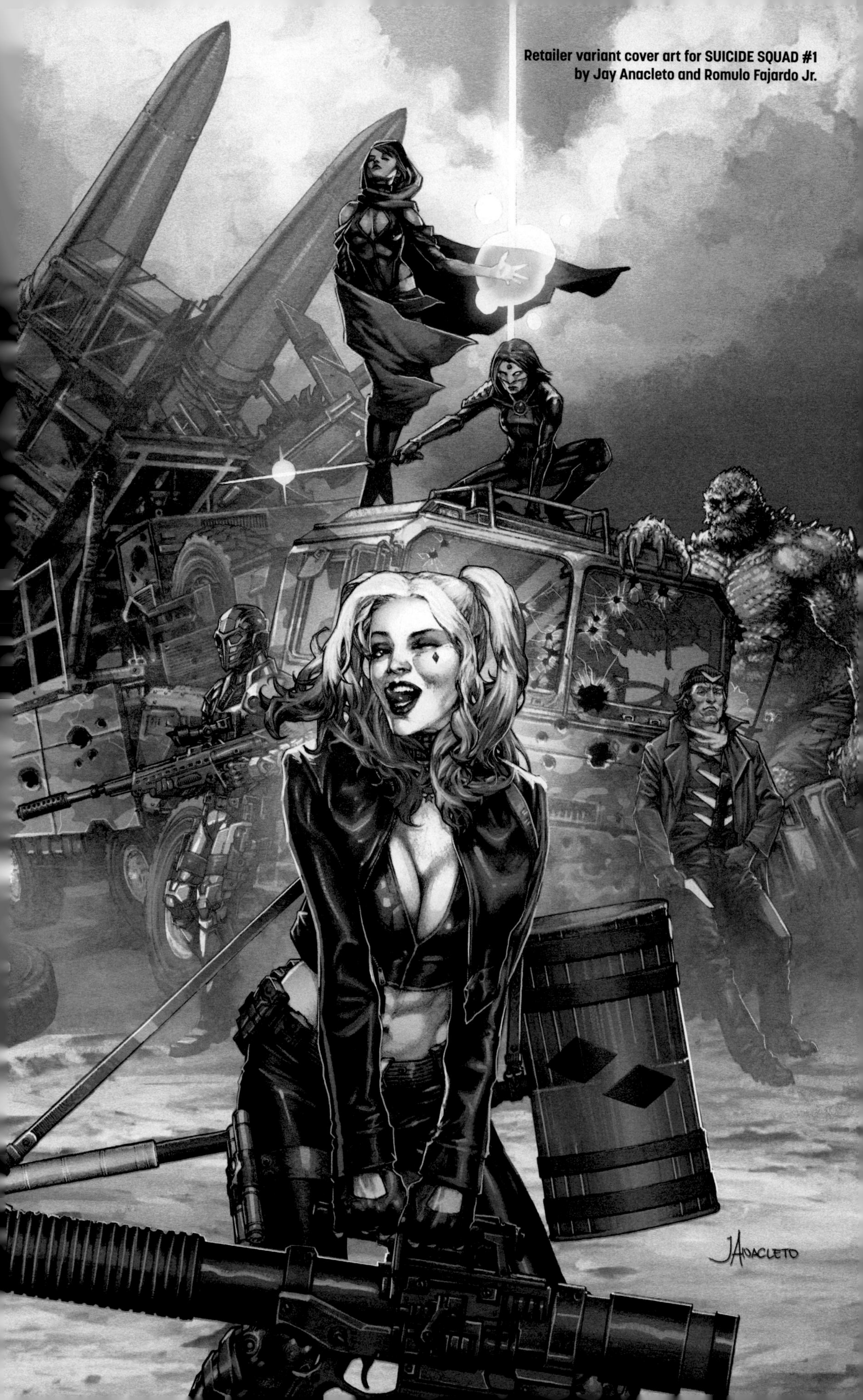

Retailer variant cover art for SUICIDE SQUAD #1
by Jay Anacleto and Romulo Fajardo Jr.

Retailer variant cover art for SUICIDE SQUAD #1
by Terry and Rachel Dodson

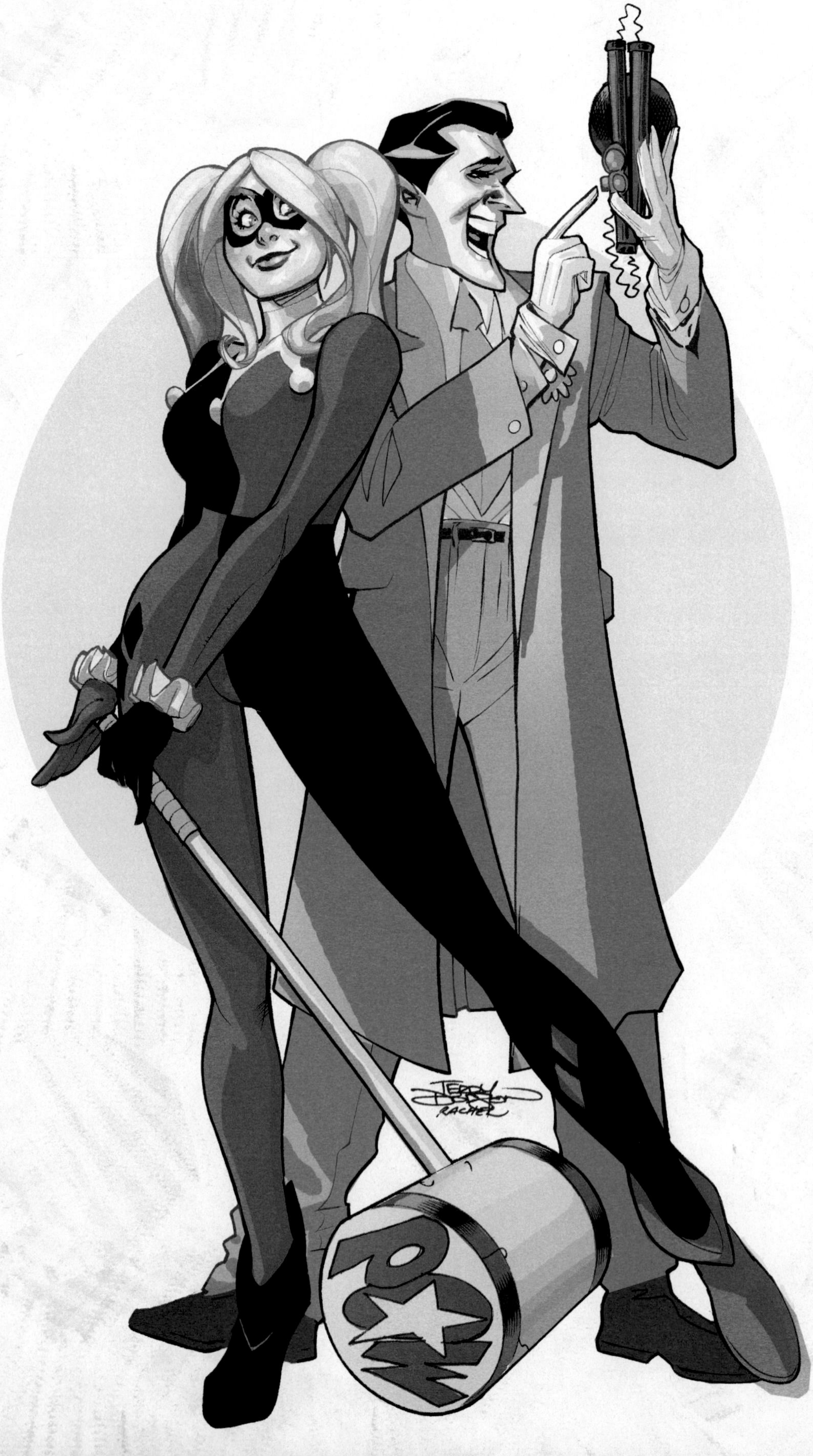
POW

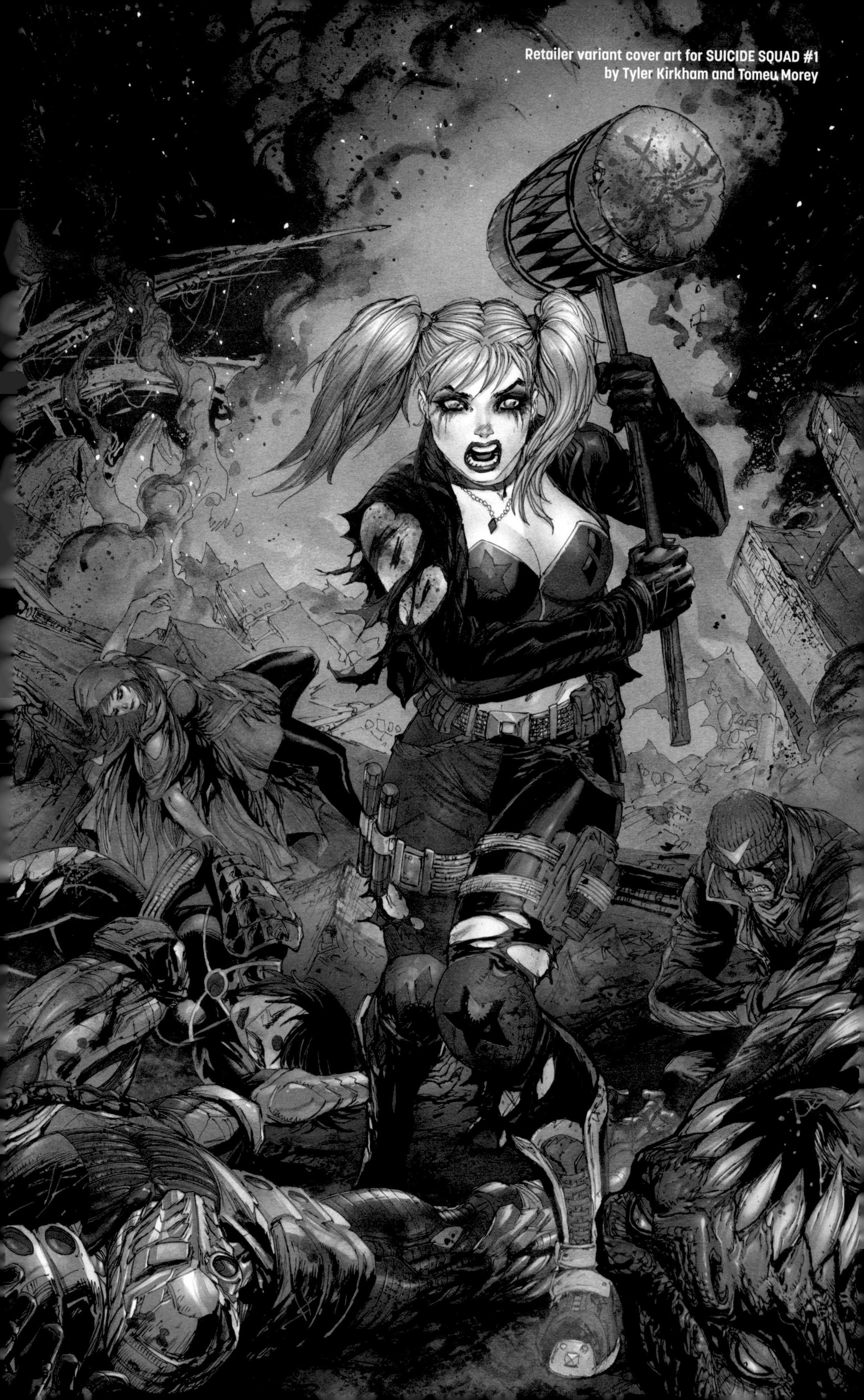

Retailer variant cover art for SUICIDE SQUAD #1
by Tyler Kirkham and Tomeu Morey

Retailer variant cover art for SUICIDE SQUAD #1 by Ben Oliver

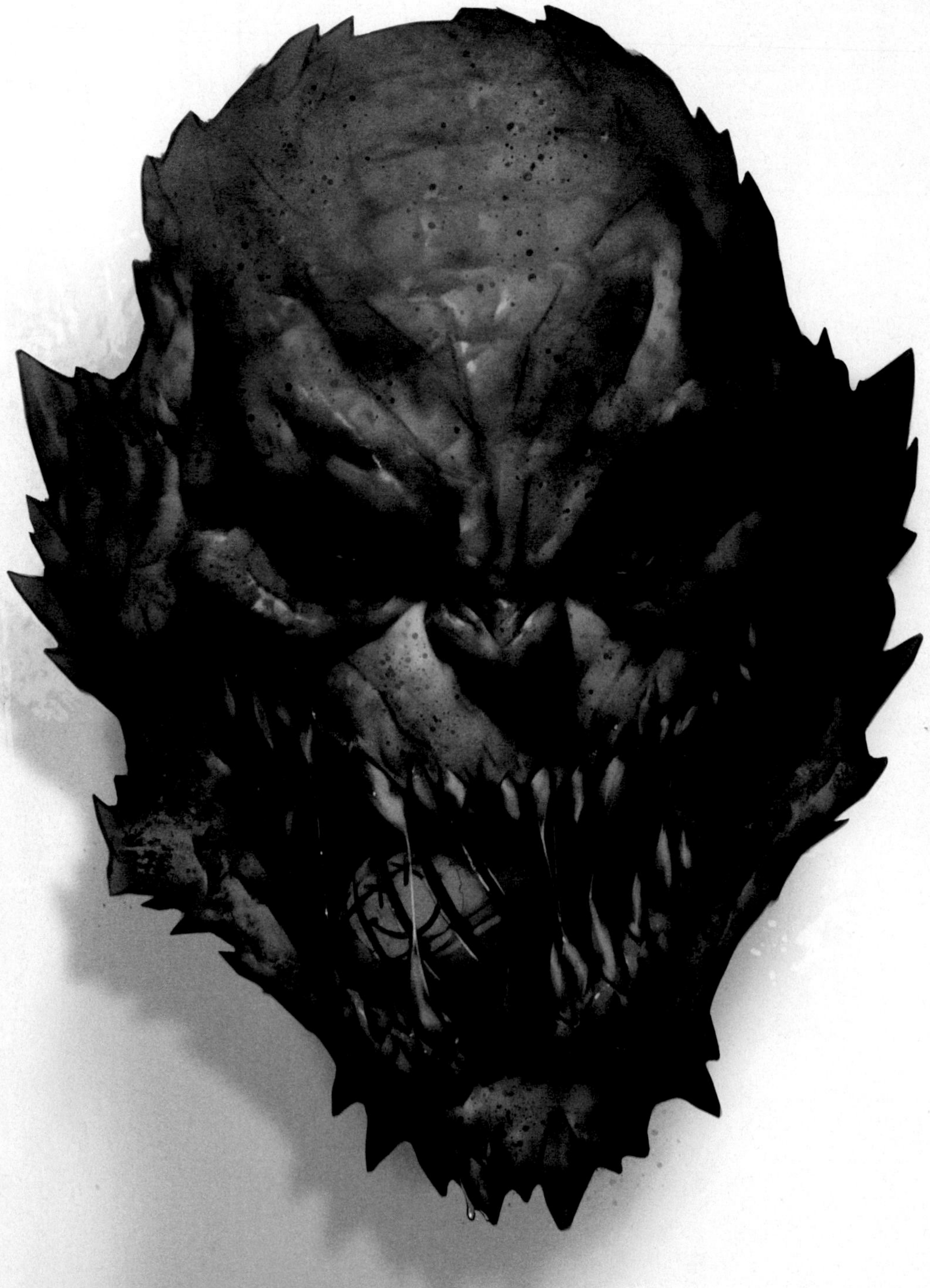

Retailer variant cover art for SUICIDE SQUAD #1 by Greg Tocchini

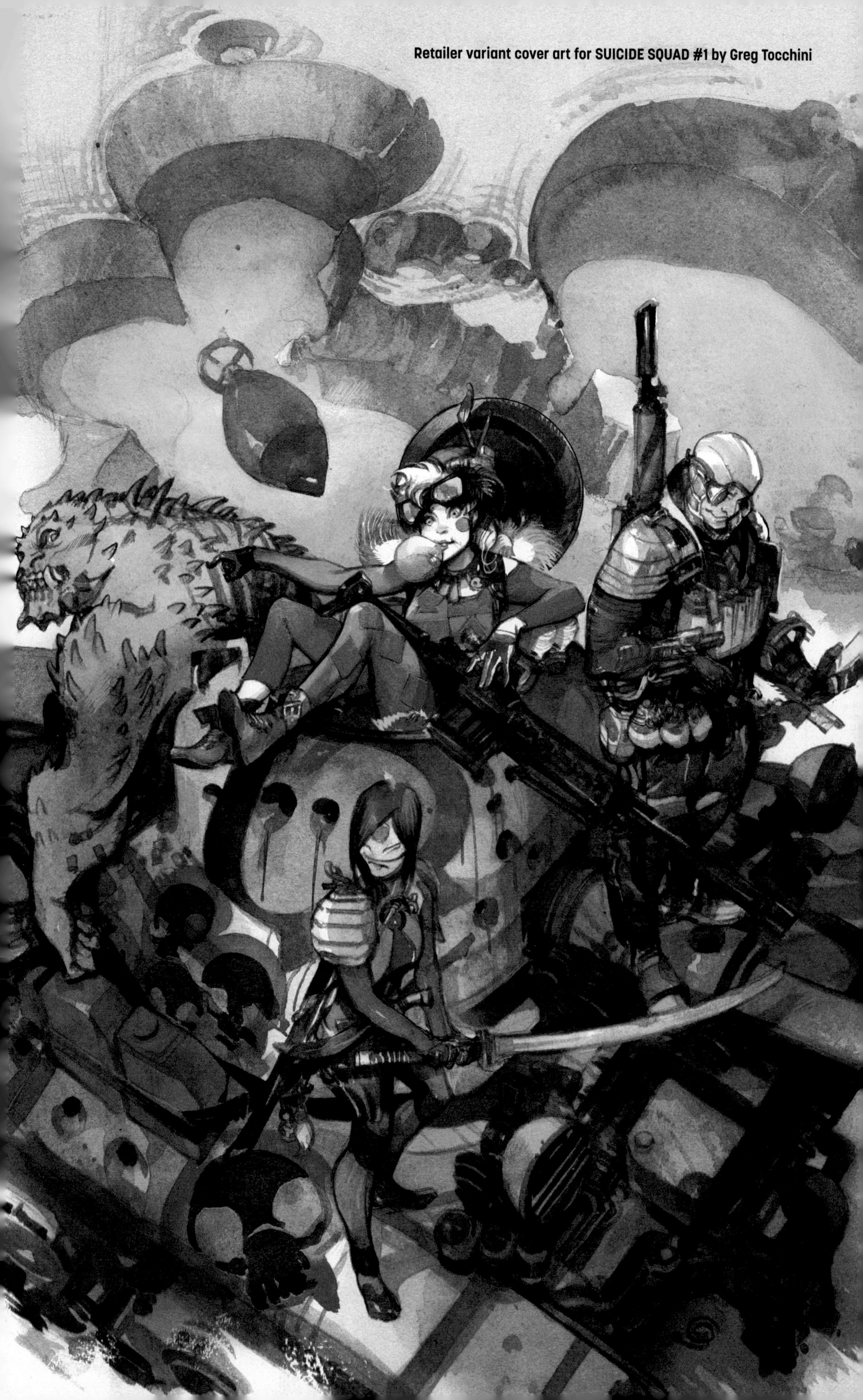

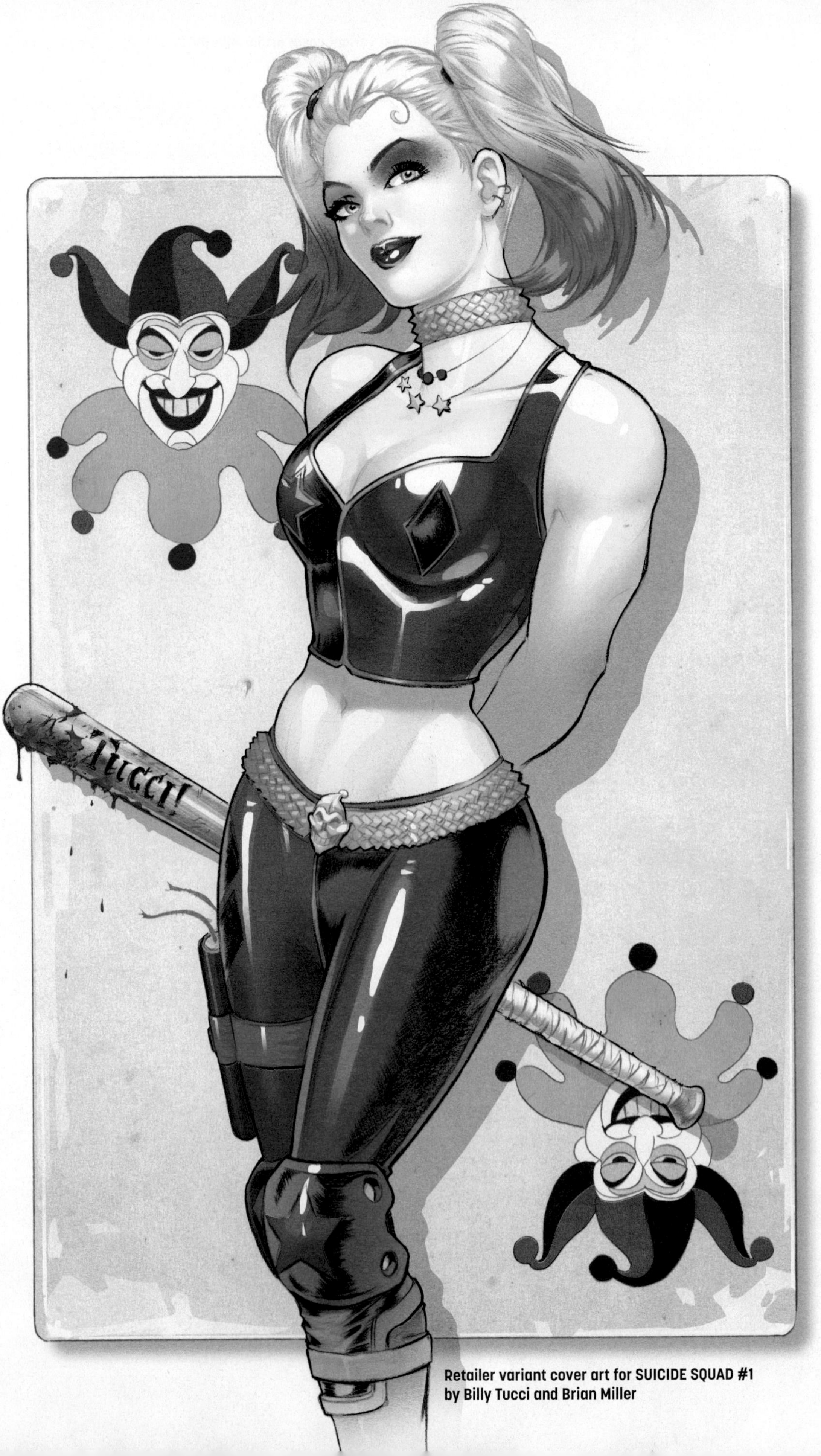
TUCCI!

Retailer variant cover art for SUICIDE SQUAD #1
by Billy Tucci and Brian Miller

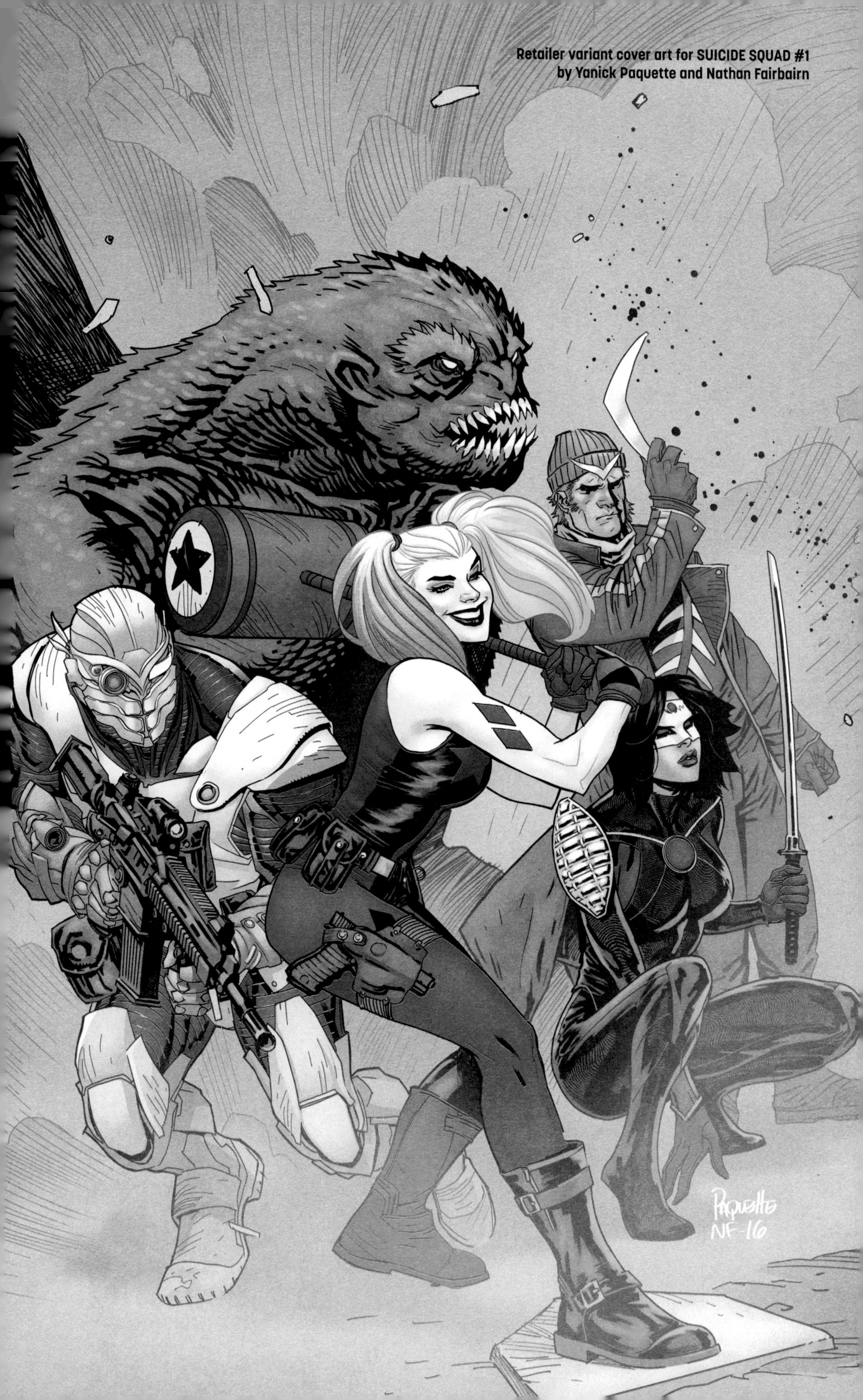
PAQUETTE
NF-16

Retailer variant cover art for SUICIDE SQUAD #1
by Yanick Paquette and Nathan Fairbairn

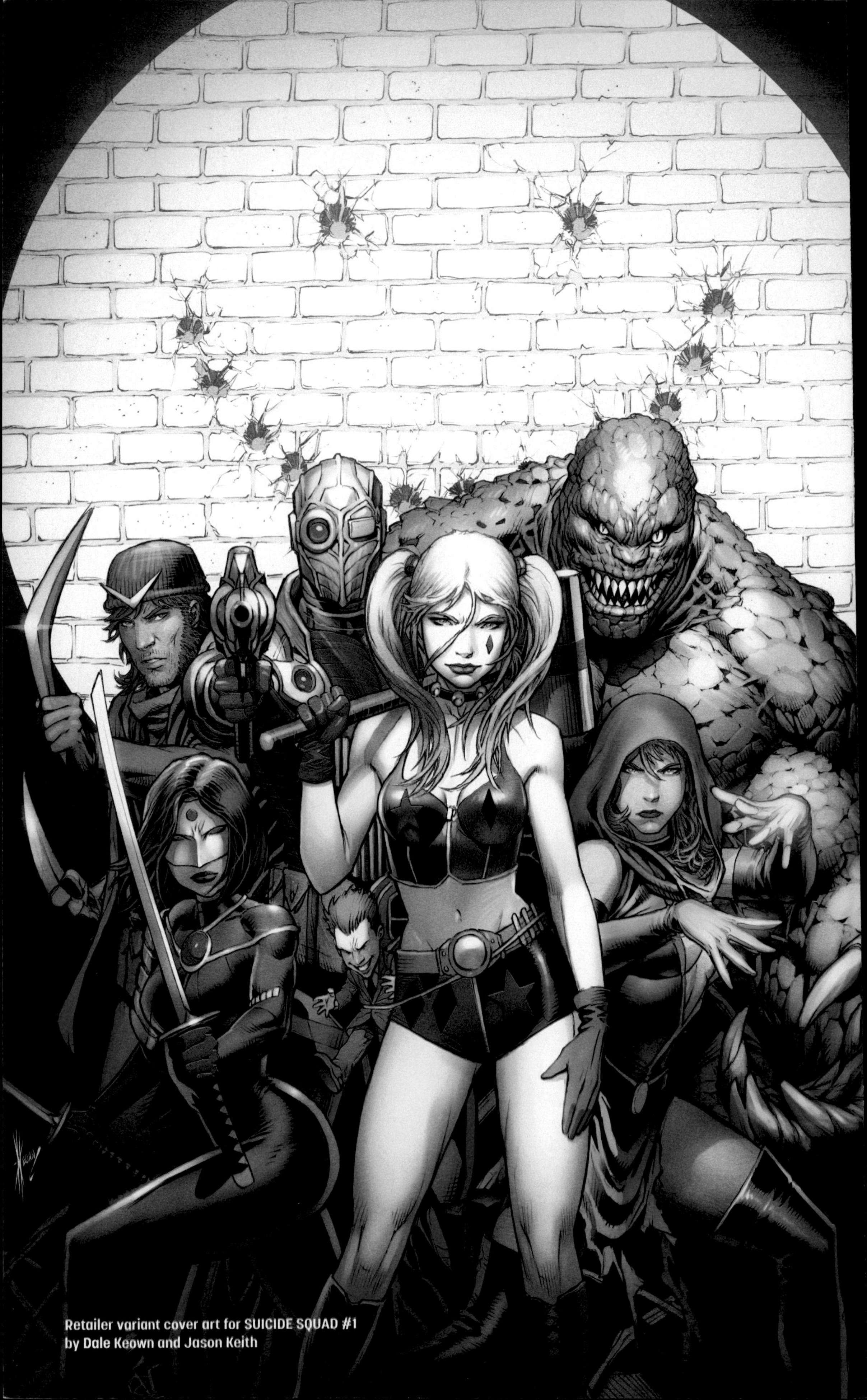

Retailer variant cover art for SUICIDE SQUAD #1
by Dale Keown and Jason Keith

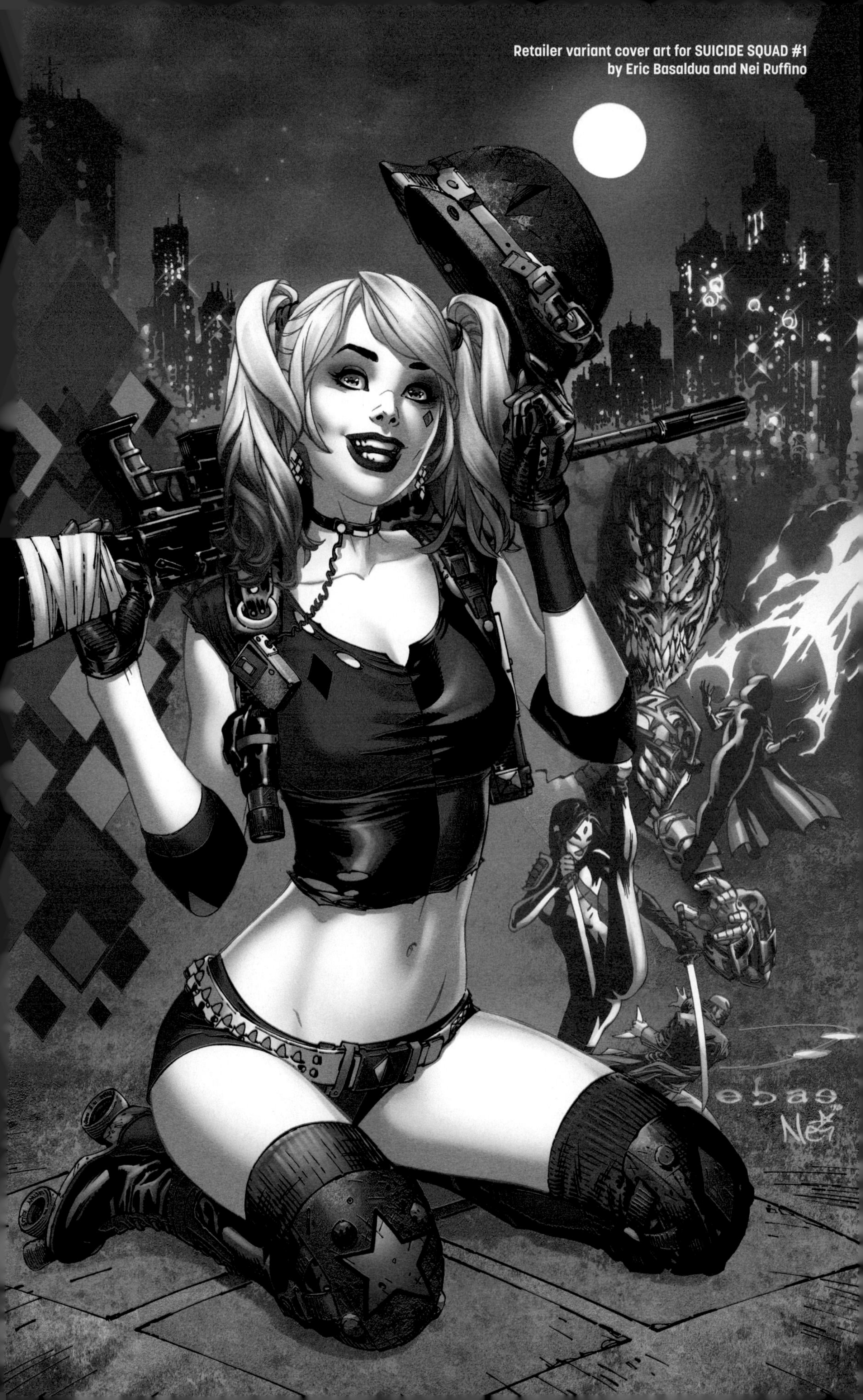
Retailer variant cover art for SUICIDE SQUAD #1
by Eric Basaldua and Nei Ruffino

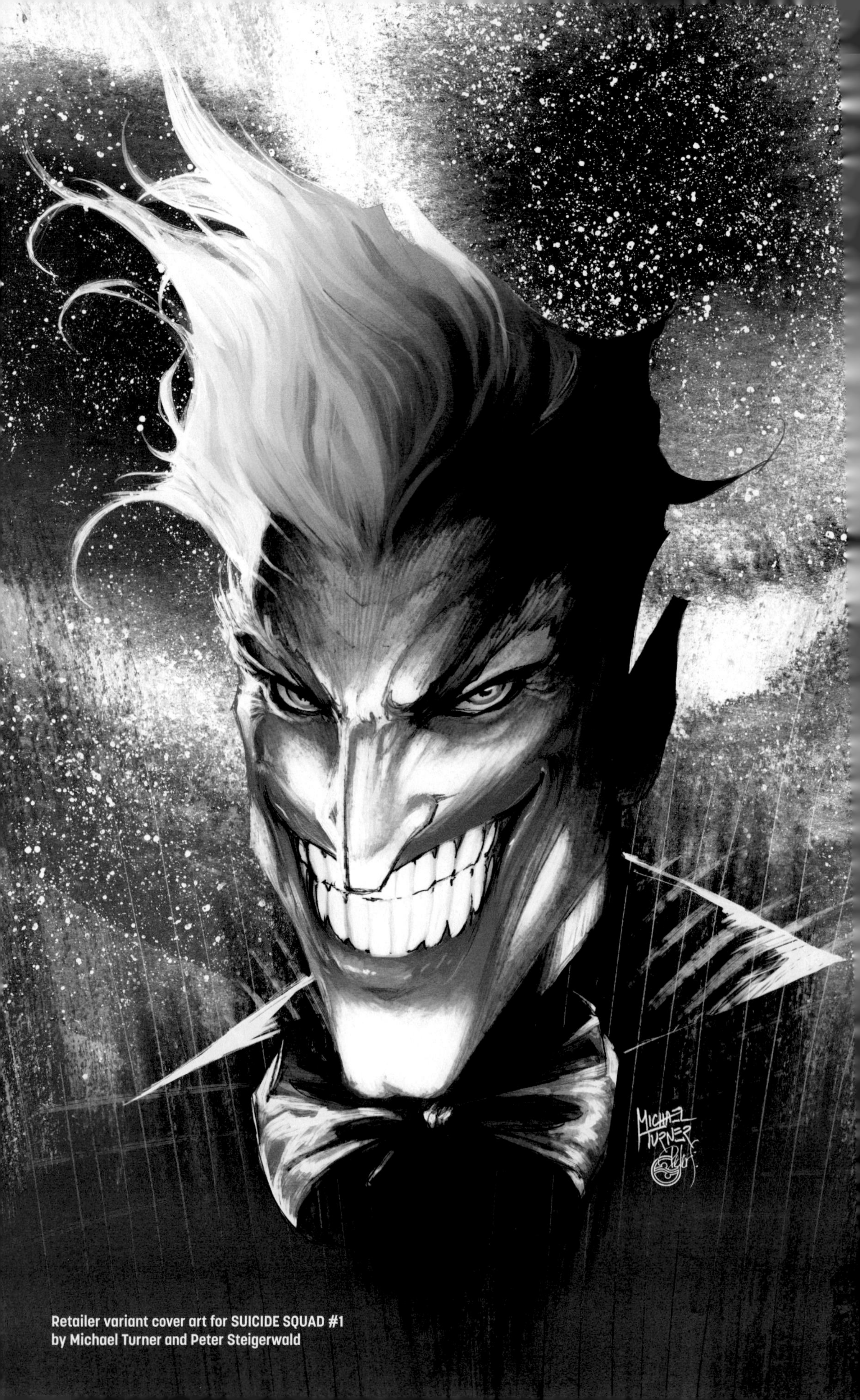
MICHAEL TURNER

Retailer variant cover art for SUICIDE SQUAD #1
by Michael Turner and Peter Steigerwald

Variant cover art for SUICIDE SQUAD #2
by Lee Bermejo

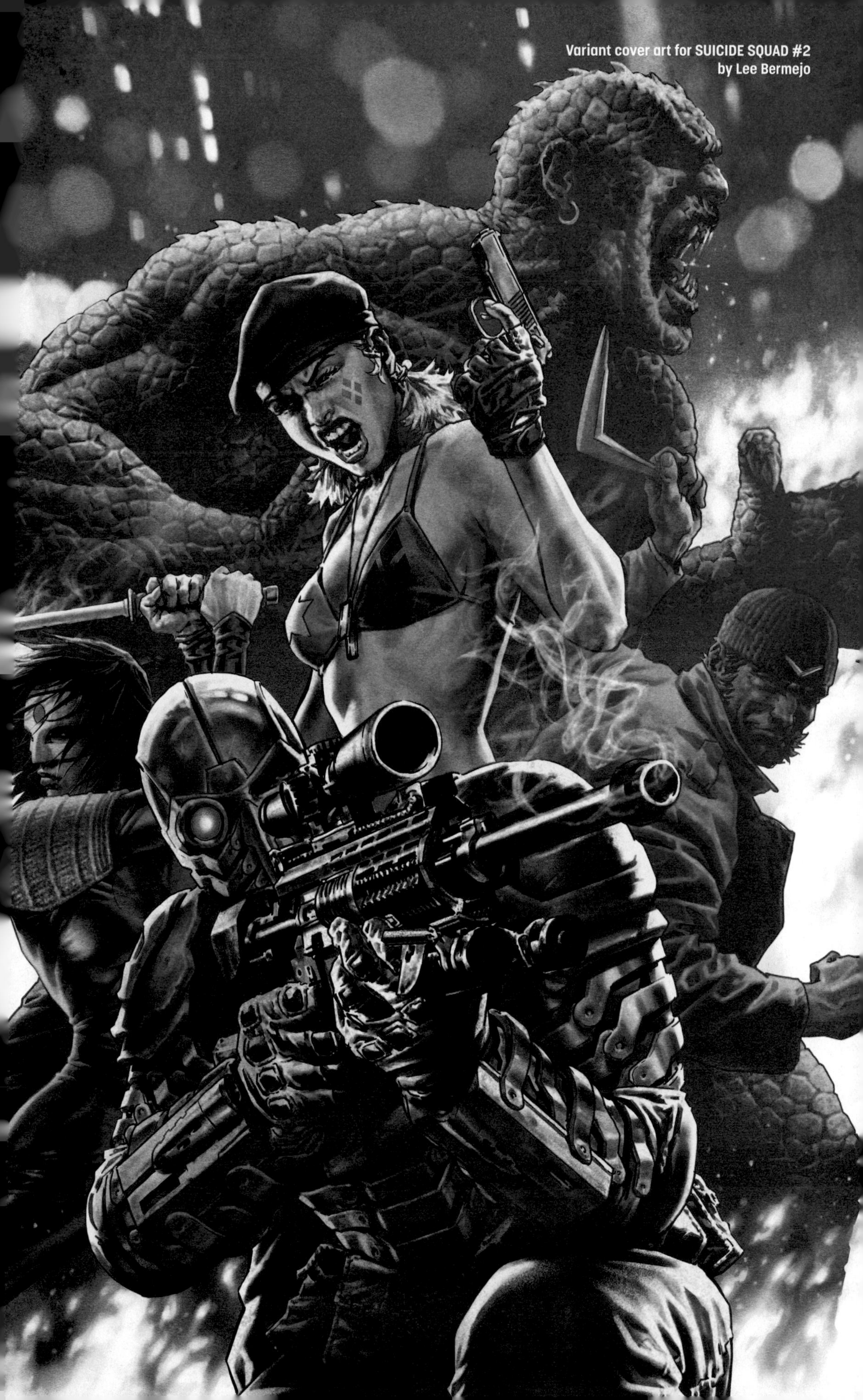

Variant cover art for SUICIDE SQUAD #3
by Lee Bermejo

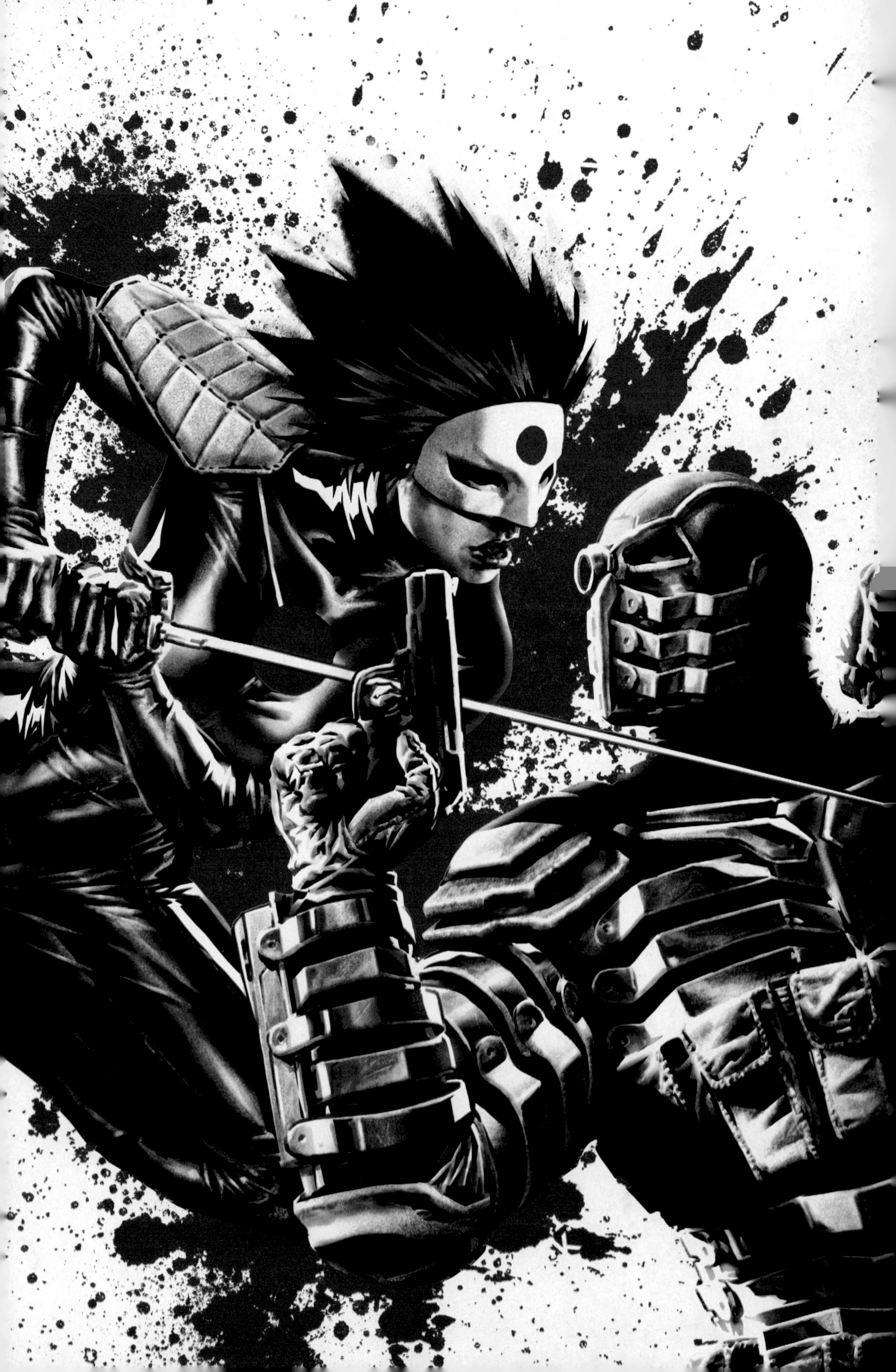

Variant cover art for SUICIDE SQUAD #4
by Lee Bermejo

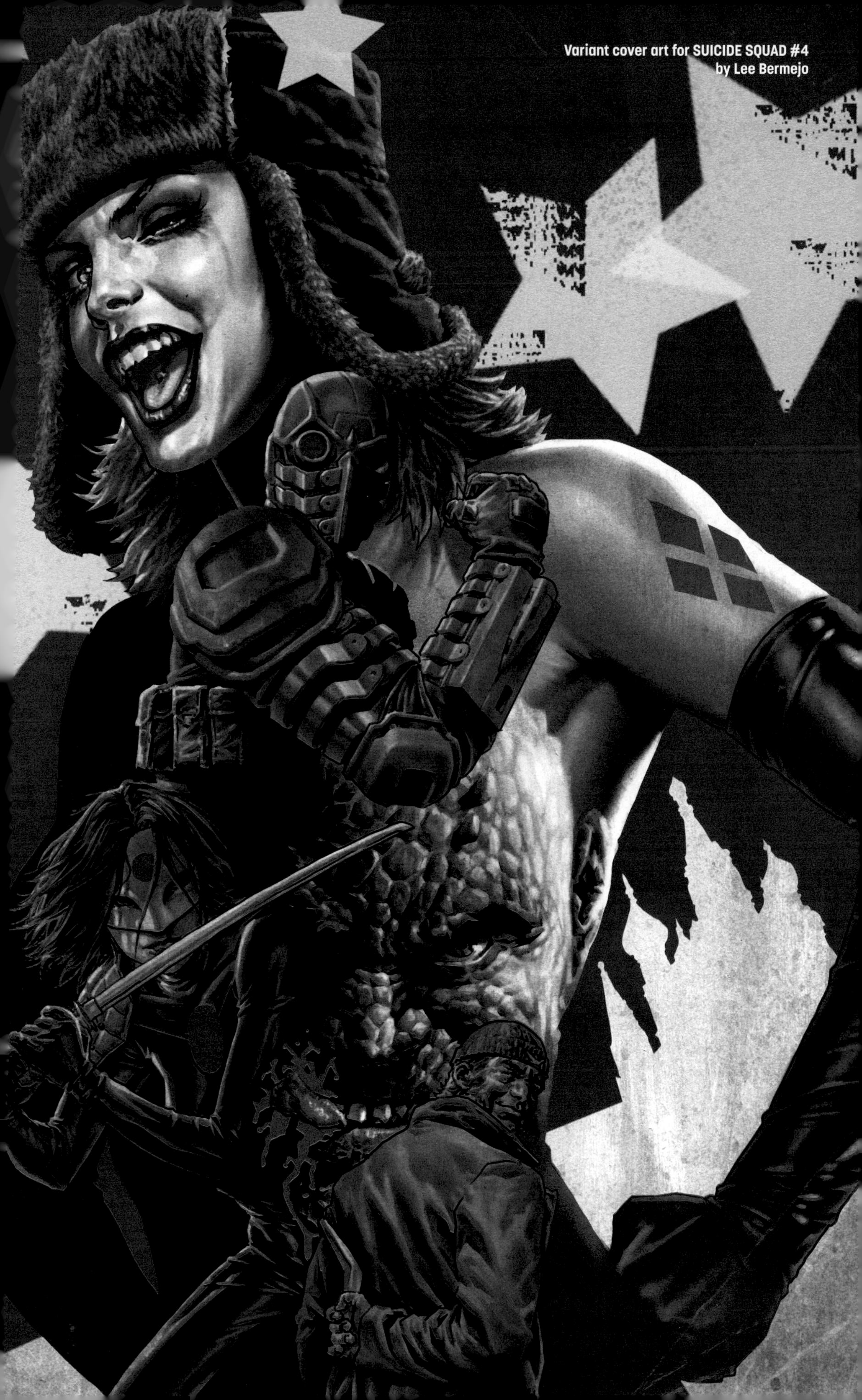

Cover rough and final pencils for SUICIDE SQUAD #1
by Jim Lee

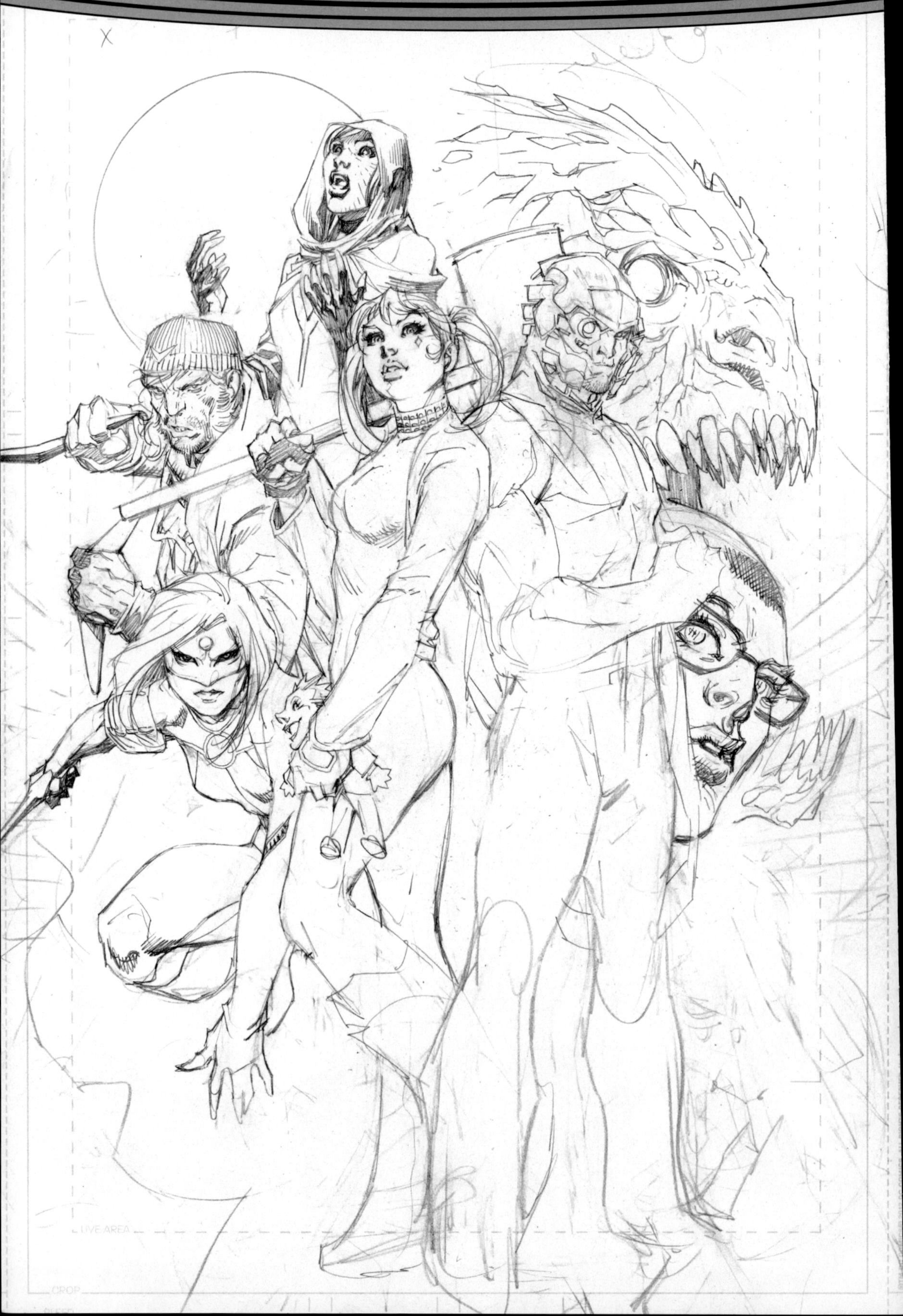
LIVE AREA
CROP

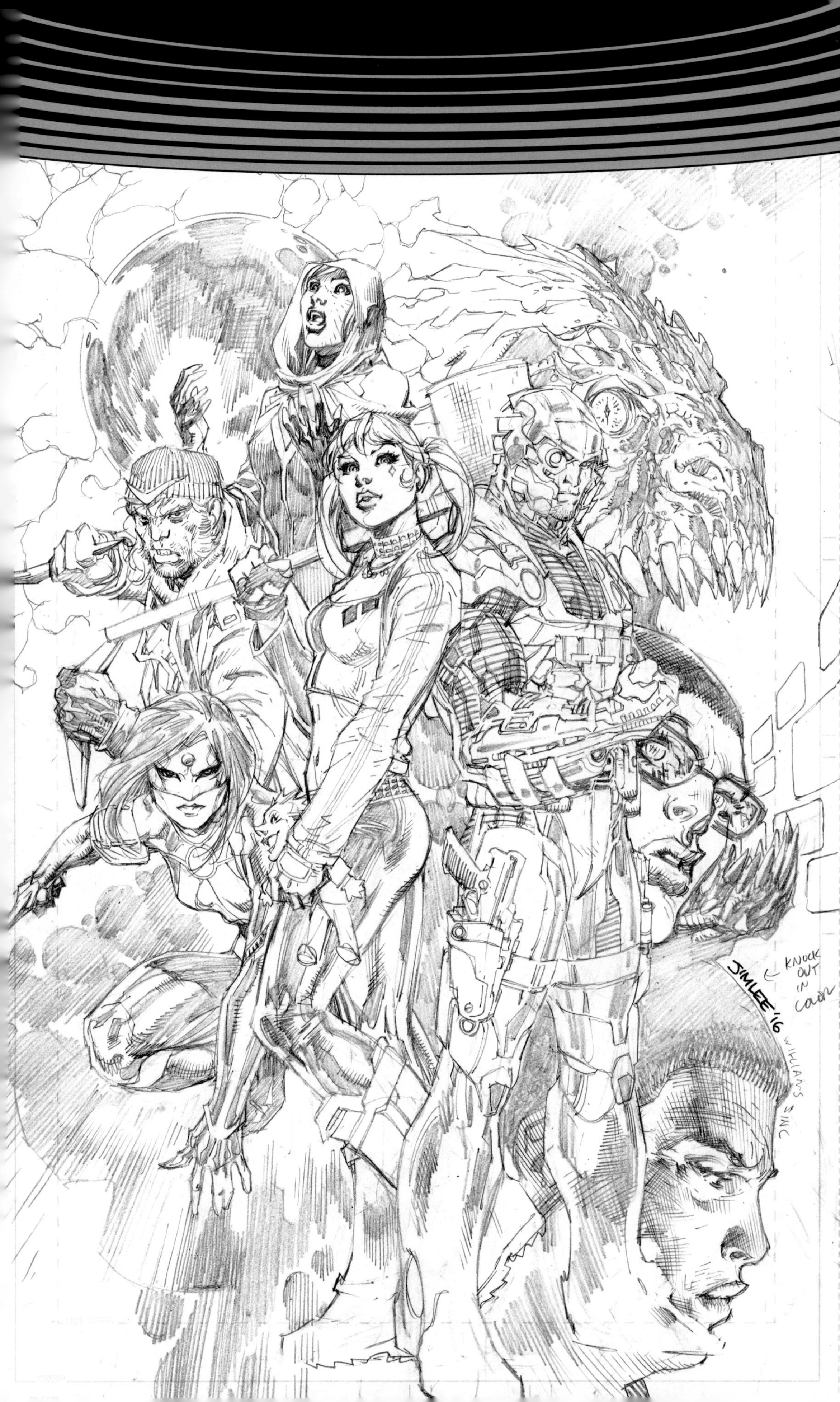

JIMLEE '16
← KNOCK OUT IN COLOR
WILLIAMS INC

Pencils from SUICIDE SQUAD: REBIRTH #1
by Philip Tan

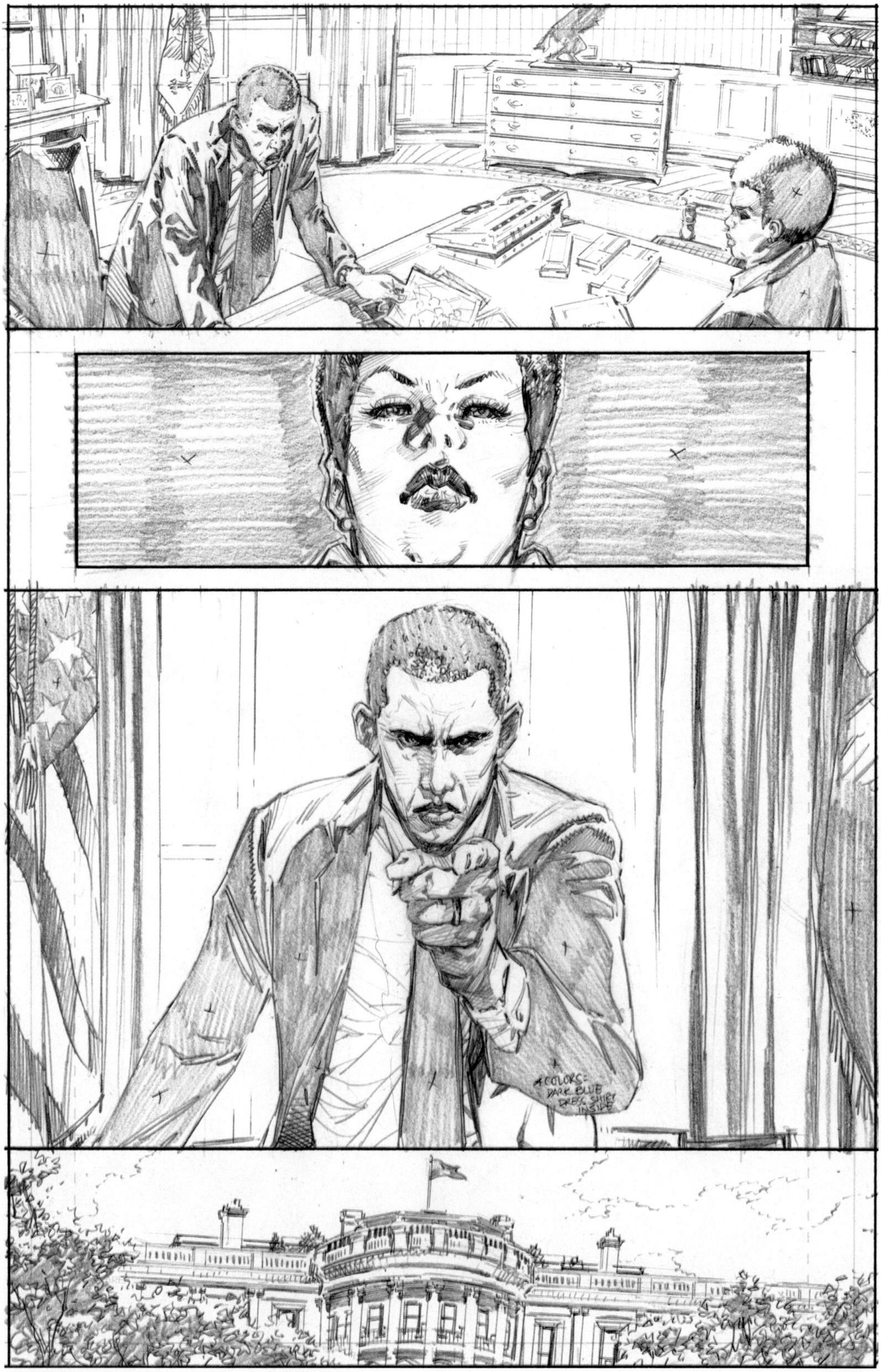
*COLORS: DARK BLUE DRESS SHIRT INSIDE

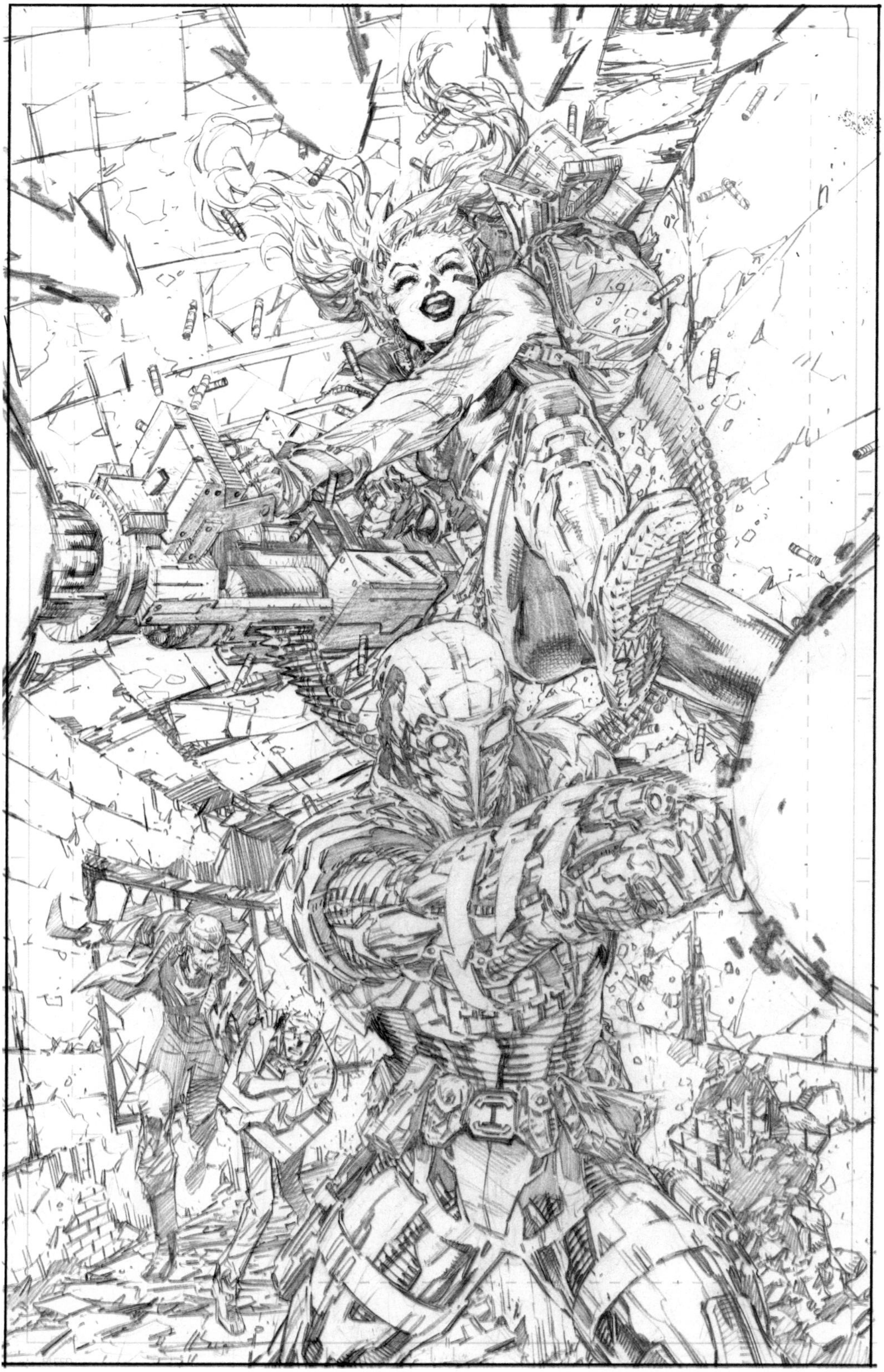

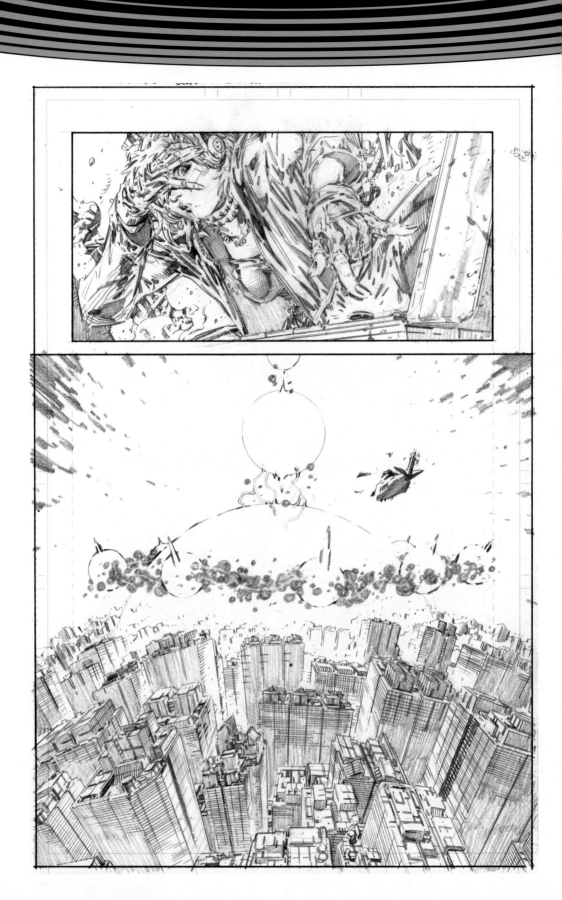

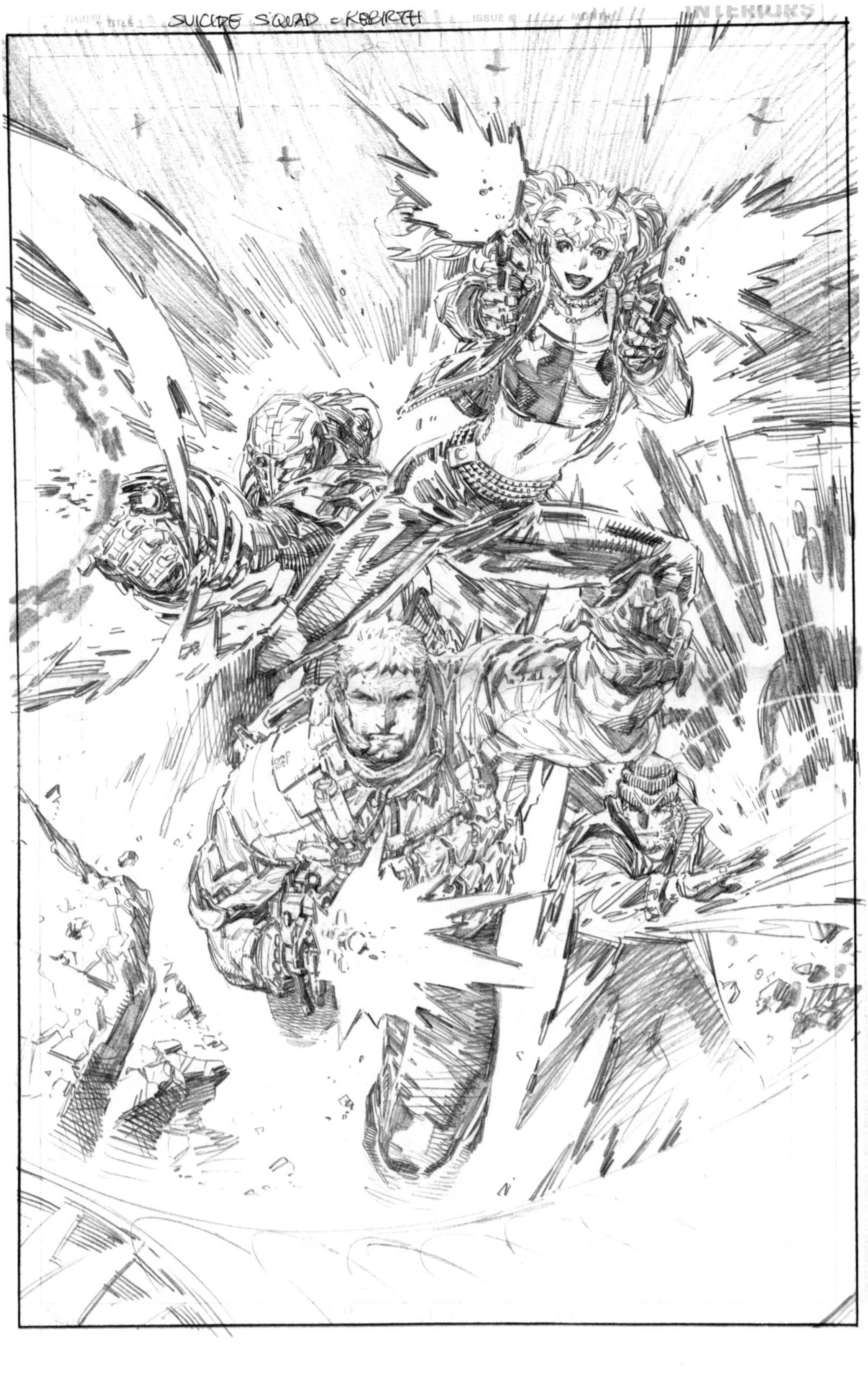
TITLE SUICIDE SQUAD - REBIRTH
ISSUE #
MONTH
INTERIORS

Pencils from SUICIDE SQUAD #1-4
by Jim Lee

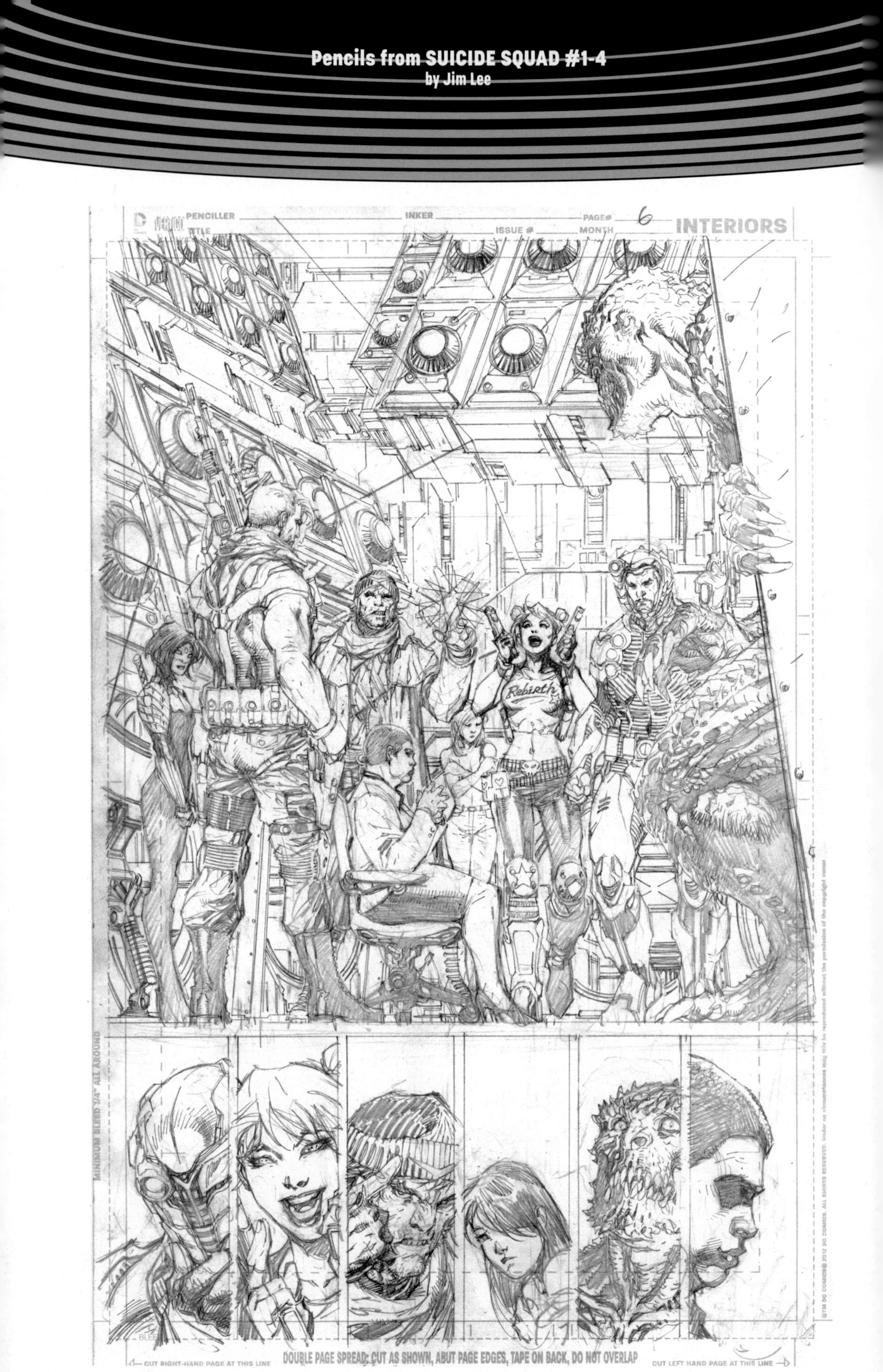
PENCILLER
INKER
PAGE# 6
TITLE
ISSUE #
MONTH
INTERIORS
Rebirth
MINIMUM BLEED 1/4" ALL AROUND
DOUBLE PAGE SPREAD: CUT AS SHOWN, ABUT PAGE EDGES, TAPE ON BACK, DO NOT OVERLAP
CUT RIGHT-HAND PAGE AT THIS LINE
CUT LEFT HAND PAGE AT THIS LINE

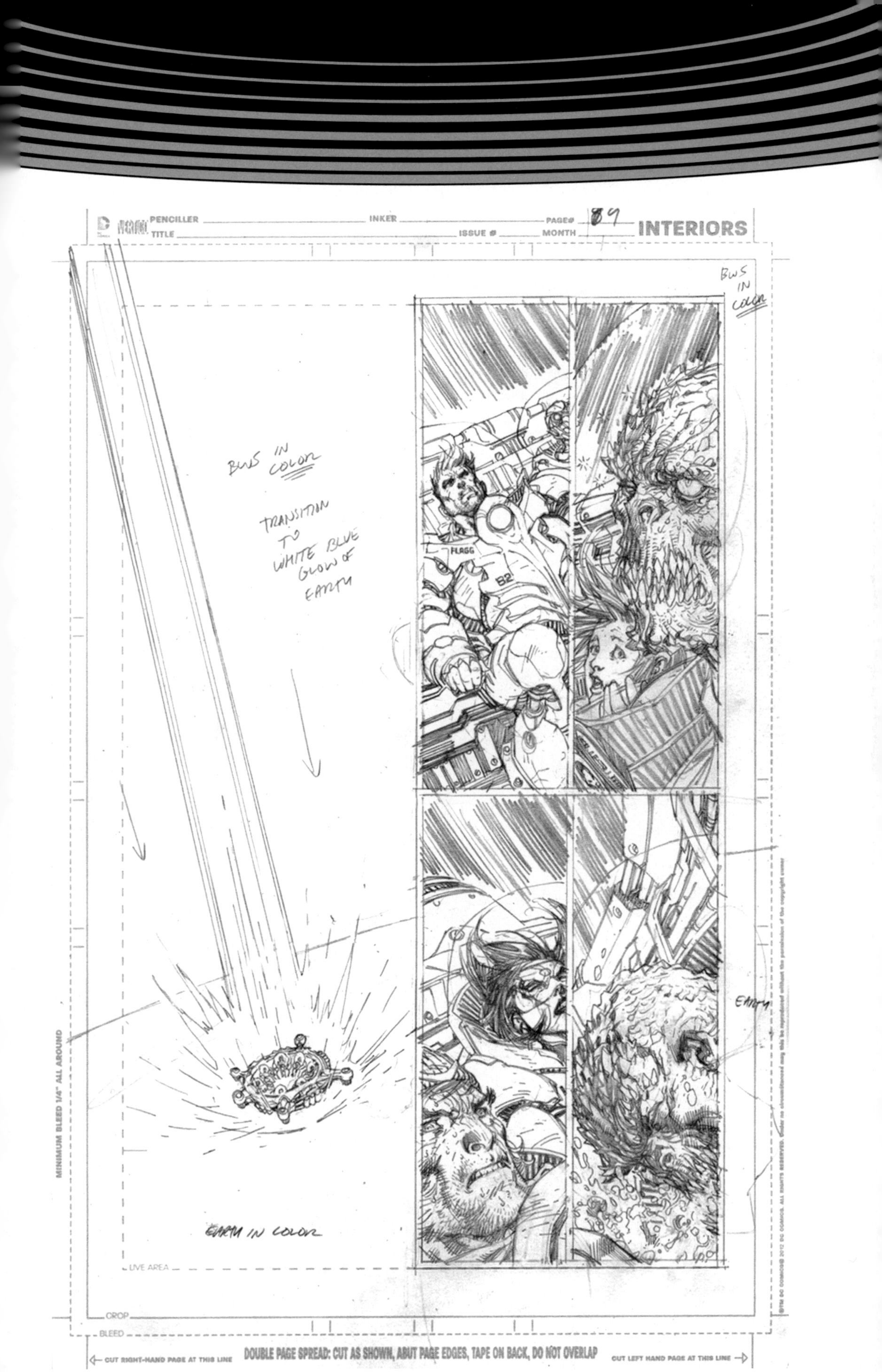

PENCILLER
INKER
PAGE# 89
INTERIORS
TITLE
ISSUE #
MONTH
BWS IN COLOR
BWS IN COLOR
TRANSITION TO WHITE BLUE GLOW OF EARTH
FLAGG
B2
EARTH
EARTH IN COLOR
LIVE AREA
CROP
BLEED
MINIMUM BLEED 1/4" ALL AROUND
CUT RIGHT-HAND PAGE AT THIS LINE
DOUBLE PAGE SPREAD: CUT AS SHOWN, ABUT PAGE EDGES, TAPE ON BACK, DO NOT OVERLAP
CUT LEFT HAND PAGE AT THIS LINE

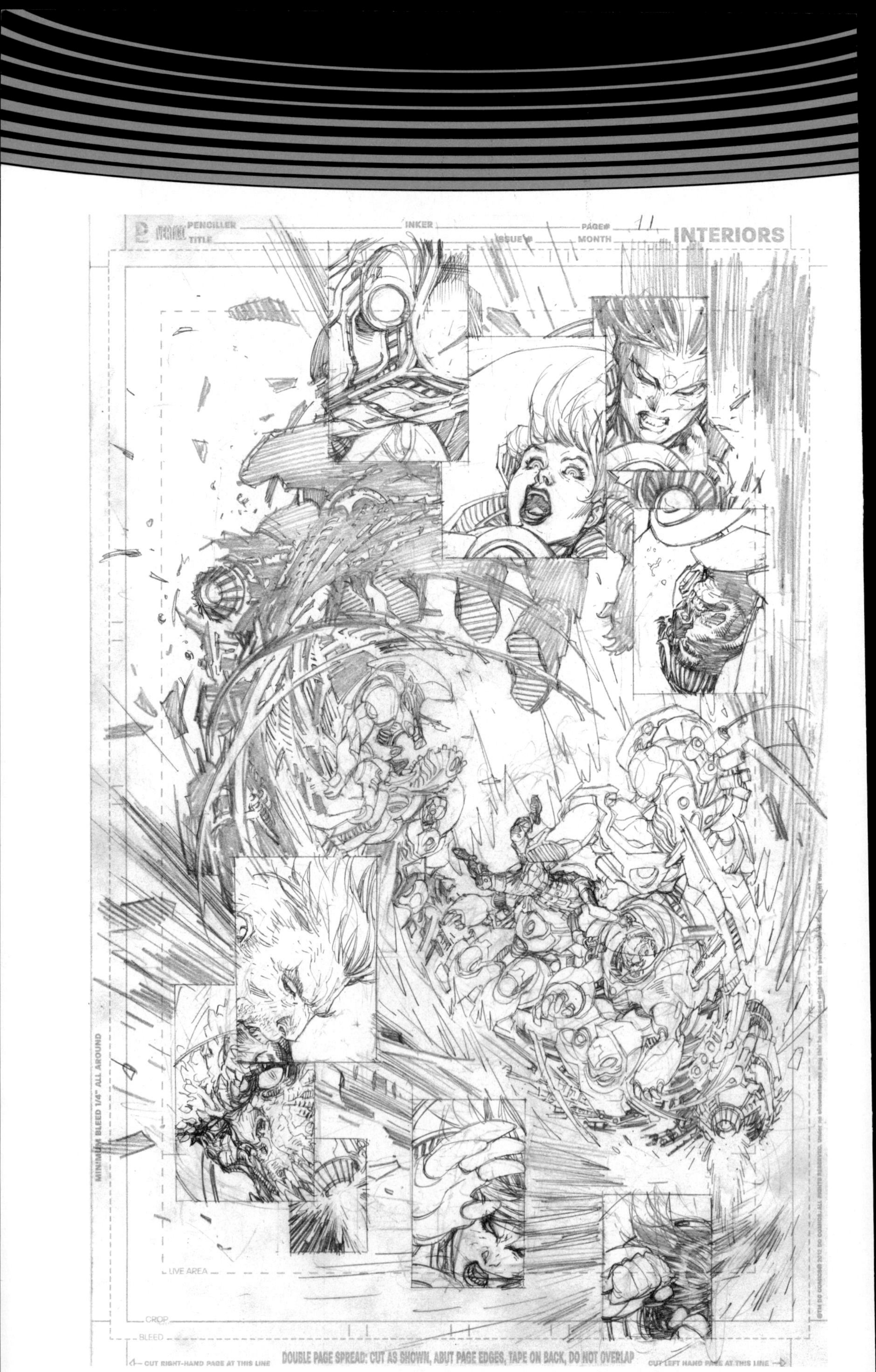
PENCILLER
INKER
PAGE# 11
TITLE
ISSUE #
MONTH
INTERIORS
MINIMUM BLEED 1/4" ALL AROUND
LIVE AREA
CROP
BLEED
CUT RIGHT-HAND PAGE AT THIS LINE
DOUBLE PAGE SPREAD: CUT AS SHOWN, ABUT PAGE EDGES, TAPE ON BACK, DO NOT OVERLAP
CUT LEFT HAND PAGE AT THIS LINE

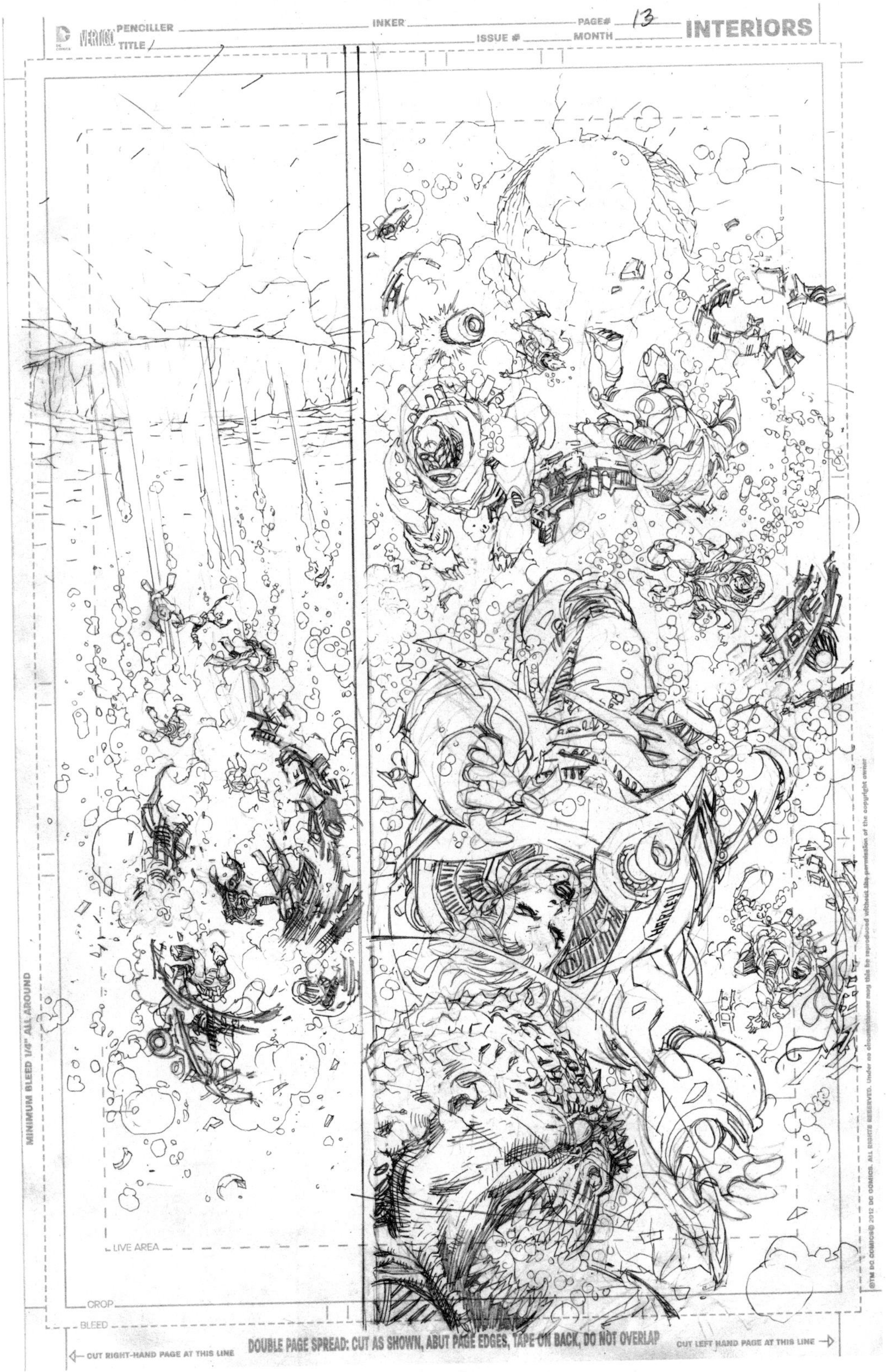

PENCILLER
INKER
PAGE# 13
INTERIORS
TITLE
ISSUE #
MONTH
VERTIGO
MINIMUM BLEED 1/4" ALL AROUND
LIVE AREA
CROP
BLEED
DOUBLE PAGE SPREAD: CUT AS SHOWN, ABUT PAGE EDGES, TAPE ON BACK, DO NOT OVERLAP
CUT RIGHT-HAND PAGE AT THIS LINE
CUT LEFT HAND PAGE AT THIS LINE

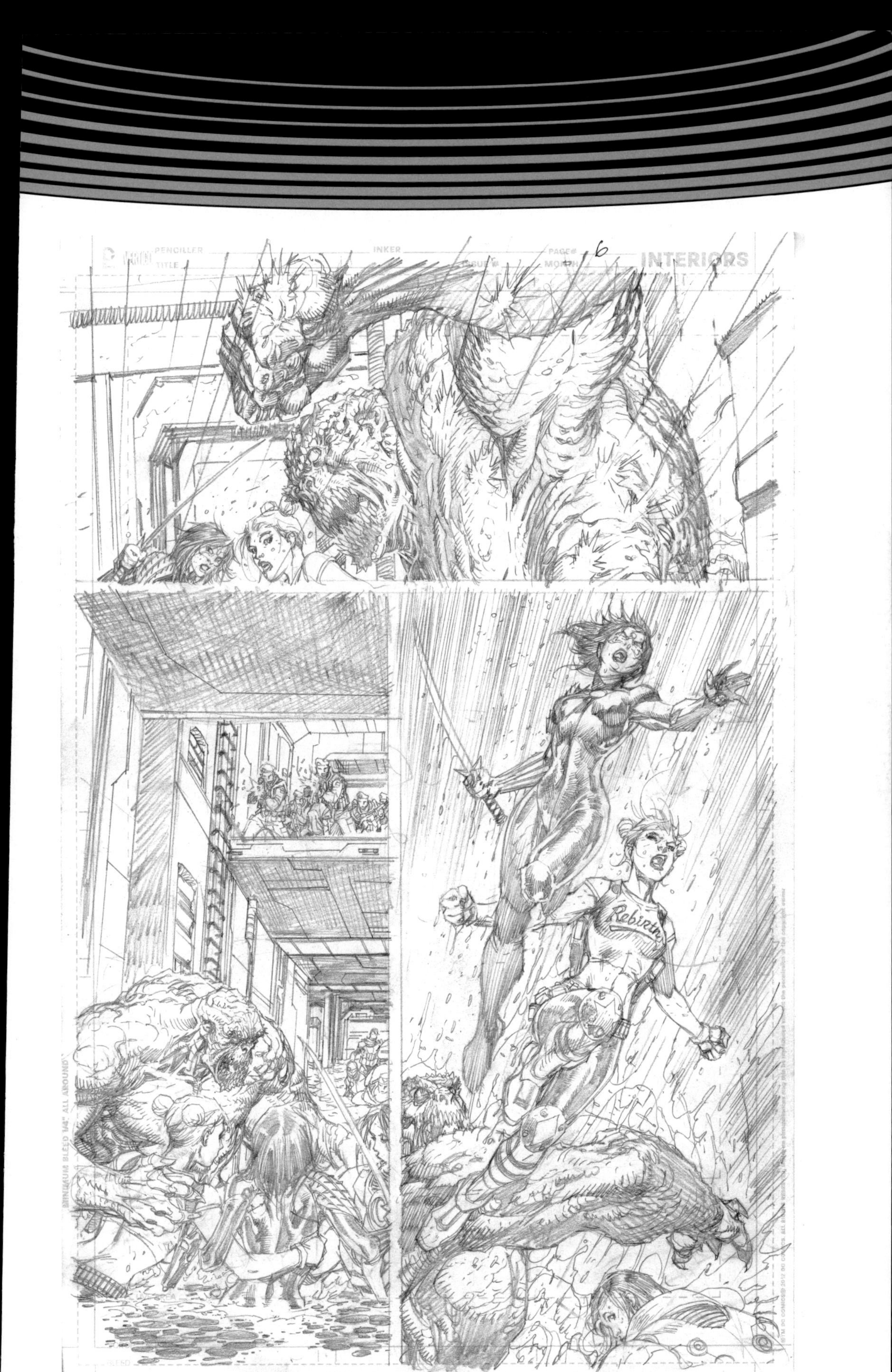
PENCILLER
TITLE
INKER
PAGE# 6
INTERIORS
Rebirth
CUT RIGHT-HAND PAGE AT THIS LINE
DOUBLE PAGE SPREAD: CUT AS SHOWN, ABUT PAGE EDGES, TAPE ON BACK, DO NOT OVERLAP
CUT LEFT HAND PAGE AT THIS LINE

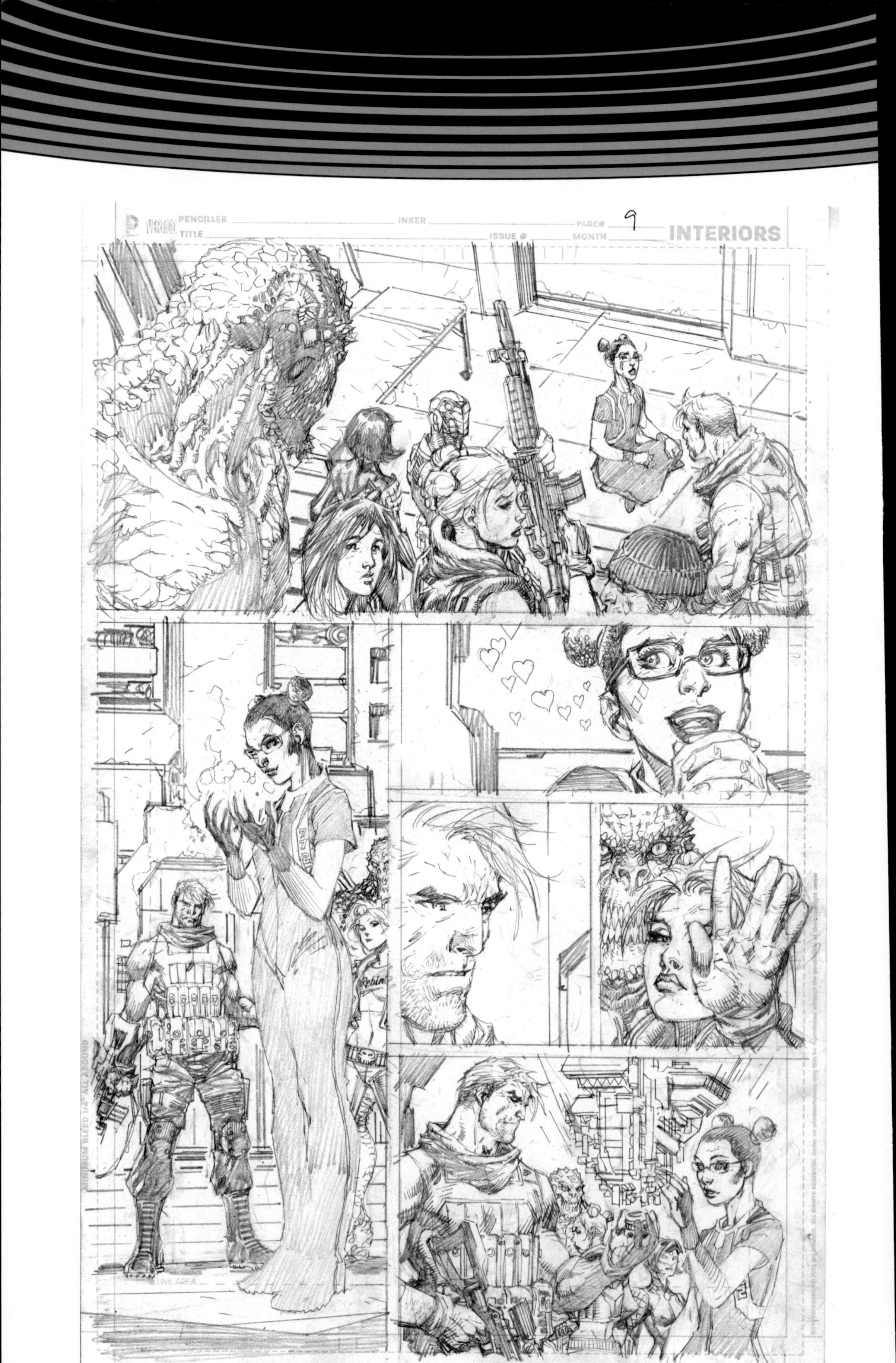
PENCILLER
INKER
PAGE# 9
TITLE
ISSUE #
MONTH
INTERIORS
CUT RIGHT-HAND PAGE AT THIS LINE
DOUBLE PAGE SPREAD: CUT AS SHOWN, ABUT PAGE EDGES, TAPE ON BACK, DO NOT OVERLAP
CUT LEFT HAND PAGE AT THIS LINE

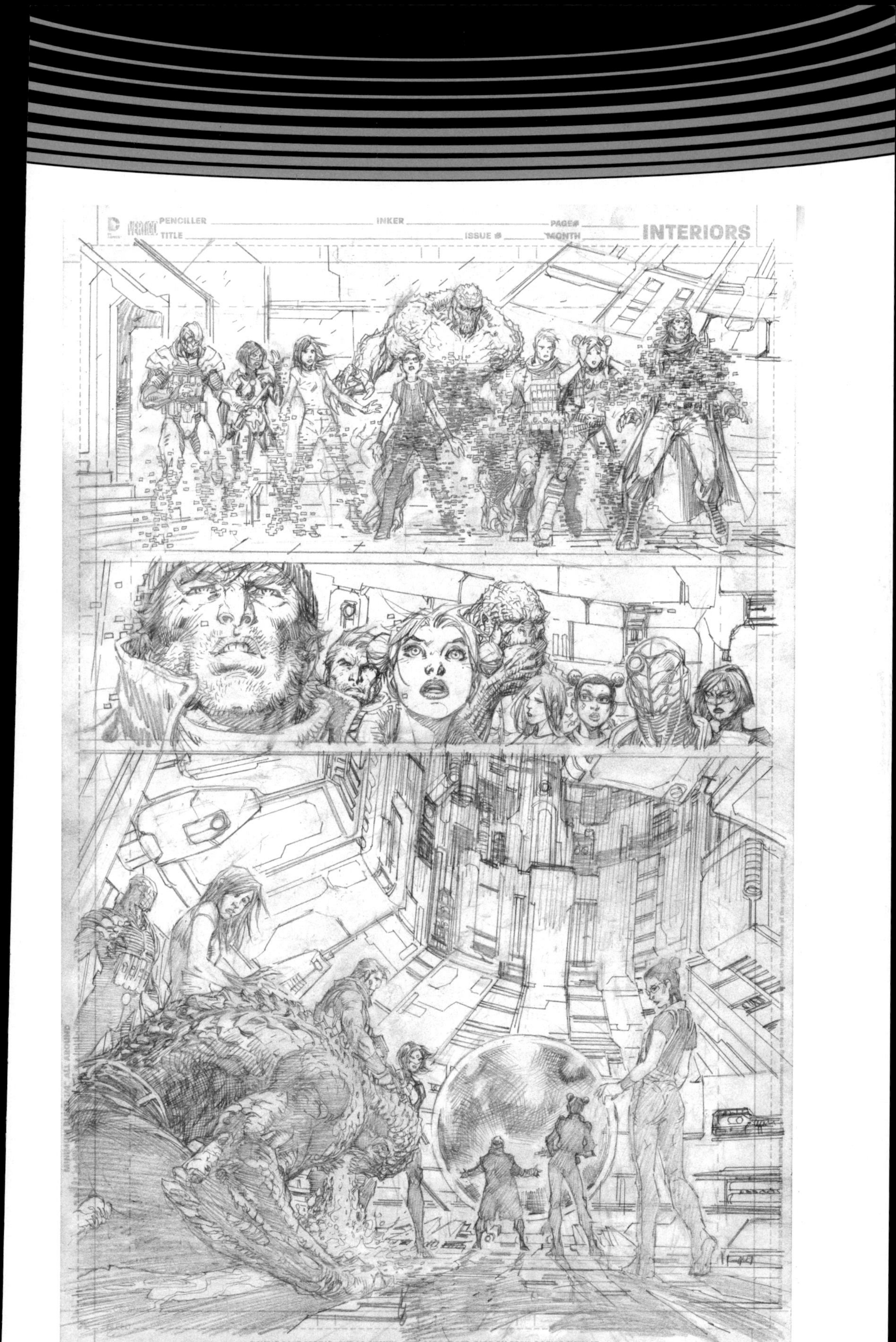
PENCILLER
INKER
PAGE#
TITLE
ISSUE #
MONTH
INTERIORS
DOUBLE PAGE SPREAD: CUT AS SHOWN, ABUT PAGE EDGES, TAPE ON BACK, DO NOT OVERLAP

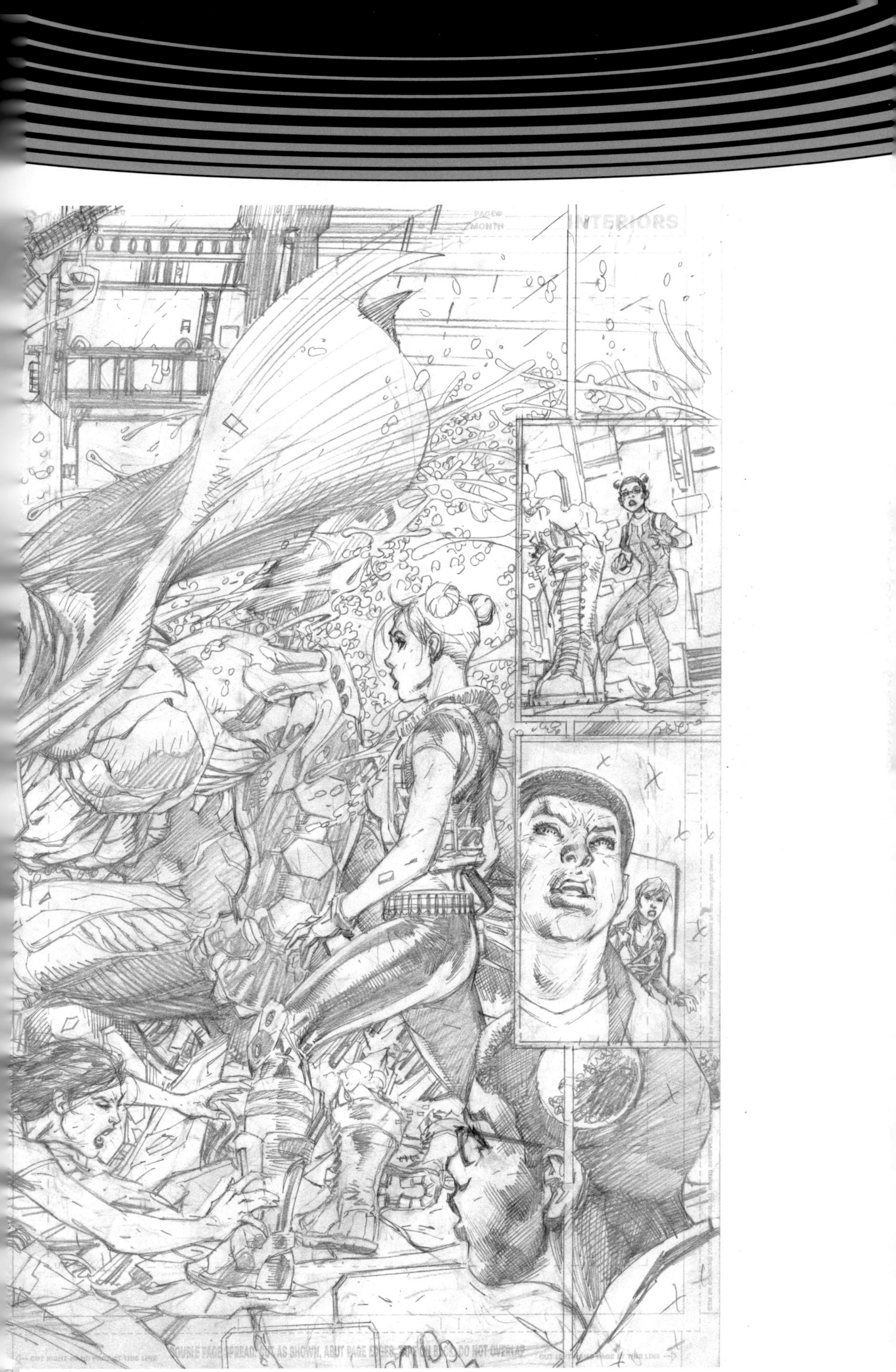
INTERIORS

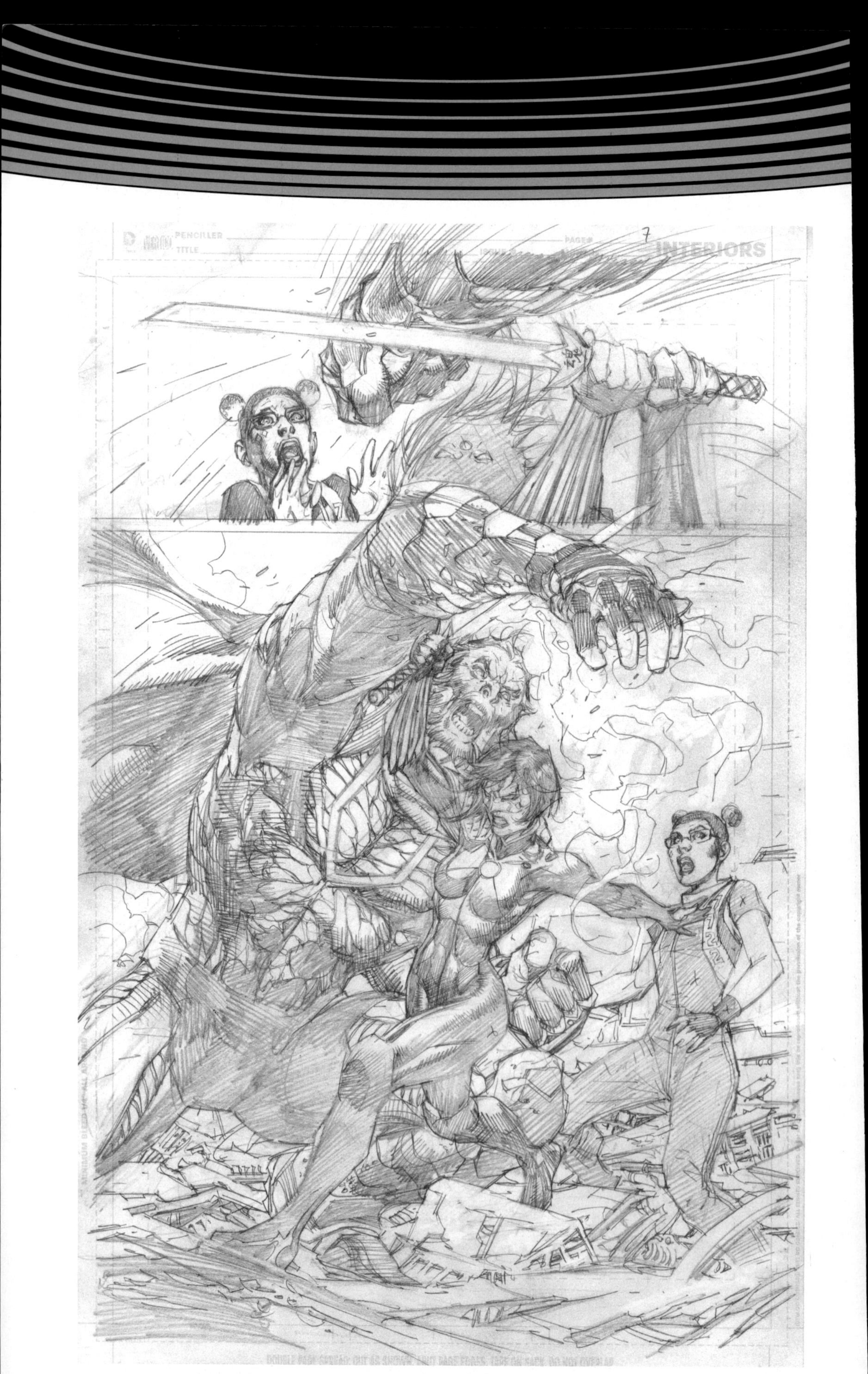
PENCILLER
TITLE
PAGE#
7
INTERIORS

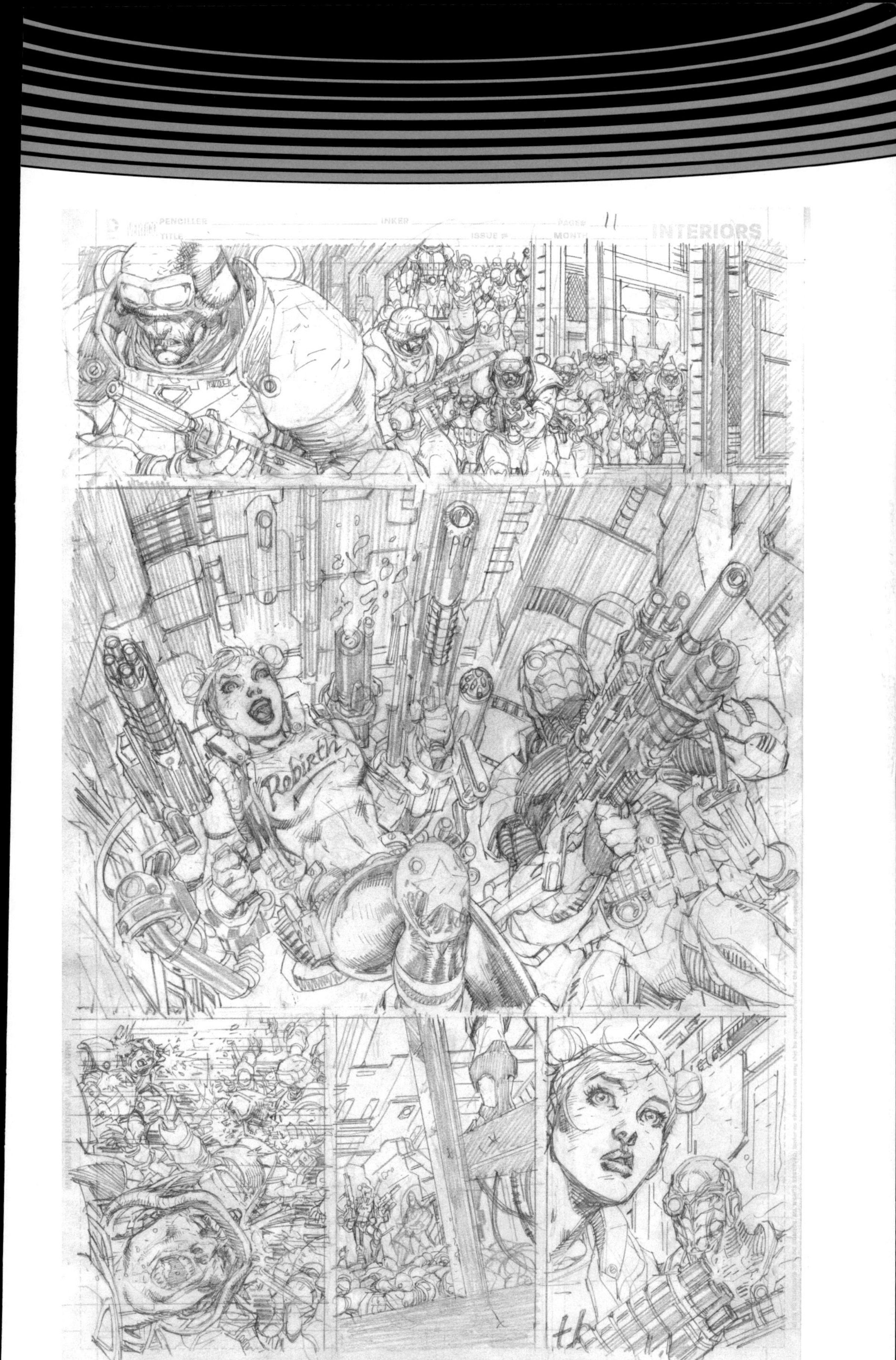
PENCILLER
INKER
PAGE#
11
TITLE
ISSUE #
MONTH
INTERIORS
Rebirth
DOUBLE PAGE SPREAD: CUT AS SHOWN, ABUT PAGE EDGES, TAPE ON BACK, DO NOT OVERLAP

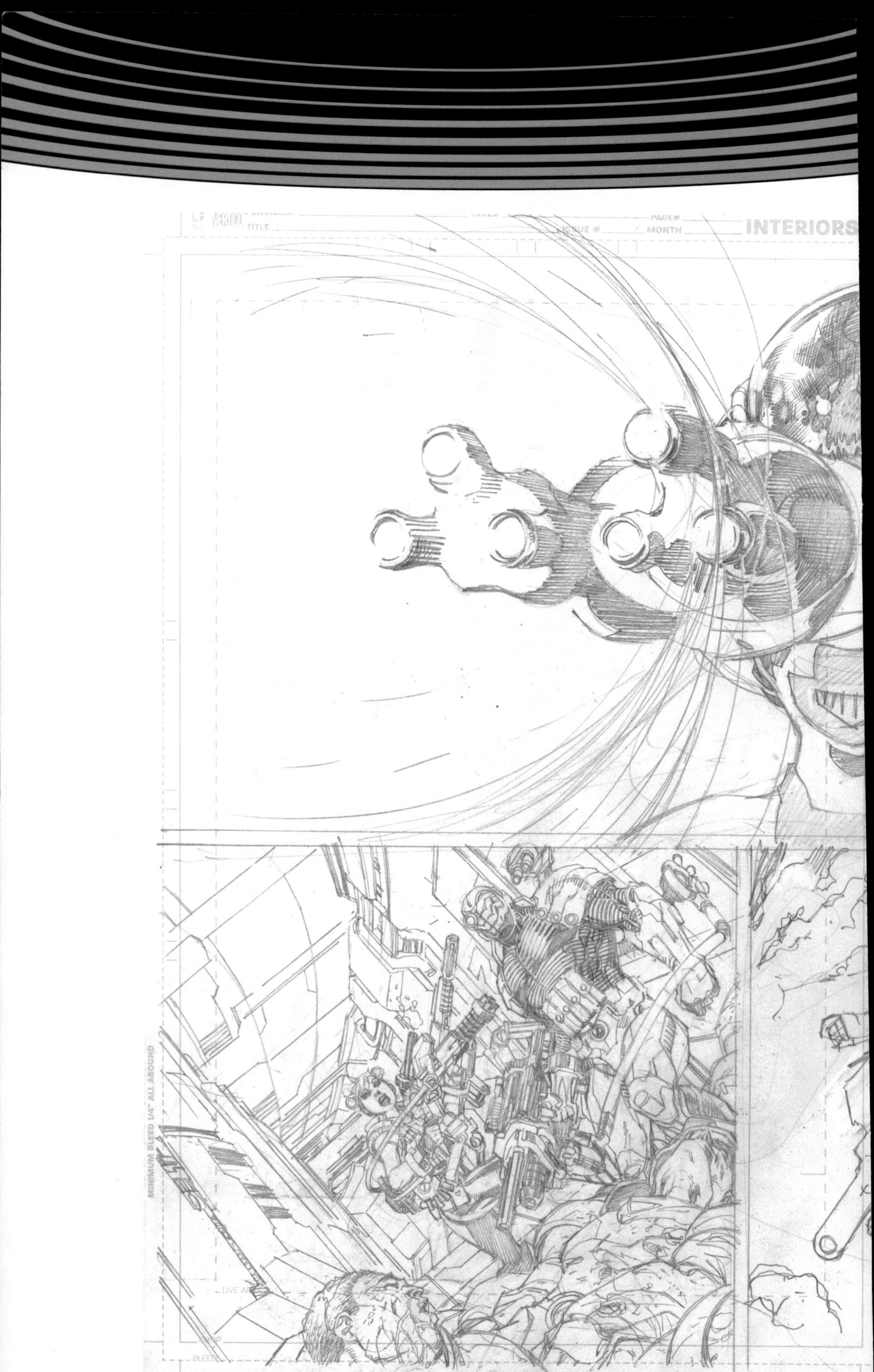
TITLE
ISSUE #
MONTH
PAGE#
INTERIORS
MINIMUM BLEED 1/4" ALL AROUND
DOUBLE PAGE SPREAD: CUT AS SHOWN, ABUT PAGE EDGES, TAPE ON BACK, DO NOT OVERLAP

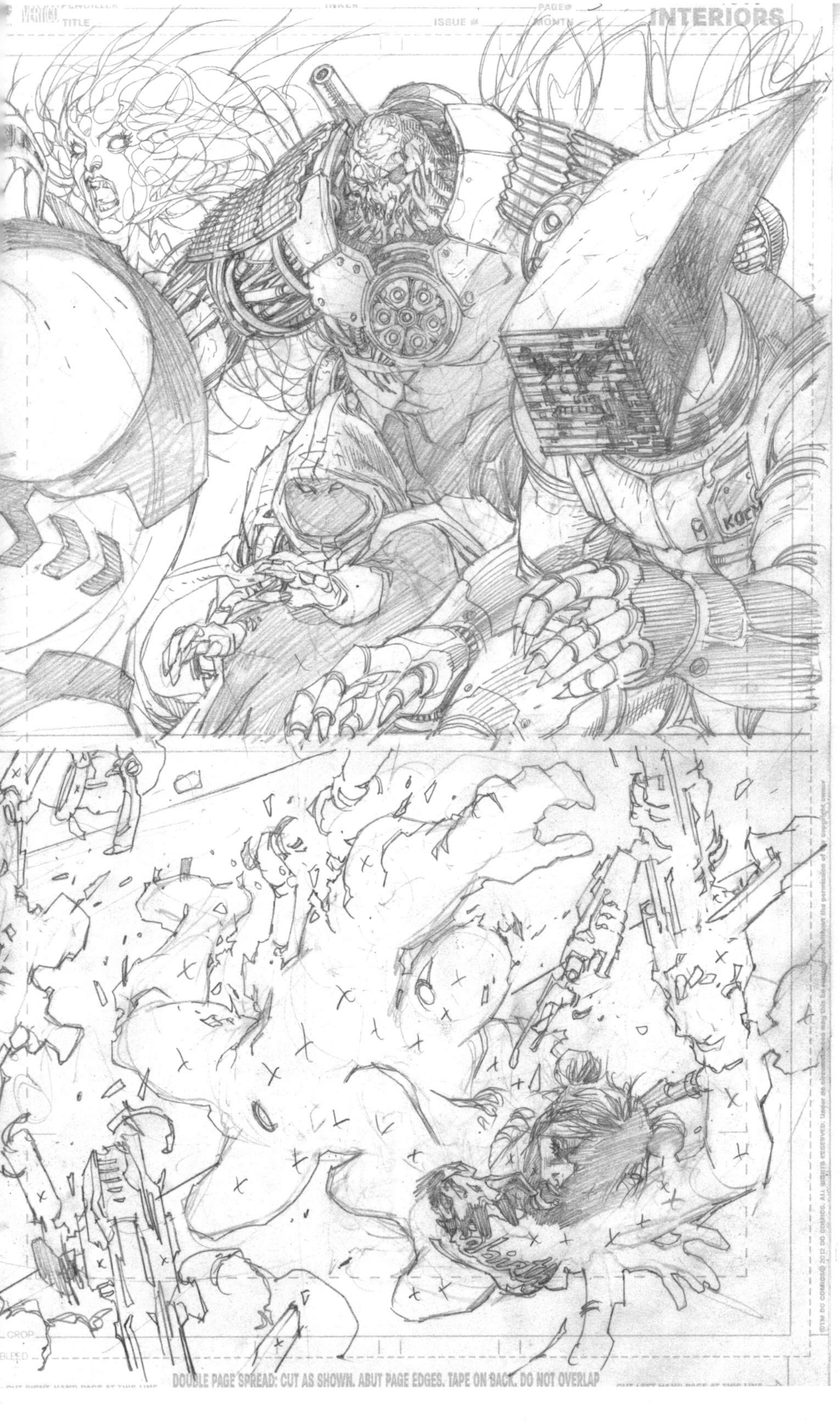
TITLE
ISSUE #
PAGE#
MONTH
INTERIORS
CROP
BLEED
DOUBLE PAGE SPREAD: CUT AS SHOWN. ABUT PAGE EDGES. TAPE ON BACK. DO NOT OVERLAP

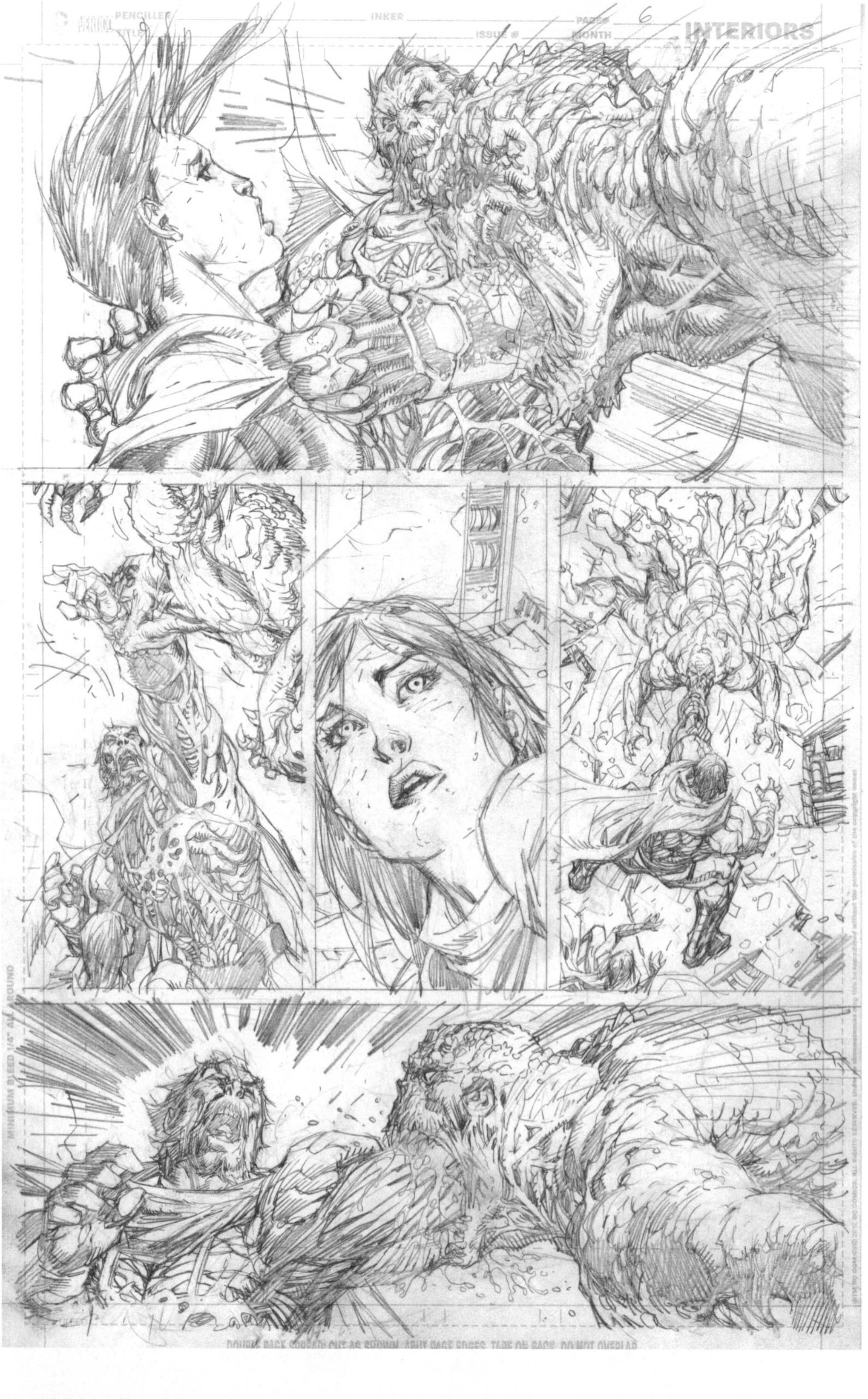
PENCILLER
INKER
PAGE
6
TITLE
ISSUE #
MONTH
INTERIORS

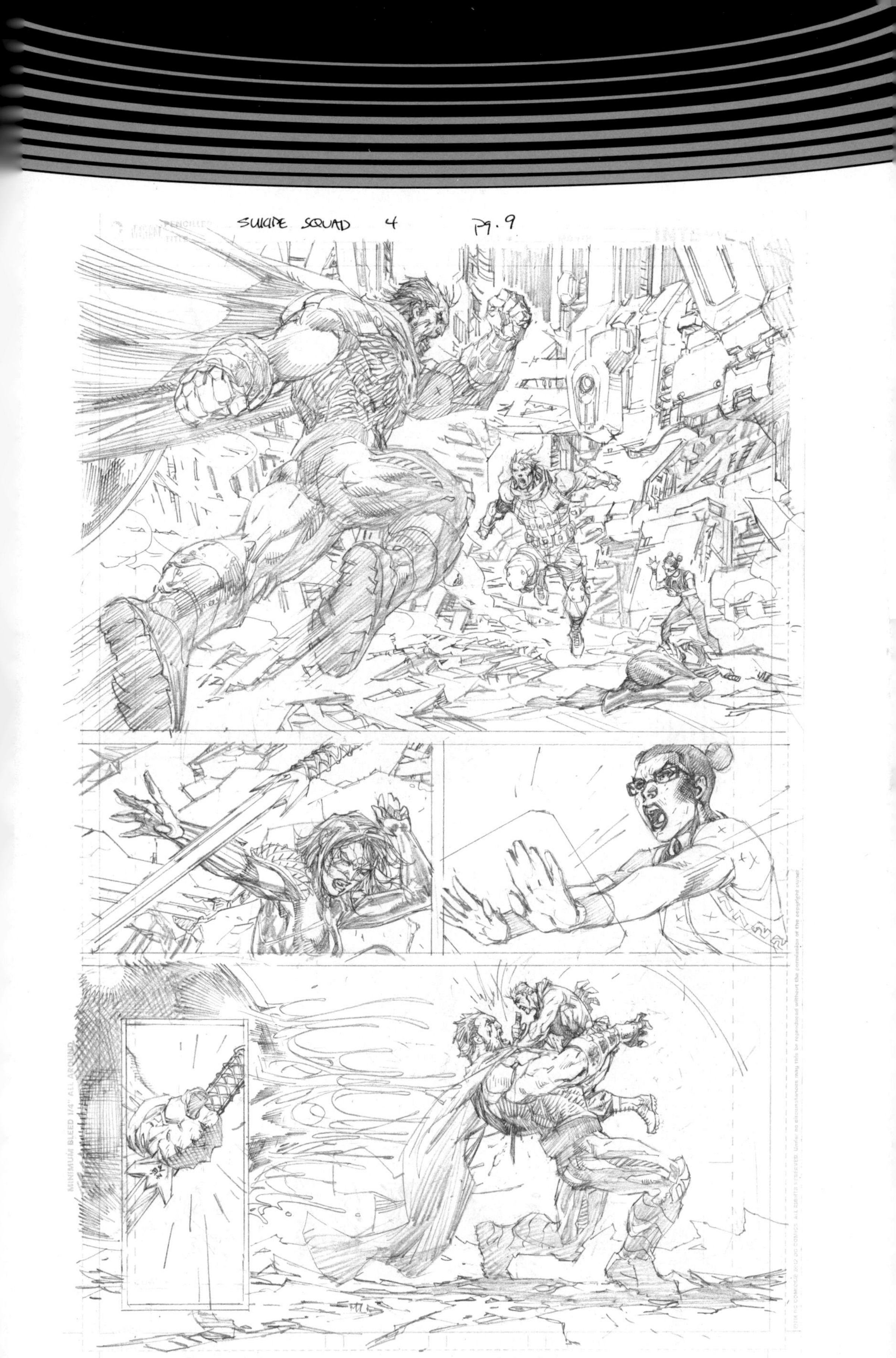
PENCILLER
TITLE
SUICIDE SQUAD 4 Pg. 9
MINIMUM BLEED 1/4" ALL AROUND
DOUBLE PAGE SPREAD: CUT AS SHOWN, ABUT PAGE EDGES, TAPE ON BACK, DO NOT OVERLA

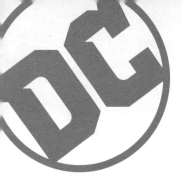

"Welcoming to new fans looking to get into superhero comics for the first time and old fans who gave up on the funny-books long ago."
– SCRIPPS HOWARD NEWS SERVICE

THE NEW YORK TIMES BESTSELLER
THE NEW 52!
JUSTICE LEAGUE
VOLUME 1 ORIGIN
"WRITTEN BY GEOFF JOHNS, WITH ART BY THE GODLY JIM LEE, JUSTICE LEAGUE IS A MUST READ."
– COMPLEX MAGAZINE
GEOFF JOHNS JIM LEE SCOTT WILLIAMS

JUSTICE LEAGUE

VOL. 1: ORIGIN

GEOFF JOHNS
and JIM LEE

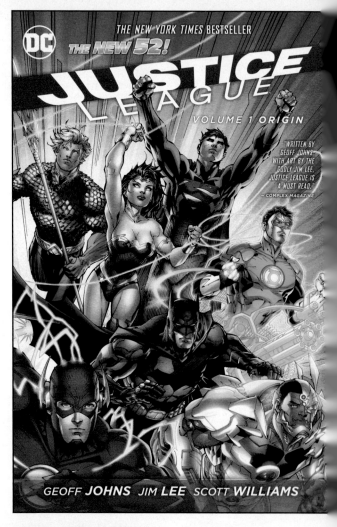

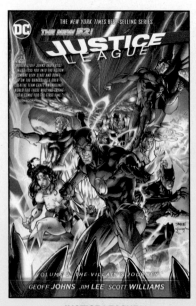

THE NEW YORK TIMES BEST-SELLING SERIES
THE NEW 52!
JUSTICE LEAGUE
VOLUME 2 THE VILLAIN'S JOURNEY
GEOFF JOHNS JIM LEE SCOTT WILLIAMS

JUSTICE LEAGUE
VOL. 2: THE VILLAIN'S JOURNEY

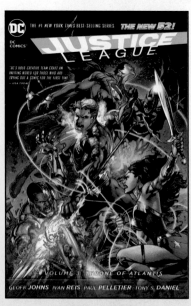

THE #1 NEW YORK TIMES BEST-SELLING SERIES
THE NEW 52!
JUSTICE LEAGUE
VOLUME 3 THRONE OF ATLANTIS
GEOFF JOHNS IVAN REIS PAUL PELLETIER TONY S. DANIEL

JUSTICE LEAGUE
VOL. 3: THRONE OF ATLANTIS

READ THE ENTIRE EPIC

JUSTICE LEAGUE VOL. 4
THE GRI

JUSTICE LEAGUE VOL. 5
FOREVER HEROES

JUSTICE LEAGUE VOL. 6
INJUSTICE LEAGUE

JUSTICE LEAGUE VOL. 7
DARKSEID WAR PART

JUSTICE LEAGUE VOL. 8
DARKSEID WAR PART 2